THE NEW GROVE

BACH FAMILY

Christoph Wolff
Walter Emery
Richard Jones
Eugene Helm
Ernest Warburton
Ellwood S. Derr

W. W. NORTON & COMPANY

NEW YORK   LONDON

Copyright © Christoph Wolff, Walter Emery, Nicholas
Temperley, Richard Jones, Eugene Helm, Ernest Warburton,
Ellwood S. Derr 1980, 1983

First published in
The New Grove Dictionary of Music and Musicians,
edited by Stanley Sadie, 1980

First American Edition in book form with additions 1983

ISBN 0-393-01684-6

Printed in Great Britain

Contents

List of illustrations

Illustration acknowledgments

We are grateful to the following for permission to reproduce
illustrative material: Bibliothèque Nationale, Paris (fig.2); Deutsche
Staatsbibliothek, Berlin (figs.3, 6 and 7); Stadtarchiv, Zwickau (fig.4);
William H. Scheide, Princeton, New Jersey/photo Willard Starks
(cover, fig.5); British Library, London (fig.8); Staatliche Galerie
Moritzburg, Halle/photo Walter Danz (fig.9); Staatliche Museen
Preussischer Kulturbesitz, Berlin (fig.10); Kunsthalle, Hamburg
(fig.11); Staatsbibliothek Preussicher Kulturbesitz, Musikabteilung,
Berlin (fig.12); Mansell Collection, London, and Alinari, Florence
(fig.13).

General abbreviations

A	alto, contralto [voice]	*Jb*	Jahrbuch [yearbook]
A	Anhang [appendix]	Jg.	Jahrgang [year of
a	alto [instrument]		publication/volume]
acc.	accompaniment,	kbd	keyboard
	accompanied by	Ky	Kyrie
add, addl	additional	lib	libretto
add, addn	addition		
Anh.	Anhang [appendix]	Mez	Mezzo
appx	appendix	movt	movement
B	bass [voice]	n.d.	no date of publication
b	bass [instrument]	n.p.	no place of publication
b	born	ob	oboe
bc	basso continuo	obbl	obbligato
Bd.	Band [volume]	opt.	optional
bn	bassoon	orch	orchestra, orchestral
BWV	Bach-Werke-Verzeichnis	orchd	orchestrated (by)
	[Schmieder, catalogue of	org	organ
	J. S. Bach's works]	ov.	overture
c	circa [about]	perf.	performance, performed
c.f.	cantus firmus		(by)
cl	clarinet	pl.	plate
collab.	in collaboration with	posth.	posthumously
conc.	concerto	pr.	printed
		pubd	published
d	died	pubn	publication
db	double bass		
ded.	dedication, dedicated to	qnt	quintet
		qt	quartet
edn.	edition		
eng hn	english horn	*R*	photographic reprint
		r	recto
F	Falck catalogue [W. F.	rec	recorder
	Bach]	recit	recitative
facs.	facsimile	red.	reduction, reduced for
fl	flute	repr.	reprinted
frag.	fragment	rev.	revision, revised (by/for)
		RISM	Répertoire International
Gl	Gloria		des Sources Musicales
gui	guitar	RV	Ryom catalogue [Vivaldi]
H	Helm catalogue [C. P. E.	S	San [Saint]; soprano [voice]
	Bach]	str	string(s)
hn	horn	sym.	symphony, symphonic
hpd	harpsichord		
inc.	incomplete	T	tenor [voice]
inst	instrument		

T	Terry catalogue [J. C. Bach]	v, vv	voice, voices
		v., vv.	verse, verses
t	tenor [instrument]	*v*	verso
timp	timpani	va	viola
tpt	trumpet	vc	cello
Tr	treble [voice]	vle	violone
tr	treble [instrument]	vn	violin
transcr.	transcription, transcribed by/for	W	Wotquenne catalogue [C. P. E. Bach]
trbn	trombone	ww	woodwind
U.	University		

Symbols for the library sources of works, printed in *italic*, correspond to those used in *RISM*, Ser. A.

Bibliographical abbreviations

AcM	*Acta Musicologica*
AMf	*Archiv für Musikforschung*
AMw	*Archiv für Musikwissenschaft*
AMZ	*Allgemeine musikalische Zeitung*
AnMc	*Analecta musicologica*
Bjb	*Bach-Jahrbuch*
BMw	*Beiträge zur Musikwissenschaft*
BurneyH	C. Burney: *A General History of Music from the Earliest Ages to the Present* (London, 1776–89)
CMc	*Current Musicology*
Cw	Das Chorwerk
DDT	Denkmäler deutscher Tonkunst
DJbM	*Deutsches Jahrbuch der Musikwissenschaft*
DTB	Denkmäler der Tonkunst in Bayern
EDM	Das Erbe deutscher Musik
EitnerQ	R. Eitner: *Biographisch-bibliographisches Quellen-Lexikon*
FétisB	F.-J. Fétis: *Biographie universelle des musiciens*
GerberL	R. Gerber: *Historisch-biographisches Lexikon der Tonkünstler*
GerberNL	R. Gerber: *Neues historisch-biographisches Lexikon der Tonkünstler*
GfMKB	*Gesellschaft für Musikforschung Kongressbericht*
HM	Hortus musicus
HMw	Handbuch der Musikwissenschaft, ed. E. Bücken (Potsdam, 1927–) [monograph series]
HMYB	*Hinrichsen's Musical Year Book*
HW	Wohlfarth catalogue [J. C. F. Bach]
IMSCR	*International Musicological Society Congress Report* [1930–]
JAMS	*Journal of the American Musicological Society*
JbMP	*Jahrbuch der Musikbibliothek Peters*
JMT	*Journal of Music Theory*
JRBM	*Journal of Renaissance and Baroque Music*
Mf	*Die Musikforschung*
MGG	*Die Musik in Geschichte und Gegenwart*
ML	*Music and Letters*
MMg	*Monatshefte für Musikgeschichte*
MQ	*The Musical Quarterly*
MR	*The Musical Review*
MT	*The Musical Times*
NM	Nagels Musikarchiv
NRMI	*Nuova rivista musicale italiana*
NZM	*Neue Zeitschrift für Musik*

ÖMz	*Österreichische Musikzeitschrift*
PRMA	*Proceedings of the Royal Musical Association*
RBM	*Revue belge de musicologie*
RiemannL	*Riemann Musik Lexikon*
SBA	**Stuttgarter Bach-Ausgabe**
SIMG	*Sammelbände der Internationalen Musik-Gesellschaft*
STMf	*Svensk tidskrift för musikforskning*
ZfM	*Zeitschrift für Musik*
ZMw	*Zeitschrift für Musikwissenschaft*

Preface

This volume is one of a series of short biographies derived from *The New Grove Dictionary of Music and Musicians* (London, 1980). In its original form, the text was written in the mid-1970s, and finalized at the end of that decade. For this reprint, the text has been re-read and modified by the original authors and corrections and changes have been made. In particular, an effort has been made to bring the bibliographies up to date and to incorporate the findings of recent research.

The fact that the texts of the books in this series originated as dictionary articles inevitably gives them a character somewhat different from that of books conceived as such. They are designed, first of all, to accommodate a very great deal of information in a manner that makes reference quick and easy. Their first concern is with fact rather than opinion, and this leads to a larger than usual proportion of the texts being devoted to biography than to critical discussion. The nature of a reference work gives it a particular obligation to convey received knowledge and to treat of composers' lives and works in an encyclopedic fashion, with proper acknowledgment of sources and due care to reflect different standpoints, rather than to embody imaginative or speculative writing about a composer's character or his music. It is hoped that the comprehensive work-lists and extended bibliographies, indicative of the origins of the books in a reference work, will be valuable to the reader who is eager for full and accurate reference information and who may not have ready access to *The New Grove Dictionary* or who may prefer to have it in this more compact form.

The lists of works in this volume are contributed by the authors of the corresponding texts, except in the case of J. S. Bach, where the list was originally prepared by

Richard Jones and has now been revised by Stephen Daw (with help from Christoph Wolff, Alfred Dürr and Robert L. Marshall), and J. C. Bach, where the list was originally prepared by Ellwood Derr and Ernest Warburton and has been revised by Stephen Roe and Dr Warburton (with help from Dr Derr and Richard Maunder). The section on the Bach Revival (J. S. Bach) was contributed by Nicholas Temperley.

S.S.

Introduction

From the 16th century to the early 19th, the Bach family produced musicians of every kind in number beyond parallel: from fiddlers and town musicians to organists, Kantors, court musicians and Kapellmeisters. The greatest among them was of course Johann Sebastian Bach, although there were distinguished musicians in earlier, contemporary and later generations.

The musician members of the family are listed below, in alphabetical order, with brief biographical notes on those who are not the subject of later chapters. This is followed by a general history of the family, and then a series of separate chapters dealing with the family's most important members. The italic numeral in parentheses following the name of each member is taken from the family genealogy (or *Ursprung*; see *Bach-Dokumente*, i, no.184) drawn up in 1735, as far as no.*53*; numbers thereafter are assigned on a continuation of the same principle (the inadvertent fusion in 1735 into one nameless individual of Caspar (*b c*1570) and Lips (*b c*1552), both with the number *3*, which was also allotted to their descendants, has been corrected, but the *3* is shown along with the new number to facilitate comparisons). The arabic numeral preceding the names of family members refers to their individual chapters below; non-musician members of the family are excluded, but some musicians of the family, who are apparently not members of the main, Wechmar line are included without numbering.

List of musicians

Carl Philipp Emanuel Bach (*46*) (*b* Weimar, 8 March 1714; *d* Hamburg, 14 Dec 1788). Son of Johann Sebastian (*24*); see chapter 9.

Caspar Bach (*3/56*) (*b c*1570; *d* Arnstadt, after 1640). Possibly a son of Hans (*54*). He was Stadtpfeifer in Gotha in 1619, and court and town musician (bassoonist) in Arnstadt, 1620–33.

Caspar Bach (*3/58*) (*b c*1600). Son of Caspar (*3/56*). He was educated as a musician (violinist) at the courts of Bayreuth (1621–3) and Dresden (1623), at the expense of the Count of Schwarzburg-Arnstadt; he probably went to Italy, and nothing further is known of him.

Christoph Bach (*5*) (*b* Wechmar, 19 April 1613; *d* Arnstadt, 12 Sept 1661). Son of Johann (*2*). He was a court musician in Weimar, then from 1642 a town musician in Erfurt and from 1654 court and town musician in Arnstadt. A musical entry by him in the album of Georg F. Reimann, Kantor in Saalfeld, survives (see *BJb*, xxv, 1928, p.175).

Ernst Carl Gottfried Bach (*81*) (*b* Ohrdruf, 12 Jan 1738; *d* Ohrdruf, 21 July 1801). Son of Johann Christoph (*42*). He was Kantor in Wechmar, 1765–72, then at St Michael's, Ohrdruf.

Ernst Christian Bach (*82*) (*b* Ohrdruf, 28 Sept 1747; *d* Wechmar, 29 Sept 1822). Son of Johann Christoph (*42*). He was Kantor in Wechmar, 1773–1819.

Georg Christoph Bach (*10*) (*b* Erfurt, baptized 8 Sept 1642; *d* Schweinfurt, 24 April 1697). Son of Christoph (*5*). He was Kantor in Themar from 1668 and in Schweinfurt from 1684. One composition by him is extant, the vocal concerto *Siehe, wie fein und lieblich ist*

es (1689) for two tenors, bass and instruments (EDM, 1st ser., ii, 1935, p.22; SBA). See F. Müller: 'Georg Christoph Bach', *Die Musik*, xxxiv (1942), 361.

Georg Friedrich Bach (*b* Tann, 17 March 1793; *d* Iserlohn, 2 Oct 1860). Not a member of the Wechmar line, he was a son of Johann Michael (see chapter 13). A flautist, he deserted from Napoleon's army and went to Sweden, where he became music teacher to the crown prince (later Oscar I). He returned to Germany and became music director in Elberfeld and Iserlohn. Manuscripts of works and a harmony textbook by him survive (*D-EIb*).

Georg Michael Bach (*74*) (*b* Ruhla, baptized 27 Sept 1703; *d* Halle, 18 Feb 1771). Son of Johann Jacob (*68*). He was Kantor at St Ulrich's, Halle, from 1747.

Gottfried Heinrich Bach (*48*) (*b* Leipzig, 26 Feb 1724; *d* Naumburg, buried 12 Feb 1763). Eldest son of Johann Sebastian (*24*) and Anna Magdalena Bach. Although he became feeble-minded at an early age, he played the keyboard well and, according to C. P. E. Bach, he showed 'a great genius, which however failed to develop'. From 1750 he lived with his brother-in-law J. C. Altnikol.

Gottlieb Friedrich Bach (*76*) (*b* Meiningen, 10 Sept 1714; *d* Meiningen, 25 Feb 1785). Son of Johann Ludwig (*3/72*). He was court organist and painter (*Kabinettsmaler*) in Meiningen.

Hans Bach: see under Johann Bach below (unnumbered, *2* and *4*).

Heinrich Bach (*3/62*) (*d* Arnstadt, buried 27 May 1635). Son of Caspar (*3/56*). He is listed in the death register as the blind son of Caspar, and is thus probably the 'blind Jonas' mentioned in the *Ursprung*. He was

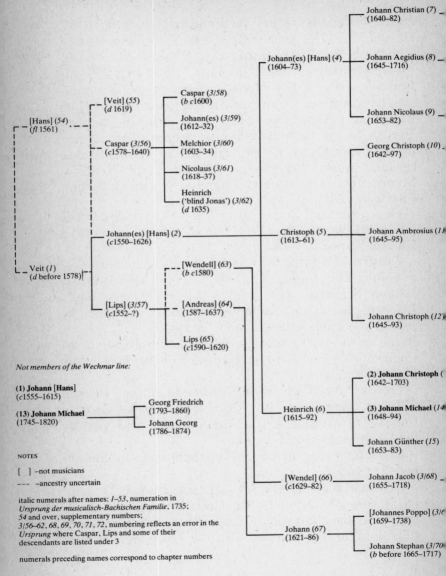

1. The Bach Family Tree

Johann Christian (7)
(1640–82)

Johann(es) [Hans] (4)
(1604–73)

Johann Aegidius (8)
(1645–1716)

Johann Nicolaus (9)
(1653–82)

Caspar (3/58)
(b c1600)

Johann(es) (3/59)
(1612–32)

Melchior (3/60)
(1603–34)

Nicolaus (3/61)
(1618–37)

Heinrich
('blind Jonas') (3/62)
(d 1635)

[Veit] (55)
(d 1619)

Caspar (3/56)
(c1578–1640)

[Hans] (54)
(fl 1561)

Georg Christoph (10)
(1642–97)

Christoph (5)
(1613–61)

Johann Ambrosius (11)
(1645–95)

Johann(es) [Hans] (2)
(c1550–1626)

Johann Christoph (12)
(1645–93)

[Wendell] (63)
(b c1580)

Veit (1)
(d before 1578)

[Lips] (3/57)
(c1552–?)

[Andreas] (64)
(1587–1637)

Lips (65)
(c1590–1620)

(2) Johann Christoph
(1642–1703)

Heinrich (6)
(1615–92)

(3) Johann Michael (14)
(1648–94)

Johann Günther (15)
(1653–83)

Not members of the Wechmar line:

(1) Johann [Hans]
(c1555–1615)

(13) Johann Michael
(1745–1820)

Georg Friedrich
(1793–1860)

Johann Georg
(1786–1874)

Johann Jacob (3/68)
(1655–1718)

[Wendel] (66)
(c1629–82)

[Johannes Poppo] (3/69)
(1659–1738)

Johann (67)
(1621–86)

Johann Stephan (3/70)
(b before 1665–1717)

NOTES

[ ] – not musicians

- - - – ancestry uncertain

italic numerals after names: *1–53*, numeration in
Ursprung der musicalisch-Bachischen Familie, 1735;
54 and over, supplementary numbers;
3/56–62, 68, 69, 70, 71, 72, numbering reflects an error in the
Ursprung where Caspar, Lips and some of their
descendants are listed under 3

numerals preceding names correspond to chapter numbers

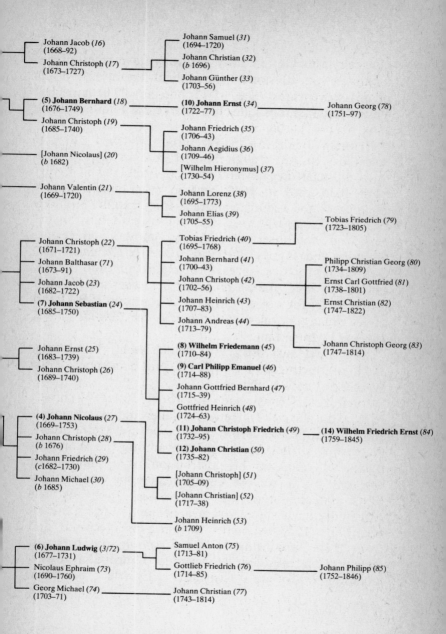

Johann Jacob (16)
(1668–92)

Johann Christoph (17)
(1673–1727)

Johann Samuel (31)
(1694–1720)

Johann Christian (32)
(b 1696)

Johann Günther (33)
(1703–56)

(5) Johann Bernhard (18)
(1676–1749)

(10) Johann Ernst (34)
(1722–77)

Johann Georg (78)
(1751–97)

Johann Christoph (19)
(1685–1740)

Johann Friedrich (35)
(1706–43)

Johann Aegidius (36)
(1709–46)

[Wilhelm Hieronymus] (37)
(1730–54)

[Johann Nicolaus] (20)
(b 1682)

Johann Valentin (21)
(1669–1720)

Johann Lorenz (38)
(1695–1773)

Johann Elias (39)
(1705–55)

Johann Christoph (22)
(1671–1721)

Johann Balthasar (71)
(1673–91)

Johann Jacob (23)
(1682–1722)

(7) Johann Sebastian (24)
(1685–1750)

Tobias Friedrich (40)
(1695–1768)

Tobias Friedrich (79)
(1723–1805)

Johann Bernhard (41)
(1700–43)

Johann Christoph (42)
(1702–56)

Philipp Christian Georg (80)
(1734–1809)

Ernst Carl Gottfried (81)
(1738–1801)

Ernst Christian (82)
(1747–1822)

Johann Heinrich (43)
(1707–83)

Johann Andreas (44)
(1713–79)

Johann Christoph Georg (83)
(1747–1814)

Johann Ernst (25)
(1683–1739)

Johann Christoph (26)
(1689–1740)

(8) Wilhelm Friedemann (45)
(1710–84)

(9) Carl Philipp Emanuel (46)
(1714–88)

Johann Gottfried Bernhard (47)
(1715–39)

Gottfried Heinrich (48)
(1724–63)

(4) Johann Nicolaus (27)
(1669–1753)

Johann Christoph (28)
(b 1676)

Johann Friedrich (29)
(c1682–1730)

Johann Michael (30)
(b 1685)

(11) Johann Christoph Friedrich (49)
(1732–95)

(14) Wilhelm Friedrich Ernst (84)
(1759–1845)

(12) Johann Christian (50)
(1735–82)

[Johann Christoph] (51)
(1705–09)

[Johann Christian] (52)
(1717–38)

Johann Heinrich (53)
(b 1709)

(6) Johann Ludwig (3/72)
(1677–1731)

Samuel Anton (75)
(1713–81)

Gottlieb Friedrich (76)
(1714–85)

Johann Philipp (85)
(1752–1846)

Nicolaus Ephraim (73)
(1690–1760)

Georg Michael (74)
(1703–71)

Johann Christian (77)
(1743–1814)

musically educated in Italy and may have received the nickname (an allusion to the biblical figure) as a result of his adventures. See M. Schneider: 'Thematisches Verzeichnis der musikalischen Werke der Familie Bach', *BJb*, iv (1907), 105.

Heinrich Bach (*6*) (*b* Wechmar, 16 Sept 1615; *d* Arnstadt, 10 July 1692). Son of Johann (*2*). He was town musician in Schweinfurt from 1629 and in Erfurt from 1635, and in 1641 became town musician and organist of the Liebfrauenkirche in Arnstadt. His funeral sermon (*MMg*, vii, 1875, p.178) calls him an experienced composer of chorales, motets, concertos, preludes and fugues. A vocal concerto *Ich danke dir, Gott* (1681) for five voices, strings and continuo (EDM, 1st ser., ii, 1935, p.3); a *lamento, Ach, dass ich Wassers genug hätte*, for voice, strings and continuo (SBA) and three organ chorales (*Orgelwerke der Familie Bach*, 1967, p.1) are extant.

Johann [Hans] Bach (*b* Andelsbuch, Vorarlberg, *c*1555; *d* Nürtingen, 1 Dec 1615). Not a member of the Wechmar line; see chapter 1.

Johann(es) [Hans] Bach (*2*) (*b* *c*1550; *d* Wechmar, 1626). Son of Veit (*1*). He was a baker and carpetmaker, and, in that he was also a *Spielmann* (minstrel, fiddler), the earliest professional musician among the Wechmar Bachs. He received his instruction as a Stadtpfeifer before 1567 at Schloss Grimmenstein in Gotha from Matz Zisecke and his predecessor (not, as has repeatedly been stated, from a person by the name of Bach). By 1577 he owned a house in Wechmar and from there, according to the *Ursprung*, he travelled widely as a musician to various Thuringian towns, including Gotha, Arnstadt, Erfurt, Eisenach,

Schmalkalden and Suhl. The Wechmar death register notes him as 'Hanss Bach ein Spielmann'.

Johann(es) Bach (*3/59*) (*b* 1612; *d* Arnstadt, buried 9 Dec 1632). Son of Caspar (*3/56*). He was a Stadtpfeifer in Arnstadt.

Johann(es) [Hans] Bach (*4*) (*b* Wechmar, 26 Nov 1604; *d* Erfurt, buried 13 May 1673). Son of Johann (*2*). He had a seven-year apprenticeship and journeyman period with the Stadtpfeifer Christoph Hoffmann in Suhl, after which he became a town musician in Erfurt; from 1636 he was organist of the Predigerkirche there. Two motets by him are extant: *Unser Leben ist ein Schatten* (six parts with a three-part echo choir; SBA) and *Sei nun wieder zufrieden* (eight voices; SBA), as well as an aria *Weint nicht um meinen Tod* for four voices and continuo (EDM, 1st ser., i, 1935, p.3; SBA). See S. Orth: 'Neues über der Stammvater der "Erfurter" Bache, Johann Bach', *Mf*, ix (1956), 447; S. Orth: 'Johann Bach, der Stammvater der Erfurter Bache', *BJb*, cix (1973), 79.

Johann Bach (*67*) (*b* Themar, 1621; *d* Lehnstedt, 12 Sept 1686). Son of the alderman Andreas (*64*) (*b* 1587; *d* Suhl, 21 April 1637). He was Kantor in Ilmenau and from 1668 deacon there; in 1680 he was appointed vicar of Lehnstedt.

Johann Aegidius Bach (*8*) (*b* Erfurt, baptized 11 Feb 1645; *d* Erfurt, buried 22 Nov 1716). Son of Johann (*4*). In 1671 he was a violinist in the Erfurt town music, becoming its director in 1682; from 1690 he also held the position of organist at St Michael's, in succession to Pachelbel.

Johann Aegidius Bach (*36*) (*b* Erfurt, baptized 4 Aug 1709; *d* Gross-Monra, nr. Kölleda, 17 May 1746). Son

of Johann Christoph (*19*). He was Kantor of Gross-Monra.

Johann Ambrosius Bach (*11*) (*b* Erfurt, 22 Feb 1645; *d* Eisenach, 20 Feb 1695). Son of Christoph (*5*) and twin brother of Johann Christoph (*12*). On 8 April 1668 he married Maria Elisabeth Lämmerhirt (*b* Erfurt, 24 Feb 1644; *d* Eisenach, buried 3 May 1694). He was Stadtpfeifer in Arnstadt and from 1667 violinist in the Erfurt town music. From 1671 he was a court trumpeter and director of the town music in Eisenach. He must have been an outstanding and versatile musician: the Eisenach town chronicler noted that 'In 1672 the new Hausmann [director of town music] made music at Easter with organ, violins, voices, trumpets and kettledrums, something never before known in the history of Eisenach'. When in 1684 he was offered the important position of director of the town band in Erfurt, the Duke of Eisenach was unwilling to allow him to go and he was compelled to decline the offer. A portrait of him, painted after 1671, is extant (*D-Bds*). See F. Rollberg: 'Johann Ambrosius Bach, Stadtpfeifer zu Eisenach von 1671–1695', *BJb*, xxiv (1927), 133; C. Freyse: 'Das Porträt Ambrosius Bach', *BJb*, xlvi (1959), 149.

Johann Andreas Bach (*44*) (*b* Ohrdruf, 7 Sept 1713; *d* Ohrdruf, 25 Oct 1779). Son of Johann Christoph (*22*). In 1733 he was an oboist in the military band in Gotha; from 1738 he was organist of the Trinity Church in Ohrdruf and from 1743 of St Michael's in the same town. He owned the so-called *Johann Andreas Bach Buch* (*D-LEm*, Sammlung Becker III.8.4), one of the principal sources of the early keyboard works of Johann Sebastian (*24*).

Johann Balthasar Bach (*71*) (*b* Eisenach, 4 March 1673; *d* Eisenach, 11 June 1691). Son of Johann Ambrosius (*11*). He was Stadtpfeifer apprentice to his father.

Johann Bernhard Bach (*18*) (*b* Erfurt, baptized 25 Nov 1676; *d* Eisenach, 11 June 1749). Son of Johann Aegidius (*8*); see chapter 5.

Johann Bernhard Bach (*41*) (*b* Ohrdruf, 24 Nov 1700; *d* Ohrdruf, 12 June 1743). Son of Johann Christoph (*22*). From 1715 to 1719 he studied with Johann Sebastian Bach in Weimar and Cöthen and from 1721 he was organist of St Michael's, Ohrdruf. A suite in E♭ and a sonata in B♭, both for keyboard, were cited by Spitta.

Johann Christian Bach (*7*) (*b* Erfurt, baptized 17 Aug 1640; *d* Erfurt, buried 1 July 1682). Son of Johann (*4*). He was a violinist in the Erfurt town music, then town musician in Eisenach; in 1667 he became director of the Erfurt town music.

Johann Christian Bach (*32*) (*b* Erfurt, 1696). Son of Johann Christoph (*17*). He was a musician in Sondershausen.

Johann Christian Bach (*50*) (*b* Leipzig, 5 Sept 1735; *d* London, 1 Jan 1782). Son of Johann Sebastian (*24*); see chapter 12.

Johann Christian Bach (*77*) (*b* Halle, 1743; *d* Halle, 1814). Son of Georg Michael (*74*). He studied with Wilhelm Friedemann Bach in Halle and received from him the autograph of Johann Sebastian Bach's *Clavierbüchlein für Wilhelm Friedemann*. He was a teacher at the Pedagogium (preparatory school) in Halle and is known as the 'Clavier-Bach'.

Johann Christoph Bach (*13*) (*b* Arnstadt, baptized 8 Dec 1642; *d* Eisenach, buried 2 April 1703). Son of Heinrich (*6*); see chapter 2.

Johann Christoph Bach (*12*) (*b* Erfurt, 22 Feb 1645; *d* Arnstadt, 25 Aug 1693). Son of Christoph (*5*). In 1666 he was a town musician in Erfurt, and from 1671 court and town musician (violinist) in Arnstadt.

Johann Christoph Bach (*22*) (*b* Erfurt, 16 June 1671; *d* Ohrdruf, 22 Feb 1721). Son of Johann Ambrosius (*11*). He studied in Erfurt with Pachelbel from 1685 to 1688, when he became organist of St Thomas's in Erfurt; from 1690 he was organist of St Michael's, Ohrdruf. From 1695 to 1700 he gave instruction to his brother Johann Sebastian (*24*), who lived in his house after their parents' death. He has been identified as the main copyist of two major keyboard anthologies, important sources for some of Johann Sebastian's early works: the *Johann Andreas Bach Buch* (*D-LEm*, Sammlung Becker III.8.4) and the Möllersche Handschrift (*D-B*, Mus. ms. 40644). See C. Freyse: *Die Ohrdrufer Bache in der Silhouette: J. S. Bachs ältester Bruder Johann Christoph und seine Nachkommen* (Eisenach, 1957) and H.-J. Schulze: *Studien zur Bach-Überlieferung im 18. Jahrhundert* (diss., U. of Rostock, 1977).

Johann Christoph Bach (*17*) (*b* Erfurt, baptized 13 Jan 1673; *d* Gehren, buried 30 July 1727). Son of Johann Christian (*7*). He was Kantor in Erfurt from 1695 and Kantor and organist in Gehren from 1698.

Johann Christoph Bach (*28*) (*b* Eisenach, baptized 29 Aug 1676). Son of Johann Christoph (*13*). He was a harpsichordist in Erfurt, and travelled to England via Hamburg (where evidence of him is dated 1708–9) and

Rotterdam (1717–20); it seems that he never returned to his home country. See C. Oefner: 'Neues zur Biographie von Johann Christoph Bach (geb.1676)', *DJbM*, xiv (1969), 121.

Johann Christoph Bach (*19*) (*b* Erfurt, baptized 17 Aug 1685; *d* Erfurt, buried 15 May 1740). Son of Johann Aegidius (*8*). He was a member of the Erfurt town music from 1705 and became its director in 1716.

Johann Christoph Bach (*26*) (*b* Arnstadt, 12 Sept 1689; *d* Blankenhain, buried 28 Feb 1740). Son of Johann Christoph (*12*). In 1714 he was organist in Keula and from 1729 organist, teacher and merchant in Blankenhain.

Johann Christoph Bach (*42*) (*b* Ohrdruf, 12 Nov 1702; *d* Ohrdruf, 2 Nov 1756). Son of Johann Christoph (*22*). He was Kantor in Ohrdruf from 1728.

Johann Christoph Friedrich Bach (*49*) (*b* Leipzig, 21 June 1732; *d* Bückeburg, 26 Jan 1795). Son of Johann Sebastian (*24*); see chapter 11.

Johann Christoph Georg Bach (*83*) (*b* Ohrdruf, 8 May 1747; *d* Ohrdruf, 30 Dec 1814). Son of Johann Andreas (*44*). He was organist of St Michael's in Ohrdruf from 1779.

Johann Elias Bach (*39*) (*b* Schweinfurt, 12 Feb 1705; *d* Schweinfurt, 30 Nov 1755). Son of Johann Valentin (*21*). He studied theology at Jena from 1728 and at Leipzig from 1738. He lived with Johann Sebastian (*24*) as his private secretary, pupil and tutor of his younger children until 1742. In 1743 he became Kantor of St John's in Schweinfurt and inspector of the church boarding-school. See K. Pottgiesser: 'Die Briefentwürfe des Johann Elias Bach', *Die Musik*, xii (1912–13), 3; F. Beyschlag: 'Ein Schweinfurter Ableger der thüringischen

Musikerfamilie Bach', *Schweinfurter Heimatblätter*, xi (1925).

Johann Ernst Bach (*25*) (*b* Arnstadt, 5 Aug 1683; *d* Arnstadt, 21 March 1739). Son of Johann Christoph (*12*). He studied in Hamburg and Frankfurt and in 1707 became organist of the Neukirche at Arnstadt, succeeding Johann Sebastian (*24*). During winter 1705–6 he had deputized for Johann Sebastian during the latter's journey to Lübeck to visit Buxtehude. From 1728 he was organist of the Liebfrauenkirche, Arnstadt.

Johann Ernst Bach (*34*) (*b* Eisenbach, baptized 30 Jan 1722; *d* Eisenach, 1 Sept 1777). Son of Johann Bernhard (*18*); see chapter 10.

Johann Friedrich Bach (*29*) (*b* Eisenach, *c*1682; *d* Mühlhausen, buried 8 Feb 1730). Son of Johann Christoph (*13*). After attending the University of Jena, he succeeded Johann Sebastian (*24*) as organist of St Blasius's church in Mühlhausen in 1708. An organ fugue in G minor by him is extant (*D-Bds*).

Johann Friedrich Bach (*35*) (*b* Erfurt, baptized 22 Oct 1706; *d* Andisleben, nr. Erfurt, buried 30 May 1743). Son of Johann Christoph (*19*). He was organist in Quedlinburg and by 1735 a schoolmaster in Andisleben.

Johann Georg Bach (*78*) (*b* Eisenach, baptized 2 Oct 1751; *d* Eisenach, 1797). Son of Johann Ernst (*34*). In 1777 he succeeded his father as court and town organist, titular Kapellmeister, notary and town treasurer in Eisenach.

Johann Georg Bach (*b* Güstrow, *c*1786; *d* Elberfeld, 6 Dec 1874). Not a member of the Wechmar line, he was a son of Johann Michael (see chapter 13) and a music teacher in Elberfeld.

Johann Gottfried Bernhard Bach (*47*) (*b* Weimar, 11

May 1715; *d* Jena, 27 May 1739). Son of Johann Sebastian (*24*). He was a pupil of his father; in 1735 he became organist of St Mary's in Mühlhausen and in 1737 of the Jakobikirche in Sangerhausen (a post his father had applied for in 1702). By spring 1738 he had left that position. In a letter of 26 May 1738 Johann Sebastian complained bitterly about his 'undutiful son', who displayed an unstable character and had incurred debts. He enrolled as a law student at the University of Jena on 28 January 1739 but died soon afterwards; the cause is unknown.

Johann Günther Bach (*15*) (*b* Arnstadt, baptized 17 July 1653; *d* Arnstadt, buried 10 April 1683). Son of Heinrich (*6*). He was assistant organist to his father in Arnstadt from 1682 and was also active as a keyboard and violin maker.

Johann Günther Bach (*33*) (*b* Gehren, 4 April 1703; *d* Erfurt, buried 24 Oct 1756). Son of Johann Christoph (*17*). He was a town musician (tenor and viola player) and a teacher in Erfurt by 1735. His *Orgelbuch*, an anthology of keyboard music of J. Pachelbel, J. C. F. Fischer, and other 17th-century masters, but also including works of J. S. Bach, has been preserved in the Lowell Mason Collection (*US-NH* LM 4983).

Johann Heinrich Bach (*43*) (*b* Ohrdruf, 4 Aug 1707; *d* Oehringen, 20 May 1783). Son of Johann Christoph (*22*). He was a pupil of Johann Sebastian (*24*) and one of his principal copyists (formerly known as 'Hauptkopist C') at the Leipzig Thomasschule, 1724–8. He then became assistant organist to his father in Ohrdruf and in 1735 was appointed Kantor at Oehringen.

Johann Heinrich Bach (*53*) (*b* Hamburg, baptized 4 Nov 1709). Son of Johann Christoph (*28*). According

to the *Ursprung* he was 'a good keyboard player'.

Johann Jacob Bach (*3/68*) (*b* Wolfsbehringen, 12 Sept 1655; *d* Ruhla, 11 Dec 1718). Son of Wendel (*66*) (*b* Wechmar, 1629 or 1631; *d* Wolfsbehringen, 18 Dec 1682), a farmer 'who could also sing well', and grandson of Wendel (*63*) (*b* c1580). Johann Jacob went to school in Eisenach, and was later organist in Thal, Kantor in Steinbach, Kantor in Wasungen (1690–94) and thereafter in Ruhla.

Johann Jacob Bach (*16*) (*b* Erfurt, baptized 14 Aug 1668; *d* Eisenach, buried 29 April 1692). Son of Johann Christian (*7*). He served his Stadtpfeifer apprenticeship and journeyman period under Johann Ambrosius Bach (*11*) in Eisenach.

Johann Jacob Bach (*23*) (*b* Eisenach, baptized 11 Feb 1682; *d* Stockholm, 16 April 1722). Son of Johann Ambrosius (*11*). He received instruction as a Stadtpfeifer in Eisenach with Johann Heinrich Halle, his father's successor, and in 1704 became an oboist with the Swedish guard. He went with the Swedish army under Charles XII to Turkey and took flute lessons in Constantinople with P. G. Buffardin. From 1713 he was a chamber musician at the Stockholm court. About 1704 Johann Sebastian (*24*) wrote a Capriccio (BWV992) on Johann Jacob's departure from his home country. See A. Protz: 'Johann Sebastian Bachs Capriccio sopra la lontananza del suo fratello dilettissimo', *Mf*, x (1957), 405.

Johann Lorenz Bach (*38*) (*b* Schweinfurt, 10 Sept 1695; *d* Lahm im Itzgrund, 14 Dec 1773). Son of Johann Valentin (*21*). He was a pupil of Johann Sebastian (*24*) in Weimar, 1715–17, and from 1718 was organist and Kantor in Lahm. An organ fugue in D by him is extant (*Orgelwerke der Familie Bach*, 1967,

p.31); the manuscript of the prelude belonging to it (incipit in *BJb,* xxxvii, 1949–50, p.108) was lost in World War II. See O. Kaul: *Zur Musikgeschichte der ehemaligen Reichstadt Schweinfurt* (Würzburg, 1935).

Johann Ludwig Bach (*3/72*) (*b* Thal, nr. Eisenach, 4 Feb 1677; *d* Meiningen, buried 1 May 1731). Son of Johann Jacob (*3/68*); see chapter 6.

Johann Michael Bach (*14*) (*b* Arnstadt, baptized 9 Aug 1648; *d* Gehren, 17 May 1694). Son of Heinrich (*6*); see chapter 3.

Johann Michael Bach (*30*) (*b* Eisenach, baptized 1 Aug 1685). Son of Johann Christoph (*13*). He left Eisenach in 1703; nothing is certainly known of his later life except that he was active in Stockholm as an organ builder.

Johann Michael Bach (*b* Struth, nr. Schmalkalden, 9 Nov 1745; *d* Elberfeld, 1820). Not a member of the Wechmar line but from a Hessian branch of the family; see chapter 13.

Johann Nicolaus Bach (*9*) (*b* Erfurt, baptized 5 Feb 1653; *d* Erfurt, buried 30 July 1682). Son of Johann (*4*). From 1673 he was an Erfurt town musician (viol).

Johann Nicolaus Bach (*27*) (*b* Eisenach, 10 Oct 1669; *d* Jena, 4 Nov 1753). Son of Johann Christoph (*13*); see chapter 4.

Johann Philipp Bach (*85*) (*b* Meiningen, 5 Aug 1752; *d* Meiningen, 2 Nov 1846). Son of Gottlieb Friedrich (*76*). From 1790 he was court organist and painter (*Kabinettsmaler*) in Meiningen.

Johann Samuel Bach (*31*) (*b* Niederzimmern, 4 June 1694; *d* Gundersleben, 1 July 1720). Son of Johann Christoph (*17*). He was a musician and teacher in Sondershausen and Gundersleben.

Johann Sebastian Bach (*24*) (*b* Eisenach, 21 March

1685; *d* Leipzig, 28 July 1750). Son of Johann Ambrosius (*11*); see chapter 7.

Johann Stephan Bach (*3/70*) (*b* Ilmenau, before 1665; *d* Brunswick, 10 Jan 1717). Son of Johann (*67*). He was Kantor at the Cathedral of St Blasius in Brunswick from 1690; he also wrote sonnets.

Johann Valentin Bach (*21*) (*b* Themar, 6 Jan 1669; *d* Schweinfurt, 12 Aug 1720). Son of Georg Christoph (*10*). He was town musician and head tower watchman (*Obertürmer*) in Schweinfurt from 1694.

Lips [Philippus] Bach (*65*) (*b* Wechmar, c1590; *d* Wechmar, 10 Oct 1620). Son of the carpetmaker Lips (*3/57*) (*b* c1552) who was a son of Veit (*1*); see p.22ff. The younger Lips was a musician.

Melchior Bach (*3/60*) (*b* 1603; *d* Arnstadt, buried 7 Sept 1634). Son of Caspar (*3/56*). He was a Stadtpfeifer in Arnstadt.

Nicolaus Bach (*3/61*) (*b* Arnstadt, 1618; *d* Arnstadt, buried 1 Oct 1637). Son of Caspar (*3/56*). He was a Stadtpfeifer in Arnstadt.

Nicolaus Ephraim Bach (*73*) (*b* Wasungen, baptized 26 Nov 1690; *d* Gandersheim, 1760). Son of Johann Jacob (*3/68*). In 1708 he was appointed musician and in 1719 organist at the Meiningen court. In 1724 he became organist in Gandersheim.

Philipp Christian Georg Bach (*80*) (*b* Ohrdruf, 5 April 1734; *d* Wernigshausen, 18 Aug 1809). Son of Johann Christoph (*42*). He was Kantor of St Michael's, Ohrdruf, 1759–72, and thereafter a vicar in Wernigshausen.

Samuel Anton Bach (*75*) (*b* Meiningen, 26 April 1713; *d* Meiningen, 1781). Son of Johann Ludwig (*3/72*). He studied with Johann Sebastian (*24*) in

Leipzig around 1732; later he was court organist in Meiningen and for a time also court painter.

Tobias Friedrich Bach (*40*) (*b* Ohrdruf, 21 July 1695; *d* Udestedt, 1 July 1768). Son of Johann Christoph (*22*). He was organist of the Trinity Church in Ohrdruf from 1714 until 1717, when he became court Kantor in Gandersheim. In 1720 he became Kantor in Pferdingsleben and the next year in Udestedt.

Tobias Friedrich Bach (*79*) (*b* Udestedt, 22 Sept 1723; *d* Erfurt, 18 Jan 1805). Son of Tobias Friedrich (*40*). In 1747 he became Kantor of the Reglerkirche in Erfurt and in 1762 of the Franciscan Church there.

Veit Bach (*1*) (*b* ?Pressburg [now Bratislava]; *d* Wechmar, before 1578). A baker by trade, he was the earliest member of the family to show musical proclivities and was head of the Wechmar line; see p.21ff.

Wilhelm Friedemann Bach (*45*) (*b* Weimar, 22 Nov 1710; *d* Berlin, 1 July 1784). Son of Johann Sebastian (*24*); see chapter 8.

Wilhelm Friedrich Ernst Bach (*84*) (*b* Bückeburg, baptized 27 May 1759; *d* Berlin, 25 Dec 1845). Son of Johann Christoph Friedrich (*49*); see chapter 14.

Family history

The Bach family lived and worked in central Germany, primarily in Thuringia, with the duchies and principalities of Saxe-Eisenach, Saxe-Gotha, Saxe-Meiningen, Saxe-Weimar, the county of Schwarzburg-Arnstadt and the town of Erfurt, belonging to the Mainz electorate. The region, bitterly split politically though unified denominationally, had its own cultural traditions and, despite the turmoils of war and other vicissitudes, enjoyed a varied and firmly based economic life. In these

conditions a lively musical atmosphere flourished, encouraged by the ambitious displays of magnificence of the small courts, by the individual towns' need for prestige, and by the consciousness of a strong musical tradition and post-Reformation zeal in the church in this the home country of Lutheranism. The growth and decline of the Bach family, like that of other families of musicians (for example the Hasses), is closely linked with these social conditions: initially with the rapid expansion of musical practice in courts, towns and churches towards the end of the 16th century, then with the decline in importance of the leading musical institutions such as court orchestras, Stadtpfeifer bands and church choirs in the face of the increasingly popular bourgeois music culture of the later 18th century.

The musical life of Thuringia was small in scale but varied. The region – perhaps in the aftermath of the Thirty Years War – had no important centre, such as a city or court with a large opera company, and hence held no particular attraction for musicians of standing. A sound, ordinary ability served to accord members of the Bach family a pre-eminent position in local musical life; only a few achieved anything extraordinary, and most of those drifted away from their original environment.

The unusual concentration of musical talent within a single family and territory has long interested scholars concerned with genealogy, heredity and talent. The continual reappearance of musical talent during several generations (the singular culmination being Johann Sebastian Bach) within an increasingly large and then sharply declining number of prominent family members remains a unique phenomenon. The prerequisite for the

18

development of such a dynasty of musicians was a general emphasis on craftsmanship in practical musical activities, so that from early childhood a musical career was virtually prescribed for the male members of the family. Musical training was given for the most part within the family group – by fathers, brothers, uncles, cousins or more distant relations. This is typical even of the later generations: for instance, Johann Sebastian taught six of his relatives (Johann Lorenz (*38*), Johann Bernhard (*41*), Johann Elias (*39*), Johann Heinrich (*43*), Samuel Anton (*75*), Johann Ernst (*34*)) as well as his own sons; Carl Philipp Emanuel (*46*) took his youngest brother Johann Christian (*50*) into his care, and Wilhelm Friedemann (*45*) taught his relative Johann Christian (*77*). Studies outside the region or educational journeys were certainly unusual, though Caspar's sons (*3/58–62*), Johann Nicolaus (*27*) and finally Johann Christian (*50*) went to Italy. In these circumstances, even Johann Sebastian's journey to study with Buxtehude in Lübeck must be considered out of the ordinary.

In a milieu so self-sufficient and so governed by guild thinking and professional regulations, intermarriage between families of musicians was frequent. This was certainly the case in Thuringia in, for example, the Wilcke, Lämmerhirt, Hoffmann and Bach families. Precisely these families were, in fact, mutually associated. The first wife of Johann (*4*), like that of his brother Heinrich (*6*), was a Hoffmann, and his second was a Lämmerhirt. Johann Sebastian too was typical: his mother was a Lämmerhirt (as, incidentally, was J. G. Walther's), his first wife a Bach and his second a Wilcke. Common social standing, professional interdependence

and musical interests created a close unity within the family, and their social status as 'outsiders' (during the 17th century musicians of lower rank were not normally permitted citizenship) was a significant factor in the family's solidarity. Strict religious attitudes also had an important role, and some members of the family even showed a tendency to sectarian religious behaviour. To deepen the manifold connections, there were regular family gatherings, which must have resembled small music festivals; Forkel wrote:

Since the company consisted of none but Kantors, organists and town musicians, all of whom had to do with the church . . . first of all, when all were assembled, a chorale was sung. From this devotional opening they proceeded to jesting, often in strong contrast to it. For now they would sing folksongs, the contents of which were partly comic and partly indelicate, all together and extempore, but in such a way that the several improvised parts made up a kind of harmony, although the text was different for each voice. They called this kind of extempore harmonizing [*Zusammenstimmung*] a quodlibet . . . and enjoyed a hearty laugh at it.

Johann Sebastian's early Quodlibet (BWV524), only partly extant, provides a characteristic example of this family speciality.

The family was keenly aware of its position as bearers of a musical tradition. It was with that consciousness that Johann Sebastian, in a letter to G. Erdmann (28 October 1730), described his children as 'born *musici*'; and as early as 1732 J. G. Walther's *Musicalisches Lexicon*, in which the first brief biography of Johann Sebastian appeared, referred expressly to the great master's roots in an unusual family of musicians. His obituary notice of 1754 made the point more fully. And it was Johann Sebastian himself who systematically investigated the family's history and musical heritage. His genealogy of the family, written down in 1735, is still the most reliable documentary evidence of the family history, above all in respect to the early generations.

(The original manuscript of the *Ursprung* is lost, but several copies are extant, among them a particularly important one of 1774–5 written for Forkel by Anna Carolina Philippina Bach, with additions by her father, Carl Philipp Emanuel.) Further, Johann Sebastian's estate contained a manuscript collection of compositions by the most important earlier members of the family, under the title 'Alt-Bachisches Archiv' (when acquired by the Berlin Singakademie in the 19th century it contained 20 works; that collection was lost in World War II, but other manuscripts originally in the 'Archiv' survived individually – ed. in EDM, 1st ser., i–ii, 1935). A number of entries are in the hand of Johann Ambrosius (*11*), suggesting that it was he who initiated the collection; Johann Sebastian later reordered it, adding some new title-pages, and put it to practical use (he prepared some instrumental parts).

*

The *Ursprung* traces the family as far back as Veit (*1*) in the mid-16th century. Up to the generation of Veit's grandsons, however, much remains unclear, and the lack of available archival documents in church records and elsewhere makes it impossible to clarify this period in the family's history. The supposition, found in some Bach literature, that Veit was a son of Hans (*54*) is untenable; this Hans, who can be traced in Wechmar in 1561, must have been a brother, cousin or other relative. Nothing is known of his profession. Although Hans is the earliest bearer of the name of Bach to be found in Wechmar, no further conclusion can be drawn from that. By this time the name of Bach (also often spelt 'Baach', hinting at the phonetic value of a long 'a', as in 'father'; see *Bach-Dokumente*, ii, nos.1 and 6) was

21

widespread in the Thuringian region, and it can be traced back to the 14th century, though there is no evidence that any of these earlier members of the family were involved in musical activity. The *Ursprung* says of Veit, who was a baker by trade, that his hobby was playing the 'cythringen' (a small cittern). There is an explicit additional sentence – 'this was, as it were, the beginning of music in his descendants' – which probably indicates that none of Veit's ancestors was a professional musician. Neither was Veit himself. He had most likely been driven from Moravia or Slovakia about 1545 as a result of the expulsion of Protestants in the Counter-Reformation, at the time of the Schmalkaldian War (1545–7). The reference to 'Hungary' in the *Ursprung* is not to be taken literally and in accordance with the terminology of the time must signify in general terms the central lands of the Habsburg Empire (including present-day Austria and Czechoslovakia). Veit took up residence in Wechmar – a small town located between Gotha and Ohrdruf – and must have died by 1577 as for that year his sons Johann (*2*) and Lips (*3/57*) are recorded as house-owners in Wechmar. Contrary to current opinion (which is based on the assumption that Hans was Veit's father), Veit did not migrate from Wechmar or Thuringia but (according to Korabinsky, 1784) was born in Moravia or Slovakia, as the son of an earlier migrant, possibly in or near Pressburg (now Bratislava). There, and elsewhere in the Habsburg lands, various people by the name of Bach can be traced in the 16th and 17th centuries, among them musicians such as the *Spielmann* (violinist) and jester Johann or Hans Bach (see chapter 1). It seems noteworthy that Count Questenberg, with whom J. S. Bach had connections,

employed a certain Maria Rosina Bach in 1721 as a maid at his Moravian castle Jaroměřice.

Another Veit Bach (*55*) died in Wechmar in 1619; nothing further is known of him. He should not be confused with Veit (*1*), the head of the Wechmar line of the Bach family; he may have been a son of Veit or Hans. In the 16th and early 17th centuries there were in Thuringia branches of the family which may have been connected either directly or indirectly with the Wechmar line and in which musicians are occasionally found (for example Eberhard Heinrich Bach, son of a Heinrich Bach, a trumpeter from Rohrborn near Erfurt who went to the Netherlands and emigrated to Indonesia about 1598). However, the *Ursprung* wisely limits itself to the smaller circle which can strictly be considered the musical family of Bachs.

Johann Bach (*2*), Veit's son, was the first member of the family to receive a thorough musical training and to pursue a musical career, even though he also pursued other activities. His sons were the first to follow music exclusively. By accepting salaried positions they became sedentary and distinct from non-organized musicians (or 'beer-fiddlers'), thereby taking the first step towards citizenship and breaking with the tradition of the *Spielmann* – although in their varied occupations as instrumentalists their background continued to have its effect.

Genealogical difficulties arise over a series of family members who were in some way connected with the main Wechmar line but whose precise extraction remains unclear. Indeed, the *Ursprung* has a lacuna concerning the brother of Johann (*2*). His name is not given, but his trade (carpetmaker) is mentioned and his

sons are briefly described. This has led to a confusion between two family members, Caspar (*3/56*) and Lips (*3/57*). According to the *Ursprung*, the sons of Johann's brother visited Italy; that can refer only to Caspar's sons who, it has been established, were encouraged to go there by the Count of Schwarzburg-Arnstadt. Further, Caspar had a blind son Heinrich (*3/62*), who must surely be the 'blind Jonas' mentioned in the *Ursprung*; and the ancestors of Johann Ludwig (*3/72*), connected with Johann's brother, can be related only to Lips. Thus either Johann had two brothers, or Caspar and Lips must at least have been so closely related that family tradition could plausibly merge them into one. It appears that Lips's descendants were farmers. The connection between Andreas (*64*) and Lips remains unclear: Andreas was an alderman in Themar, and his son Johann (*67*) was Kantor and later vicar, as were several of his descendants. In the *Ursprung* Johannes Poppo (*3/69*), brother of Johann Stephan (*3/70*), is listed as a priest, and the presence of Georg Michael (*74*) at his funeral in 1738 implies that they came from closely related branches of the family. Most probably the two lines had a common origin in Lips.

Almost all the Bachs were first and foremost instrumentalists; they were mainly keyboard players, but virtually all other instruments were represented, and in the true Stadtpfeifer tradition most of them learnt to play several instruments. Several of them were also active in instrument manufacture, for example Johann Michael (*14*), Johann Günther (*15*), Johann Nicolaus (*27*) and Johann Michael (*30*). This interest in the quality and functioning of instruments, alongside his skill as a performer, is marked in Johann Sebastian,

who was a considerable expert on the organ, stimulated the development of the viola pomposa and the Lauten-klavier, and offered constructive criticism of Silbermann's early pianoforte. Most of the earlier Bachs concentrated on learning and playing instruments; composition ordinarily remained in the background, and was reserved for those who had the necessary training and from whom a supply of music was expected. Almost without exception among the 17th-century Bachs, that meant the organists; so it is hardly surprising that no compositions by even such eminent family members as Johann Ambrosius (*11*) were handed down. At all events, composing must have been a peripheral activity for the court trumpeter, if indeed he composed at all, whereas his two cousins, the organists Johann Christoph (*13*) and Johann Michael (*14*), were avid composers. Their vocal works were not primarily for liturgical use – the supply of music for the liturgy was the Kantors' responsibility – so they wrote mostly funeral motets, doubtless a well-paid side activity.

By the turn of the 17th century the musical family was so widespread in the Thuringian region that the name 'Bach' had come to be regarded as synonymous with 'musician'. In many places, particularly Erfurt and Arnstadt, they held the principal positions, and it was typical that the successor to a position vacated by a Bach would be another Bach. When Johann Christoph (*13*) left Arnstadt, his younger brother Johann Michael (*14*) replaced him; Johann Sebastian's position in Mühlhausen went to his cousin Johann Ernst (*25*); and the post held by Johann Christoph (*22*) was even passed down through two generations (*41*, *79*). Carl Philipp Emanuel's application for his father's post as Kantor of

the Thomaskirche in 1750 may be seen as in the same tradition. This almost automatic succession of musical positions, however, grew ever more difficult: the institutions which had given rise to a musician class organized by guilds – and thus the very means of existence to a family like the Bachs – began to crumble.

Having risen from simple *Spielmann* beginnings, the Bachs had gradually reached every level of the musical hierarchy, in the three spheres of contemporary musical activity (court, town, church): court musician, court Konzertmeister or Kapellmeister; Stadtpfeifer or director of the town music; organist or Kantor. By the middle of the 18th century, social change had affected the structure of each of these areas, and broke the patterns that for so long had governed the lives of the Bach family. Further, the sons of the thenceforth middle-class Bachs had quite different professional opportunities because of their new educational prospects (almost all the members of the generation of J. S. Bach's sons attended university); formerly they had had little alternative but to become musicians. It is natural that fewer took up music as a profession. Several members of the family turned to another artistic field, painting: the descendants of Johann Ludwig (*3/72*) were court painters, and Johann Sebastian (1748–78), the son of Carl Philipp Emanuel, studied with Goethe's friend Adam F. Oeser and was a highly respected landscape painter (he went to Italy and died in Rome at the age of 30: for his works see *BJb*, xxxvii, 1940–48, p.163ff). Considering the proliferation of musical gifts over more than six generations of the Bach family it may appear surprising, though understandable in the light of historical developments, that in 1843, at the ceremonial unveiling in front

of the Thomaskirche of the Leipzig Bach monument, donated by Mendelssohn, Wilhelm Friedrich Ernst (*84*) was the solitary representative of a musical family with a tradition of more than 250 years.

EDITIONS

Alt-Bachisches Archiv aus Johann Sebastian Bachs Sammlung von Werken seiner Vorfahren, ed. M. Schneider, EDM, 1st ser., i–ii (1935)

Music of the Bach Family: an Anthology, ed. K. Geiringer (Cambridge, Mass., 1955)

Orgelwerke der Familie Bach, ed. D. Hellmann (Leipzig, 1967)

Stuttgarter Bach-Ausgaben (Stuttgart, 1968–) [and other works pubd by Hänssler-Verlag (1950–); for catalogue see M. Jödt, ed.: *Johann Sebastian Bach und die Bach-Familie in Ausgaben des Hänssler-Verlages* (Stuttgart, 1980; Eng. edn., 1981)] [SBA]

BIBLIOGRAPHY

CATALOGUES, BIBLIOGRAPHIES

M. Schneider: 'Thematisches Verzeichnis der musikalischen Werke der Familie Bach (I. Teil)', *BJb*, iv (1907), 103–77 [continuations never appeared]

W. Schmieder, ed.: 'Das Bachschrifttum 1945–1952', *BJb*, xl (1953), 119–68; for 1953–7, *BJb*, xlv (1958), 127; for 1958–62, ed. E. Francke, *BJb*, liii (1967), 121–69; for 1963–7, ed. R. Nestle, *BJb*, lix (1973), 91–150; for 1968–72, ed. R. Nestle, *BJb*, lxii (1976), 95; for 1973–7, ed. R. Nestle, *BJb*, lxvi (1980), 87–152

K. Geiringer: *The Bach Family: Seven Generations of Creative Genius* (London, 1954; Ger. trans., enlarged, 1958) [bibliography, 490ff; Ger. edn., 542ff]

P. Kast: *Die Bach-Handschriften der Berliner Staatsbibliothek*, Tübinger Bach-Studien, ii–iii (Trossingen, 1958)

J. F. Richter: 'Johann Sebastian Bach und seine Familie in Thüringen', *Bach-Festbuch Weimar 1964*, 50

SOURCES

[J. S. Bach]: *Ursprung der musicalisch-Bachischen Familie*, 1735 [original MS lost]; ed. W. Neumann and H.-J. Schulze in *Bach-Dokumente*, i (Kassel, 1963), no.184

M. Korabinsky: *Beschreibung der königlichen ungarischen Haupt- Frey und Krönungsstadt Pressburg*, i (Pressburg, 1784), 110ff

M. Schneider: *Bach-Urkunden: Ursprung der musikalisch-Bachischen Familie* (Leipzig, 1917) [facs. of copy by C. P. E. and A. C. P. Bach]

C. S. Terry: *The Origin of the Family of Bach Musicians* (London, 1929)

J. Müller-Blattau: *Genealogie der musikalisch-Bachischen Familie* (Kassel, 1950)

MONOGRAPHS

RiemannL 12

C. F. M.: 'Bemerkungen zu dem Stammbaum der Bachischen Familie', *AMZ*, xxv (1823), 187

Kawaczynsky: 'Über die Familie Bach: eine genealogische Mitteilung', *AMZ*, xlv (1843), 537

P. Spitta: *Johann Sebastian Bach*, i (Leipzig, 1873–80, 5/1962; Eng. trans., 1884–99/*R*1951)

A. Lorenz: 'Ein alter Bach-Stammbaum', *NZM*, lxxxii (1915), 281

G. Thiele: 'Die Familie Bach in Mühlhausen', *Mühlhäuser Geschichtsblätter*, xxi (1920–21), 62

H. Lämmerhirt: 'Bachs Mutter und ihre Sippe', *BJb*, xxii (1925), 101–37

C. S. Terry: *Bach: a Biography* (London, 1928/*R*1962)

E. Borkowsky: *Die Musikerfamilie Bach* (Jena, 1930)

H. Helmbold: 'Die Söhne von Johann Christoph und Johann Ambrosius Bach auf der Eisenacher Schule', *BJb*, xxvii (1930), 49

C. S. Terry: 'Has Bach Surviving Descendants?', *MT*, lxxi (1930), 511

E. Lux: 'Der Familienstamm Bach in Gräfenroda', *BJb*, xxviii (1931), 107

H. Miesner: 'Urkundliche Nachrichten über die Familie Bach in Berlin', *BJb*, xxix (1932), 157

H. Lämmerhirt: 'Ein hessischer Bach-Stamm', *BJb*, xxxiii (1936), 53–89

L. Bach: 'Ergänzungen und Berichtigungen zu dem Beitrag "Ein hessischer Bach-Stamm" von Hugo Lämmerhirt', *BJb*, xxxiv (1937), 118

K. Fischer: 'Das Freundschaftsbuch des Apothekers Friedrich Thomas Bach: eine Quelle zur Geschichte der Musikerfamilie Bach', *BJb*, xxxv (1938), 95

C. U. von Ulmenstein: 'Die Nachkommen des Bückeburger Bach', *AMf*, iv (1939), 12

W. G. Whittaker: 'The Bachs and Eisenach', *Collected Essays* (London, 1940)

H. Löffler: ' "Bache" bei Bach', *BJb*, xxxviii (1949–50), 106

Bibliography

R. Benecke: 'Bach, Familie', *MGG*

Bach in Thüringen: Gabe der Thüringer Kirche an das Thüringer Volk zum Bach-Gedenkjahr 1950 (Berlin, 1950)

H. Besseler and G. Kraft, eds.: *Johann Sebastian Bach in Thüringen: Festgabe zum Gedenkjahr 1950*, Quellenkundliche Studien thüringischer Musikforscher (Weimar, 1950)

K. Geiringer: 'Artistic Interrelations of the Bachs', *MQ*, xxxvi (1950), 363

W. Rauschenberger: 'Die Familien Bach', *Genealogie und Heraldik*, ii (1950), 1

E. Wölfer: 'Naumburg und die Musikerfamilie Bach', *Programmheft zu den Bach-Tagen Naumburg 1950*, 9

C. Schubart: 'Anna Magdalena Bach: neue Beiträge zu ihrer Herkunft und ihren Jugendjahren', *BJb*, xl (1953), 29

K. Geiringer: *The Bach Family: Seven Generations of Creative Genius* (London, 1954; Ger. trans., enlarged, 1958; enlarged, 2/1977)

C. Freyse: 'Wieviel Geschwister hatte J. S. Bach?', *BJb*, xlii (1955), 103

G. Kraft: 'Zur Enstehungsgeschichte des "Hochzeitsquodlibet" (BWV 524)', *BJb*, xliii (1956), 140

G. von Dadelsen: *Bemerkungen zur Handschrift Johann Sebastian Bachs, seiner Familie und seines Kreises*, Tübinger Bach-Studien, i (Trossingen, 1957)

K. Müller and F. Wiegand: *Arnstädter Bachbuch: J. S. Bach und seine Verwandten in Arnstadt* (Arnstadt, 1957)

K. Geiringer: 'Unbekannte Werke von Nachkommen J. S. Bachs in amerikanischen Sammlungen', *IMSCR*, vii *Cologne 1958*, 110

G. Kraft: 'Neue Beiträge zur Bach-Genealogie', *BMw*, i (1959), 29–61

A. Schmiedecke: 'Johann Sebastian Bachs Verwandte in Weissenfels', *Mf*, xiv (1961), 195

H.-J. Schulze: 'Marginalien zu einigen Bach-Dokumenten', *BJb*, xlviii (1961), 79

G. Kraft: *Entstehung und Ausbreitung des musikalischen Bach-Geschlechtes in Thüringen: mit besonderer Berücksichtigung des Wechmarer Stammes* (Habilitationsschrift, U. of Halle, 1964)

F. Wiegand: 'Die mütterlichen Verwandten Johann Sebastian Bachs in Erfurt – Ergänzungen und Berichtigungen zur Bachforschung', *BJb*, liii (1967), 5

E. Zavarský: 'Zur angeblichen Pressburger Herkunft der Familie Bach', *BJb*, liii (1967), 21

G. Kraft: 'Das mittelthüringische Siedlungszentrum der Familien Bach und Wölcken', *Musa–mens–musici: im Gedenken an Walther Vetter* (Leipzig, 1969), 153

P. M. Young: *The Bachs: 1500–1800* (London, 1970)

CHAPTER ONE

Johann Bach

Johann (or Hans) Bach was born in Andelsbuch, near
Voralberg, in about 1555. He became a *Spielmann*
(violinist) and jester at the Stuttgart court of Duke
Ludwig of Württemberg about 1585, and in 1593 he
followed the widowed Duchess Ursula to the court of
Nürtingen, where he remained until his death (1
December 1615). He apparently often travelled, both
alone and in the court entourage. Of his work all that
survives is the text of a narrative song of 1614 describing
a visit to the town of Weil (*Hanss Baachens Lobspruch
zur Weil der Statt*: 'Es ist nun über zwantzig Jahr'); its
manner is reminiscent of the late medieval style of
Oswald von Wolkenstein. There are two extant portraits
of him, an etching of about 1605 and an engraving of
1617 (fig.2). The etching bears the inscription:

> Hie siehst du geigen/Hansen Bachen
> Wenn du es hörst/so mustu lachen
> Er geigt gleichwol/nach seiner Art
> Und tregt ein hipschen/Hans Bachen Bart.

Nothing is known of his extraction; he was probably
related in some way (perhaps nephew) to Veit Bach of
the Wechmar line – Johann was Protestant (no matter of
course in the Catholic south) and like Veit he came from
Habsburg lands. C. P. E. Bach's ownership of the 1617
portrait of him suggests that he was traditionally considered a member of the family, although the fact that

2. *Johann Bach: engraving (1617)*

C. P. E. Bach's *Verzeichniss des musikalischen Nach-lasses* of 1790 incorrectly cited him as 'Bach (Hans) a Gotha musician', perhaps confusing him with Johann (2), may imply that his true identity was unknown to C. P. E. Bach.

BIBLIOGRAPHY
W. Wolffheim: 'Hans Bach', *BJb*, vii (1910), 70
W. Irtenkauf and H. Maier: 'Gehört der Spielmann Hans Bach zur Musikerfamilie Bach?', *Mf*, ix (1956), 450

CHAPTER TWO

Johann Christoph Bach (*13*)

Johann Christoph was born in Arnstadt and baptized on 8 December 1642. He received a thorough musical grounding from his father, Heinrich Bach (*6*), and on 20 November 1663 was appointed organist of the Arnstadt castle chapel. Two years later he was invited by the Eisenach town council to apply for the post of town organist at St George's (where the Kantor was Andreas Christian Dedekind); after an audition on 10 December 1665 he was appointed to that position and also to the post of organist and harpsichordist in the court Kapelle of the Duke of Eisenach. He retained both positions until his death; he was buried in Eisenach on 2 April 1703.

Little is known of his work in the court Kapelle. For some years the Kapellmeister was Daniel Eberlin, the father-in-law of Telemann, who was later to conduct the Kapelle on occasion, and for a short while Pachelbel was a member of the Kapelle. During most of his time there, Johann Christoph was a colleague of his cousin, the trumpeter Johann Ambrosius (*11*); Ambrosius often served as his copyist, and their relationship was doubtless a close one. The young Johann Sebastian must have received his first impressions of the organ from his uncle. While Johann Christoph's court position was one of high standing, his tenure of the civic one was marred by a succession of quarrels between him and the town council, for which he was not entirely blameless. These

mostly involved matters of salary and the council's refusal to provide an official residence for him, a deficiency eventually made good by the court. For many years he also battled with the council over the restoration (or reconstruction) of the organ at St George's; he was successful only in 1696, and then did not live to see the completion (by J. C. Stertzing) of the famous instrument in 1707 (his copious, expert notes on the organ's reconstruction are extant; see Freyse). He died in 1703, just ten days after the death of his wife; her illnesses and those of their children, as well as other family difficulties, had plagued him throughout his Eisenach years.

Within the family Johann Christoph was highly respected as a composer (a 'profound' one according to the *Ursprung*). In Johann Sebastian's obituary notice of 1754 he is mentioned expressly as one who 'was as good at inventing beautiful thoughts as he was at expressing words. He composed, to the extent that current taste permitted, in a *galant* and *cantabile* style, uncommonly full-textured . . . On the organ and the keyboard [he] never played with fewer than five independent parts'. Johann Sebastian performed some of his motets and vocal concertos (including the 22-part *Es erhub sich ein Streit*) in Leipzig (as did C. P. E. Bach later in Hamburg), and he added a final chorale (BWV Anh.159) to the motet *Ich lasse dich nicht*. Although Johann Christoph was primarily an organist and harpsichordist, his extant keyboard works are few, but they show him as a capable composer, stylistically akin to Pachelbel though in general less pedantic. The E♭ prelude and fugue is a significant work, and his organ chorales (probably in effect written-down improvisations) demonstrate

his mastery of the small form. His vocal works, in particular the motets and concertos, are notable for the variety of their settings. The concertos are characterized by their full instrumental writing, with unusually interesting inner part-writing. While the vocal writing is for the most part technically undemanding (bearing in mind the needs of elementary choirs), the instrumental parts are usually highly elaborate. There is much solo–tutti alternation. Basically the motets follow the central German type of the aria motet and the chorale motet, which indeed culminated in the works of Johann Christoph and his brother (3) Johann Michael (*14*). The older style of writing, with alternating chordal and imitative sections, still predominated; but the newer style, with its livelier lines (including melismatic semiquaver passages) and looser, more concertante writing, is found in *Sei getreu bis in den Tod* and *Der Mensch, vom Weibe geboren*, obviously later works. The lack of documentation and the small number of the surviving works preclude the establishment of a clear chronology of Johann Christoph's music.

WORKS

VOCAL

Arias: Es ist nun aus, 4vv, bc; Mit Weinen hebt sichs an, 1691, 4vv, bc: ed. in EDM, 1st ser., i (1935)

Motets: Der Mensch, vom Weibe geboren, 5vv, ed. in EDM, 1st ser., i (1935); Fürchte dich nicht, 5vv, ed. V. Junk (Leipzig, 1922); Herr, nun lässest du deinen Diener, 8vv, ed. V. Junk (Leipzig, 1922); Ich lasse dich nicht, 8vv, BWV Anh.159, ed. in Johann Sebastian Bachs Werke, xxxix (Leipzig, 1892); Lieber Herr Gott, 8vv, 1672, ed. V. Junk (Leipzig, 1922); Sei getreu bis in den Tod, 5vv, ed. in EDM, 1st ser., i (1935); Unsers Herzens Freude, 8vv, ed. K. Straube (Leipzig, 1924), ed. P. Steinitz (London, 1968): all ed. in SBA; Der Gerechte, ob er gleich zu zeitlich stirbt, 1676, 5vv, ed. in EDM, 1st ser., i (1935)

Konzerte: Die Furcht des Herrn, 5vv, 2 vn, 2 va, bc, ed. in EDM, 1st ser., ii (1935); Es erhub sich ein Streit, 10vv, 4 tpt, timp, 2 vn, 4 va, bc; Lamentatio: Ach, dass ich Wassers genug hätte, A, vn, 3 va, bc, *D-B*; Lamentatio: Wie bist du denn, O Gott, ed. in DTB, x, Jg.vi/1 (1905), attrib. J. P. Krieger, ed. in SBA; Dialogue, Herr, wende dich, 4vv, 2 vn, 2 va, bc, *B*; Dialogue, Meine Freundin, du bist schön (wedding piece), 4vv, 4 vn, 3 va, bc, ed. in EDM, 1st ser., ii (1935)

INSTRUMENTAL

Aria Eberliniana pro dormente Camillo (1690) [15 variations], hpd, ed. C. Freyse, Veröffentlichungen der Neuen Bachgesellschaft, Jg.xxxix/2 (1940)

Sarabande, G [12 variations], hpd, ed. H. Riemann (Leipzig, n.d.)

Aria, a [15 variations], hpd, ed. G. Birkner (Zurich, 1973)

Praeludium und Fuge, E♭, BWV Anh.177, org, ed. D. Hellmann, *Orgelwerke der Familie Bach* (Leipzig, 1967)

44 chorales with preludes, org, ed. M. Fischer (Kassel, 1936)

BIBLIOGRAPHY

M. Schneider: 'Thematisches Verzeichnis der musikalischen Werke der Familie Bach', *BJb*, iv (1907), 132–77

M. Fischer: *Die organistische Improvisation bei Johann Christoph Bach* (Kassel, 1928)

F. Rollberg: 'Johann Christoph Bach: Organist zu Eisenach 1665–1703', *ZMw*, xi (1929), 945

C. Freyse: 'Johann Christoph Bach', *BJb*, xliii (1956), 36

R. Benecke: 'Bach, Johann Christoph', *MGG*

CHAPTER THREE

Johann Michael Bach (*14*)

Johann Michael Bach was born in Arnstadt and baptized on 9 August 1648. He received a solid musical training from his father, Heinrich Bach (*6*), and from the Kantor in Arnstadt, Jonas de Fletin; the influence of the latter may account for his early interest in vocal music. In 1665 he succeeded his brother (2) Johann Christoph (*13*) as organist of the Arnstadt castle chapel. After an audition on 5 October 1673 he succeeded J. Effler (who later preceded Johann Sebastian as castle organist in Weimar) as town organist in Gehren. He was also active as an instrument maker there and held the important administrative post of town clerk, remaining in Gehren until his death (17 May 1694). On 17 October 1707 his youngest daughter, Maria Barbara (*b* Gehren, 20 Oct 1684), married her distant cousin (7) Johann Sebastian (*24*).

A pamphlet issued by the Gehren council refers to Johann Michael as a 'quiet, withdrawn and artistically well-versed subject'; within the family he was considered a 'capable composer' (*Ursprung*). As a composer, in fact, he is on almost the same level as his brother Johann Christoph. Especially in the chorale motet, the vocal form to which he almost exclusively devoted himself, he composed works of real significance. His convincing treatment of spoken declamation is particularly notable. As in his brother's music, the older, strongly homophonic style predominates; but in such

works as *Sei lieber Tag willkommen* he turned to the new, freer style with melismatic passages. His works for double chorus stand firmly in the tradition of Schütz, Scheidt and Praetorius. His vocal concertos are less extended than those of his brother, but he too favoured full-textured orchestration. His arias with obbligato instruments are particularly charming; here, as in the concertos, his use of a virtuoso solo violin part is noteworthy. His organ chorales are typical of the central German tradition of practical settings in smooth counterpoint.

WORKS

VOCAL

Arias: Ach, wie sehnlich wart ich der Zeit, S, vn, 3 va da gamba, bc; Auf, lasst uns den Herrn loben, A, vn, 3 va da gamba, bc, ed. in SBA: both ed. in EDM, 1st ser., ii (1935)

Motets: Das Blut Jesu Christi, 5vv; Dem Menschen ist gesetzt einmal zu sterben, 8vv; Fürchtet euch nicht, 8vv; Herr du lässest mich erfahren, 8vv; Herr ich warte auf dem Heil, 8vv; Herr, wenn ich nur dich habe, 5vv; Ich weiss, das mein Erlöser lebt, 5vv; Nun hab ich überwunden, 8vv; Sei lieber Tag willkommen, 6vv; Unser Leben währet siebenzig Jahr, 5vv: all ed. in EDM, 1st ser., i (1935), ed. in SBA; Ehre sei Gott in der Höhe, 8vv, ed. in DDT, xlix–1 (1915); Halt, was du hast, 8vv, ed. in EDM, 1st ser., i (1935); Sei nun wieder zufrieden, 8vv; Unser Leben ist ein Schatten, 9vv: both ed. F. Naue (Leipzig, n.d.)

Konzerte: Ach bleib bei uns, Herr Jesu Christ, 4vv, 2 vn, 3 va, bc; Es ist ein grosser Gewinn, S, 4 vn, bc: both ed. in EDM, 1st ser., ii (1935); see also under (4) J. N. Bach (27)

Dialogue: Liebster Jesu, hör mein Flehen, 5vv, 2 vn, 2 va, bc, ed. in EDM, 1st ser., ii (1935)

Benedictus, 5vv, *A-Wgm*, cited by Eitner

INSTRUMENTAL

72 org chorales, cited in *GerberL*, incl. Partita, Wenn wir in höchsten Nöten sein; Dies sind die heilgen zehn Gebot; Wenn mein Stündlein vorhanden ist: all ed. D. Hellmann, *Orgelwerke der Familie Bach* (Leipzig, 1967); Wo Gott, der Herr, nicht bei uns hält, *D-B*; Wenn wir in höchsten Nöten sein, *B*; In dich hab ich gehoffet, Herr, ed. in EDM, 1st ser., ix (1937); Nun freut euch lieben Christen gmein, *B*; Von Gott will ich nicht lassen, *B*

Ensemble sonatas, further kbd works cited in *GerberL*

BIBLIOGRAPHY

M. Schneider: 'Thematisches Verzeichnis der musikalischen Werke der Familie Bach', *BJb*, iv (1907), 109

CHAPTER FOUR

Johann Nicolaus Bach (27)

Johann Nicolaus Bach, a son of (2) Johann Christoph Bach (13), was born in Eisenach on 10 October 1669. He received his early musical training at home and in 1690 he entered the University of Jena, pursuing his musical studies with J. N. Knüpfer (son of S. Knüpfer, Kantor of the Leipzig Thomaskirche). After a journey to Italy, the purpose and duration of which is not known, he succeeded Knüpfer in 1694 as organist of the town church at Jena. The university authorities were however reluctant to allow him to act in addition as organist at the Kollegienkirche, as Knüpfer had done, and it was not until 1719 that he finally took on the double post of town and university organist. In 1703 he had refused an appointment in Eisenach as successor to his father, primarily, no doubt, because of the better salary in Jena, where he lived in modest prosperity. Possibly he was in contact with his relative Johann Gottfried Bernhard (47) during the latter's spell in Jena, 1738–9. From 1745, in consideration of his age, he was provided with an assistant. In the *Ursprung* Johann Sebastian called him 'present senior of all the Bachs still living'. Also according to Johann Sebastian, correcting a reference in J. G. Walther's *Musicalisches Lexicon* (1732), it was Johann Nicolaus who discovered that 'the letters BACH are melodic in their arrangement' (see *Bach-Dokumente*, ii, no.323). He died in Jena on 4 November 1753.

Johann Nicolaus Bach

Johann Nicolaus was a skilful composer; but the small number of his extant works hardly permits a characterization of his style. There are, however, no noticeable Italianate aspects such as might have resulted from his stay in Italy. Apart from being an organist, the leader of the university's collegium musicum and a composer, he was also an instrument maker, particularly of harpsichords. Adlung called him the inventor of the Lautenklavier. As an expert on organs he supervised the reconstruction of an instrument with three manuals and 44 stops in the Kollegienkirche, 1704–6. Among his pupils was F. E. Niedt, writer of the well-known thoroughbass method.

WORKS

Mass, sopra cantilena Allein Gott in der Höhe, e, 1716 [Ky–Gl], ed. V. Junk (Leipzig, 1920), ed. in SBA [beginning of Gl by J. S. Bach]
Der Jenaische Wein- und Bierrufer (student music), ed. F. Stein (Leipzig, 1921)
Konzert, Herr, wie sind deine Werke, *D-B*, also attrib. (3) J. M. Bach (*14*)
Org chorale, Nun freut euch lieben Christen gmein, *Bds*
Kbd suites, cited in J. Adlung, *Anleitung zu der musikalischen Gelahrtheit* (Erfurt, 1758/*R*1953, 2/1783)

BIBLIOGRAPHY

H. Koch: 'Johann Nicolaus, der "Jenaer" Bach', *Mf*, xxi (1968), 290

CHAPTER FIVE

Johann Bernhard Bach (*18*)

Johann Bernhard was born in Erfurt and baptized on 25 November 1676. He studied with his father, Johann Aegidius Bach (*8*), and about 1695 took up his first post, as organist at the Kaufmannskirche in Erfurt; he then went to Magdeburg, and in 1703 he replaced his uncle (2) Johann Christoph (*13*) as town organist and court harpsichordist in Eisenach, where he occasionally worked under Telemann. Repeated rises in salary show the esteem in which he was held, particularly at court. He died in Eisenach on 11 June 1749.

His only extant works are instrumental; some of the organ works are in copies by one of his Erfurt pupils, Johann Gottfried Walther. Johann Sebastian Bach evidently valued his orchestral suites, for he had four of them copied (he himself was involved in some of the copying) for his collegium musicum in Leipzig. The obituary notice of 1754 says that Johann Bernhard 'composed many beautiful overtures in the manner of Telemann', no doubt particularly referring to his use, in the French tradition, of programmatic movement titles.

WORKS

4 ovs., orch: g, ed. A. Fareanu (Leipzig, 1920); G; e; D, ed. K. Geiringer, *Music of the Bach Family* (Cambridge, Mass., 1955): all *D-Bds*

Org works: fugue, F, ed. H. Riemann (Leipzig, n.d.); fugue, D, ed. A. G. Ritter, *Zur Geschichte des Orgelspiels*, ii (Leipzig, 1884) [ed. G. Frotscher as *Geschichte des Orgel-Spiels und der Orgel-Komposition* (Berlin, 1935–6, enlarged 3/1966)]; Chaconne, B♭

Org chorales: Du Friedefürst, Herr Jesu Christ; Vom Himmel hoch: both ed. D. Hellmann, *Orgelwerke der Familie Bach* (Leipzig, 1967); Christ lag in Todesbanden; Nun freut euch lieben Christen: both ed. in EDM, 1st ser., ix (1937); Wir glauben all an einen Gott [3 versions]; Jesus, Jesus, nichts als Jesus

BIBLIOGRAPHY

H. Kühn: 'Vier Organisten Eisenachs aus Bachischem Geschlecht', *Bach in Thüringen: Gabe der Thüringer Kirche* (Berlin, 1950)

S. Orth: 'Zu den Erfurter Jahren Johann Bernard Bachs (1676–1749)', *BJb*, lvii (1971), 106

CHAPTER SIX

Johann Ludwig Bach (*3/72*)

Johann Ludwig was born in Thal, near Eisenach, on 4 February 1677. Nothing is known of his musical training, although he may have received some instruction from his father, Johann Jacob Bach (*3/68*); he attended the Gotha Gymnasium, 1688–93, and then began to study theology. From 1699 he was a court musician at Meiningen, from 1703 Kantor and from 1711 court Kapellmeister. In 1706 he had unsuccessfully applied to succeed A. C. Dedekind as Kantor of St George's, Eisenach, although he had been interested only in the musical and not the teaching duties of the post. His lifelong patron Duke Ernst Ludwig died in 1724 and Johann Ludwig wrote the music for his funeral. On 1 May 1731 he was buried in Meiningen.

Johann Ludwig wrote an imposing number of vocal works. Although orchestral music was probably his principal activity from 1711 onwards, hardly any material is extant. The preservation of the cantatas is due entirely to Johann Sebastian, who performed 18 of them, as well as the two masses, in Leipzig in 1726; some were given again between 1735 and 1750. *Denn du wirst meine Seele* was long considered an early work by Johann Sebastian (BWV15). The cantatas constitute the most significant part of Johann Ludwig's work; in contrast with the main corpus of Johann Sebastian's cantatas, they represent the older type of mixed cantata, before Neumeister, which consists essentially of biblical

text and chorale, in the following scheme: text from the Old Testament; recitative; aria; text from the New Testament; aria; recitative; chorus; chorale. The standard scoring is for four-part choir, strings and (usually) two oboes; in one cantata two horns are required, but there are no solo woodwind. These works had at least some small influence on Johann Sebastian, for example in his use of strings to the words of Jesus.

WORKS

19 cantatas, all *D-B*: Gott ist unser Zuversicht; Der Gottlosen Arbeit wird fehlen; Darum will ich auch erwählen; Darum säet euch Gerechtigkeit; Ja, nun hast du Arbeit gemacht; Wie lieblich sind auf den Bergen; Ich will meinen Geist in auch geben; Die mit Tränen säen, ed. in SBA; Mache dich auf, werde Licht; Es ist aus der Angst und Gericht; Er machet uns lebendig; Und ich will ihnen einen einigen Hirten erwecken; Der Herr wird ein neues im Land erschaffen; Die Weisheit kommt nicht in eine boshafte Seele; Durch sein Erkenntnis; Ich aber ging für dir über; Siehe ich will meinen Engel senden; Denn du wirst meine Seele nicht in der Hölle lassen, BWV15, ed. in Johann Sebastian Bachs Werke, ii (Leipzig, 1851); Klingt vergnügt (secular cantata)

8 motets: Das ist meine Freude, 8vv, ed. in SBA; Die richtig für sich gewandelt haben, 10vv; Gedenke meiner, mein Gott, 8vv; Gott sei mir gnädig, 9vv; Ich will auf den Herrn schauen, 8vv; Sei nun wieder zufrieden, 8vv, ed. in Cw, xcix (1964); Uns ist ein Kind geboren, 8vv (Leipzig, 1930); Unser Trübsal, 6vv, ed. in Cw, xcix (1964)

Magnificat, 8vv

Mass, g [Ky–Gl], BWV Anh.166, ed. V. Junk (Leipzig, n.d.); Mass, c [Ky–Gl]; Christe by J. S. Bach, BWV242, BWV Anh.26, *D-Bds*

Funeral music, Ich suche nur das Himmelleben, 1724, ed. K. Geiringer, *Music of the Bach Family* (Cambridge, Mass., 1955)

Funeral music, O Herr, ich bin, *Bds*

Passion; cantata cycle for 1713: lost, cited in S. Kümmerle, *Encyklopädie der evangelischen Kirchenmusik*, i (Gütersloh, 1888/R1974), 67

Ov., orch, G, 1715 (Vienna, 1939)

BIBLIOGRAPHY

A. Dörffel: 'Verzeichnis der Kirchenkompositionen des Johann Ludwig Bach in Meiningen', *Johann Sebastian Bachs Werke*, xli (1894), 275

A. M. Jaffé: *The Cantatas of Johann Ludwig Bach* (diss., Boston U., 1957)

W. H. Scheide: 'Johann Sebastian Bachs Sammlung von Kantaten seines Vetters Johann Ludwig Bach', *BJb*, xlvi (1959), 52–94; xlviii (1961), 5; xlix (1962), 5

W. Blankenburg: 'Eine neue Textquelle zu sieben Kantaten J. S. Bachs und achtzehn Kantaten J. L. Bachs', *BJb*, lxiii (1977), 7

K. Hofmann: 'Forkel und die "Köthener Trauermusik" Joh. Seb. Bachs', *BJb*, lxix (1983) [re: funeral music, O Herr, ich bin]

CHAPTER SEVEN

Johann Sebastian Bach (*24*)

Johann Sebastian Bach is the most important member of the family. His genius combined outstanding performing musicianship with supreme creative powers in which forceful original inventiveness and intellectual control are perfectly balanced. While it was in the former capacity, as a virtuoso, that in his lifetime he acquired an almost legendary fame, it is the latter virtues and accomplishments, as a composer, that have earned him a unique historical position. His art was of an encyclopedic nature, drawing together and surmounting the techniques, the styles and the general achievements of his own and earlier generations and leading on to new perspectives which later ages have received and understood in a great variety of ways.

The first authentic posthumous account of his life, with a summary catalogue of his works, was put together by his son Carl Philipp Emanuel and his pupil J. F. Agricola before March 1751 (published as *Nekrolog*, 1754). J. N. Forkel planned a detailed Bach biography in the early 1770s and carefully collected first-hand information on Bach, chiefly from his two eldest sons; the book appeared in 1802, by when the Bach Revival had begun and various projected collected editions of Bach's works were under way; it continues to serve, together with the 1754 obituary and the other 18th-century documents, as the foundation of Bach biography.

1 **Childhood**

The parents of Johann Sebastian were Johann Ambrosius Bach (*11*) and Maria Elisabeth Lämmerhirt (1644–94), daughter of a furrier in Erfurt, Valentin Lämmerhirt (*d* 1665). Another Lämmerhirt daughter became the mother of Bach's cousin J. G. Walther, suggesting that Lämmerhirt blood was perhaps not unimportant for the musical talents of the Bach family's greatest son. Ambrosius and Elisabeth were married on 8 April 1668, and had eight children. Johann Sebastian, the last, was born in Eisenach on 21 March 1685; he was one of the four (three sons, nos.*22*, *71* and *23*, and one daughter, Maria Salome) who did not die young. The date of his birth was carefully recorded by Walther in his *Lexicon*, by Sebastian himself in the family genealogy, and by his son as the co-author of the obituary. It is supported by the date of baptism (23 March; these dates are old style) in the register of the Georgenkirche. His godfathers were Johann Georg Koch, a forestry official, and Sebastian Nagel, a Gotha Stadtpfeifer. The house of his birth no longer stands; it is not the handsome old structure (Frauenplan 21) acquired by the Neue Bachgesellschaft in 1907 as the 'Bachhaus' and established as a Bach Museum.

Like Luther, also an Eisenach boy, Sebastian attended the Lateinschule, which offered a sound humanistic and theological education. He probably entered in spring 1692. At Easter 1693 he was 47th in the fifth class, having been absent 96 hours; in 1694 he lost 59 hours, but rose to 14th and was promoted; at Easter 1695 he was 23rd in the fourth class, in spite of having lost 103 hours (perhaps owing to the deaths of his parents as much as to illness). He stood one or two

45

places above his brother Jacob, who was three years older and less frequently absent. Nothing more is known about his Eisenach career; but he is said to have been an unusually good treble and probably sang under Kantor A. C. Dedekind at the Georgenkirche, where his father made instrumental music before and after the sermon and where his relation (2) Johann Christoph Bach (*13*) was organist. His musical education is matter for conjecture; presumably his father taught him the rudiments of string playing, but (according to Emanuel) he did not study keyboard instruments until he went to Ohrdruf. He later described Johann Christoph as 'a profound composer'; no doubt he was impressed by the latter's organ playing as well as by his compositions.

Elisabeth Bach was buried on 3 May 1694, and on 27 November Ambrosius married Barbara Margaretha, née Keul (daughter of a former mayor of Arnstadt, and already twice widowed). He died, however, on 20 February 1695. On 4 March the widow appealed to the town council for help; but she received only her legal due, and the household broke up. Sebastian and Jacob were taken in by their elder brother Johann Christoph (*22*), organist at Ohrdruf.

Both were sent to the Lyceum. Jacob left at the age of 14 to be apprenticed to his father's successor at Eisenach; Sebastian stayed on until 1700, when he was nearly 15, and thus came under the influence of an exceptionally enlightened curriculum. Inspired by the educationist Comenius, it embraced religion, reading, writing, arithmetic, singing, history and natural science. Sebastian entered the fourth class probably about March 1695, and was promoted to the third in July: on 20 July 1696 he was first among the seven new boys

and fourth in the class; on 19 July 1697 he was first, and was promoted to the second class; on 13 July 1698 he was fifth; on 24 July 1699 second, and promoted to the first class, in which he was fourth when he left for Lüneburg on 15 March 1700. It has been claimed that he was always a year or so younger than the average for his class; but the register nowhere gives his age correctly, and may be equally untrustworthy over the others, so this remains uncertain.

In the obituary, Emanuel stated that his father had his first keyboard lessons from Christoph, at Ohrdruf; in 1775, replying to Forkel, he said that Christoph might have trained him simply as an organist, and that Sebastian became 'a pure and strong fuguist' through his own efforts. That is likely enough; Christoph is not known to have been a composer. Several biographers have told the story of how Christoph would not allow his brother to use a certain manuscript; how Sebastian copied it by moonlight; how Christoph took the copy away from him; and how he did not recover it until Christoph died. Emanuel and Forkel assumed that Christoph died in 1700, and that Sebastian, left homeless, went to Lüneburg in desperation. Later authors, knowing that Christoph lived on until 1721, and that the brothers had been on good terms, have tended to reject the story – perhaps unnecessarily, for it may illustrate contemporary attitudes to discipline and restraint. In fact, the story fits in well with the little that is known of the Ohrdruf years, and with the idea that Sebastian taught himself composition by copying. Most probably he recovered his copy when he went to Lüneburg. As for its contents, Forkel implied that it contained works by seven named composers, three of

them northerners. He probably misunderstood Emanuel's reply to another of his questions; according to the obituary, the manuscript was exclusively southern (Froberger, Kerll, Pachelbel) – as one would expect, since Johann Christoph had been a Pachelbel pupil. The larger of the two organs at Ohrdruf was in almost unplayable condition in 1697, and Sebastian no doubt picked up some of his expert knowledge of organ building while helping his brother with repairs.

II Lüneburg

According to the school register, Sebastian left 'ob defectum hospitiorum'. This has been taken to mean 'for lack of a free place', but it is simpler to suppose that Christoph no longer had room for his brother. Since the latter's arrival, he had had two children; by March 1700 a third was expected; and (if local tradition can be trusted) his house, now destroyed, was a mere cottage. The brothers' problem seems to have been solved by Elias Herda, Kantor and a master at the Lyceum. He had been educated at Lüneburg, and no doubt it was he who arranged for Sebastian to go north; probably he similarly helped Georg Erdmann, a fellow pupil of Sebastian's, three years older, who left the school just before Bach (for the same reason) and who may have been his travelling companion – both were at Lüneburg on 3 April 1700.

The Michaeliskirche, Lüneburg, had two schools associated with it: a Ritteracademie for young noblemen, and the Michaelisschule for commoners. There were also two choirs: the 'chorus symphoniacus' of about 25 voices was led by the Mettenchor (Matins choir), which numbered about 15, and was limited to poor boys with

good voices. Members of the Mettenchor, which Bach and Erdmann joined, received free schooling at the Michaelisschule, up to one thaler per month according to seniority, their keep, and a share in fees for weddings and other occasions (Bach's share in 1700 has been put at 14 marks). From the arrangement of the pay-sheets it has been deduced that they were both trebles. Bach was welcomed for his unusually fine voice; but it soon broke, and for eight days he spoke and sang in octaves. After that he may or may not have sung, but no doubt he made himself useful as an accompanist or string player. As the last extant pay-sheet is that for 29 May 1700, no details are known; but it is clear that the school was short of instrumentalists at just this time.

At school, Bach's studies embraced orthodox Lutheranism, Latin, arithmetic, history, geography, genealogy, heraldry, German poetry and physics. The Kantor was August Braun, whose compositions have disappeared; the organist, F. C. Morhard, was a nonentity. The organ was repaired in 1701 by J. B. Held, who had worked at Hamburg and Lübeck; he lodged in the school, and may have helped Bach to study organ building. There was a fine music library, which had been carefully kept up to date; but whether choirboys were allowed to consult it is uncertain. If Braun made good use of it, Bach must have learnt a good deal from the music he had to perform; but his chief interests probably lay outside the school. At the Nikolaikirche was J. J. Löwe (1629–1703), distinguished but elderly. The Johanniskirche was another matter, for there the organist was Georg Böhm (1661–1733), who is generally agreed to have influenced Bach. It has been argued that the organist of the Johanniskirche would not have

been accessible to a scholar of the Michaelisschule, since the two choirs were not on good terms, and that Bach's knowledge of Böhm's music must have come later, through J. G. Walther. But Emanuel Bach stated in writing that his father had studied Böhm's music; and a correction shows that his first thought was to say that Böhm had been his father's teacher. This hint is supported by the fact that in 1727 Bach named Böhm as his northern agent for the sale of Partitas nos.2 and 3. That seems to imply that the two were on friendly terms; it is likelier that they became so between 1700 and 1702 than at any later date.

Bach went more than once to Hamburg, some 50 km away; probably he visited his cousin Johann Ernst (*25*), who is said to have been studying there about this time. The suggestion that he went to hear Vincent Lübeck cannot be taken seriously, for Lübeck did not go to Hamburg until August 1702, by which time Bach had almost certainly left the area. He may have visited the Hamburg Opera, then directed by Reinhard Keiser, whose *St Mark Passion* he performed during the early Weimar years and again in 1726; but there is no solid evidence that he was interested in anything but the organ and organist of the Catharinenkirche. Marpurg's familiar anecdote makes the point neatly: how Bach, returning almost penniless to Lüneburg, once rested outside an inn; how someone threw two herring heads out on the rubbish heap; how Bach – a Thuringian, to whom fish were a delicacy – picked them up to see if any portion were edible; how he found that they contained two Danish ducats, and was thus able not only to have a meal, but also 'to undertake another and a more comfortable pilgrimage to Herr Reincken'.

J. A. Reincken (1623–1722), a pupil of Sweelinck and organist of the Catharinenkirche since 1663, was a father figure of the north German school. Böhm may have advised Bach to hear him; and his showy playing, exploiting all the resources of the organ, must have been a revelation to one brought up in the reticent tradition of the south. As for the organ itself, Bach never forgot it; in later years he described it as excellent in every way, said that the 32′ Principal was the best he had ever heard, and never tired of praising the 16′ reeds. Whether he actually met Reincken before 1720 is uncertain. If he did, Reincken might have given him a copy of his sonatas; Bach's reworkings of them (the keyboard pieces BWV954, 965 and 966) are more likely to have been made soon after 1700 than 20 years later, when Bach no longer needed to teach himself composition. Some 80 km south of Lüneburg lay Celle, seat of a duke who had acquired a Parisian veneer and maintained an orchestra consisting largely of Frenchmen. Bach had access to this household, but how, and in what capacity, is not known. He must have had a friend at court, and that friend could have been Thomas de la Selle, who was a member of the orchestra and also dancing-master at the Ritteracademie, next door to Bach's school in Lüneburg. Emanuel Bach knew only that his father had 'heard' this French music; but perhaps de la Selle took him to Celle as a performer, or, more likely, Bach heard the Celle orchestra in or near Lüneburg at one of the castles belonging to the Celle court.

The date of Bach's departure from Lüneburg is not recorded, and the reason for it is not known; but that reason must have been urgent, for he left without hearing Buxtehude, and took extraordinary pains to do so in

winter 1705–6. All that is definitely known is that the organist of the Jakobikirche, Sangerhausen, was buried on 9 July 1702, and that Bach competed successfully for the post, but the Duke of Weissenfels intervened and had J. A. Kobelius, an older man, appointed in November. Bach is next heard of on 4 March 1703 at Weimar, when he was paid as a lackey; in the *Ursprung* he described himself as a court musician. This was at the minor Weimar court, that of Duke Johann Ernst, younger brother of the Duke Wilhelm Ernst whom Bach served from 1708 to 1717. Possibly the Duke of Weissenfels, having refused to accept Bach at Sangerhausen, found work for him at Weimar; another possibility is that Bach owed his appointment to a distant relation of his, David Hoffmann, another lackey–musician.

Of the musicians with whom Bach now became associated, three are worth mentioning. G. C. Strattner (*c*1644–1704), a tenor, became vice-Kapellmeister in 1695, and composed in a post-Schütz style. J. P. von Westhoff (1656–1705) was a fine violinist and had travelled widely, apparently as a diplomat, and is said to have been the first to compose a suite for unaccompanied violin (1683). J. Effler (*c*1640–1711) was the court organist: he had held posts at Gehren and Erfurt (where Pachelbel was his successor) before coming in 1678 to Weimar, where about 1690 he moved to the court. He may have been willing to hand over some of his duties to Bach, and probably did something of the kind, for a document of 13 July 1703 at Arnstadt, where Bach next moved, describes Bach as court organist at Weimar – a post that was not officially his until 1708.

III **Arnstadt**

The Bonifaciuskirche at Arnstadt had burnt down in 1581, and was subsequently rebuilt, in 1676–83; it then became known as the Neukirche, and so remained until 1935, when it was renamed after Bach. In 1699 J. F. Wender contracted to build an organ, which by the end of 1701 had become usable; on 1 January 1702 Andreas Börner was formally appointed organist. The organ was complete by June 1703, and was examined before 3 July; there were more examiners than one, but only Bach was named and paid, and it was he who 'played the organ for the first time'. The result was that on 9 August Bach was offered the post over Börner's head; at the same time, 'to prevent any such "collisions" as are to be feared', Börner was given other work. Bach accepted the post 'by handshake' on 14 August 1703. The exact date of his removal to Arnstadt is not known, nor is his address. As his last board and lodging allowance was paid to Feldhaus, he probably spent at least that year in either the Golden Crown or the Steinhaus, both of which belonged to Feldhaus. Considering his age, and local standards, he was well paid; and his duties, as specified in his contract, were light. Normally, he was required at the church only for two hours on Sunday morning, for a service on Monday, and for two hours on Thursday morning; and he had only to accompany hymns. He thus had plenty of time for composition and organ playing, and he took as his models Bruhns, Reincken, Buxtehude (all northerners) and certain good French organists. There is no evidence as to whether he took part in the theatrical and musical entertainments of the court or the town.

The *Capriccio sopra la lontananza del suo fratello*

dilettissimo was presumably written when Bach's brother Jacob went to Poland, to be an oboist in the army of Charles XII of Sweden. It has been suggested that this was in 1706, when the army came nearest to Thuringia; but the date given in the *Ursprung* is 1704, and that seems to have Bach's authority. 1703 is perhaps more likely still. When making biographical notes, about 1735, Bach may have remembered only that his brother left in the year when he himself went to Arnstadt; he dated his own appointment 1704 and may also have been wrong about his brother's departure.

Bach was in no position to put on elaborate music at Arnstadt. The Neukirche, like the other churches, drew performers from two groups of schoolboys and senior students. Only one of these groups was capable of singing cantatas; it was supposed to go to the Neukirche monthly in the summer, but there does not appear to have been a duty roster. The performers naturally tended to go to the churches that had an established tradition and friendly organists; and Bach had no authority to prevent this, for he was not a schoolmaster and was younger than many of the students. Further, he never had much patience with the semi-competent, and was apt to alienate them by making offensive remarks. One result was his scuffle with J. H. Geyersbach (*b* 1682). On 4 August 1704 he and his cousin Barbara, elder sister (aged 26) to his future wife, fell in with six students who had been to a christening feast; one of these was Geyersbach, who asked why Bach had insulted him (or his bassoon), and struck him in the face with a stick. Bach drew his sword, but another student separated them. Bach complained to the consistory that it would be unsafe for him to go about the streets if

Geyersbach were not punished, and an inquiry was held. The consistory told Bach that he ought not to have insulted Geyersbach and should try to live peaceably with the students; further, he was not (as he claimed) responsible only for the chorales but was expected to help with all kinds of music. Bach replied that if a musical director were appointed, he would be willing enough.

Bach, unimpressed, asked for four weeks' leave, and set off for Lübeck – 'what is more, on foot', says the obituary, adding that he had an overwhelming desire to hear Buxtehude. Dates and distance cast some doubts on his straightforwardness. He left Arnstadt about 18 October, and was therefore due to be back, or well on his way back, by about 15 November; he would thus have been unable to hear even the first of Buxtehude's special services, which were given on various dates from 15 November to 20 December. Perhaps, like Mattheson and Handel before him, he went primarily to see if there was any chance of succeeding Buxtehude, and was put off by the prospect of marrying Buxtehude's daughter, aged 30; in any case, by 1705 there was a rival in the field. However that may be, he stayed almost three months at Lübeck, and was absent altogether for about 16 weeks, not returning to Arnstadt until shortly before 7 February 1706, when he communicated.

On 21 February the consistory asked Bach why he had been away for so long; his replies were unsatisfactory and barely civil. They next complained that his accompaniments to chorales were too elaborate for congregational singing, and that he still refused to collaborate with the students in producing cantatas; further, they could not provide a Kapellmeister for him, and if he

continued to refuse they would have to find someone
more amenable. Bach repeated his demand for a musical
director, and was ordered to declare himself within eight
days. From the next case that the consistory heard that
day it seems that there had been actual 'disordres' in the
church between Bach and the students. There is no
evidence that Bach declared himself, and the consistory
dropped the matter for eight months. They brought it up
again on 11 November, and Bach undertook to answer
them in writing. They also accused him of inviting a
'stranger maiden' to make music in the church, but
for this he had obtained the parson's permission; presumably the girl was his cousin and future wife, and
she had simply sung to his accompaniment for practice.

Neither Bach nor the consistory took further action;
no doubt they saw that the problem would soon solve
itself. Probably Bach had come back from Lübeck with
exalted ideas about church music, requiring facilities
that Arnstadt could not provide. His ability was becoming known; on 28 November he helped to examine an
organ at Langewiesen. Forkel said that various posts
were offered to him; and with the death of J. G. Ahle, on
2 December, a sufficiently attractive vacancy seemed to
have arisen.

iv Mühlhausen

Ahle had been a city councillor of Mühlhausen, organist of the church of St Blasius and a composer of
minor rank. Musical standards had fallen during his
tenure of office, but the post was a respectable one and
various candidates gave trial performances. One was to
have been J. G. Walther, the future lexicographer; he
sent in two compositions for 27 February 1707

(Sexagesima), but withdrew after being told privately
that he had no hope. Bach played at Easter (24 April)
and may have produced Cantata no.4. At the city council meeting on 24 May no other name was considered,
and on 14 June Bach was interviewed. He asked for the
same salary that he was receiving at Arnstadt (some 20
gulden more than Ahle's); the councillors agreed, and an
agreement was signed on 15 May. At Arnstadt, his
success became known; his cousin Johann Ernst (*25*)
and his predecessor Börner applied for the Neukirche
on 22 and 23 June. He resigned formally on 29 June,
and presumably moved to Mühlhausen within a few
days. It was perhaps in July that he wrote Cantata
no.131; this was clearly intended for a penitential service, perhaps connected with a disastrous fire of 30
May. It was not Bach's own Pastor Frohne who commissioned this cantata, but Pastor Eilmar of St Mary's;
a fact whose possible significance will be seen later.

On 10 August Tobias Lämmerhirt, Bach's maternal
uncle, died at Erfurt; it is reasonable to suppose that
Cantata no.106 was performed at his funeral on 14
August. Tobias left Bach 50 gulden, more than half his
salary, and thus facilitated his marriage to Maria
Barbara (*b* 20 Oct 1684), daughter of (3) Johann
Michael Bach (*14*) and Catharina Wedemann. The wedding took place on 17 October at Dornheim, a village
near Arnstadt; the pastor, J. L. Stauber (1660–1723),
was a friend of the family and himself married Regina
Wedemann on 5 June 1708.

Pupils began to come to Bach at about this time, or
perhaps even earlier. J. M. Schubart (1690–1721) is
said to have been with him from 1707 to 1717, and J. C.
Vogler (1696–1763) to have arrived at the age of ten (at

Arnstadt), to have left for a time, and to have returned from about 1710 until 1715. These two were his immediate successors at Weimar; from their time onwards he was never without pupils.

On 4 February 1708 the annual change of council took place, and Cantata no.71 was performed. It must have made an impression, for the council printed not only the libretto, as was usual, but also the music. Bach next drew up a plan for repairing and enlarging the St Blasius organ; the council considered this on 21 February, and decided to act on it. Cantata no.196 may have been written for Stauber's wedding on 5 June. At about this time Bach played before the reigning Duke of Weimar, Wilhelm Ernst, who offered him a post at his court. On 25 June Bach wrote to the council asking them to accept his resignation.

No doubt the larger salary at Weimar was an attraction, particularly as Bach's wife was pregnant. But it is clear, even from his tactful letter to these councillors who had treated him well, that there were other reasons for leaving. He said that he had encouraged 'well-regulated church music' not only in his own church, but also in the surrounding villages, where the harmony was often 'better-fashioned' (Spitta found a fragment, BWV223, at nearby Langula). He had also gone to some expense to collect 'the choicest sacred music'. But in all this members of his own congregation had opposed him, and were not likely to stop. Some people no doubt disliked the type of music that he was trying to introduce. Further, Pastor Frohne may have distrusted his organist; an active Pietist, he was at daggers drawn with the orthodox Pastor Eilmar of St Mary's – Bach had begun his Mühlhausen career by working with

Eilmar, and they had become intimate enough for
Eilmar and his daughter to be godparents to Bach's first
two children.

The council considered his letter on 26 June and
reluctantly let him go, asking him only to supervise the
organ building at St Blasius. However badly Bach may
have got on with his congregation, he was evidently on
good terms with the council. They paid him to come and
perform a cantata at the council service in 1709, and
possibly also in 1710 (all trace of these works is lost). In
1735 he negotiated on friendly terms with the new
council on behalf of his son Johann Gottfried Bernhard
(*47*). He is not known to have been paid for supervising
or opening the St Blasius organ, but he may have done
so.

v **Weimar**

When he announced his resignation from Mühlhausen, Bach said that he had been appointed to the
Duke of Weimar's 'Capelle und Kammermusik'; and
it was long thought that he did not become organist at
once. In fact, Weimar documents show that on 14 July
1708, when his 'reception money' was paid over, he
was called 'the newly appointed court organist', and that
he was almost always so called until March 1714, when he
became Konzertmeister as well. Effler, it seems, was
pensioned off on full salary (130 florins); on 24 December
1709 he received a small gift as 'an old sick servant', and
he died at Jena on 4 April 1711.

It is said that Bach wrote most of his organ works at
Weimar, and that the duke took pleasure in his playing.
His salary was from the outset larger than Effler's (150
florins, plus some allowances); it was increased to 200

from Michaelmas 1711, 215 from June 1713, and 250 on his promotion in 1714. On 20 March 1715 it was ordered that his share of casual fees was to be the same as the Kapellmeister's. Moreover, he seems to have had a fair amount of spare time, in which, for instance, to cultivate the acquaintance of Telemann while the latter was at Eisenach (1708–12). Together with the violinist Pisendel he copied a concerto in G of Telemann's (*D-Dlb*), probably during Pisendel's visit to Weimar in 1709.

Six of Bach's children were born at Weimar: Catharina (baptized 29 Dec 1708; *d* 14 Jan 1774); (8) Wilhelm Friedemann (*45*) (*b* 22 Nov 1710); twins (*b* 23 Feb 1713; both died in a few days); (9) Carl Philipp Emanuel (*46*) (*b* 8 March 1714); and Johann Gottfried Bernhard (*47*) (*b* 11 May 1715). The various god-parents show that Bach and his wife kept in touch with relations and friends from Ohrdruf, Arnstadt and Mühlhausen, besides making fresh contacts at Weimar; it is noteworthy that Telemann was godfather to Emanuel.

On 13 March 1709 Bach, his wife, and one of her sisters (probably the eldest, Friedelena, who died at Leipzig in 1729) were living with Adam Immanuel Weldig, a falsettist and Master of the Pages. They probably stayed there until August 1713, when Weldig gave up his house, having secured a similar post at Weissenfels. Weldig was godfather to Emanuel; Bach (by proxy) to a son of Weldig's in 1714. Weldig's house was destroyed in 1944; where Bach lived before and after the given dates is not known.

Since 29 July 1707, J. G. Walther (the lexicographer) had been organist of the Stadtkirche; he was related to

Bach through his mother, a Lämmerhirt, and the two became friendly. On 27 September 1712 Bach stood godfather to Walther's son. Forkel told a story of how Walther played a trick on Bach, to cure him of boasting that there was nothing he could not read at sight. Their relations did not deteriorate, as Spitta supposed; in 1735 Bach negotiated on Walther's behalf with the Leipzig publisher J. G. Krügner, and Walther's references to Bach in his letters to Bokemeyer carry no suggestion of any coolness. From one such letter it seems that during his nine years at Weimar Bach gave Walther some 200 pieces of music, some by Buxtehude, others compositions of his own.

Of Bach's pupils, Schubart and Vogler have already been mentioned. The pupil for whom Bach was paid by Ernst August's account in 1711–12 was not Duke Ernst August himself but a page called Jagemann. J. G. Ziegler (1688–1747) matriculated at the University of Halle on 12 October 1712, but before that he had studied with Bach for a year or so, and had been taught to play chorales 'not just superficially, but according to the sense of the words'; Bach's wife stood godmother to his daughter in 1718, and in 1727 Bach employed him as agent, in Halle, for Partitas nos.2 and 3. P. D. Kräuter of Augsburg (1690–1741) set out for Weimar in March 1712, and stayed until about September 1713. Johann Lorenz Bach (*38*) probably arrived in autumn 1713; he may have left Weimar by July 1717. Johann Tobias Krebs (1690–1762) studied with Walther from 1710, with Bach from about 1714 until 1717. Johann Bernhard Bach (*41*) worked with his uncle from about 1715 until March 1719, alongside Samuel Gmelin (1695–1752), who appears to have left in 1717. C. H.

Dretzel of Nuremberg (1697–1775) may have been briefly with Bach. In 1731, when applying for a post, T. C. Gerlach (1694–1768) implied that Bach had been teaching him by correspondence for 14 years, but his confused phraseology should not be taken literally.

The specification of the organ in the castle chapel, published in 1737, has not always been reprinted correctly; in any case, it does not represent the organ that Bach left in 1717. Extensive alterations were made in 1719–30. Still less does the specification represent the organ that Bach was faced with in 1708, for he himself had made even more extensive alterations in 1713–14. The organ is said to have been built by Compenius in 1657–8. It was overhauled in 1707–8, and a sub-bass added, by J. C. Weishaupt, who carried out further maintenance work in 1712. A contract for alterations had however been signed on 29 June 1712 with H. N. Trebs (1678–1748), who had moved from Mühlhausen to Weimar in 1709. Bach and he had worked together on a new organ at Taubach in 1709–10, opened by Bach on 26 October 1710; in 1711 he gave Trebs a handsome testimonial, and in 1713 he and Walther became godfathers to Trebs's son. Bach and Trebs collaborated again about 1742, over an organ at Bad Berka. Trebs's new organ was usable during 1714; he had done 14 days' tuning by 19 May, and was paid off on 15 September. Of this rebuild nothing is known, except that either Bach or the duke was determined that the instrument include a glockenspiel; great trouble was taken over obtaining bells from dealers in Nuremberg and Leipzig, and it seems that the original set of 29 (a number hard to account for) had to be replaced because of difficulties over blend and pitch. In 1737 the organ had a glockenspiel on the *Oberwerk*, but alterations had

been made in 1719–20 and it does not follow that the glockenspiel of 1714 was on a manual.

In December 1709 and February 1710 Bach was paid for repairing harpsichords in the household of the junior dukes, Ernst August and Johann Ernst. On 17 January 1711 he became godfather to a daughter of J. C. Becker, a local burgher. In February 1711 Duke Johann Ernst went to the University of Utrecht. From 21 February 1713 Bach was lodged in the castle at Weissenfels. Duke Christian's birthday fell on 23 February, and it is now thought that Cantata no.208 was performed in this year, not in 1716. The earlier date is stylistically suitable; moreover, it is compatible both with the watermark of the autograph score, and with the fact that in this score Bach contradicted sharps by flats rather than by naturals – an old-fashioned habit that he gave up progressively during 1714.

About May 1713 the young duke returned from Utrecht, apparently with a good deal of music, for in the year from 1 June there were bills for binding, copying and shelving (some of the music came from Halle). In February 1713 he had been in Amsterdam, and may have met the blind organist J. J. de Graff who was in the habit of playing recent Italian concertos as keyboard solos. This may have given rise to the numerous concerto arrangements made by Walther and Bach.

On 7 September 1713 Bach was probably at Ohrdruf, standing godfather to a nephew; and on 6 November he took part in the dedication of the new Jakobikirche at Weimar (there is no evidence that he composed any of the music). On 27 November he was at Weimar, as godfather to Trebs's son. At about this time he seems to have gone to Halle, perhaps to buy music, and to have become accidentally involved with the auth-

orities of the Liebfrauenkirche. The organist there (Zachow, Handel's teacher) had died in 1712, and the organ was being enlarged to a three-manual of 65 stops. The story has to be pieced together from hints in an incomplete correspondence; but it looks as if the pastor, J. M. Heineccius, pressed Bach to apply for the vacant post. Bach composed and performed a cantata, attended a meeting on 13 December 1713, was offered the post, and let the committee suppose that he had accepted it, although he had not had time to find out what his casual fees would amount to. On 14 December they sent him a formal contract. Bach replied on 14 January 1714, saying cautiously that he had not been released from Weimar, was uneasy about his salary and duties, and would write again within the week. Whether he did so is not known; but on 1 February the committee resolved to tell him that his salary was not likely to be increased. Thus at Halle he could expect a slightly smaller salary than he was already getting; the attraction was the organ, more than twice as large. Bach must then have approached the duke, for on 2 March, 'at his most humble request', he became Konzertmeister (ranking after the vice-Kapellmeister), with a basic salary of 250 florins from 25 February. In finally refusing the Halle post, he probably mentioned that figure, for the committee accused him of having used their offer as a lever to extract more money from the duke. This he denied on 19 March, in a letter so reasonable and so obviously honest that he remained on good terms with Halle and was employed there as an organ examiner in 1716. Gottfried Kirchhoff had meanwhile been appointed organist on 30 July 1714.

Few cantatas (apart from the secular no.208) can be

ascribed to these early Weimar years. No.150 may date from 1708–9; no.18 may be as early as 1713, or may have been performed at Sexagesima in 1715, to show the duke what his organist could do. The work performed at Halle in December 1713 was formerly thought to be no.21, in an early version; but no.63 now seems just as likely. We know it as a Christmas work, but the music has no Christmas features, and the original words may have been different. As Bach seems to have spent the first half of December 1713 at Halle, he may possibly have written this work for 10 December, the second Sunday in Advent.

On 23 March 1714 it was ordered that cantatas should in future be rehearsed in the chapel, not at home or in lodgings; and on Palm Sunday, 25 March, Bach performed no.182. This was the fourth Sunday after his appointment as Konzertmeister, when he had become responsible for writing a cantata every four weeks. As he evidently hoped to complete an annual cycle in four years, he did not keep strictly to this rule; having written a cantata for Advent Sunday in 1714, he wrote for the last Sunday after Trinity in 1715, and for the second Sunday in Advent in 1716 (in 1717 he was in prison). Apart from such intentional irregularities, there are gaps in the series, and the strange thing is that these gaps became suddenly more numerous after the end of 1715. From 1717 there are no cantatas at all. A tentative explanation will be suggested for this; but it is hard to see why Bach's usual allowance of paper was paid for on 16 May 1716 when he is not known to have performed any church cantatas between 19 January and 6 December.

The young Duke Johann Ernst died at Frankfurt on 1

August 1715, and on 12 August Bach received an allowance for mourning garments (not for illness); court mourning may explain why there are no cantatas for 11 August or 8 September.

On 4 April 1716 Bach, like the librettist Salomo Franck and 'the book-printer', was paid for 'Carmina', bound in green taffeta, that had been 'presented' on some unspecified occasion; perhaps on 24 January, when Duke Ernst August had married Eleonore, sister of the Prince of Cöthen. Ernst's birthday was celebrated in April; two horn players from Weissenfels came to Weimar, possibly brought over for a repeat performance of Cantata no.208.

Meanwhile, the new organ at Halle had been making progress, and on 17 April the council resolved that Bach, Kuhnau of Leipzig and Rolle of Quedlinburg should be invited to examine it on 29 April. They all accepted; each was to receive 16 thalers, plus food and travelling expenses. The examination began at 7 a.m., and lasted three days – until some time on 1 May, when the experts wrote their report, a sermon was preached and fine music was performed. On 2 May the organist and the three examiners met the builder to discuss details. The council, who behaved liberally, gave a tremendous banquet, whose date is usually given as 3 May (1 May seems more likely).

On 31 July 1716 Bach and an Arnstadt organ builder signed a testimonial for J. G. Schröter, who had built an organ at Erfurt. In 1717 Bach was mentioned in print for the first time: in the preface to Mattheson's *Das beschützte Orchestre*, dated 21 February, Mattheson referred to Bach as 'the famous Weimar organist' saying that his works, both for the church and for keyboard,

led one to rate him highly, and asked for biographical information.

It is against this background that Bach's departure from Weimar has to be considered. In 1703 he had been employed by Duke Johann Ernst; since his return in 1708, by Duke Wilhelm, Johann's elder brother. The brothers had been on bad terms, and when Johann Ernst died in 1707 and his son Ernst came of age in 1709, things became no better. For some time the ducal disagreements do not seem to have affected Bach; perhaps they were kept within bounds by Superintendent Lairitz, and Ernst's younger brother (Johann, the composer) may have had some influence. But the latter died in 1715, Lairitz on 4 April 1716, and the new superintendent certainly failed to cope with the 'court difficulties'; like the rest of Wilhelm's household, he was forbidden to associate with Ernst. The musicians, though paid by both households, were threatened with fines of ten thalers if they served Ernst in any way.

No extant Bach cantata can be securely dated between 19 January and 6 December 1716; it may seem unlikely that this long, continuous gap was due to casual losses. It is tempting to suppose that Bach found his position embarrassing (owing to his early connection with the junior court) and expressed disapproval of Duke Wilhelm's behaviour by evading his own responsibilities. In fact, Bach does not seem to have disapproved of the duke's behaviour until he discovered that a new Kapellmeister was being sought elsewhere. Drese senior died on 1 December 1716; his son, the vice-Kapellmeister, was by all accounts a nonentity. Bach composed Cantatas nos.70*a*, 186*a* and 147*a* for 6, 13 and 20 December (three successive weeks, not months),

but there were no more, as far as is known. By Christmas, Bach may have found out that the duke was angling for Telemann. Negotiations with Telemann came to nothing; but apparently Bach now set about looking for a post as Kapellmeister. He was offered one by Prince Leopold of Cöthen, brother-in-law to Duke Ernst (Bach and the prince had probably met at Ernst's wedding in January 1716) and the appointment was confirmed on 5 August 1717. No doubt Bach then asked Duke Wilhelm's permission to leave, and no doubt he was refused – the duke being annoyed because his nephew had obviously had a hand in finding Bach a job that carried more prestige and, at 400 thalers, was better paid.

The duke and Bach must nevertheless have remained on speaking terms for the time being, for at some date hardly earlier than the end of September Bach was in Dresden and free to challenge the French keyboard virtuoso Louis Marchand. Versions of this affair differ, but according to Birnbaum (who wrote in 1739, probably under Bach's supervision), Bach 'found himself' at Dresden, and was not sent for by 'special coach'. Once there, some court official persuaded him to challenge Marchand to a contest at the harpsichord; the idea that they were to compete at the organ seems to have crept in later. Whatever may be the truth about these and other details, it is universally agreed that Marchand ran away.

On his birthday, 30 October 1717, Duke Wilhelm set up an endowment for his court musicians; and the second centenary of the Reformation was celebrated from 31 October to 2 November. Presumably Bach took part in these ceremonies, though there is no

evidence that he set any of the librettos that Franck had provided. Emboldened, perhaps, by the Marchand affair, he then demanded his release in such terms that the duke had him imprisoned from 6 November until his dismissal in disgrace on 2 December. Terry's attractive idea that the *Orgel-Büchlein* was planned and partly written in prison is unfortunately untenable.

The Cöthen court had paid Bach 50 thalers on 7 August. Some have supposed that this was for travelling expenses, and that Bach had his wife and family moved to Cöthen soon after; but it seems unlikely that the duke would have allowed them to move until he had agreed to let Bach go. The younger Drese became Kapellmeister in his father's place and Bach's pupil J. M. Schubart became court organist. The post of Konzertmeister disappeared.

VI Cöthen

Except during the last few months of his Weimar period, Bach had been on good terms with Duke Wilhelm; but his relations with that martinet must always have been official. At Cöthen, until the end of 1721, things were different; Prince Leopold was a young man who, as Bach himself said, loved and understood music. He was born in 1694, of a Calvinist father and a Lutheran mother. The father died in 1704, the mother ruled until Leopold came of age on 10 December 1715. There was no court orchestra until October 1707, when Leopold persuaded his mother to take on three musicians. While studying in Berlin in 1708, he met A. R. Stricker; from the end of 1710 to 1713 he was on the usual Grand Tour, during which he studied with J. D. Heinichen at Rome. He returned capable of singing

bass, and of playing the violin, viola da gamba and harpsichord. The Berlin court orchestra had broken up in 1713, and from July 1714 he employed Stricker as Kapellmeister and his wife as soprano and lutenist; by 1716 he had 18 musicians. In August 1717 Stricker and his wife seem to have resigned, leaving the prince free to appoint Bach.

At Cöthen the Jakobikirche organ was in poor condition. The court chapel was Calvinist; it had an organist, but no elaborate music was performed there, and the two-manual organ had only 13 or 14 stops, though it may have had a complete chromatic compass to pedal *e'* and manual *e'''*. The Lutheran Agnuskirche had a two-manual organ of 27 stops, again with an exceptional pedal compass. There is not the slightest reason to suppose that Bach wrote any particular work to exploit these pedal compasses, but no doubt he used one or both of the organs for teaching and private practice. He communicated at the Agnuskirche, and took part in the baptisms at the court chapel, but had no official duties in either. He may, however, have been involved in the affair of May 1719, when a cantata was put on for the dedication festival of the Agnuskirche, and 150 copies of (presumably) the libretto were printed. The printer's bill for one thaler and eight groschen was endorsed by the pastor: 'The churchwardens can give him 16 groschen; if he wants more, he must go to those who gave the order'.

Bach's basic salary, 400 thalers, was twice Stricker's, and extra allowances made it up to about 450. Only one court official was paid more, and there is other evidence that Bach was held in high esteem. On 17 November 1718 the last of his children by his first wife (a short-

lived son) was named after the prince, who himself was a godfather. Bach's residence in Cöthen is not definitely known, but it seems likely that he began as a tenant in Stiftstrasse 11; in 1721, when that house was bought by the prince's mother for the use of the Lutheran pastor, he moved to Holzmarkt 12. The orchestra needed a room for their weekly rehearsals; the prince supplied it by paying rent to Bach (12 thalers a year from 10 December 1717 to 1722). Presumably there was a suitable room in Bach's first house. Whether he continued to use that room after his move in 1721, and why he was not paid rent after 1722, is not clear.

The date of the first rent payments suggest that Bach and his household moved to Cöthen a day or two after he was released from prison (2 December); and that, after hasty rehearsals, he helped to celebrate the prince's birthday on 10 December. That would normally have been his duty. The court accounts suggest that something connected with the birthday was either printed or bound in 1717, as also in 1719 and 1720 (Anh.7); Bach certainly wrote a cantata in 1722, and Cantatas nos.66*a* and Anh.5 in 1718 (the latter was performed in church). In 1721 there may have been no birthday celebrations, for the prince was married, at Bernburg, the next day. Cantata no.173*a* was undoubtedly a birthday work, but Bach probably wrote it after he had left Cöthen; 36*a*, an arrangement of 36*c* (1725), was put on at Cöthen on 30 November 1726, for the birthday of the prince's second wife.

New Year cantatas also were expected. No.134*a* dates from 1719, Anh.6 from 1720, Anh.8 from 1723. There is no evidence for 1718, 1721 or 1722; printers' and binders' bills paid on 5 January 1722 may have

been for music performed in December 1721. Bach may well have been unable to put on a wedding cantata, but there seems no reason why he should not have offered something for the prince's birthday. Nos.184 and 194 (Leipzig, 1724, and Störmthal, 1723) seem to be arrangements of Cöthen works, and so perhaps are parts of no.120. Whether or not Bach performed a cantata at Cöthen on 10 December 1717, he was at Leipzig on 16 December examining the organ at the university church (St Paul's). The work had been done by Johann Scheibe, with whose son Bach was later in dispute. Bach is not known to have done any other work of this kind while at Cöthen.

On 9 May 1718 the prince went to drink the waters at Carlsbad for about five weeks, taking with him his harpsichord, Bach and five other musicians. Early in 1719 Bach was in Berlin, negotiating for a new harpsichord. About this time he seems to have been busy composing or buying music, for between July 1719 and May 1720 some 26 thalers were spent on binding. During 1719 Handel visited his mother at Halle, only some 30 km away; it is said that Bach tried, but failed, to make contact with him. Bach also disregarded a renewed request from Mattheson for biographical material.

W. F. Bach was nine in 1719; the title-page of his *Clavier-Büchlein* is dated 22 January 1720. In May Bach again went to Carlsbad with the prince. The date of their return does not seem to have been recorded; but apparently it was after 7 July, for that was the date of Maria Barbara's funeral, and there is no reason to doubt Emanuel's story that his father returned to find her dead and already buried.

His wife had been nearly 36. Her death may well

72

have unsettled Bach, and even led him to think of returning to the service of the church; but there was a more
practical reason for his taking an interest in the
Jakobikirche at Hamburg. The organist there, H. Friese,
died on 12 September 1720; Bach had known Hamburg
in his youth, and must have been attracted by the organ,
a four-manual Schnitger with 60 stops. There is no
evidence that Bach was actually invited to apply for the
post; but he may well have made inquiries of his own.

At all events, his name was one of eight being considered on 21 November, and he was in Hamburg at
about that time. A competition was arranged for 28
November, but Bach had had to leave for Cöthen five
days before. Three candidates did not appear, and the
judges were not satisfied with the other four. An approach was made to Bach, and the committee met on 12
December; as Bach's reply had not arrived, they met
again a week later, when they found that Bach had
refused. Perhaps he was unable, or unwilling, to contribute 4000 marks to the church funds, as the successful
candidate actually did.

From the way in which the committee kept the post
open for Bach, one may suppose that they had heard his
recital at the Catharinenkirche. Exactly how this performance was arranged, no-one knows; but the obituary
(Emanuel) states that Bach played before Reincken
(aged 97), the magistracy and other notables; that he
played for more than two hours in all; and that he
extemporized in different styles on the chorale *An
Wasserflüssen Babylon* for almost half an hour, just as
the better Hamburg organists had been accustomed to
doing at Saturday Vespers. As a fantasia on this chorale
was one of Reincken's major works, this may seem a

tactless choice; but the obituary makes it clear that the chorale was chosen by 'those present' and not by Bach himself. Reincken is reported to have said, 'I thought this art was dead, but I see it still lives in you', and showed Bach much courtesy. A later remark of Mattheson's has been taken to imply that Bach also played the G minor Fugue BWV542, but there are good reasons to doubt it.

During 1720 Bach made fair copies of the works for unaccompanied violin, and must have been preparing the Brandenburg Concertos, whose autograph full score was dedicated on 24 March 1721 to the Margrave Christian Ludwig, before whom Bach had played in Berlin while negotiating for the new Cöthen harpsichord, between June 1718 and March 1719. What he played is not known; but he was invited to send in some compositions. As he himself said, he took 'a couple of years' over this commission, and then submitted six works written to exploit the resources of Cöthen. Such resources do not seem to have been available to the Margrave of Brandenburg, and it is not really surprising that he did not thank Bach, send a fee or use the score.

One of Bach's friends at Cöthen was the goldsmith C. H. Bähr; Bach stood godfather to one of Bähr's sons in 1721, and deputized for a godfather to another in 1723. About the beginning of August 1721 he gave a performance of some unspecified kind for Count Heinrich XI Reuss, of Schleiz; this may have been arranged by J. S. Koch, Kantor there, who had held a post at Mühlhausen, though possibly not in Bach's time there.

On 15 June 1721 Bach was the 65th communicant at the Agnuskirche; one 'Mar. Magd. Wilken' was the

14th. This may well have been Bach's future wife – the mistake in the first name is an easy one – but Anna Magdalena makes no formal appearance until 25 September, when Bach and she were the first two among the five godparents of a child called Hahn. This baptism is recorded in three registers. In two of them Anna is described as 'court singer', in the third, simply as 'chamber musician' (*Musicantin*). In September Anna was again a godmother, to a child called Palmarius; again the registers differ in describing her occupation. Her name does not appear in court accounts until summer 1722, when she is referred to as the Kapellmeister's wife; her salary (half Bach's) is noted as paid for May and June 1722.

Practically nothing is known of her early years. She was born on 22 September 1701 at Zeitz. Her father, Johann Caspar Wilcke, was a court trumpeter; he worked at Zeitz until about February 1718, when he moved to Weissenfels where he died on 30 November 1731. The surname was variously spelt. Anna's mother (Margaretha Elisabeth Liebe, *d* 7 March 1746) was daughter of an organist and sister of J. S. Liebe who, besides being a trumpeter, was organist of two churches at Zeitz from 1694 until his death in 1742. As a trumpeter's daughter, Anna may well have met the Bachs socially. The stories that she was a public figure, having sung at Cöthen and the other local courts since the age of 15, have been discredited; they are said to have arisen through confusion with her elder brother, a trumpeter. However, she was paid for singing, with her father, in the chapel at Zerbst on some occasion between Easter and midsummer 1721. By September 1721, aged just 20, she was at Cöthen, well acquainted with Bach (aged

75

36), and ready to marry him on 3 December. The prince saved Bach ten thalers by giving him permission to be married in his own lodgings. At about this time Bach paid two visits to the city cellars, where he bought first one firkin of Rhine wine, and later two firkins, all at a cut price, 27 instead of 32 groschen per gallon.

On 11 December 1721 the prince married his cousin Friderica, Princess of Anhalt-Bernburg. The marriage, which took place at Bernburg, was followed by five weeks of illuminations and other entertainments at Cöthen. This was not however an auspicious event for Bach: he was to leave Cöthen partly because the princess was 'not interested in the Muses' and broke up the happy relationship between Bach and her husband. Perhaps her unfortunate influence had made itself felt even before she was married.

A legacy from Tobias Lämmerhirt (Bach's maternal uncle) had facilitated Bach's first marriage; Tobias's widow was buried at Erfurt on 12 September 1721, and Bach received something under her will too, though not in time for his second marriage. On 24 January 1722 Bach's sister Maria, together with one of the Lämmerhirts, challenged the will, saying that Bach and his brothers Jacob (in Sweden) and Christoph (at Ohrdruf) agreed with them (Christoph had died in 1721). Bach heard of this only by accident; and on 15 March he wrote to the Erfurt council on behalf of Jacob as well as himself. He objected to his sister's action, and said that he and his absent brother desired no more than was due to them under the will. On 16 April Jacob died; and the matter seems to have been settled on these lines towards the end of the year. Bach's legacy must have amounted to rather more than a year's pay.

In summer 1722 there was no Kapellmeister at the court of Anhalt-Zerbst, and Bach was commissioned to write a birthday cantata for the prince; for this he was paid ten thalers in April and May. The birthday was in August, and payments made during that month presumably refer to the performance. If so, the work, which seems to have disappeared, was scored for two oboes d'amore and 'other instruments'.

Several didactic works for keyboard belong to the Cöthen period. One is the *Clavierbüchlein* for Anna Magdalena Bach. 25 leaves are extant, about a third of the original manuscript; there is a kind of title-page, on which Anna Magdalena (probably) wrote the title and the date and Bach (certainly) noted the titles of three theological books. Despite the sceptics, it remains reasonable to suppose that Bach gave the book to his wife early in 1722. It seems to have been filled by 1725. The autograph of *Das wohltemperirte Clavier* (book 1 of the '48') is dated 1722 on the title-page but 1732 at the end. The writing is uniform in style, and for various reasons it is incredible that he did not finish the manuscript until 1732. This handsome fair copy was preceded by drafts, like those in W. F. Bach's *Clavier-Büchlein* (begun in 1720); and some of the movements look earlier than that. Presumably they were brought together for convenience, partly to serve as the last step in Bach's keyboard course, partly to exhibit the advantages of equal temperament. As in book 2, no doubt Bach transposed some of the pieces, to fill gaps in his key scheme; the odd pairing of the prelude in six flats with the fugue in six sharps suggests that the former was originally in E minor, the latter in D minor.

The title-page was almost certainly the only part of

3. *Autograph MS of Bach's organ chorale 'Der Tag, der ist so freudenreich' BWV605 (completed in new German organ tablature) from the 'Orgel-Büchlein', composed c1713–17*

the *Orgel-Büchlein* that Bach wrote while at Cöthen, but as another educational work it is best mentioned here. It was meant to be a collection of chorale-preludes, not only for the ordinary church seasons but also for occasions when such subjects as the Lord's Prayer, or Penitence, were being emphasized. The paper is of a kind that Bach used, as far as is known, only in 1714. A few items date from about 1740; in the rest, the writing resembles that of the cantatas of 1715–16. Of the 164 preludes Bach allowed for, he completed fewer than 50.

Last in this group of works come the Inventions and Sinfonias, whose autograph fair copy is dated 'Cöthen, 1723'. Its contents had already appeared, in earlier versions and under different titles, in W. F. Bach's *Clavier-Büchlein* of 1720.

The story of Bach's move to Leipzig begins with the death of Kuhnau, Kantor of the Thomasschule there, on 5 June 1722. Six men applied for the post, among them Telemann, who was still remembered for the good work he had done at Leipzig 20 years before. He had been doing a similar job at Hamburg for about a year, and was probably the most famous of German musicians actually living in Germany. One of the Kantor's duties was to teach Latin. Telemann refused to do that; nevertheless, he was appointed on 13 August. But the Hamburg authorities would not release him, and offered to increase his pay; by 22 November he had declined the Leipzig post. On that day Councillor Platz said that Telemann was no loss; what they needed was a Kantor to teach other subjects besides music. Of the remaining five candidates, three were invited to give trial performances; two dropped out, one because he would not teach Latin. By 21 December two Kapellmeisters had applied, Bach and Graupner. The other candidates were Kauffmann of Merseburg, Schott of the Leipzig Neukirche, and Rolle of Magdeburg. Of the five candidates, Graupner was preferred; he was a reputable musician, and had studied at the Thomasschule. He successfully performed his test (two cantatas) on 17 January 1723. But on 23 March he too withdrew, having been offered more pay at Darmstadt. Meanwhile, Bach had performed his test pieces (Cantatas

nos.22 and 23) on 7 February 1723. Rolle and Schott had also been heard, and possibly Kauffmann too. The Princess of Cöthen died on 4 April, too late to affect Bach's decision. On 9 April the council considered Bach, Kauffmann and Schott. Like Telemann, none of them wished to teach Latin. Councillor Platz said that as the best men could not be got, they must make do with the mediocre. The council evidently resolved to approach Bach, for on 13 April he obtained written permission to leave Cöthen. On 19 April he signed a curious document that reads as if he were not yet free from Cöthen, but could be free within a month; he also said he was willing to pay a deputy to teach Latin. On 22 April the council agreed on Bach, one of them hoping that his music would not be theatrical. On 5 May he came in person to sign an agreement; on 8 and 13 May he was interviewed and sworn in by the ecclesiastical authority; on 15 May the first instalment of his salary was paid; and on 16 May he 'took up his duties' at the university church, possibly with Cantata no.59. With family and furniture, he moved in on 22 May, and performed Cantata no.75 at the Nikolaikirche on 30 May. On 1 June, at 8.30 a.m., he was formally presented to the school.

This story has been told in some detail, because it throws light on the circumstances in which Bach worked at Leipzig. To him, the Kantorate was a step downwards in the social scale, and he had little respect for his employers. To the council, Bach was a third-rater, a mediocrity, who would not do what they expected a Kantor to do – teach Latin, as well as organize the city church music. The stage was set for trouble, and in due course trouble came. Councillor Platz on

Telemann is curiously echoed by Councillor Stieglitz, ten days after Bach's death: 'The school needs a Kantor, not a Kapellmeister; though certainly he ought to understand music'.

VII **Leipzig: 1723–9**

The position of Kantor at the Thomaskirche, held conjointly with that of civic director of music, had been associated with a wealth of tradition since the 16th century. It was one of the most notable positions in German musical life both in this and in the esteem it commanded; and there can be little doubt that the general attractiveness of the position in itself played a decisive part in Bach's decision to move from Cöthen to Leipzig. His subsequent remark about the social step down from Kapellmeister to Kantor must be seen in the context of his later disagreements with the Leipzig authorities, as indeed the letter in question (to Erdmann, a friend of his youth, on 28 October 1730) makes unequivocally clear. In any event, Bach was not the only Kapellmeister to apply for the post, and it seems that the Leipzig councillors were less interested in a common Kantor than in a reputable Kapellmeister to take charge of and upgrade the city's musical affairs. For Bach the duties attaching to the Leipzig position were incomparably more varied and demanding than those in Cöthen, Weimar, Mühlhausen or Arnstadt, and more or less corresponded to those undertaken by Telemann in Hamburg – it cannot have been mere chance that he wanted to tackle a range of duties comparable with those of his friend. There was also the greater economic security of a flourishing commercial town, the advantages of a relatively stable civic magistracy as an employer com-

pared with a less dependable private patron, and the superior schooling facilities for his growing sons.

The 'Cantor zu St. Thomae et Director Musices Lipsiensis' was the most important musician in the town; as such, he was primarily responsible for the music of the four principal Leipzig churches – St Thomas's (the Thomaskirche), St Nicolas's (the Nicolaikirche), St Matthew's (the Matthaeikirche or Neukirche) and St Peter's (the Petrikirche) – as well as for any other aspects of the town's musical life controlled by the town council. In carrying out his tasks he could call above all on the pupils of the boarding-school attached to St Thomas's, the Thomasschule, whose musical training was his responsibility, as well as the town's professional musicians. Normally the pupils, about 50 to 60 in number, were split up into four choir classes (*Kantoreien*) for the four churches. The requirements would vary from class to class: polyphonic music was required for St Thomas's, St Nicholas's (the civic church) and St Matthew's, with figural music only in the first two; at St Peter's only monodic chants were sung. The first choir class, with the best 12 to 16 singers, was directed by the Kantor himself, and sang alternately in the two principal churches; the other classes were in the charge of prefects, appointed by Bach, who would be older and therefore more experienced pupils of St Thomas's.

Musical aptitude was a decisive factor in the selection of pupils for the Thomasschule, and it was the Kantor's responsibility to examine them and later to train them. This was furthered by the daily singing lessons, mostly given by the Kantor. There was also instrumental instruction for the ablest pupils, which Bach had to provide free of charge: he could thus help to make good

any shortage of instrumentalists for his performances. Indeed, the number of professional musicians employed by the town (four Stadtpfeifer, three fiddlers and one apprentice) was held throughout his period of office at the same level as had obtained during the 17th century. For further instrumentalists Bach drew on the university students. In general the age of the Thomasschule pupils ranged between 12 and 23. Remembering that voices then broke at the age of 17 or 18, it is clear that Bach could count on solo trebles and altos who already had some ten years' practical experience – an ideal situation, impossible in boys' choirs today.

As far as church music was concerned, Bach's duties centred on the principal services on Sundays and church feasts, as well as some of the more important subsidiary services. In addition, he could be asked for music for weddings and funerals, for which he would receive a special fee. Such additional income was important to Bach, as his salary as Kantor of the Thomaskirche and director of music came to only 87 thalers and 12 groschen (besides allowances for wood and candles, and payments in kind, such as corn and wine). Including payments from endowments and bequests as well as additional income, Bach received annually more than 700 thalers. Further, he had the use of a spacious official residence in the south wing of the Thomasschule, which had been renovated at a cost of more than 100 thalers before he moved in in 1723. Inside the Kantor's residence was the so-called 'Komponirstube' ('composing room'), his professional office containing his personal music library and the school's. The buildings of the old Thomasschule were, scandalously, demolished in 1903 to make room for what is now the senior minister's quarters; it was also then that the west façade of the

Thomaskirche was rebuilt in the neo-Gothic style.

During his early Leipzig years, Bach involved himself in church music with particular thoroughness and extreme energy. This activity centred on the 'Hauptmusic' composed for Sundays and church feasts, a cantata, whose text generally related to the Gospel – a tradition inherited from previous Kantors. Even so, Bach engaged on a musical enterprise without parallel in Leipzig's musical history: in a relatively short time he composed five complete cycles of cantatas for the church year, with about 60 cantatas in each, making a repertory of roughly 300 sacred cantatas. The first two cycles were prepared immediately, for 1723–4 and 1724–5; the third took rather longer, being composed between 1725 and 1727. The fourth, to texts by Picander, appears to date from 1728–9, while the fifth once again must have occupied a longer period, possibly extending into the 1740s. The newly established chronology of Bach's vocal works makes it clear that the main body of the cantatas was in existence by 1729, and that Bach's development of the cantata was effectively complete by 1735. The existence of the fourth and fifth cycles has been questioned, because of their fragmentary survival compared with the almost complete survival of the first, second and third; but until a positive argument for their non-existence can be put forward the number of five cycles, laid down in the necrology of 1754, must stand. Compared with the high proportion of Bach's works of other kinds that are lost (orchestral and chamber music, for instance), the disappearance of about 100 cantatas would not be exceptional. (The preservation of Bach's works is discussed below, §XI; see §XV for the correspondence of excess chorales in the Breitkopf collection to the number of lost cantatas.)

The first cycle begins on the first Sunday after Trinity 1723 with Cantata no.75, which was performed 'mit gutem applausu' at the Nicolaikirche, followed by no.76, for the second Sunday after Trinity, performed at the Thomaskirche (see the calendar of cantata performances, *BJb*, xliv, 1957). The two largest churches in Leipzig are both Gothic in style, and in Bach's time they contained stone and wooden galleries. The choir lofts were on the west wall of the nave above the council gallery. The organs too were in the choir lofts (the 'Schüler-Chor'): the Nicolaikirche and the Thomaskirche each had a three-manual organ with 36 and 35 stops respectively (*Oberwerk, Brustwerk, Rückpositiv, Pedal*). The Thomaskirche had a second organ, fitted to the east wall as a 'swallow's nest', with 21 stops (*Oberwerk, Brustwerk, Rückpositiv, Pedal*); this fell into dilapidation and was demolished in 1740. The organs were always played before cantata performances, during which they would provide continuo accompaniment; they were played by the respective organists at each church – Bach himself, who had not held a regular appointment as an organist since his time in Weimar, directed the choir and the orchestra, and would not normally be playing the organ. However, he frequently must have directed his church ensemble from the harpsichord, as is documented for the performance of BWV198 in 1727. At any rate, the harpsichord was often, if not regularly, employed as a continuo instrument in addition to the organ.

The cantata was an integral part of the Leipzig Lutheran liturgy. It followed immediately on the reading from the Gospel, preceding the Creed and the sermon (the second part of a two-part cantata or, sometimes, a second cantata would follow the sermon,

'sub communione'). Apart from organ playing and the congregational singing of hymns, selected by the Kantor, the other musical constituent of the liturgy was the introit motet, which would be taken from the *Florilegium Portense* (1618) by Erhard Bodenschatz, a collection mainly drawn from the 16th century (Lassus, Handl etc), and was performed *a cappella* with harpsichord continuo. Services began at about 7 a.m. and lasted three hours; this allowed a mere half-hour for the cantata, and Bach rarely overstepped this duration. The normal performing forces consisted of some 16 singers and 18 instrumentalists; it was rare for the total number of singers and players to fall below 25 or to exceed about 40 (the figure required on exceptional occasions, like the *St Matthew Passion*). Ordinarily the forces were made up by students of St Thomas's (the first Kantorei), the seven salaried town musicians (until 1734 headed by J. G. Reiche, thereafter by J. C. Gentzmer) and their apprentices and helpers, students from the University as well as one or two paid assistants.

In the first weeks of Bach's holding office in Leipzig there was a funeral service for the postmaster's widow, Johanna Maria Keese (18 July 1723); it was probably for this occasion that he wrote the motet *Jesu meine Freude* BWV227. By 9 August (though possibly as early as 16 May, with the performance of Cantata no.59 in the university church, St Paul's) Bach had taken up his duties as musical director to the university, an office traditionally held by the Thomaskantor: on this occasion he performed the Latin Ode BWV Anh.20 (now lost) at festivities on the birthday of Duke Friedrich II of Saxe-Gotha. On 30 August he introduced Cantata

no.119, as part of the celebrations for the change of town council in Leipzig. The enormous scope of Bach's new responsibilities, as well as his vast work-load, may be gauged from the fact that the day before (14th Sunday after Trinity) Cantata no.25 was heard for the first time, and the first performance of no.138 (for the 15th Sunday) was soon to follow.

September 1723 saw the start of Bach's protracted wrangle over the responsibility for services at the university. In a written request for payment, he laid claim to the traditional right of the Thomaskantor to be responsible for the so-called 'old' services (special feast days and academic ceremonies) and the 'new' services (normal Sundays and feast days); the 'new' services, however, together with the designation 'director of music', had in April 1723 been entrusted by the university to J. G. Görner, organist of the Nicolaikirche. On 28 September Bach's request was turned down, and he was paid only half the fee. He would not give in, and turned to the Elector of Saxony in Dresden with three petitions. The intervention of the Dresden court was apparently to little avail: the university left Görner in charge of the 'new' services and awarded Bach the 'old', with payment as before. After this, Bach seems to have withdrawn from the 'old' services too by 1726 and to have limited his activities at the university to festive occasions.

About 2 November 1723 Bach inaugurated a new organ (which he had previously appraised) in Störmthal, outside Leipzig, with Cantata no.194. Then, from the second Sunday in Advent to the fourth, came his first break in the weekly routine of composing and performing cantatas; in Leipzig, unlike Weimar, this period was

a 'tempus clausum', as was Lent up to and including Palm Sunday. On Christmas Day figural music returned, in a particularly splendid manner, with Cantata no.63, the *Magnificat* BWV243a (E♭ version) and probably the D major Sanctus BWV238. In Leipzig it was usual to have Latin mass settings on church feast days.

At the end of the next 'tempus clausum', Lent 1724, Bach produced his first large-scale choral work for Leipzig, the *St John Passion* BWV245. In its original version, it had its first performance at Vespers at the Nicolaikirche on Good Friday (7 April). Performances of Passion oratorios had been introduced to Leipzig by Kuhnau in 1721, and immediately became established as a tradition, alternating annually between the two main churches. There is no documentary evidence of a Passion performance under Bach's direction on Good Friday 1723, from which the older dating of the *St John Passion* derives. The work had several further performances, including three in revised versions: 1725, about 1730 and 1746–9.

With the first Sunday after Trinity 1724 (11 June) Bach began his second cycle; these were chorale cantatas. On 25 June he was in Gera for the dedication of the organ at the Salvatorkirche. In July he went to Cöthen with Anna Magdalena for a guest appearance as a performer; he had retained the title of Court Kapellmeister there, and it lapsed only on the death of Prince Leopold in 1728. There is evidence of further visits to Cöthen, with Bach performing alongside his wife (who sang as a soprano), in December 1725 and January 1728. During 1725 Bach started to prepare a second *Clavierbüchlein* for Anna Magdalena. On 23 February 1725 he performed Cantata no.249a at the

Weissenfels court for the birthday of Duke Christian; this was the original version of the *Easter Oratorio* BWV249, first given at Leipzig the following 1 April. No.249*a* represents the beginning of a long-standing collaboration with the fluent Leipzig poet Christian Friedrich Henrici (Picander), the chief supplier of texts for Bach's later Leipzig vocal works.

Bach produced congratulatory cantatas for two Leipzig University professors in May and August (nos.36*c* and 205). On 19–20 September he played on the Silbermann organ at the Dresden Sophienkirche before the local court musicians, thus continuing his practice of giving virtuoso organ performances on concert tours (as he undoubtedly did in Leipzig, too, although he held no post as an organist). Early in 1726 – during the third cycle, which had started in June 1725 – there was an interruption of Bach's production of cantatas, for reasons that remain obscure: between February and September 1726 he performed 18 cantatas by his cousin (6) Johann Ludwig Bach (*3/72*). In particular, between Purification and the fourth Sunday after Easter, he performed none of his own music at the main Sunday services; even on Good Friday he used a work by another composer, Reinhard Keiser's *St Mark Passion*. Difficulties with performers may have been partly responsible; the instrumental forces required in J. L. Bach's cantatas are more modest than those Bach himself normally used. Even apart from this, however, the pattern of Bach's cantata production – as far as can be judged from the available material – changed during the third cycle; there are considerable gaps as early as the period after Trinity Sunday 1725, and it seems that the third cycle extended over two years. In the gaps,

cantatas by other composers and further performances of Bach's own works were given.

Michaelmas 1726 saw the appearance in print of Partita no.1: with this Bach began his activity, later to increase in scope, as a publisher of keyboard music. Partita no.1, published singly, was followed by nos.2 and 3 (1727), no.4 (1728), no.5 (1730) and no.6 (1730 or 1731; no copy is known). According to an advertisement of 1 May 1730 the series was to have comprised seven partitas. There are early versions of nos.3 and 6 in the second book for Anna Magdalena of 1725. Bach sent no.1, with a dedicatory poem, to the court at Cöthen as a form of congratulation on the birth of an heir, Prince Emanuel Ludwig (born 12 September 1726).

In December 1726, on the installation of Dr Gottlieb Kortte as university professor, Bach produced a more sizable occasional work, the *dramma per musica*, Cantata no.207. It is probable that the first performance of the *St Matthew Passion* took place on Good Friday of 1727: this would be in the earlier version, BWV244*b*. Recent scholarship has produced evidence (the dating of Picander's text, the repairing of the second organ at the Thomaskirche, etc) which calls into question the traditional belief that the first performance was on Good Friday 1729. The *St Matthew Passion* would then come at the beginning of the cycle of cantatas planned by Bach and Picander for 1728–9. Bach had composed his first setting of a Picander Sunday cantata text for Septuagesima 1727 (no.84), and it seems that this was subsequently included in the later cycle. The texts for all the cantatas have survived, in the third volume of Picander's poems, but the music is extant of only nine

pieces and a fragment (nos.84, 149, 188, 197*a*, 171, 156, 159, 145, 174). It is scarcely open to doubt, however, that Bach – named in Picander's foreword to his *Cantaten auf die Sonn- und Festtage durch das gantze Jahr* (1728) as the composer of the music of the cycle – set at least a large proportion of the texts, and indeed he probably did so in the weekly sequence that he followed in the first two cycles.

An important work composed by Bach in October 1727 was the *Trauer Ode*, Cantata no.198. The university planned a memorial ceremony on the death of Electress Christiane Eberhardine, the wife of August the Strong of Saxony, and commissioned Bach to set a text by the Leipzig professor of poetry, Johann Christoph Gottsched. This became a somewhat controversial affair, as the university director of music, Görner, felt he had been slighted. Bach however retained the commission and performed the two parts of his work, 'composed in the Italian manner', directing it from the harpsichord, in the university church, on 17 October. Between 7 September 1727 and 6 January 1728 there was a period of national mourning, with no other musical performances.

In September 1728 a brief dispute with the church authorities flared up. The sub-deacon, Gaudlitz, demanded that he himself should choose the songs to be sung before and after the sermon at Vespers; as it was usual for the Kantor to select these songs, Bach felt that his rights had been encroached upon. The dispute was settled in the sub-deacon's favour. Bach must have seen this as a setback, for once again his grievances had not been met; but his relations with the ecclesiastical authorities were on the whole good throughout his time at

Leipzig. His relations with the town council and the head teachers of the Thomasschule went less smoothly, and were to become even more difficult in the 1730s. Documents dealing with the various disputes show Bach to have been a stubborn defender of the prerogatives of his office who frequently reacted with excessive violence and was often to blame if there was a negative outcome. It would be wrong, however, to draw hasty inferences about Bach's personality and his relations with the world about him. It is unfortunate that about a half of Bach's surviving correspondence is concerned with generally trivial but often protracted disputes over rights. This material is extant in public archives, while utterances of kinds not appropriate to archival preservation, which might have complemented this rather austere view of his personality, have survived in only small quantity. From Bach's behaviour during these disputes it can be seen that, under pressure, he would defy bureaucratic regulations in order to preserve his independence and to clear himself an artistic breathing-space. His taking over of the collegium musicum in 1729, to be directed under his own management, must be seen in this context, as it represents something more than an incidental biographical fact.

Early in 1729 Bach spent some time at the Weissenfels court in connection with the birthday celebrations in February of Duke Christian, with whom he had long been associated. On this occasion the title of court Kapellmeister of Saxe-Weissenfels was conferred on him (his Cöthen title had lately expired); he retained the title until 1736. At the end of March he went to Cöthen to perform the funeral music for his former employer. On 15 April (Good Friday) the *St Matthew*

Passion was performed again at the Thomaskirche. On the second day of Whit week (6 June), what was probably the last cantata of the Picander cycle was performed, no.174. This cantata, with its rich orchestral forces and weighty sinfonia (based on the first movement of the Brandenburg Concerto no.3), announces the beginning of Bach's work with the collegium musicum. The manuscript, uniquely for Bach, is dated ('1729'); perhaps this represents some sort of final gesture after a heavy, six-year involvement in cantata composition. During this time instrumental music remained in the background. Besides the few harpsichord works already mentioned, his only instrumental productions were, it seems, a few organ pieces connected with his activities as a recital organist.

In June 1729 an invitation to visit Leipzig was delivered to Handel, then in Halle, by Wilhelm Friedemann, in place of his father, who was ill at the time; but nothing came of it. Thus Bach's second and last attempt to establish contact with his highly esteemed London colleague met with failure.

VII Leipzig: 1729–39

On his appointment as director of the collegium musicum, decisive changes came about in Bach's activities in Leipzig; and at the same time new possibilities were opened up. The collegium had been founded by Telemann in 1702 and had most recently been directed by G. B. Schott (who left to become Kantor at Gotha in March 1729); it was a voluntary association of professional musicians and university students that gave regular weekly (and during the fair season even more frequent) public concerts. Such societies played an important part

in the flowering of bourgeois musical culture in the 18th century, and with his highly reputed ensemble Bach made his own contribution to this in the commercial metropolis of Leipzig. He took over the direction before the third Sunday after Easter – in other words, by April 1729 – and retained it in the first place until 1737. Bach must have had strong reasons for wanting to take on this fresh area of work in addition to his other duties. To some extent it is possible to guess those reasons. For six years he had immersed himself in the production of sacred music, and he had created a stock of works sufficient to supply the requirements of his remaining time in office. In his efforts to provide sacred music that was at once fastidious and comprehensive he had met with little appreciation from the authorities, and no additional facilities (for example, much needed professional instrumentalists) had been placed at his disposal: it would be understandable if he now felt resigned to the situation. Further, as a former Kapellmeister, he must have been attracted by the prospect of working with a good instrumental ensemble. He must have felt that, as director of the collegium, he would be able to establish an area of musical activities where he would be completely independent and free to pursue his own ideas. This new position may also have involved some additional income.

Nothing, unfortunately, is known about the programmes of the 'ordinaire' weekly concerts. But it is generally acknowledged that Bach must have given performances of many of his Cöthen instrumental works, some of them in revised versions, as the surviving performing parts for the orchestral suites BWV1066–9 and the flute sonatas BWV1030 and 1039 testify. And there can be no doubt that the seven harpsichord concertos

BWV1052–8, gathered together in a Leipzig manuscript collection, belong with these works. No evidence survives as to the extent to which Bach composed new music specially for collegium performances. But he often performed works by other composers, including orchestral suites by his cousin Johann Ludwig. Further, Bach's many musical acquaintances from other places must have made frequent appearances, including his colleagues in the Dresden court orchestra (there is evidence of visits from J. A. Hasse, Georg Benda, S. L. Weiss, C. H. Graun and J. D. Zelenka). C. P. E. Bach's remark that 'it was seldom that a musical master passed through [Leipzig] without getting to know my father and playing for him' must refer to performances of the collegium musicum, which took place on Wednesdays between 4 and 6 p.m. in the coffee-garden 'before the Grimmisches Thor' in the summer and on Fridays between 8 and 10 p.m. in Zimmermann's coffee-house in the winter. In addition, there were 'extraordinaire' concerts, to mark such events as visits of the Dresden court; on these occasions, during the 1730s, Bach performed his large-scale secular cantatas. His activities with the collegium must have made heavy demands on him, and the reduction in his production of sacred music is easy to understand.

This does not, however, mean that his interest in sacred music was diminished (as has been claimed, with undue emphasis in the light of the revised dating of his works). Such a view is contradicted not only by the major ecclesiastical works written after 1730 but also by the simple fact that, throughout his period of office, Bach provided performances of his cantatas, a repertory largely completed before 1729, every Sunday at the two

main Leipzig churches. His reference in 1739 to the 'onus' of such undertakings, in connection with a projected performance of the Passion, might just as well have been made in the 1720s. Admittedly, his difficulties became particularly acute around 1730, as his important memorandum of 23 August 1730, dealing with the state of church music in Leipzig and outlining his remedies, testifies. His letter of 28 October that year, to his old friend Erdmann in Danzig, may be read in the same sense; sheer frustration that the memorandum had proved ineffectual drove him to consider leaving Leipzig. It would seem that his work with the collegium musicum had not yet brought about the intended equilibrium in his activities.

The situation had been aggravated by other, external factors. The old headmaster Johann Heinrich Ernesti had died in 1729 (Bach had performed a motet BWV226 at his funeral in October). During the subsequent interim in the Thomasschule's direction the organization of school life was disturbed. Problems of space appear to have arisen too. It was in this context that complaints were made about Bach's neglect of his school duties (the dropping of singing lessons, absence on journeys without leave); in August 1730 there was even a question of reducing his salary 'because the Kantor is incorrigible'. It would appear that things were put right by J. M. Gesner, who took over the headship of the school in the summer, and who seems soon to have established friendly and familiar relations with Bach.

On Good Friday 1730 Bach apparently performed a *St Luke Passion*, not of his own composition. From 25 to 27 June the jubilee of the Confession of Augsburg

was celebrated across Lutheran Germany, and Bach wrote three cantatas for the event (nos.190*a*, 120*b*, Anh.4*a*: all were parody cantatas). They are not untypical of his church compositions of this period, most of which were put together as parodies; and that is also true of the major vocal works like the *St Mark Passion*, the B minor Mass, the small masses and the *Christmas Oratorio*. Bach's only sacred cantatas composed as completely original works after 1729 seem to be nos.117 (1728–31), 192 (1730), 51 (*c*1730), 29, 112 and 140 (1731), 177 (1732), 97 (1734), 9 and 100 (1732–5), 14 (1735), 195 (after 1737), 197 (*c*1742) and 200 (fragment, *c*1742).

In 1731 a collected edition of the six partitas appeared as op.1, as the first part of the *Clavier-Übung*. From the wording of the title it is clear that Bach planned a series of 'keyboard exercises', which he now proceeded to produce. His new and continuing interest in publishing his own compositions is a clear indication of his change of attitude over an independent and freely creative activity of his own. The first performance of the *St Mark Passion*, predominantly a parody work, took place on Good Friday of that year. At the end of June 1731 Bach and his family had to move to temporary quarters while rebuilding and extension work were being carried out on the Thomasschule. His residence must have become increasingly cramped, for his family was growing. At the beginning of Bach's period in Leipzig Anna Magdalena had borne a child every year, to whom members of leading local families (noblemen, merchants, professors, theologians) had stood as godparents. But few of the children survived infancy:

Christiana Sophia Henrietta (*b* spring 1723; *d* 29 June 1726)
Gottfried Heinrich (*48*)
Christian Gottlieb (baptized 14 April 1725; *d* 21 Sept 1728)
Elisabeth Juliane Friederica (baptized 5 April 1726; *d* Naumburg, 24 Aug 1781)
Ernestus Andreas (baptized 30 Oct 1727; *d* 1 Nov 1727)
Regina Johanna (baptized 10 Oct 1728; *d* 25 April 1733)
Christiana Benedicta (baptized 1 Jan 1730; *d* 4 Jan 1730)
Christiana Dorothea (baptized 18 March 1731; *d* 31 Aug 1732)
Johann Christoph Friedrich (*49*)
Johann August Abraham (baptized 5 Nov 1733; *d* 6 Nov 1733)
Johann Christian (*50*)
Johanna Carolina (baptized 30 Oct 1737; *d* Leipzig, 18 Aug 1781)
Regina Susanna (baptized 22 Feb 1742; *d* Leipzig, 14 Dec 1809)

Joy and sorrow were everyday matters. But Bach's family life must have been harmonious in more than one sense; in 1730 he reported, as a proud paterfamilias, that with his family he could form a vocal and instrumental concert ensemble. The family moved into the new residence the next April. The school was reconsecrated on 5 June 1732 with a cantata, BWV Anh.18. In September 1731 Bach had been to Dresden for the first performance of Hasse's opera *Cleofide* and to give concerts at the Sophienkirche and at court (there were enthusiastic reports in the newspapers). In September 1732 he went with his wife to Kassel for the examination and inauguration of the organ of St Martin's, where he probably played the 'Dorian' Toccata and Fugue in D minor BWV538.

With the death of Elector Friedrich August I of Saxony on 1 February 1733 a five-month period of national mourning began. The collegium musicum obtained permission to restart its performances in the middle of June, when a new harpsichord was introduced (possibly in harpsichord concertos). During the mourn-

ing period Bach worked on the Kyrie and the Gloria of the B minor Mass, which, in the hope of obtaining a title at the court Kapelle, he presented to the new Elector Friedrich August II in Dresden, with a note dated 27 July 1733, as a *Missa* in a set of parts. Recent investigations suggested that the *Missa* was performed at this time, perhaps at the Sophienkirche in Dresden, where W. F. Bach had been working as an organist since June 1733. Bach may have stayed in Dresden from the middle of July to organize such a performance. Not until November 1736, however, was the title 'Hofkomponist' conferred on Bach, and even then only through the intervention of his patron Count Keyserlingk after a further letter of application. As a gesture of thanks, Bach paid his respects to the Dresden royal household and an enthusiastic public with a two-hour organ recital on the new Silbermann instrument at the Frauenkirche on 1 December 1736.

After the dedication of the *Missa* in July 1733, Bach kept the Saxon royal family's interests in mind with his 'extraordinaire' concerts of the collegium musicum. On 3 August, the name day of the new elector, Bach began his remarkable series of secular cantatas of congratulation and homage with BWV Anh.12 (music lost), followed by Cantata no.213 (5 September, for the heir to the electorate), no.214 (8 December, for the electress), no.205a (19 February 1734, for the coronation of the elector as King of Poland; music lost), an unknown work (24 August, again for the elector), and no.215 (5 October, also for the elector, who was at the performance). In these and similar later works Bach came closest to opera, not just in terms of the dramatic nature of some of the librettos but also stylistically. They

99

indicate that he was not only thoroughly familiar with current operatic style, since his frequent visits to the Dresden opera house, but actually indebted to opera as a musical stimulus, more than his remark on 'the lovely Dresden ditties' ('die schönen Dresdner Liederchen', reported by Forkel) suggests. Much of the festive music was performed in the open air with splendid illuminations, and according to newspaper reports the music benefited from a resounding echo. (On the day after the performance of no.215 Bach's virtuoso trumpeter and the leader of the Leipzig Stadtpfeifer, Gottfried Reiche, died as a result of the exertions of his office.) During the following Christmas season Bach gave the people of Leipzig a chance to hear much of the music from his secular festive cantatas in modified form, as the *Christmas Oratorio*, which was heard in six sections between Christmas Day 1734 and Epiphany 1735 (and consisted predominantly of parodies of Cantatas nos.213–15).

On 21 November 1734 the new headmaster of the Thomasschule, Johann August Ernesti, was greeted with a cantata, BWV Anh.19 (Gesner had moved to the University of Göttingen). Bach's dealings with the directors of the school had been untroubled for four years, thanks to his friendly relations with Gesner; but with Ernesti he experienced the most violent of all his controversies. A dispute flared up during August 1736 over the authority to nominate choral prefects, in which the interests of the Kantor and the headmaster were diametrically opposed. With his neo-humanist educational ideals, whereby he set great store by the academic quality of training in school, Ernesti showed little appreciation of the musical traditions. In line with prevailing trends during the Enlightenment, the ten-

dency at the Thomasschule, at least from the start of Bach's period of office, had been to restrict musical activities or at any rate to reduce their proportions; Bach, on the other hand, demanded the best-qualified pupils to assist him, and certainly he often made excessive demands (for music copying, rehearsals and so on). Against what were to some extent unfair arguments on the headmaster's part, his struggles were doomed to failure. The grievances over prefects were taken before the courts in Dresden; the affair, which led to Bach's having disciplinary difficulties with his pupils, was settled early in 1738 (the precise outcome is not recorded).

Among the more important events of 1735 was the appearance of the second part of the *Clavier-Übung* at Easter. In the context of Bach's activities as a publisher it should also be mentioned that by 1729 he was involved in the distribution of musical publications by other authors and kept a stock, including Heinichen's book on figured bass, Walther's *Lexicon* and keyboard works by Hurlebusch, Krebs and his own sons. On 19 May the *Ascension Oratorio* (Cantata no.11) was first performed; probably the *Easter Oratorio* was heard on the preceding Easter Sunday. In June he travelled to the town where he had spent his youth, Mühlhausen, to appraise the rebuilt organ in the Marienkirche, where his son Johann Gottfried Bernhard (*47*) had just been appointed organist. During Advent 1735, when no music was performed, and Lent 1736 Bach was probably engaged on the revision of the *St Matthew Passion* and in making a carefully laid-out fair copy of the new version. In this form, characterized by its writing for double chorus (with two continuo parts), the work was performed in the Thomaskirche on 30 March

1736, with the cantus firmus parts in the opening and closing choruses of part 1 played on the 'swallow's nest' organ. Also at Easter the Schemelli Hymnbook, on whose tunes and figured basses Bach had collaborated, was published.

In summer 1737 Bach temporarily resigned the direction of the collegium musicum, For the last 'extraordinaire' concert on 7 October 1736 he had written the congratulatory Cantata no.206 on the birthday of the elector. Only two further works of homage are known from 1737–8 (BWV30a and Anh.13). He now turned to keyboard music, working on the second part of *Das wohltemperirte Clavier*, and on the third part of the *Clavier-Übung*, the largest of his keyboard works. This collection of organ pieces, freely based on chorales, with large-scale works for the church organ and small-scale ones for domestic instruments, appeared at Michaelmas 1739. Probably he also devoted himself more particularly about this time to private music teaching. Around this time J. F. Agricola (his pupil 1738–41) and J. P. Kirnberger (up to 1741) – his most important pupils apart from his own sons – were in Leipzig. Over the years Bach had something like 80 private pupils; among them were C. F. Abel (c1743), J. C. Altnikol (1744–8), J. F. Doles (1739–44), G. F. Einicke (1732–7), H. N. Gerber (1724–7), J. C. G. Gerlach (1723–9), J. G. Goldberg (from 1737), G. A. Homilius (1735–42), J. C. Kittel (1748–50), J. L. Krebs (1726–35), L. C. Mizler (?–1734), J. G. Müthel (1750), J. C. Nichelmann (1730–33), J. G. Schübler (after 1740), G. G. Wagner (1723–6) and C. G. Wecker (1723–8).

In October 1737 Bach's nephew Johann Elias (*39*) came to live with the family, as private secretary and

4. *Bach's autograph letter (24 August 1735) of recommendation for his pupil Johann Ludwig Krebs*

tutor for the younger children; he remained until 1742. The surviving drafts of letters he prepared give a lively picture of Bach's correspondence in these few years. At this period Bach gave close attention to the study of works by other composers. He was a subscriber to

Telemann's Parisian flute quartets of May 1738; but more typical is his preoccupation with Latin polyphonic liturgical compositions. The *stile antico* tradition seems to have held a particular fascination for him. In the first place he owed his knowledge of this repertory, to which he marginally contributed by making transcriptions (works by Palestrina, Caldara, Bassani etc), to his connections at Dresden. His knowledge of Pergolesi's *Stabat mater* of 1736, which he reworked during the 1740s as a psalm setting, *Tilge, Höchster, meine Sünden* (not in BWV), is also surprising; the earliest trace of Pergolesi's work north of the Alps thus leads to Bach – a sign of the latter's remarkable knowledge of the repertory. His interest in Latin liturgical music relates not only to his plans for and completion of the B minor Mass, but also, in the late 1730s, to the composition of the small masses in A and G (BWV234, 236). These may have been written for the Protestant court services in Dresden, but that would not exclude performances in Leipzig.

On 14 May 1737 J. A. Scheibe, in his journal *Der critische Musikus*, published a weighty criticism of Bach's manner of composition. This seems to have come as a severe blow to Bach. The Leipzig lecturer in rhetoric Johann Abraham Birnbaum responded with a defence, printed in January 1738, which Bach distributed among his friends and acquaintances. The affair developed into a public controversy which was pursued in 1739 with further polemical writings by Scheibe and Birnbaum, and by Mizler's Correspondirende Societät der Musicalischen Wissenschaften (who supported Bach), and was concluded by Scheibe in 1745 with a conciliatory review of the Italian Concerto.

Scheibe acknowledged Bach's extraordinary skill as a performer on the organ and the harpsichord, but sharply criticized his compositions, claiming that Bach 'by his bombastic and intricate procedures deprived them of naturalness and obscured their beauty by an excess of art'. Birnbaum's not particularly skilful replies fail to recognize the true problem, which lies in a clash of irreconcilable stylistic ideals. His factual definition of what is natural and what artificial in Bach's style (in which he drew a historical parallel with Lotti and Palestrina – of whose works Bach possessed transcripts – as precedents) could not, ultimately, counter Scheibe's criticisms.

IX Leipzig: 1739–50

In October 1739 Bach resumed the direction of the collegium musicum, which had meanwhile been in the charge of C. G. Gerlach (organist at the Neukirche and a pupil of Bach). A composition for the birthday of the elector (7 October; the music is lost) dates from this time, but it would seem that Bach's ambitions and activities in connection with the 'ordinaire' and 'extraordinaire' concerts were considerably diminished. There were few performances of congratulatory cantatas, and these were probably repeats of earlier works. Nor is there evidence of any chamber music being produced during this period. However, the preparation of the score for the seven harpsichord concertos BWV1052–8 probably belongs to this time. Bach withdrew from the collegium musicum again in 1741. With the death of the Coffee-house owner Gottfried Zimmermann (30 May 1741) the collegium had lost its landlord and organizer, and without him it could not long continue. In 1744 its 40 years as an important

institution came to an end (possibly Bach still gave occasional performances up to that date). Civic musical life in Leipzig found a new focal point in the Grosse Concert, founded in 1743 and sponsored by a growing circle of musical dilettantes and hence less professional than the collegium.

In August 1741 Bach went to Berlin, probably to visit Carl Philipp Emanuel who in 1738 had been appointed court harpsichord player to Crown Prince Frederick of Prussia (later Frederick the Great). In the two previous years Bach had made brief journeys to Halle (early 1740) and Altenburg (September 1739; he gave an organ recital in the castle church). In November 1741 there was a further journey, this time to Dresden, where he visited Count Keyserlingk. The 'Aria with 30 Variations', the so-called Goldberg Variations, appeared in 1741–2 as the fourth part of the *Clavier-Übung* (published by Schmidt of Nuremberg). Bach's visit to Dresden may lie behind the anecdote related by Forkel, according to which the variations were written as a commission for the count. But the lack of any formal dedication in the original edition suggests that the work was not composed to a commission. It is however known that Bach presented the count with a copy, apparently for the use of his young resident harpsichord player Johann Gottlieb Goldberg, who was a pupil of both J. S. and W. F. Bach. In a copy of the variations which came to light in 1975, Bach added a series of 14 enigmatically notated canons on the bass of the Aria (BWV1087); these appear at the outset of a period of intensive involvement in canonic writing.

On 30 August 1742, on the Kleinzschocher estate near Leipzig, a 'Cantata burlesque' (known as the

Peasant Cantata, no.212) was performed in homage to the new lord of the manor, Carl Heinrich von Dieskau; this work is unique in Bach's output for its folklike manner. The thoroughly up-to-date characteristics of parts of the work show that Bach was not only intimately acquainted with the musical fashions of the times but also knew how to adapt elements of the younger generation's style for his own purposes (as he also did in the lute piece BWV998 and the third movement of the trio sonata from the *Musical Offering*).

Alongside this work, apparently his last secular cantata, only isolated sacred cantatas were composed or arranged during the 1740s: 197, 200 and possibly 195. Instead Bach gave regular repeat performances of his cantata revisions besides retouchings of earlier, larger works, such as the *St Matthew* and *St John Passions*, and also turned to performances of works by other composers: an anonymous *St Luke Passion*, Handel's *Brockes Passion*, a Passion Oratorio by Graun, and passion pasticcios by Keiser and Handel, Graun and Telemann, and Kuhnau and Altnikol. The only new composition of any considerable scope was the 'Symbolum Nicenum' of the B minor Mass, in which Bach's preoccupation of the late 1730s with Latin polyphonic music is again seen. The occasion for its composition and performance is unknown, so it cannot be firmly dated (it was probably some time between 1742 and 1745). Recent research has however managed to establish that the work was written out only during Bach's last years, perhaps about 1748. The so-called 'B minor Mass' as an exemplary collection of the standard sections of the mass was completed with a Sanctus (composed in 1724) and the closing movements, from

the 'Osanna' onwards (all parodies).

Instrumental music, however, again came to the fore in the 1740s. But before then Bach had begun to sift through his older organ chorales. Some of the Weimar pieces were extensively reworked and gathered into a new manuscript collection (the '18', BWV651–68). These revisions may have been undertaken with a view to the subsequent appearance of the chorales in print, as happened with the six chorales on movements from the cantatas (the 'Schübler Chorales') about 1748. Apparently Bach was still engaged in work on the chorales in the last months of his life. The copying from dictation of the chorale *Vor deinen Thron* BWV668, later the subject of legend, was in fact probably confined to an improvement of an existing work (the chorale BWV641 from the Weimar *Orgel-Büchlein*).

Bach retained his interest in organ building. In 1746 there were two important examinations and inaugurations of organs: on 7 August in Zschortau and on 26–9 September at St Wenceslas, Naumburg. The Naumburg appraisal was one of Bach's most important; Bach subjected the instrument to the most searching examination, both of its technical reliability and of its tone quality. He took a critical interest in Gottfried Silbermann's building of pianofortes, proposing alterations in the mechanism, which Silbermann adopted. Bach publicly praised Silbermann's later pianos and helped to sell them (a receipt for one sold to Poland, dated 6 May 1749, survives). On his visit to Potsdam Bach played on a series of Silbermann pianos.

The visit to the court of Frederick the Great in May 1747 is one of the most notable biographical events in Bach's unspectacular life. The invitation probably came

about through Count Keyserlingk, the royal envoy in Dresden, who was then in Berlin. Bach's encounter with Frederick began on 7 May at the palace of Potsdam with an exercise in fugal improvisation; Bach's execution on the piano of an improvisation on a theme supplied by the king met with general applause. The next day Bach gave an organ recital in the Heiliggeist Church in Potsdam, and during chamber music that evening he improvised a six-part fugue on a theme of his own. He also visited the new Berlin opera house, and possibly went to look at organs in Potsdam and Berlin. On his return, probably in the middle of May, he worked industriously on an 'elaboration of the King of Prussia's fugue theme', beginning with writing down the fugue he had improvised (a three-part ricercare), which, while in Potsdam, he had announced that he would print. But he now decided on a larger project and under the title *Musikalisches Opfer* ('Musical Offering') he prepared a work in several movements dedicated to Frederick the Great; this work was printed in its entirety by the end of September (Michaelmas) 1747. The royal theme serves as the basis for all the movements (two ricercares, in three and six parts, for keyboard; a trio sonata for flute, violin and continuo; and various canons for flute, violin and continuo with harpsichord obbligato).

In June 1747, after some hesitation, Bach joined the Correspondirende Societät der Musicalischen Wissenschaften founded by Lorenz Mizler. It was probably in 1747 that he submitted, as a 'scientific' piece of work, his canonic composition on *Vom Himmel hoch* BWV769. At the same time he sent the members an offprint of the six-part canon from the series on the bass of the Goldberg Variations. He seems, however, to have taken no further

interest in the society's affairs as (according to C. P. E. Bach) he thought nothing of the 'dry, mathematical matters' that Mizler wanted to discuss. Besides his long acquaintance with his pupil Mizler, Bach's most likely reason for joining the society was that prominent colleagues such as Telemann and Graun were fellow members.

The beginnings of his work on *Die Kunst der Fuge* ('The Art of Fugue') seem to date from around 1740, or before. It is impossible to give an exact date as the original composing score is now lost. However, a complete autograph version survives from the 1740s, preceding the published one. During his last years Bach worked at a revision which he intended to have printed – a process he himself still supervised to a large extent. The printing was probably largely complete by about the end of 1749 (in other words, before his son Johann Christoph Friedrich, who had contributed to this task, left to join the court at Bückeburg in January 1750). But Bach was not to see the entire work in print; his sons, probably C. P. E. in particular, took charge of the publication and the work appeared posthumously in autumn 1751. The organ chorale BWV668 (*Vor deinen Thron*) served as a supplement to mitigate the work's incompleteness.

In his final years (possibly even from the early or middle 1740s) Bach suffered from eye trouble, specifically cataract; ultimately he was totally blind. By the beginning of 1749 he was apparently incapable of working at full capacity; otherwise the Leipzig town council would surely not have been so tactless as to allow J. G. Harrer, a protégé of the Dresden prime minister Count Brühl, to take the examination for the post of Kantor on 8 June 1749. Out of consideration for Bach the

110

cantata performance was in a concert hall rather than one of the churches. The town chronicle reported that the authorities were counting on Bach's death. After the beginning of 1749 Bach composed only on the most exceptional occasions. The last known examples of his handwriting, which give an impression of increasing irregularity, clumsiness and cramping, date from May 1749. On the baptism of his grandson Johann Sebastian Altnikol (his pupil Johann Christoph Altnikol had married Elisabeth Juliane Friederica Bach) on 6 October 1749 Bach was unable to be present as godfather.

During his last year, Bach's state of health and his ability to work must have fluctuated. But he was not entirely inactive. In the spring of 1749 he is known to have corresponded with Count Johann Adam von Questenberg, apparently about a commission or some other project. Although no details are known this reaffirms Bach's obviously well-established connections with some major noble patrons from the area of Bohemia (Count Sporck of Lissa and Kukus), Moravia (Count Questenberg of Jароměřice) and Silesia (the Haugwitz family). From May 1749 to June 1750 he was engaged in a controversial correspondence about the Freiberg headmaster Biedermann. In May 1749 Biedermann had violently attacked the cultivation of music in schools; Bach immediately felt himself called into battle, and among other things he gave a repeat performance of the satirical cantata about the controversy between Phoebus and Pan, no.201. His involvement is understandable, for he must have seen parallels with the state of affairs at the Thomasschule. Bach solicited a rejoinder on the part of C. G. Schröter, a member of Mizler's society, and even Mattheson joined

5. *Johann Sebastian Bach: replica (1748) by Elias Gottlob Haussmann of his portrait (1746) showing the composer holding a copy of his six-part canon* BWV1076

in, from Hamburg. Once again, the affair throws characteristic light on the increasingly unfavourable conditions surrounding the traditional role of music in schools during the Enlightenment.

At the end of March Bach underwent an eye operation, performed by the English eye specialist John Taylor (who was later to perform a similar operation on Handel). It was only partly successful, however, and had to be repeated during the second week of April. The second operation too was ultimately unsuccessful, and indeed Bach's physique was considerably weakened. Yet as late as the beginning of May 1750 Johann Gottfried Müthel could go to Leipzig, stay at Bach's house and become his last pupil. To what extent regular instruction was possible under these circumstances remains uncertain. In the next two months Bach's health had so deteriorated that, on 22 July, he had to take his last Communion at home. He died only six days later, on the evening of 28 July, after a stroke. He was buried two or three days later at St John's cemetery.

His wife, Anna Magdalena, who in addition to her domestic tasks was a loyal and industrious collaborator, participating in performances and copying out music, survived him by ten years. She died in abject poverty in 1760. On his death Bach had left a modest estate consisting of securities, cash, silver vessels, instruments – including eight harpsichords, two lute-harpsichords, ten string instruments (among them a valuable Stainer violin), a lute and spinet – and other goods, officially valued at 1122 thalers and 22 groschen; this had to be divided between the widow and the nine surviving children of both marriages.

x Iconography

The coffin containing Bach's remains was exhumed in 1894: a detailed anatomical investigation by Professor Wilhelm His confirmed their identity and showed that Bach was of medium build. From a skull impression Carl Seffner, in 1898, modelled a bust, which shows an undoubted similarity with the only likeness of Bach that can be guaranteed as authentic, that of the Leipzig portraitist Elias Gottlob Haussmann. That portrait exists in two versions, one dating from 1746 (Historisches Museum der Stadt Leipzig) and one of 1748 (William H. Scheide Library, Princeton; see fig.5). The earlier, signed 'E. G. Haussmann pinxit 1746', was presented to the Thomasschule in 1809 by August Eberhard Müller, later a Thomaskantor, on his retirement in 1809. It is not known whence Müller had obtained the painting. It seems improbable that the portrait had been presented to Mizler's society; probably none was ever presented, and this one was painted for his own family. The Thomasschule picture had been severely damaged and repeatedly painted over. In 1912–13 it was restored, but it remains inferior to the excellently preserved replica of 1748, which came from C. P. E. Bach's estate and was long owned by the Jenke family, in Silesia and then in England, before being identified by Hans Raupach in 1950.

All the other portraits allegedly of Bach are at best doubtful. Perhaps the least improbable is that by Johann Jacob Ihle, dating from about 1720, which purports to show him as Kapellmeister in Cöthen; yet coming from the palace at Bayreuth (and identified as a 'picture of Bach' only in 1897), the portrait gives no concrete indication of whom it represents, and its provenance is

uncertain. Portraits of probable authencity that no longer survive were once in the possession of J. C. Kittel (from the estate of the Countess of Weissenfels) and of J. N. Forkel. A pastel, again from C. P. E. Bach's collection, has not survived. There must have been at least one further replica of Haussmann's portrait, according to early Bach literature (from the estate of W. F. Bach), but all trace of it has been lost. A valuable copy of the 1746 portrait, dating from 1848 (before it had been restored) and possibly by G. A. Friedrich, was formerly in the possession of the Burckhardt family of Leipzig and is now in that of Baron H. O. R. Tuyll van Serooskerken, Alabama, USA.

During the 18th and 19th centuries many copies were made of the Haussmann portraits, both in oils and by printing processes. Of these, the engraving (1774) by Samuel Gottlieb Kütner, an art student at Leipzig with C. P. E. Bach's son, Johann Sebastian Bach (1748–78), is of particular value; C. P. E. Bach described it to Forkel as 'a fair likeness'. In addition, numerous apocryphal 'pictures of Bach' exist (including the so-called Erfurt portrait and the Volbach picture); most are of the 'old-man-with-a-wig' type and have nothing to do with Bach. The nearest we can nowadays get to his true physiognomy is probably in the 1748 version of Haussmann's portrait, wherein, as a man in his early 60s, Bach is represented as a learned musician, with a copy of the enigmatic six-part canon BWV1076 in his hand to demonstrate his status.

XI Sources, repertory

The earliest catalogue of Bach's compositions – admittedly a very rough one – was drawn up by C. P. E.

Bach and J. F. Agricola; together with the first authentic posthumous account of his life it was published as *Nekrolog* in 1754. It scarcely provides an adequate idea of the extent of Bach's works. But most of those printed during Bach's lifetime (Cantata no.71 and its lost Mühlhausen counterpart; the four parts of the *Clavier-Übung*; the Schemelli Hymnbook; the *Musical Offering*; the Canonic Variations BWV769; the Schübler chorales; the *Art of Fugue*; the canons BWV1074 and 1076) and a great many compositions surviving only in manuscript are included. Palpable losses appear to have occurred among the cantatas (more than 100 works: nearly two cycles of church cantatas and several secular occasional works) and among the orchestral and chamber music (the extent of these losses is unknown, but must be considerable); beyond these, there are isolated known losses of works in every genre.

In general, the materials of Bach's works were essentially kept together during his lifetime, and the losses occurred only on the division of his legacy in 1750, when the manuscripts, especially of the vocal works, were divided between the eldest sons and Bach's widow; according to Forkel, most of them went to Wilhelm Friedemann. He, unfortunately, was compelled for financial reasons to sell them off item by item, and the material is not simply scattered but for the most part lost. Only a few of the items owned by Johann Christian, including a printed copy of the *Musical Offering* and the autograph score of the organ Prelude and Fugue in B minor BWV544 (signed with his nickname 'Christel'), can be traced; and nothing is known of any material that may have passed to five of his brothers and sisters. C. P. E. Bach's and Anna Magdalena's

shares were better preserved. Bach's widow gave her portion (the parts of the cycle of chorale cantatas) to the Thomasschule while most of C. P. E. Bach's estate passed through Georg Pölchau's collection into the Berlin Königliche Bibliothek (later the Preussiche Staatsbibliothek, now divided between the Staatsbibliothek, West Berlin, and the Deutsche Staatsbibliothek, East Berlin). This collection forms the basis of the most important collection of Bach archives. During the 19th century this library acquired further, smaller Bach collections, notably those from the Singakademie and the estates of Forkel, Franz Hauser and Count Voss-Buch (in some of which fragments from W. F. Bach's inheritance appear).

Besides the original manuscripts – the autograph scores, and parts prepared for performances under Bach's direction – which, in their essentials, Bach kept by him, many copies were made in the circle of his pupils, particularly of organ and harpsichord music. As many of the autograph scores of the keyboard works are lost, this strand is specially significant for the preservation of Bach's works. For example, important copies have come down through Bach's pupils Krebs and Kittel. After Bach's death Breitkopf in Leipzig became a centre for the dissemination of his music (again, primarily the keyboard music). In Berlin a notable Bach collection was made for Princess Anna Amalia of Prussia, under the direction of Kirnberger, in which all facets of Bach's creative output were represented. These secondary sources often have to serve when autograph material is not available – relatively often with the instrumental works, more rarely with the vocal ones.

Research into source materials, notably in conjunc-

tion with the Neue Bach-Ausgabe, has proved fruitful. Most of the copyists who worked for Bach have been catalogued and some have been identified (e.g. Johann Andreas Kuhnau, 1703–?, formerly 'Hauptkopist A'; Christian Gottlob Meissner, 1707–60, formerly 'Hauptkopist B'; Johann Heinrich Bach, 1707–83, formerly 'Hauptkopist C'); papers, inks and binding have been analysed; and examinations of Bach's handwriting have revealed its various stages of development. A far-reaching revision of the chronoloy of Bach's works (only some 40 of the originals are dated) has been made possible. For the vocal works this new dating is now basically complete; sometimes it is precise to the actual day. With the instrumental works the situation is more complicated, because the original manuscripts are often lost; in consequence, results have been less precise since the history of the secondary sources permits of only vague conclusions about composition dates (for example, copies originating from the circle around Krebs and J. G. Walther point to a date in the Weimar period); this makes it unlikely that any complete and exact chronology can be established for the instrumental works, though a relative one is now largely achieved. Investigations of source material have also led to the solution of crucial questions of authenticity, particularly in connection with the early works. For example, Cantata no.15, hitherto regarded as Bach's earliest cantata, has now been identified as by Johann Ludwig Bach; similarly, Cantata nos.53, 189 and 142 have been excised from the list of his works. Several instrumental works too have gone, such as bwv553–60, 834–5, 838–9, 964, 990, 1036 and 1070. However, an important early organ work, bwv739, has now been authenticated.

XII **Background, style, influences**

Bach's output, unparalleled in its encylopedic character, embraces practically every musical form of his
time besides opera. The accepted genres were significantly added to by Bach (notably with the harpsichord
concerto and chamber music with obbligato keyboard);
further, he opened up new dimensions in virtually every
department of creative work to which he turned, in
format, density and musical quality, and also in technical demands (a work like the *St Matthew Passion* is
unique in music up to and including the 18th century).
At the same time Bach's creative production was inex-
tricably bound up with the external factors of his places
of work and his employers, as was normal in his time.
The composition dates of the various repertories thus
reflect Bach's preoccupations in his various official
capacities. Thus most of the organ works were composed while he was active as an organist at Arnstadt,
Mühlhausen and Weimar; most of his output of chamber music comes from the period when he was
Kapellmeister at Cöthen; and the main vocal works
belong to the period of his Kantorate at Leipzig. But
Bach's production was by no means wholly dependent
on the duties attaching to his office at the time. Thus
during his Leipzig period he found time to produce a
body of keyboard music to meet his requirements for
concerts, for advertisement, for teaching and other purposes. And his career may be seen as a steady and
logical process of development: from organist to
Konzertmeister, then to Kapellmeister, and finally to
Kantor and director of music – a continual expansion of
the scope of his work and responsibilities. This is no
matter of chance. Bach chose his appointments, and

chose the moment to make each move. If he was unable to accomplish what he required (as was often the case in Leipzig), he was capable of turning his attention elsewhere in pursuit of his creative aims. Bach was a surprisingly emancipated and self-confident artist for his time.

The uncertainty about the dating of Bach's early works makes it difficult to reconstruct and assess the beginnings of his work as a composer. The Capriccio BWV992 of 1703–4 is the earliest of his works that can be dated within two or three years; and it is doubtful whether he had composed much music before then. He took no formal lessons with an established composer, like Handel with Zachow; but it would be mistaken to call him self-taught as a composer, for the significance of his belonging to a long-standing family of professional musicians should not be underestimated. Composing was probably overshadowed by instrumental playing in Ambrosius Bach's family; this must certainly have applied to the young Johann Sebastian, and probably he devoted more attention to his training as an instrumentalist, especially as an organist, than to composition studies. But the art of improvisation – in those days inseparably bound up with practice on the instrument – would at worst prepare the ground for his work as a composer. This reciprocity between performing and composing is reflected in the unruly virtuoso and improvisatory elements in Bach's early works.

As composers who influenced the young Bach, C. P. E. Bach cited (to Forkel) Froberger, Kerll, Pachelbel, Frescobaldi, Fischer, Strungk, certain French composers, Bruhns, Buxtehude, Reincken and Böhm – almost exclusively keyboard composers; C. P. E. Bach

also said that Bach formed his style through his own efforts and developed his fugal technique basically through private study and reflection. In his letter of resignation from Mühlhausen Bach himself wrote of having procured a 'grossen Apparat' ('large supply') of vocal compositions, suggesting that in vocal music too he was decisively stimulated by the study of other composers' music. Bach came into personal contact with the last three of the composers named by C. P. E.; there was no question of any teacher–pupil relationship. As later influences, C. P. E. Bach named Fux, Caldara, Handel, Keiser, Hasse, the two Grauns, Telemann, Zelenka and Benda. This list, though certainly less representative than the earlier one, suggests that Bach's main interests still lay in his great contemporaries, whose music he not only heard but also studied in transcripts. His one-sided attention to earlier masters of organ music had disappeared, but his interest in the retrospective style represented by Fux and Caldara, complemented by his enthusiasm (mentioned by Birnbaum, 1737) for Palestrina and Lotti, is notable, and is borne out by tendencies in his music from the mid-1730s. Clearly he also became interested in, and ready to follow, more recent stylistic trends, particularly after the time of his contact with the Dresden court (for example in the 'Christe eleison' of what was to become the B minor Mass); also in such works as the Peasant Cantata, the Goldberg Variations and the *Musical Offering*. Mizler, in an article of 1739 on Bach's cantata style, referring to the Scheibe–Birnbaum controversy, mentioned a work (BWV Anh.13, lost) composed 'perfectly in accordance with the newest taste' ('vollkommen nach dem neuesten Geschmack eingerichtet').

The literary sources, surprisingly, nowhere mention Vivaldi and other contemporary Italian composers. Yet it was Vivaldi who exercised what was probably the most lasting and distinctive influence on Bach from about 1712–13, when a wide range of the Italian repertory became available to the Weimar court orchestra. Bach drew from Vivaldi his clear melodic contours, the sharp outlines of his outer parts, his motoric and rhythmic conciseness, his unified motivic treatment and his clearly articulated modulation schemes. His confrontation with Vivaldi's music in 1713–14 provoked what was certainly the strongest single development towards Bach's personal style, and that style's unmistakable identity came about through his coupling of Italianisms with complex counterpoint, marked by busy interweavings of the inner voices as well as harmonic refinement. It is impossible to describe Bach's personal style by means of simple formulae; but the process of adaptation and mutation that can be felt throughout his output seems to have taken a particularly characteristic turn at that point in 1713–14 whose principal landmarks are the *Orgel-Büchlein* and the first Weimar series of cantatas. His adaptation and integration of various contemporary and retrospective styles represent his systematic attempt at shaping and perfecting his personal musical language and expanding its structural possibilities and its expressive powers.

An essential component of Bach's style can be seen in his combination of solid compositional craftsmanship with instrumental and vocal virtuosity. The technical demands made by his music reflect his own prowess as an instrumentalist. Bach's own versatility – his early involvement in singing (it is not known whether he was

later active as a singer), and his experience as a keyboard player, violinist and violist – was partly responsible for the fact that demanding technical standards became the norm for every type of composition he wrote. This led to Scheibe's famous criticism: 'Since he judges according to his own fingers, his pieces are extremely difficult to play; for he demands that singers and instrumentalists should be able to do with their throats and instruments whatever he can play on the keyboard. But this is impossible'. It makes no essential difference at what level these demands are made (for instance between the Inventions and the Goldberg Variations, the four-part chorale and the choral fugue); everywhere Bach's requirements are the antithesis of conventional simplicity. Yet technical virtuosity never predominates; it becomes a functional element within the composition as a whole. Bach's impulse towards integration is also manifested in the typically instrumental idiom in which he cast his vocal parts. He thus produced in his music for voices and instruments a homogeneous language of considerable density. Even so, he differentiated between instrumentally and (less often) vocally dominated types of writing; but even in such vocally dominated pieces as the Credo of the B minor Mass he maintained both the density and the uncompromising, yet appropriate technical standard. It is of course significant, both as regards matters of technique and the quality of his music in general that, as far as we know, he wrote almost exclusively for himself, performing groups of his own pupils, and never for a broader public (let alone a nonprofessional one). This partly explains why his music – unlike, say, Telemann's or Handel's – was disseminated within unusually narrow confines.

XIII **Cantatas**

About two-fifths of Bach's sacred cantatas must be considered lost; of the secular cantatas, more are lost than survive. Thus it is difficult to draw firm conclusions about the evolution of the cantata in Bach's hands, even though the surviving repertory is considerable and is roughly proportional to the number of cantatas composed at each place where he worked.

The earliest surviving cantatas, and probably Bach's first, date from the Mühlhausen period and include nos.131 and 106 (c1707). The only others from this time are nos.71 and 196 (1708) and nos.4 and 150 (c1708 or a little later). These are not cantatas of the type established by Neumeister in 1700 but rely closely on central German tradition. The texts were mostly taken from the Bible or the chorale repertory; more rarely they were freely conceived poetry. Musically they are marked by their varied sequence of sections representing different kinds of composition: concerto, motet, (strophic) aria and chorale, thus attaining a particularly high degree of interdependence and correspondence between text (even individual words and phrases) and music, in line with the Lutheran ideal of 'proclamation of the word'. His cantatas were put together from combinations of these formal sections adapted from the late 17th-century motet and the vocal concerto tradition, even the unique chorale cantata *per omnes versus* no.4. Bach did not call these works cantatas: generally he reserved that term for the solo cantata of the Italian type (like nos.211 and 212), calling his sacred cantatas 'Concerto', and in earlier works 'Motetto', sometimes 'Dialogus' (depending on the text) or simply 'Music'.

Bach's early cantatas are distinguished from their

124

central German precursors by his tendency to give each movement a unified structure, assuring its artistic independence, and his development of a broad formal scheme. Further, he found the means to unify movements that are not self-contained by the use of motivic material, in solo movements, and, in choral ones, with the 'permutational fugue', his earliest type of choral fugue, in which the subject and its counterpoints are retained and continually interchanged. Reacting against the use of a haphazard sequential form, with its danger of formal dissolution and small-scale, motet-like articulation, he began to use strictly symmetrical sequences of movements: for example, chorus–solos–chorus–solos–chorus (no.106).

During his early Weimar years, organ music must have dominated his output; at any rate, no vocal works have survived from then. His first secular cantata, the *Jagd-Kantate* no.208, written to a commission from the Weissenfels court, probably dates from 1713. Newly acquainted with the Italian style, he here began to take up the recitative and the modern kind of aria (for preference the da capo aria), a step which had a decisive effect on the subsequent sacred cantatas. The first of these seems to have been no.21, probably written in connection with his application for the position in Halle in December 1713. Then, with his nomination as court Konzertmeister in March 1714, he began his first cantata series with a view to producing an entire cycle over four years. The principle of cycles is closely bound up with the history of the cantata from Neumeister on; the texts too were for the most part collected and published in cycles. Bach, however, never adhered strictly to a single poet (except in the lost Picander cycle of 1728–

9). In Weimar he turned for the first time to librettos by Neumeister (nos.18 and 61) and used texts by G. C. Lehms (1684–1717; nos.199 and 54), but evidently preferred texts by the Weimar court poet Salomo Franck (1659–1725), the author of extremely original and profoundly felt sacred and secular poetic texts, among the best Bach set. The sequence of the Weimar cantatas is: 1714 – nos.182, 12, 172, 54, 199, 61, 152, (?)18; 1715 – 80a, 31, 165, 185, 161, 162, 163, 132; 1716 – 155, 70a, 186a, 147a (?unfinished). No.21 may precede 1714.

Musically the works are of particular importance for the development they show in Bach's personal style of writing for voices and instruments. There is a wide variety of treatments. Bach gradually established a number of types of setting, which remain basically unchanged even in the later Leipzig cantatas. Solo movements prevail, especially arias, which become longer and vocally (as well as instrumentally) more virtuoso, and are generally in da capo form. For the first time Bach used recitative, usually with syllabic declamation. At first he also used extended, arioso-like passages, corresponding with the relatively reserved, speech-song manner of the recitative 'senza battutta' (as in no.182). The contrast between the more melodious arioso, often marked by characteristic motifs, and the free, harmonically more daring recitative is later much stronger. The choruses too embrace a multiplicity of principles of construction, among them fugue and canon (no.182), passacaglia (12), concerto (172), motet (21) or French overture (61). They fall into two general categories (from which numerous mixed forms derive): concertante style in the manner of the aria and sectionalized

polyphony in the manner of the motet. Bach also interspersed instrumental and vocal formal schemes, inserted choral sections into solo movements and used instrumental elaborations of chorale melodies. The instrumentation is sometimes extraordinarily colourful; within the smallest of performing ensembles Bach tried out a great variety of combinations. Following the Italian ideal, his orchestral writing moved away from the French practice of five-part writing, with two violas, which predominates in the early cantatas towards a more flexible four-part style. Instead of the harmonic weight of the middle voices in five-part writing Bach provided a rhythmically and melodically active viola part that is particularly characteristic.

In Cöthen, corresponding to Bach's official responsibilities, only secular cantatas were composed (with the single exception of BWV Anh.5) and those were mostly written for New Year celebrations or the prince's birthday. Bach's librettist was C. F. Hunold ('Menantes', 1681–1721). Among the Cöthen cantatas, many survive only as verbal texts or are lost altogether. These pieces mostly exemplify the 'serenata' type of work, with succinct operatic treatment in dialogues between allegorical figures. It is not surprising that they reflect Bach's contemporary contact with the instrumental concerto or that dance characteristics appear, notably in the solo movements.

At Leipzig the performance of sacred cantatas on Sundays and feast days (some 60 a year) was one of Bach's chief tasks, and he produced a large number of new works. His vast work-load meant that within the first cycle he not only had to rely on repeat performances of earlier sacred cantatas (often revised) but also

127

6. *Autograph MS of Bach's Serenata 'Durchlauchtster Leopold' bwv173a, composed ?c1722, with the text of the sacred cantata 'Erhöhtes Fleisch und Blut' bwv173 added 1724*

had to resort to parodies on secular cantatas written at Cöthen. Nevertheless, his first cycle (1723–4) contains the following new compositions: nos.75, 76, 24, 167, 136, 105, 46, 179, 69*a*, 77, 25, 119, 138, 95, 148, 48, 109, 89, 194, 60, 90, 40, 64, 190, 153, 65, possibly 154, 73, 81, 83, 144, possibly 181, 67, 104, 166, 86, 37 and 44; to these must be added his test works (nos.22 and 23, for Quinquagesima 1723). Apart from no.24 (Neumeister) and nos.64, 69*a* and 77 (Knauer), the poet or poets are unknown.

In these works Bach used many different forms, free from any schematicism. Three favourite groundplans are: biblical text–recitative–aria–recitative–aria–chorale (nos.46, 105, 136 etc); biblical text–recitative–chorale–aria–recitative–aria–chorale (nos.40, 48, 64 etc); biblical text–aria–chorale–recitative–aria–chorale (nos.86, 144, 166 etc). A constant feature, characteristic of the Leipzig cantatas as a whole, is the framework, comprising an introductory choral movement in the grand style (solo pieces appear rarely at the start) and closing four-part chorales, simple but expressive. Compared with the Weimar cantatas, the instrumentation is more refined though in some ways less colourful. The orchestral forces are larger. From no.75 onwards the brass (mainly trumpets and horns) are more strongly deployed, the flute is brought into play increasingly after 1724, and the oboe d'amore (from no.75) and the oboe da caccia (from no.167) are introduced as new instruments. Instrumental virtuosity is heightened, and the melismatic quality of the vocal writing is further developed. The 'prelude and fugue' type of movement is frequently used for the introductory chorus (as in no.46).

With the second cycle, dating from 1724–5, Bach

turned to the concept of a cantata cycle based on a unifying theme. It consists mainly of a series of freshly composed chorale cantatas: nos.20, 2, 7, 135, 10, 93, 107, 178, 94, 101, 113, 33, 78, 99, 8, 130, 114, 96, 5, 180, 38, 115, 139, 26, 116, 62, 91, 121, 133, 122, 41, 123, 124, 3, 111, 92, 125, 126, 127 and 1. From Easter 1725, this series was continued with cantatas in the usual form, *Easter Oratorio,* nos.6, 42 and 85, and then with nine cantatas to texts by Marianne von Ziegler (1695–1760): 103, 108, 87, 128, 183, 74, 68, 175 and 176. 1724–5 was not only the most productive year for cantatas; it also, with the chorale cantata, saw the beginnings of a type that perhaps represents Bach's most important contribution to the history of the genre. What is particularly striking is his endeavour to lay out the introductory movements as large-scale cantus firmus compositions, using a great variety of structural principle. Cohesion between the cantata's movements is guaranteed, at least from the textual point of view, by their relationship to the fundamental chorale (with chorale paraphrases for the solo pieces, as opposed to the procedure in no.4); often it is further emphasized by references to the cantus firmus and by the use of various ways of intermingling cantus firmus and free material. The author of the texts for the chorale cantatas is not known – Pastor Weiss of Leipzig is a possibility, but not Bach himself, as has been supposed. The way in which Ziegler's texts are set is not essentially different from the manner of the first cycle.

With the third cycle, from 1725–7, the continuous production of cantatas ends, or so the sources indicate. The forms include solo and dialogue cantatas, and large-scale works in two parts. Bach showed a wide

variety of approaches. He continued the cycle of chorale cantatas with further works of that type (no.137), reverted to texts by Neumeister (28), Franck (72), Lehms (110, 57, 151, 16, 32, 13, 170, 35) or from a Rudolstadt textbook of 1726 (17, 39, 43, 45, 88, 102, 187), and experimented with forms using two different texts – one from the Old Testament and one from the New (the former in the introductory movement, the latter in a central one). The third cycle, and also the fourth, make extensive use of pre-existing concerto material, perhaps from Cöthen, as instrumental sinfonias at the beginning of a number of cantatas (nos.110, 156, 174, 120*a*). From late 1726 obbligato organ parts appear (nos.35, 146, 169, 49, 188). The third cycle was followed by the 1728–9 cycle on texts by Picander, which has disappeared – all that remains are nine pieces and a fraction of a tenth. A chief feature of the Picander texts appears to be the interpolation of chorale and free poetry in arias and choruses, giving opportunities for various sorts of combinatorial technique (see the second movements of nos.156 and 159; also the first movement of the *St Matthew Passion*). The cantatas written after 1729 contribute nothing essentially new. It is interesting to find modifications of the chorale cantata type among later works in the genre (nos.117, 192, 112, 177, 97, 100); at the same time, Bach abandoned freely composed texts, although the central movements (unlike those in no.4) are constructed in the manner of recitatives and arias. His increasing receptiveness towards new stylistic trends should be noted in several arias in the later cantatas.

Besides the cantatas composed in connection with the church year, Bach also wrote sacred cantatas for other occasions, like changes of town council, weddings, fun-

erals, the jubilee celebrations of the Confession of Augsburg (1730) and inaugurations of organs; in style these are essentially indistinguishable from the other works. The body of cantatas, for all its variety, has an unusually self-contained character, maintained above all by its constant high musical quality and its unfailing expressive profundity. Bach's expressive urge, as seen in individual arias and choruses, was not confined to single words as the primary bearers of expression, but from the outset was geared to movements and formal sections as a whole, in keeping with Baroque formal models (like the *ABA* of the da capo aria). Only within the context of a movement's structural and expressive unity did he regard the special treatment of single words as possible or logical. Among the tools of Bach's craft the traditions of *musica poetica* and musical rhetoric (the theory of musical figures) must certainly be reckoned. They were deeply rooted in him. Yet to reduce Bach's intentions to their rhetorical and figural components, or even to emphasize those components, would be to diminish their true breadth. Over and above this objective of expressive unity, Bach was always primarily concerned with the contrapuntal organization of melodic–rhythmic and harmonic textures to establish coherence. That is a principal reason why his cantata movements lend themselves so readily to parody. The technical prerequisites for producing a parody work – which Bach did so often – are metrical similarity and expressive affinity; a further essential requirement is self-sufficiency of the musical substance. Its flexibility leaves considerable scope for the musical interpretations of a new text.

During his early Leipzig years Bach wrote only isolated secular cantatas. These were produced for vari-

ous occasions: university ceremonies (nos.36*b*, 198, 205, 207), celebrations at the Thomasschule (BWV Anh.18, Anh.19, 36*c*), festivities in the houses of noblemen and prominent citizens (216, 210, 249*b*, 30*a*, 210*a*, 212) and commissions from court (249*a*, 36*a*). Most of his large-scale congratulatory and homage cantatas written for the electoral house of Saxony were produced at the collegium musicum. A favourite format was the operatic *dramma per musica*, with a simple plot suited to the nature of the festivities, with characters from mythology, shepherds or allegorical characters (nos.213, 206, 214, 207*a*, 215). The more lyrical cantatas such as no.204, or the two Italian works, nos.203 and 209, would certainly have been performed at the collegium musicum. The Coffee and Peasant Cantatas (nos.211 and 212), to some extent tinged with folk style, are distinguished by their lifelike and humorous characterization. The librettist of most of the works of 1725–42 was the versatile Picander, the only other important poet for Bach's cantatas during this period being J. C. Gottsched (1700–66), the influential Leipzig professor of rhetoric (no.198, *Auf! süss entzückende Gewalt* (not in BWV) and Anh.13).

XIV Oratorios, Passions, Latin works

The three works known as 'oratorios' fall within a very short period: the *Christmas Oratorio* of 1734–5, the *Easter Oratorio* and *Ascension Oratorio* of 1735. The librettists are not known for certain. The place of the oratorio in the Lutheran liturgy is the same as that for the cantata; the oratorio can be distinguished from the cantata only in that it has a self-contained plot. In this Bach's use of the term differs from its usual application.

In the *Christmas Oratorio* the normal character of a single self-contained work is contradicted by its being split into sections for six different services between Christmas Day and Epiphany, and this is further emphasized by Bach in his use of different performing forces for the sections (although these are based on an underlying general scheme, and are grouped round six scenes from the Bible, with certain divergences from the allocation of lessons to be read at the various services). All three works are essentially based on parodies of secular cantatas whose music, initially associated with a particular occasion, could reasonably be re-used in this way (the *Christmas Oratorio* from nos.213, 214 and 215 among other works; the *Easter Oratorio* by a re-working of parts of BWV249a; the *Ascension Oratorio* above all from BWV Anh.18). However, there is so much that is new and individual in the *Christmas Oratorio*, especially in the biblical choruses and the chorales and in the *Ascension Oratorio*, that the works are in no sense subordinate to their originals. The pervasive use of texts from the Gospels, moreover, gives the works a special status, linking them with the Protestant *historia* and thus ultimately with the Passion.

Of the five Passions mentioned in the necrology two survive (*St Matthew* and *St John*), for one the text survives (*St Mark*; the only known copy was destroyed in World War II, although some of the music survives in its original form in Cantatas nos.54 and 198, and one movement was revised for the *Christmas Oratorio*) and the other two are lost. The unauthentic *St Luke Passion* was probably included among Bach's works in error because the score, dating from about 1730, was copied in Bach's hand and contained additions by him. This

means that only one Passion remains to be accounted for. Recent research on the *St John* and *St Matthew* has shown that some of their movements must have originated in a Passion setting dating from Bach's pre-Leipzig days, probably from his Weimar period, notably the chorus 'O Mensch bewein' (used in both works) as well as the three arias 'Himmel, reisse', 'Zerschmettert mich' and 'Ach windet euch nicht so' (*St John*). Hilgenfeldt (1850) mentioned a Passion by Bach dating from 1717, giving no indication of the source of his information. In Weimar, before 1714, Bach made a transcript of Keiser's *St Mark Passion*, so his interest in the genre is established for this period; the missing fifth Passion may thus well be a lost Weimar work.

The three known works represent the same type of Passion oratorio, in the tradition of the *historia*, in which the biblical text is retained as a whole (for the soloists – Evangelist, Jesus, Pilate etc – and the turba choruses), and is interrupted by contemplative, so-called 'madrigal' pieces set to freely composed verse, as well as by chorales. A special feature of Bach's Passions is the unusual frequency of the chorales, which are set in extremely expressive four-part writing. From the textual point of view the *St John Passion* of 1724 lacks unity. The freely composed parts of the text rely mainly on the famous Passion poem by B. H. Brockes (*Der für die Sünde der Welt gemarterte und sterbende Jesus*, 1712) and the *St John Passion* libretto by C. H. Postel (*c*1700). Besides this, the Evangelist's part contains interpolations from *St Matthew*. Musically, various allusions to the Postel *St John Passion* long attributed to Handel, now tentatively ascribed to Böhm, can be enumerated. Bach made countless alterations in the work

135

for its various performances. In 1725 the opening and closing choruses were interchanged and arias were added; the new additions may well be from the lost Weimar Passion. In a third version, dating from around 1730, the interpolations from *St Matthew* were deleted and replaced by a (lost) sinfonia. In a fourth and final version, dating from Bach's last years (1746–9), the original sequence of movements was largely re-established, and the performing forces were augmented.

The history of the *St Matthew Passion*, with its double chorus, is less complicated, though not entirely straightforward. In this case the date of the first performance is now established (1727), but because of lacunae in the source material it is not clear which items (apart from 'O Mensch bewein', which was incorporated in 1736 from the second version of the *St John Passion*) originated with an earlier Passion or Passion cantata of 1725 on a text by Picander – if indeed Bach set that text. The *St Matthew Passion*, however, right from its foundations in Picander's libretto, was essentially conceived as a unity; and its increased scope for arias and 'madrigal' pieces in general (the coupling of arioso with aria being especially typical) allowed for a greater breadth of design. A special feature, following an older tradition, is the inclusion of the strings to provide an accompanying halo in Jesus's recitatives. Clearly it was planned as a unity in a sense that the *St John Passion* was not: witness the relationships between the chorales, the distribution of tonalities, the couplings of movements; the *St John*, by comparison, lacks a structural centre (see Smend, 1926). The *St Matthew Passion* had at least two subsequent performances: in 1736, with the continuo part strictly divided between the two chor-

uses, a simple chorale replaced by 'O Mensch bewein' at the end of part I, and the viola da gamba replacing the lute in 'Komm süsses Kreuz'; and in the 1740s, with some changes in the manner of performance and certain minor revisions.

In its main sections, that is in the 'madrigal' pieces, the *St Mark Passion* of 1731 is a parody work whose main sources are the *Trauer Ode* (Cantata no.198) and the Funeral Music for Leopold (BWV244*a*). Although only the text survives, the music can in part be reconstructed from these works; the possibility of adding movements from Cantatas nos.54 and 7, the *Christmas Oratorio* and some chorales has been suggested by Smend (1940–48) in particular.

In Bach's time Latin polyphonic music was still often used in ordinary Lutheran Sunday worship, and particularly at important church feasts. Further, the concerted *Magnificat* continued to hold its place in Vespers, notably at Christmas and Easter. Bach had been interested in Latin polyphonic music at least by his Weimar period, as his copies of pieces by other composers demonstrate (Peranda, Johann Ludwig and Johann Nicolaus Bach, Pez, Wilderer, Bassani, Caldara, Lotti, Palestrina etc; catalogue in Wolff, 1968). He also wrote insertions in this style for other composers' works, and made some arrangements (Sanctus BWV241; Credo intonation for a mass by Bassani; 'Suscepit Israel' for a *Magnificat* by Caldara). His earliest surviving work of this type is probably the Kyrie BWV233*a* on the cantus firmus 'Christe, du Lamm Gottes'. Then in his first year at Leipzig came the *Magnificat*, first the E♭ version, with four inserted Christmas pieces (BWV243*a*), revised in D major in 1728–31, without the Christmas pieces, for

7. *Autograph MS of the Sinfonia (arranged from the Prelude of the Partita for violin* BWV1006*) from Bach's cantata 'Wir danken dir, Gott'* BWV29, *1731*

use on any major feast day (BWV243). Among the various Sanctus settings attributed to Bach probably only BWV238 is an original composition (1723–4); BWV241 has been identified as an arrangement after J. C. Kerll's *Missa superba*. The two short masses in F and G minor (BWV233 and 235) probably date from the mid-1720s; like their later companion-pieces in A and G (BWV234 and 236) of 1735–40 they are for the most part parody works based on cantata movements (nos.11, 102, 40, Anh.18; 102, 72, 187; 67, 179, 79, 136; 179, 79, 138, 17). The Latin Christmas music Cantata no.191 comes from the Gloria of BWV232.

Bach's masterpiece in this genre is of course the work known – though not conceived as a unity – as the B minor Mass. Its genesis stretched over more than two decades. Bach's aim seems to have been to bring together a collection of large-scale mass movements to serve as models rather than to create a single, multi-movement work on an unprecedented scale. The oldest section is the Sanctus of 1724. The Kyrie and Gloria come from the 1733 *Missa* dedicated to the Dresden court, while the Credo or 'Symbolum Nicenum' was composed only during Bach's last years. In many respects these two main sections represent Bach's ideals of Latin polyphonic music: in their stylistic many-sidedness, with deliberately archaic styles contrasted with modern ones; in their abandonment of the da capo aria and the recitative; and in their formal autonomy. The Credo is a particularly good example of Bach's self-contained and symmetrical layout. The *Missa* and the Credo have a series of parody originals (Cantatas nos.29, 46; 171, 12, 120); in the latter only the 'Credo' and the 'Confiteor' seem to be original compositions. Further, the

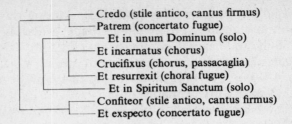

Credo (stile antico, cantus firmus)
Patrem (concertato fugue)
Et in unum Dominum (solo)
Et incarnatus (chorus)
Crucifixus (chorus, passacaglia)
Et resurrexit (choral fugue)
Et in Spiritum Sanctum (solo)
Confiteor (stile antico, cantus firmus)
Et exspecto (concertato fugue)

last four pieces are parody movements that Bach added in 1748–9 ('Osanna', BWV Anh.11; 'Benedictus', an unknown aria; Agnus, Cantata no.11; 'Dona' from the *Missa*), alongside the old Sanctus, to complete the collection.

XV Motets, chorales, songs

In Bach's time motets were sung as introits for services and on certain special occasions. The tradition established at Leipzig was to select introit motets from *Florilegium Portense* (1618), a classical repertory from the 16th century compiled by Erhard Bodenschatz. For this reason, in Leipzig – no Weimar compositions of this kind are known – Bach wrote motets only for special occasions, probably only for burial services, although in only one case, *Der Geist hilft*, is there documentary evidence of this. Bach's motet texts, following the tradition, are based on biblical quotations and chorales; freely composed poetry is used in only one case, and even this is songbook poetry (*Komm, Jesu, komm*, Paul Thymich). On the occasions for which the motets were composed, Bach normally had more than the school choristers at his disposal; he was thus able to use between five- and eight-part writing, as he did in five pieces (BWV225–9). It was a rule in the performance of motets at

Leipzig, including those from *Florilegium Portense*, that a
continuo part should be included – to be precise, a
harpsichord and string bass. The performing parts that
have survived for *Der Geist hilft*, with strings (first chorus)
and reed instruments (second chorus) doubling the voices,
cannot necessarily be taken as applicable to the other
motets; a similar special case, with partly obbligato
instruments, is BWV118, *O Jesu Christ* (often referred to as
a cantata, but in fact a motet).

Bach's use of double chorus and his exposition of
forms of chorale treatment link the motets with the
central German tradition. Among the movements
closest to that tradition are the closing section of
Fürchte dich nicht, in its combination of cantus firmus
('Warum sollt ich mich denn grämen') and freely
imitative writing, and the opening section of *Komm,
Jesu, komm*, with its chordal writing for double chorus.
As a whole, the style of BWV118 too is retrospective,
with its archaic instrumentation and its homophonic
choral writing. By contrast, most movements in the
motets have a markedly polyphonic vocal manner,
dominated by instrumental style and showing unifying
motivic work. Another characteristic is the clear formal
articulation, with multi-movement works demonstrating
different kinds of treatment. Thus *Jesu, meine Freude*,
the longest work of this kind, in 11 movements, is the
most strictly (that is, symmetrically) conceived: the
opening and closing movements are identical, the second
and the tenth use the same material, and the third to fifth
largely correspond with the seventh to ninth; the central
sixth is a fugue. *Der Geist hilft* begins with a concerto-
like movement, followed by a double fugue and a simple
chorale setting (apparently taken from the lost cantata of

the preceding Whit Sunday, in the Picander cycle). The form of the instrumental concerto (fast–slow–fast) is used in *Singet dem Herrn*. For a repeat performance in the 1740s, *O Jesu Christ*, originally composed about 1736–7, was revised in its instrumentation, with strings, oboes, bassoons and horns; the original had only two *litui*, cornett and three trombones. The authenticity of *Lobet den Herrn* has been questioned (Geck, *BJb*, liii, 1967); the paucity of comparative material makes conclusions difficult. Bach's arrangement of Pergolesi's *Stabat mater* with the psalm text 'Tilge, Höchster, meine Sünden', dating from 1744–8, should be counted among the motets.

Bach's composition of chorales is most closely associated with his production of cantatas. Four-part chorale style, or *stylus simplex* (but generally with elaborate bass parts and contrapuntally active middle voices), was normal for his closing movements, particularly in the Leipzig cantatas; it also often occurred at the ends of subsections in large-scale works, notably the Passions. Bach's chorale writing is characterized by the 'speaking' quality of the part-writing and the harmonies – meaning that they aim to be a direct interpretation of the text. The posthumously published collections (Birnstiel, 2 vols., 1765, 1769; Breitkopf, 4 vols., 1784–7) contain almost 200 of the chorales known from Bach's vocal works, some under different titles; about 50 known chorales are lacking. The Breitkopf edition, prepared by C. P. E. Bach and Kirnberger, contains 371 chorales, among them more than 100 not found in the extant vocal works. This provides an important pointer to the lost vocal music, and though extremely difficult to follow up it has borne

some fruits, as in the reconstruction of the *St Mark Passion* or the Picander cycle. It is worth remarking that the number of excess chorales more or less corresponds to the number thought to exist in the lost cantata cycles and oratorio-type compositions.

Only three of the chorales are known to have been written for special occasions – BWV250–52, intended for weddings. The repertory of 348 known from the Breitkopf edition (23 of the 371 are duplicates) was already available before the printed edition in more or less complete manuscript collections circulating among Bach's pupils. As a teacher of composition Bach laid particular emphasis on chorale writing, and a specially didactic character may be ascribed to the chorale collections. According to C. P. E. Bach, his father treated chorale writing as the final stage of instruction in figured bass: he asked his pupils to write middle parts between a given melody and bass, or, at a more advanced level, required them to add a bass to a given melody. This procedure recalls his own approach to composition (outer parts first, then inner parts) and also his approach in adapting chorales from other sources (like Vopelius's *Neu Leipziger Gesangbuch*, 1682), where he would take over the outer parts and write new inner ones.

Under the generic heading of 'sacred songs' come the 69 melodies with figured bass in G. C. Schemelli's *Musicalisches Gesang-Buch* (1736). According to the foreword, Bach edited the figured basses of all the pieces; but only three melodies (BWV452, 478, 505) are demonstrably his. He seems to have been only peripherally occupied with the composition of songs and strophic arias, as the limited surviving repertory, for which the only source is the second *Clavierbüchlein* for

Anna Magdalena Bach (1725), indicates (BWV508–17).

Unique among his vocal works is a multi-sectional Quodlibet for four voices and continuo (BWV524) which has survived only in fragmentary form. It was probably composed for a wedding in 1707, and is evidently connected with the playing, in contrapuntal combinations, of folktunes with comic and even obscene texts, as was customary in the Bach family circle.

XVI Organ music

Unlike the vocal music and the chamber and orchestral works, Bach's keyboard output covers his entire creative life. There are times of heightened activity – organ music in the Weimar and pre-Weimar years, harpsichord music in the Cöthen period and around 1730. As a whole, however, Bach seems to have cultivated the two genres alongside each other. It is thus the more surprising that, right from the beginning, in full awareness of the consequences, and in defiance of inherited 17th-century tradition, he abandoned under Buxtehude's influence the conventional community of repertory between organ and harpsichord, choosing to write specifically for the one or the other. The uncompromising use of obbligato pedals, in particular, is a distinguishing mark of Bach's organ style. Only exceptionally (for example in the chorale partitas and the small chorale arrangements from the third part of the *Clavier-Übung*) do the performing possibilities coincide so that organ and harpsichord become truly interchangeable.

Since most of Bach's keyboard works from the pre-Leipzig years survive in copies (generally made in the circle of Bach's pupils) rather than in autograph scores, it is not possible to establish a precise chronology. Even

a relative one is possible only in general terms, with considerations of style and authenticity holding the balance. In the earliest works the influence of Bach's model is pronounced. These include the chorale partitas BWV766–8, wrought in the manner of Böhm (BWV768 was expanded during Bach's Weimar period); but it is difficult to judge whether these pieces date back to the Lüneburg years. The Canzona BWV588, the *Allabreve* BWV589 and the Pastorale BWV590 show late 17th-century south German and Italian characteristics, while the Fantasia in G BWV572 looks to the French style. The chorale BWV739, one of Bach's earliest autographs, reveals clearly a north German orientation. With its sectional layout and other north German features, the Prelude and Fugue in E BWV566 must have been written under Buxtehude's immediate influence, suggesting a date around 1706; its G minor counterpart BWV535*a*, which from the autograph can be dated before 1708, shows a marked movement away from Buxtehude in its more sharply defined prelude-and-fugue structure.

The extraordinary harmonic boldness and the richness of fermata embellishment in the pieces BWV715, 722 and 732, intended to accompany chorales, imply that they belong to the Arnstadt period where Bach's treatment of chorales caused confusion among the congregation. The fugues after Legrenzi and Corelli, BWV574 and 579, should probably be placed among the early works; and to these must be added a further series of organ pieces, both based on chorales and freely composed, all markedly indebted to his brother's teacher Pachelbel and owing their impression of personal style basically to unusual harmonies and distinct virtuosity while following traditional models in form and in many

other respects. Bach's early interest in pedal virtuosity is attested by the *Exercitium* BWV598.

The models recede in importance from the Mühlhausen period, at the latest, and Bach's individuality begins to pervade every note of his compositions. This applies particularly to the many extended organ chorale settings probably dating from between 1709 and 1712–13 (BWV651, etc). In his freely composed organ works (toccatas, preludes, fantasias and fugues) Bach tightened up the formal scheme, preparing the way for the two-movement prelude and fugue through an intermediate type in which the fugue was a long, self-contained complex but the prelude was not yet a unified section (such as BWV532). Probably the most important work of these years is the Passacaglia in C minor BWV582. In about 1713–14 a decisive stylistic change came about, stimulated by Vivaldi's concerto form. Bach's encounter with Vivaldi's music found immediate expression in the concertos after Vivaldi's opp.3 and 7 (BWV593, etc). Features adapted from Vivaldi include the unifying use of motivic work, the motoric rhythmic character, the modulation schemes and the principle of solo–tutti contrast as means of formal articulation; the influence may be seen in the Toccata in C BWV564. Apparently Bach experimented for a short while with a free, concerto-like organ form in three movements (fast–slow–fast) but finally turned to the two-movement form, as in BWV534 and 536. Of comparable importance to the introduction of the concerto element is his tendency towards condensed motivic work, as in the *Orgel-Büchlein*. Bach's conception of this new type of miniature organ chorale, combining rhetorical and expressive musical language with refined counterpoint, probably dates back to

1713–14; among the earliest examples are BWV601, 608, 627 and 630, and around 1715–16 Bach added BWV615, 623, 640 and 644 (to cite some typical examples). By the end of the Weimar period the *Orgel-Büchlein* was complete in all essentials; only the fragment *O Traurigkeit* and BWV613 (added in about 1740) are later. The number of pieces, fewer than 50, is considerably below the 164 originally projected by Bach; evidently he lost interest in this most original form.

Among the few organ pieces composed at Cöthen are the C major Fantasia BWV573 of about 1722 and apparently at least the earlier version of BWV653 (*An Wasserflüssen*) and a revision of the Fantasia and Fugue in G minor BWV542, these last two probably prepared for Bach's Hamburg candidature in 1720. Then, in Leipzig about 1727, the trio sonatas appeared, a new genre of organ work in three-part contrapuntal writing (the six works are at least in part based on chamber works); these were followed by a series of preludes and fugues, now always in two sections with the preludes as important as the fugues – surely a consequence of the '48'. There is a final flourish of virtuosity in works like the E minor Prelude and Fugue BWV548, though always in a clearcut form (BWV548 provides a rare example of a da capo fugue).

The organ music from this time on must be seen in conjunction with Bach's extensive activities as a recitalist. In 1739, as the third part of the *Clavier-Übung*, he published a comprehensive and very varied group of organ works. Framed by a Prelude and Fugue in E♭ (BWV552), there are nine chorale arrangements for Mass and 12 for the catechism followed by four duets. Bach's encyclopedic intentions can be seen in the form

of the work – that of a collection of specimen organ pieces for large church instruments and smaller domestic ones (including the harpsichord), symbolized in his invariable coupling of a large piece with a small; they can equally be seen in the variety of his contrapuntal methods, whereby he constantly produced fresh kinds of cantus firmus treatment. At the very end of Bach's output for the organ are such disparate works as the 'Schübler' chorales (arrangements after solo movements from cantatas) and the canonic variations on *Vom Himmel hoch* BWV769. The latter, written for Mizler's society in 1747, survives in two original versions, printed and autograph, whose different sequence of movements shows Bach experimenting with symmetrical form and the placing of climaxes.

XVII **Harpsichord and lute music**

Bach's early compositions for harpsichord – including those for clavichord, appropriate in music of a more intimate type – are in a similar situation to the corresponding organ works as regards dating and evaluation. There are no works which can be firmly dated, but before 1712–13 there were countless individual pieces like toccatas, preludes and fugues (these last mainly using a 'repercussive' thematic technique, like the early organ fugues); variation form is represented by the *Aria variata* BWV989. In the toccatas (BWV910, etc), Italian, north German and French influences conjoin in equal importance (BWV912 is an interesting counterpart to the organ work BWV532); Bach's penchant for the French style is particularly evident in his abundant use of the *style brisé*. After 1712 the particular influence of

148

Vivaldi's concertos can be seen in Bach's numerous concerto arrangements (BWV972, etc). The so-called English Suites BWV806–11 of the late Weimar years are mature examples of Bach's masterly integration of the Italian and French styles in his keyboard music.

To the early years in Cöthen belong several single works, such as the Chromatic Fantasia and Fugue BWV903, and also the *Clavier-Büchlein* for Wilhelm Friedemann, of 1720, which is predominantly didactic in layout. It is however less important for its instruction in playing technique (the *Applicatio* BWV994 gives fingering and tables of ornaments after D'Anglebert) than as a book of instruction in composition. For Bach himself, the two could not be dissociated: and the *Clavier-Büchlein* contains the beginnings of the '48' as well as early versions of the Inventions and Sinfonias, under such titles as 'preambulum' and 'fantasia'. To some extent the 1722 *Clavierbüchlein* for Anna Magdalena is a companion work, though differently laid out.

Then followed, also in 1722, *Das wohltemperirte Clavier* (book 1 of the '48'), with its 24 preludes and fugues in all the major and minor keys, surpassing, in logic, in format and in musical quality, all earlier endeavours of the same kind by other masters, like J. C. F. Fischer's *Ariadne musica*. The work shows a perfectly balanced contrast between free and strict styles, each represented by several different types of prelude and fugue. Bach's writing in book 1 of the '48' in the most varied fugues – from two- to five-part, in styles from the traditional slow ricercare to a brilliant Italianate manner, and using a wide range of technical device – represents the culmination of a 20-year process

149

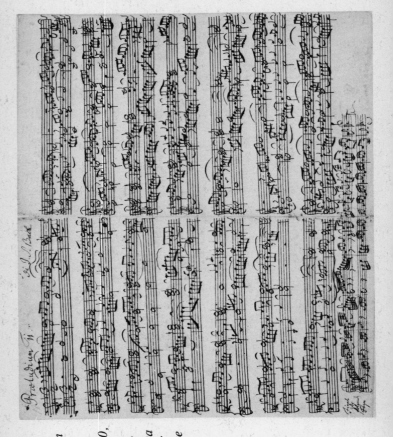

8. Autograph MS
of Bach's Prelude
and Fugue no.11 in
F from 'Das
wohltemperirte
Clavier', ii, BWV880,
composed c1740
(the first column is
in the hand of Anna
Magdalena Bach);
the final bars of the
fugue are at the
foot of the first
column

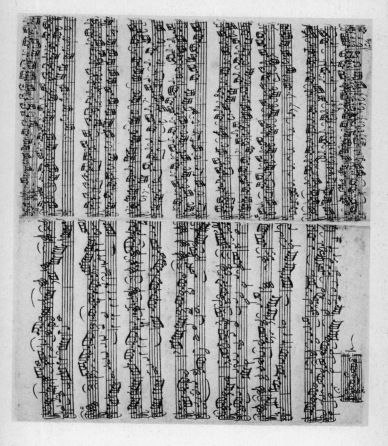

151

of maturation and stands unparalleled in the history of music. The final version of the two- and three-part Inventions and Sinfonias, also arranged by key, but representing a different method of composition whose object (according to Bach's foreword) was 'to teach clear playing in two and three obbligato parts, good inventions [i.e. compositional ideas] and a cantabile manner of playing', dates from 1723.

The first traces of the subsequent great works of the Leipzig period are to be found in the 1725 *Clavierbüchlein* for Anna Magdalena, which in fact anticipates the so-called French Suites BWV812–17 and the Partitas BWV825–30, respectively small-scale and large-scale suite types. The Partitas in particular represent a further culmination in Bach's output for the harpsichord; whereas the '48' shows the prelude and fugue type developed to its most consummate maturity, these present similarly matured specimens of the most popular harpsichord genre of the time, the partita, comprising a suite of dance movements and 'galanteries'. These – the burlesca, capriccio, and the like – do not appear in the English or French Suites; as in the English Suites, each of which begins with a prelude, usually in concerto style, each partita begins with a large-scale movement, each differently titled and each in a different style, among them pieces in the manner of an invention (no.3) and a French overture (no.4). Later, with the collected publication of all six in 1731, Bach inaugurated his series of published works under the general title *Clavier-Übung* (the title was borrowed from a publication by Kuhnau, his predecessor in office). In 1735 appeared the second part, whose contents were intended to be representative of the most prominent and

fashionable kinds of style: the Concerto in the Italian Style BWV971 embodies the ultimate stage in the process of transcribing instrumental concertos for the harpsichord, and stands in contrast to an Overture in the French Manner BWV831 which, more markedly than the partitas, represents what was specifically French in harmony, rhythm, ornamentation and melodic invention. 1741–2 eventually saw the end of the *Clavier-Übung* series with the aria and 30 variations known as the Goldberg Variations. Apparently Bach had not cultivated the variation form since his youth, so that the contrast between the Goldberg Variations and the early works (chorale partitas, the *Aria variata*) is the more marked. This work outshines all others as far as performing technique is concerned. The large-scale sequential layout (based on a grouping of 10 × 3 movements, incorporating a series of nine canons, one at every chord variation, arranged in order of ascending intervals to move towards a climax, with a final quodlibet) is without precedent. The basis of the composition is a ground bass of 32 bars, developed from the Ruggiero and related bass patterns, first presented in the aria and then subjected to free and canonic elaboration in a wide variety of ways. In their monothematic and emphatically contrapuntal conception, the Goldberg Variations set the scene for Bach's last keyboard works – the *Musical Offering, Vom Himmel hoch* variations and *Art of Fugue*.

Besides the harpsichord works published in the 1730s and 1740s, the only other major work is the second part of *Das wohltemperirte Clavier* (not so titled – the complete autograph does not survive). This companion-piece is less unified than book 1 and was partly assembled from existing preludes and fugues, some of

them transposed. The freshly composed pieces probably date chiefly from the late 1730s; some of the preludes, particularly, show elements of the *galant* style. The work was complete by 1742.

The dates of composition of the seven surviving works for lute – apparently his total output for the instrument – cover at least 30 years. The earliest work is the Suite in E minor BWV996, which dates from the middle of the Weimar period; it already shows a surprisingly balanced construction. The Prelude in C minor BWV999 shows an affinity with the '48', and may thus belong to the Cöthen or early Leipzig period. All the other lute works were composed in Leipzig, starting with the Fugue in G minor BWV1000, an expanded polyphonic development from the violin fugue (in BWV1001), which is in a tablature copied by Bach's friend, the Leipzig lawyer and lutenist Christian Weyrauch. The Suite in G minor BWV995 (after 1011, for cello) dates from the period 1727–31 and is dedicated to an unidentifiable 'Monsieur Schouster'. The Suite in E (BWV1006a, after 1006 for violin) survives in autograph form and is a much less demanding arrangement of its model as compared with BWV1000 and 995, and dates from the second half of the 1730s. Bach must have composed the Suite in C minor BWV997 before 1741; this is an original lute composition and is laid out in a similar virtuoso fashion to the Prelude, Fugue and Allegro in E♭ BWV998 which can be ascribed to the 1740s. The late works, with their markedly *galant* flavour, may have been written for the Dresden lutenists S. L. Weiss and J. Kropffgans, and in any case were probably played by them. There is evidence that Weiss and Kropffgans performed at Bach's house at least once,

in 1739. Bach's contributions to the repertory of the lute, long past its heyday but enjoying a final flowering in the German-speaking countries, represent, along with the works of Weiss, the culmination of the instrument's 18th-century repertory. They require a 14-string instrument, but in Bach's day were at least occasionally played on the lute-harpsichord, an instrument in whose construction Bach had assisted. The indistinct line between lute and harpsichord music is illustrated by the autograph of BWV998, marked 'pour La Luth ò Cembal'.

XVIII **Orchestral music**

Many of Bach's orchestral works must be presumed lost. The surviving repertory can in any case give only an incomplete idea of his output for larger instrumental ensembles, for he must have written many further works during his years at Cöthen and while he was working with the collegium musicum in Leipzig. Traces of lost concerto movements may be found in numerous cantatas, such as no.42, and other large-scale vocal works; and various of the surviving harpsichord concertos, in particular, invite inferences about lost originals. In the score bearing the dedication to Margrave Christian Ludwig of Brandenburg, the so-called Brandenburg Concertos are dated 24 March 1721. This is merely a *terminus ante quem*, for the concertos themselves must have been written over a considerable period before being assembled in 1721 as a collection of 'Concerts avec plusieurs instruments' (not as a single work in several parts). It cannot be proved that Bach composed instrumental music in his capacity as Konzertmeister in Weimar; but his position there and his preoccupation with the Italian concerto style during those years make

155

it seem probable that he did. Of the Brandenburg Concertos, three (nos.1, 3 and 6) point to the Weimar period, and not only because of their particular structural and motivic indebtedness to the Italian type of concerto. The sinfonia version of no.1 (BWV1046a) apparently served as an instrumental introduction to Cantata no.208, perhaps for the performance which took place in 1716. The homogeneous string instrumentation of nos.3 and 6 also suggests an early date; the unusual combination of low strings in no.6 otherwise appears only in pre-Cöthen cantatas. Other concertos may also belong to the Weimar period, for example the violin version of BWV1052 with its markedly Vivaldian features; but no firm conclusions should be drawn about a Weimar orchestral repertory.

The special significance of the Brandenburg Concertos resides in the fact that, as a group, they abandon the standard type of concerto grosso and use a variety of solo combinations. The originality of Bach's solutions extends far beyond Vivaldi's, as do the density of the compositional texture and the level of professional virtuosity. The devising of concise head-motifs, particularly in the first movements, shows a strong Italian influence. Most of Bach's instrumentations are unprecedented. They feature all kinds of combinations, from homogeneous string sound (no.3, with its unusual three-way symmetries deriving from the use of three each of violins, violas and cellos with continuo; and no.6, with its violas in close canon and gambas providing the inner texture) to the heterogeneous mixing of brass, woodwind, string and keyboard instruments. Just as unusual is Bach's conflation of the group concerto with the solo concerto in nos.1, 4 and 5; no.4, for

example, is both a solo violin concerto and a concerto grosso with a solo group of violin and two recorders. No.5 probably represents the latest stage in composition of the set and includes Bach's first use of the transverse flute. Possibly it was written for the inauguration of the harpsichord he brought back from Berlin early in 1719 (an earlier version survives from about this date). At the same time it marks the beginnings of the harpsichord concerto as a form.

The Orchestral Suites nos.1 and 4, with their leaning towards French style, can be dated in the Cöthen period. The only solo concertos to survive in their original form from this time are the violin concertos in A minor and in E and the two-violin concerto in D minor. Further concertos can be fairly accurately reconstructed, however, from their later arrangements as harpsichord concertos – for violin (after those in D minor and F minor, BWV1052 and 1056), oboe d'amore (A major, 1055), oboe and violin (C minor, 1060) and for three violins (C major, 1064) – and there are additionally several concerto movements, less readily reconstructed from their later transcriptions in cantatas and concertos (BWV35, 49, 169, 1053, 1059 and 1063). All these probably belong to the period spent at Weimar and Cöthen. Reconstructions of specific originals arranged by Bach are possible only up to a point, as in his transcriptions Bach never proceeded in a mechanical way; rather, he strove to give the arrangement an identity of its own by subjecting the model to further development and exhausting its potential. This often involved the addition of fresh contrapuntal parts, the alteration of detail and structural modification. Of special interest are Bach's adaptations of instrumental works into vocal ones, like

the derivation of the first chorus of Cantata no.110 from BWV1069; also of note is the wresting of the other movements of an ensemble concerto (BWV1044) out of the Prelude and Fugue in A minor for harpsichord (BWV894).

Probably only a few works are demonstrably of Leipzig origins, written for the collegium musicum concerts; these include such works as Suites nos.2 and 3, the Triple Concerto in A minor BWV1044 (using the same instrumental forces as Brandenburg Concerto no.5), the eight harpsichord concertos BWV1052–9 and the concertos for two or more harpsichords BWV1060–65, which, like the Triple Concerto, are all reworkings of older works (the four-harpsichord concerto is an arrangement of Vivaldi's Concerto in B minor for four violins, op.3 no.10). BWV1061 appears to have been written originally for two harpsichords without accompaniment (*c*1732–5). In fact, Bach's alterations and restructurings are sufficiently important – especially the deployment of the left hand of the harpsichord part and the invention of idiomatic harpsichord figuration – for works of this rank to be considered compositions in their own right. They owe their special historical importance to their occurrence (simultaneously with Handel's inauguration of the organ concerto in England) at the beginning of the history of the keyboard concerto, a form which was to be taken up above all by Bach's sons so that in Germany, until about 1750, it remained the exclusive preserve of the Bach family. A stimulus for the composition of the harpsichord concertos may have been the new instrument introduced at a concert on 17 June 1733 ('a new harpsichord, the like of which no-one here has ever yet heard'), which may be the 'fournirt Claveçin' Bach left at his death (to remain in his family's possession).

XIX **Chamber music**

As with the orchestral music, a great many chamber compositions are thought to be lost. Of the surviving works many were composed at Cöthen (except the doubtful BWV1040 trio, from early 1713). Bach became familiar with the *sonata da chiesa* repertory early in his life, as his arrangements BWV574 after Legrenzi and BWV579 after Corelli's op.3 testify, and he used the four-movement Italian sonata model for most of his trio and solo sonatas. The unusual flexibility with which he manipulated the conventional genres is analogous with his handling of the orchestral forms. Particularly important is his emancipation of the harpsichord from its role as continuo instrument and its deployment as a true partner in the sonatas for harpsichord with viola da gamba (BWV1027–9), violin (1014–19) and flute (1030, 1032). The influence of the trio sonata with continuo still remains; but it progressively disappeared in favour of a more integrated three-part style. The development of this new type of trio writing from the trio sonata is illustrated by Bach's arrangement of BWV1027 after the Trio Sonata BWV1039 for two flutes and continuo. A similar procedure stood behind his development of the organ trio sonata, as his arrangement of the first movement of BWV528 from a trio sonata movement for oboe d'amore, viola da gamba and continuo in Cantata no.76 shows. The latter movement represents a trace of some trio sonatas of the Cöthen period which have apparently survived only in partial form.

The list of surviving duo sonatas is not much longer, with the violin sonatas BWV1021 and 1023 and the flute sonatas BWV1034–5. Among the duo and trio sonatas credited to Bach, a fairly sizable proportion are unauthentic or doubtful. This also applies to some of the

sonatas with obbligato harpsichord, for example those in G minor with violin (BWV1020) and E♭ with flute (1031).

Bach's creative powers appear in a special light in the sonatas and partitas for solo violin (BWV1001–6), dating from 1720, the suites for solo cello (1007–12), which stylistically precede the violin works, and the sonata for solo flute (1013). They not only demonstrate Bach's intimate knowledge of the typical idioms and performing techniques of each instrument, but also show his ability to bring into effective play, without even an accompanying bass part, dense counterpoint and refined harmony coupled with distinctive rhythms. In this he far surpassed all his predecessors, both in the solo violin works (for example Westhoff, Biber and J. J. Walther) and the solo cello pieces (for example the solo gamba works of Schenck). Bach's experience in writing lute music must have stimulated the composition of the solo string works.

Of his chamber works composed during his period with the collegium musicum at Leipzig probably only the flute sonatas have survived. No doubt a larger repertory existed; a relic may well be the trio sonata of the *Musical Offering* – Bach's more artful, elaborate, complex and technically demanding chamber trio.

xx Canons, 'Musical Offering', 'Art of Fugue'

Bach's preoccupation with the canon as the strictest form of counterpoint can be traced back to the Weimar period. In his organ chorales and particularly in the *Orgel-Büchlein* the canonic principle plays a major role. Canonic elements are also in several of the early vocal works, particularly in cantus firmus composition. Here however it is a matter of canonic technique cropping up

in a context of complex contrapuntal construction; as a genre in its own right, the canon, in Bach's day, would appear almost exclusively as a theoretical example in composition teaching. It was in this sense that it was often favoured – generally in the form of a circular canon – by musicians for entries in students' albums: such entries were normally notated in enigmatic fashion, setting the would-be solver an intellectual exercise. Bach apparently had much fun resolving complicated canons (see his correspondence with J. G. Walther and his album entry with a solution of a 1597 riddle canon by Teodoro Riccio), let alone composing them. Bach wrote such canons in albums more than once; for the most part they are probably lost. Except for BWV1076–7 and 1087, all the surviving individual canons (1072–5, 1078, 1086) were probably dedicatory works of this kind; 1077 was re-used for this purpose. What is probably the earliest of them is dated 2 August 1713 (BWV1073, dedicatee uncertain); the latest is dated 1 March 1749 (BWV1078; dedicatee Benjamin Faber).

A new kind of theoretical canon came into being in connection with the Goldberg Variations, in which the canonic principle played a special part. In his personal copy of the Goldberg Variations Bach wrote after 1742 a series of 14 perpetual canons on the first eight bass notes of the aria ground (BWV1087), exploring the most varied canonic possibilities of the subject, subsequently arranging the individual perpetual canons in a progressive order, organized according to their increasing contrapuntal complexity. The types included range from simple, double and triple canons and retrograde canons to a quadruple proportion canon by augmentation and diminution. Nos.11 and 13 of this series are early versions of BWV1077 (from the Fulde album) and 1076

(depicted on Haussmann's Bach portrait of 1746). With this first systematically organized series of canons Bach added a new facet to his work – that of theoretical reflection, which was to play a decisive role in the concept of his contrapuntal late works.

Closely related to these are the *Vom Himmel hoch* variations, where Bach first used a strictly canonic scheme for a monothematic work in several movements of progressive difficulty. Still more important is the *Musical Offering*. Here, for a theme incomparably more complex than that of BWV1087, he devised ten canons of differing structural types, notated as puzzle canons in the original printed edition of 1747. The series of canons on the 'royal theme' includes a canonic fugue, providing a bridge between the canons, which are primarily theoretical in conception though also intended for performance, and the two keyboard fugues or ricercares in three and six parts. Not even the Ricercar *a* 6, or the canonic movements, requires instrumentation exceeding the limits of the ensemble mentioned by Bach in the original edition. A further constituent part of the *Musical Offering* is a trio sonata for flute, violin and continuo, also based on the royal theme. In its second slow movement Bach introduced echoes of the fashionable style practised at the Prussian court. The *Musical Offering*, in effect a compendium in three sections, shows Bach elaborating on the theme supplied to him by Frederick the Great in every imaginable way for an ensemble of up to three instruments.

The *Art of Fugue* constitutes the final contribution to this group of monothematically conceived works intended as representative examples of a specific principle. As a didactic keyboard work, the *Art of Fugue* in

some ways forms a counterpart to the two books of the '48', with the difference that here it is exclusively the fugue that is in question, and, what is more, the fugues are developed from a single theme. Bach's work on the *Art of Fugue* was accomplished in two separate stages – from about 1740 to about 1745, and then (in connection with preparing the work for publication) in about 1747–9 or even 1750. The extant autograph score represents the conclusion of the first stage in which the conception of the work already appears clearly: beginning with simple fugues (Bach avoided this term, speaking of 'contra-punctus'), progressing through 'counter-fugues', double fugues and triple fugues, with interpolated canons, and culminating in a mirror fugue. For the printed version the number of movements was slightly increased, by (among other things) two canons, a fourth simple fugue and most notably a closing quadruple fugue; their order was to some extent rearranged so as to expound more logically the 'chapter of instruction on fugues'. When Bach died the work may have been more 'complete' than it is in the form in which it has survived. In particular the quadruple fugue had surely been completed in all essentials, since the composition of its combinatorial section must necessarily be an early stage in the composition of a quadruple fugue. Only the three opening sections of the exposition, however, are extant, and these, further abbreviated by the editors, give the *Art of Fugue* the appearance of being a mighty torso.

xxi Methods of composition

Bach's methods of composition can be outlined only roughly: the sources, musical and literary, present no more than a fragmentary picture. 'Methods' here refers to

Bach's general procedures of composition, as far as these can be described objectively (without venturing into conjecture about creative psychology) and can be related to certain essential impulses and characteristic approaches.

Bach's vast knowledge of the musical repertory was a decisive factor behind his art. He had an intimate knowledge of the types and styles of composition of his time and in particular of the work of his most important contemporaries; moreover, he had a sound idea of the music of the past, extending back as far as Frescobaldi and Palestrina. The study of works by other masters went hand in hand with experimentation in his own. It is thus characteristic that his acquaintance with the works of Buxtehude and Böhm, with Vivaldi's concertos, with the Passions of Keiser and Handel and with the masses of Lotti and Palestrina should have left an immediate imprint on his compositions in the same genres. It was less a matter of imitation of a model than of an awareness of the possibilities, an expansion of his own manner of writing and a stimulation of his musical ideas. This is confirmed in a contemporary report by T. L. Pitschel on his manner of improvisation, according to which, before beginning his own fantasia, Bach as a rule played from music a work by another master (or perhaps one of his own) which would ignite his imagination. Further, C. P. E. Bach wrote that, in accompanying a trio, his father liked to extemporize a fourth part. This tendency to take compositions by others as a starting-point is paralleled in his late adaptations: in his arrangement of Pergolesi's *Stabat mater* an obbligato viola part is added, replacing the one following the continuo in the original; and his version of the 'Suscepit

Israel' from Caldara's *Magnificat* in C expands it from a five-part into a seven-part piece. An important aspect of Bach's procedure of composition is its systematic and encyclopedic nature. He habitually wrote works of one particular type within a relatively limited period: for example the *Orgel-Büchlein*, the '48', the solo violin sonatas and partitas, the canons, the chorale cantatas etc. He was concerned to try out, to develop, and to exhaust specific principles of composition. There are practically no completely isolated compositions. Relationships, correspondences and connections with other works can constantly be found. This approach to the procedure of composition is at once deep and yet of great natural simplicity; and it never results in mere repetition. Certainly there is repetition, of a kind, in the case of parodies or transcriptions of existing works. Yet even here it is inappropriate to speak of repetition, since in the process of parodying and transcribing, Bach always modified so that the end-product represents a fresh stage in the development of the original composition.

C. P. E. Bach related that his father did not actually compose at the keyboard – apart from some keyboard works whose material originated in improvisations – but that he often tried out his music on the keyboard afterwards. This procedure may be seen in the few instrumental works of which Bach's autograph draft survives, for example the early versions of the Inventions in the *Clavier-Büchlein* for Wilhelm Friedemann, where an abundance of inserted corrections are to be found. In the vocal music, where a wealth of source material is available, the main stages of composition can often be reconstructed. In thematically and motivically self-contained movements, like arias and

165

choruses, Bach normally began with the development and formulation of a motif, a phrase or a theme, which would be guided by the prosody of the text; he then added the contrapuntal voices, and continued in the same way, sometimes using 'continuation sketches' to plan the music's progress in advance (see the critical edition of the sketches, Marshall, 1972). In choral fugues he generally began by outlining the thematic entries, and wrote in the accompanying parts afterwards. The decisive step was the embarkation on the writing of a movement, for progress was in its essentials determined by established models (harmonic–tonal groundplan, modulation patterns, aria schemes) and governed by the principle of unified continuation ('style d'une teneur' and 'Affekteinheitlichkeit' – ensured by a unified motivic organization and interchange, permutation and transposition of component sections). The invention of the central idea was for Bach the critical moment in the process of composition, as the title-page of the Inventions specifies: 'gute inventiones zu bekommen' ('how to achieve good inventions'); and this is borne out by C. P. E. Bach's report that his first requirement of his composition pupils was the invention of ideas. With this the die was cast, down to a work's emotional content. Outlines and sketches relating to this operation can sometimes be found in the original manuscripts; typically, however, Bach hardly required more than one or two attempts before arriving at the definitive form of his principal idea. The further elaboration of the idea – the *dispositio*, *elaboratio* and *decoratio* – required mastery of his craft rather than inspiration.

In composing multi-movement vocal works, Bach, understandably, began as a rule with the self-contained

movements and only afterwards worked at the recitatives and chorales. In the recitatives he normally first wrote out the text and then added the melody and bass, section by section. In the chorales the bass was added to the melody and the middle parts were inserted later. Then all the movements were revised in detail, and sometimes corrections were made. The appearance of Bach's working drafts is thus unusually clear and neat as a whole, although it is mainly in his fair copies that the particular quality of his handwriting, a quality comparable to that of his music, is expressed.

Ultimately, for Bach, the process of composition was an unending one. Dynamic markings and indications of articulation would be inserted as he looked through the parts; he would revise and improve a work when he was copying it out, and when giving further performances would make fresh alterations and improvements. He also inserted corrections in works already in print. Throughout his life Bach was his own severest critic. Even in works which went through two or three different versions, like the chorale prelude *An Wasserflüssen Babylon* BWV653, the 'final' version does not represent a definitive one but merely a further state in the search for perfection – the central and ultimate concern of Bach's method of composition.

XXII **Bach Revival**

The rediscovery of Bach's music in the early 19th century marked the first time that a great composer, after a period of neglect, was accorded his rightful place by a later generation. Palestrina, Lully, Purcell and Handel had never been quite forgotten by the musical public, but Bach was known only to a small circle of pupils and

167

devotees until the Romantic movement stimulated a growing interest in his art. The Bach Revival was an early example of a new historicism which eventually opened all periods of Western music to discovery and performance, and which now constitutes the dominant factor in the musical taste of advanced Western societies. It began at about the same time in Germany, where most of Bach's descendants and pupils, and most of his surviving music, were to be found; and in England, where musical historicism was already well advanced by the end of the 18th century.

(*i*) *Germany and Austria*. After Bach's death, public knowledge of his music was at a low ebb. Even at the Thomaskirche, his cantatas were seldom used; the organ works, too, were rarely heard, unless they were played by one of his sons or pupils. For the rest of the century he was remembered, if at all, as a master of organ playing and of learned counterpoint. The first extended biographical notice of Bach, by J. A. Hiller, his third successor at the Thomaskirche, gave only a superficial and condescending account of his compositions (1784); while Reichardt remarked in 1782: 'Had Bach possessed the high integrity and the deep expressive feeling that inspired Handel, he would have been much greater even than Handel; but as it is he was only more painstaking and technically skilful'.

The rejection, by musicians of the succeeding generation, of the artistic principles that Bach stood for went beyond the normal changes in style that are found at other periods. His own sons played a part in it, though Philip Emanuel's feelings were ambivalent, and at the

last he published a passionate though anonymous defence of his father's art. It was indeed at Berlin, where Emanuel was employed until 1767, that the strongest group of Bach disciples was concentrated, including Kirnberger, Marpurg, Agricola and Princess Amalia, sister of Frederick the Great. It was this group that preserved and passed on most of the original manuscripts of Bach's works that have survived. From the Berlin group of Bach disciples, too, Baron van Swieten carried the tradition to Vienna, where in the 1780s meetings were held at his house at which the works of Bach and others were performed. There Mozart came to know Bach's music, and to be influenced by it, as to a lesser extent was Haydn. Beethoven, as a boy of 11 or 12, mastered the '48' to the satisfaction of his teacher, Christian Gottlob Neefe.

A more general appreciation of Bach came only as a result of the Romantic cult of the past. Arising in England, this movement was immensely strengthened in its German phase by patriotic and religious motives. The military and political humiliations of the Napoleonic period generated a desire to recover older German traditions, while a religious revival prompted the search for what was truly and distinctively religious in the cultural heritage. In this Bach was to become the archetypal figure. A leader in the nationalistic cult of Bach was J. N. Forkel, whose pioneering biography (1802) was inscribed 'for patriotic admirers of true musical art', and was dedicated to Swieten. 'This great man', Forkel wrote, 'was a German. Be proud of him, German fatherland, but be worthy of him too. . . . His works are an invaluable national patrimony with which

no other nation has anything to be compared'.

Forkel was joined by Rochlitz in the Leipzig *Allgemeine musikalische Zeitung*, whose first volume (1798) contained a portrait of Bach. Rochlitz was inclined to paint a romantic, saintly picture of the master, comparing him aesthetically and morally with Dürer, Rubens, Newton and Michelangelo. The religious aspect of Bach's art was important to another early convert, C. F. Zelter, the founder of the Berlin Singakademie (1791), one of the earliest German institutions to organize historical concerts. He had inherited an extensive collection of Bach's music from Kirnberger and Agricola, and he drew from it in his pioneering revivals of Bach's motets and other sacred works. He rehearsed the Mass in B minor in 1811 and the *St Matthew Passion* in 1815, but did not think it practical to perform them. Through Rochlitz and Zelter, Goethe in his old age came to a profound appreciation of Bach. E. T. A. Hoffmann, another influential literary figure, developed the idealized Romantic conception that Rochlitz had begun to build.

The mounting enthusiasm for Bach culminated in the performance of the *St Matthew Passion* by the Singakademie in 1829, with Mendelssohn conducting. This was the decisive turning-point in Bach's reputation, for it swiftly transformed the revival from a cult of intellectuals into a popular movement. Zelter had allowed a copy of the autograph to be made in 1823; with commendable self-effacement he turned over the honour of conducting the performance to his pupil. Mendelssohn, though at first hesitant, eventually agreed to attempt the formidable task. He made his own arrange-

ment of the music from Zelter's copy; cuts, changes and additions were made. After nearly two years of rehearsals, the performance took place on 11 March 1829, and was far more successful than the first performance exactly a century earlier. The audience was deeply moved; Hegel, who was present, later wrote of 'Bach's grand, truly Protestant, robust and erudite genius which we have only recently learnt again to appreciate at its full value'. Two more performances followed, the last conducted by Zelter. Mosevius, who also heard the work at Berlin, conducted it in 1830 at Breslau, an important centre of the Protestant religious revival and the home of Winterfeld. Königsberg was the next city to hear the Passion; it was not performed at Leipzig until 1841. Meanwhile the Berlin Singakademie produced the *St John Passion* in 1833, and a truncated version of the Mass in B minor in 1835 (the Credo had been revived by Schelbe at Frankfurt in 1828). A growing number of the cantatas were added to the choral repertory at this period.

Publication of Bach's music had also been accelerating. After Emanuel Bach's collected edition of the chorales (1784–7), the next landmark was the publication of *Das wohltemperirte Clavier* by three firms almost simultaneously, in 1801 (Simrock, Nägeli and Hoffmeister). Hoffmeister and Kühnel continued to publish the keyboard works in a collection entitled 'Oeuvres complettes' (1801–17). The motets appeared in 1802–3, the sonatas for violin and keyboard in 1804–17, the *Magnificat* in 1811, the solo violin sonatas in 1817–28, the solo cello suites in 1828. Peters's edition of the organ works appeared in 1845–7. Other works were pub-

lished, in editions of varying quality, so that by the middle of the century the bulk of Bach's organ and keyboard music was already available, but only a meagre proportion of the choral and chamber music. The most glaring deficiency was that the Mass in B minor and the bulk of the cantatas were still unpublished.

The idea of an edition in score of all Bach's works had been proposed by Forkel in 1802 and warmly advocated by Schumann in 1837; and its practicality had been proved by the success of the London Handel Society editions, beginning in 1843. At last, in 1850, the centenary of the composer's death, the Bach-Gesellschaft was formed, and during the next 50 years completed its monumental task. The volumes, though they varied in scholarly precision, were a remarkable achievement, and established the basic principles for scholarly musical editions that have been followed ever since. They completed the Bach Revival, and made it possible for Bach to take his place in public esteem beside or above other great composers whose music did not need reviving. The Bach-Gesellschaft edition remained standard until after World War II, when Bärenreiter embarked on the Neue Bach-Ausgabe (1954–); this incorporates the results of more recent research and the texts are prepared in accordance with modern editorial procedures.

(*ii*) *England*. England lacked the group of pupils and descendants who formed the nucleus of the German Bach Revival; but historicism and antiquarianism were more advanced than in Germany. The music of Handel, Corelli, Domenico Scarlatti and other late Baroque com-

posers continued to be popular throughout the 18th century, while such bodies as the Academy of Ancient Music (1710–92), the Madrigal Society (founded 1741) and the Concert of Ancient Music ('Ancient Concerts', 1776–1848) cultivated a taste for the music of the remoter past. Burney and Hawkins, though they failed to appreciate Bach's importance, gave him due mention in their histories of music – books of a kind that did not yet exist on the Continent.

There is evidence that a good deal of Bach's music was circulating in manuscript in England during the last three decades of the 18th century. Johann Christian Bach probably had little interest in his father's music, but he may have possessed some copies. Burney received a copy of book 1 of the '48' from Emanuel Bach in 1772, while Clementi possessed a partly autograph copy of book 2. Queen Charlotte owned a manuscript volume dated 1788, containing the '48', *Clavier-Übung*, iii, and the Credo from the Mass in B minor. This music may have reached the queen through either of two German musicians recently arrived in London: K. F. Horn (1762–1830), her music teacher from 1782, or A. F. C. Kollmann (1756–1829), organist at the German chapel in the court of St James's from 1784.

Clementi, Horn and Kollmann are the most important early figures in the English Bach Revival. Clementi is said to have practised Bach for hours on end during his time at Peter Beckford's house in the early 1770s. His own music shows early traces of Bach's influence which become much stronger in the late sonatas and the *Gradus ad Parnassum*. He incorporated several of the keyboard pieces in his didactic works. He must have

173

passed on his love of Bach to his two most famous pupils, J. B. Cramer, whose studies of 1804 and 1810 show an obvious influence of the '48', and Field, who astonished audiences with his playing of Bach during his European tour of 1802–3 and who taught Bach's music to his Russian pupils. Kollmann consistently stressed the importance of Bach in his theoretical works in English, beginning with the *Essay on Musical Harmony* (1796), which offered a detailed analysis of the F minor fugue from book 2 of the '48'. In 1799 he advertised a plan to issue an analytical edition of the entire '48', but the scheme was anticipated by the three continental editions of 1801, two of which were reissued in London. He published the Chromatic Fantasia in 1806, with 'additions' by himself, analysed 12 Bach fugues in his *Quarterly Musical Register* (1812), and translated Forkel's life of Bach into English (1820). Horn arranged 12 organ fugues for string quartet – with figured bass – and published them in 1807, and later collaborated with Wesley in the first English edition of the '48'.

The movement quickly spread to native English musicians. William Shield's *Introduction to Harmony* (1800) gave due place to Bach, and incorporated the D minor prelude from book 1 of the '48'. George Pinto, a close friend of Field's, tried to imitate Bach in his C minor Fantasia and Fugue (published posthumously, *c*1808), and it was he who first introduced Samuel Wesley to Bach's preludes and fugues, according to Wesley's memoirs. Wesley took up the cause with feverish intensity, shown in his well-known letters to Benjamin Jacob, another English Bach enthusiast. He edited, with Horn, the six organ trios, published (for the

174

first time anywhere) in 1809–10 in instalments, and a
'new and correct edition' of the '48' in 1810–13. In
1808 he began a series of concerts of Bach's music at
Surrey Chapel, with Jacob, who was organist there; and
soon afterwards he began a similar series at the
Portuguese Embassy chapel, where his friend Vincent
Novello was organist and soon became a Bach convert.

Wesley saw Bach as a superhuman genius, even
though there is a touch of whimsy in the nicknames he
used for him – 'Saint Sebastian', 'The Man', 'Our
Apollo' and so on. He felt that militant propaganda was
needed to persuade the English that any musician could
be superior to Handel. He won many converts, including even the aged Burney who at last recanted his earlier
criticism of Bach. William Crotch was recruited to the
cause, and was the first to play the 'St Anne's' fugue in
public (on the piano). Both Wesley and Crotch gave
prominence to Bach in lectures on the history of music.

As well as the keyboard works, Wesley endeavoured
to promote other music of Bach. The motet *Jesu, meine
Freude* was sung at his concert in the Hanover Square
Rooms on 3 June 1809, and the following year he
presented to the Madrigal Society a score of the same
work (with text translated into Latin). He played the
sonatas for violin and keyboard many times with Jacob,
and on 6 June 1814 he played one with Salomon at the
latter's benefit. Nevertheless, for many years Bach was
known in England more by reputation than by experience. Mendelssohn's visits of 1829 and 1832 were a fresh
stimulus, and his performances of organ works at St
Paul's Cathedral, played with pedals, and with a degree of
confidence and understanding that no English musician
could equal, were undoubtedly a revelation to English

audiences. Moscheles also played his part; he performed the D minor keyboard concerto (with additional orchestral parts of his own) at the King's Theatre on 13 May 1836, and the following year included preludes and fugues from the '48' at several concerts. Monck Mason announced Bach's Passion oratorios for the 1832 season of oratorio concerts at the King's Theatre, but nothing came of this. Parts of the *St Matthew Passion*, B minor Mass and *Magnificat* were given at the Birmingham Festival (1837) and at the Ancient Concerts. Prince Albert, after his marriage to Victoria in 1840, introduced music by Bach into concerts at Buckingham Palace and Windsor Castle and at aristocratic musical societies in which he was concerned. Sterndale Bennett was another champion of Bach, performing keyboard and chamber works at many of his concerts and editing some of the music, including the *St Matthew Passion*, for publication. At Cambridge in the 1840s T. A. Walmisley lectured on Bach and taught his students to revere him above all other composers.

The English Bach Revival culminated in the formation of the Bach Society, founded by Sterndale Bennett. The first meeting, on 27 October 1849, at Bennett's house in Russell Place, formulated the objects of the society, which included the collection and promotion, but not publication, of the works of the master (though the society did publish a volume of the motets, with English text added, in 1851). A number of concerts were given, and at last the *St Matthew Passion* had its first English performance (with English words) at the Hanover Square Rooms on 6 April 1854, Bennett conducting. Several other important works were revived before the society disbanded in 1870. The populariza-

tion of Bach was completed when his choral master-pieces were accepted alongside Handel's and Mendelssohn's. The *St Matthew Passion* was introduced at the Three Choirs Festival in 1871, and the London Bach Choir undertook the regular performance of the larger choral works, beginning with the Mass in B minor in 1876.

WORKS

Scoring. Bach did not always define instruments unambiguously. 'Corno' could mean the normal horn of his time, the need for a brass player but not necessarily a trumpeter, or possibly the most suitable brass instrument (horn, cornett, slide-trumpet [tromba da tirarsi] etc). Parts for 'three oboes' at Leipzig may indicate any combination of oboes, oboes d'amore, tailles (tenor oboes in F, with no solo material) or oboes da caccia (a specific local tenor type, designed for obbligato work). Four trombones indicate SATB and three ATB (usually below a cornett).

Dates of later copies or performances are given only if modifications are involved.

Editions: J. S. Bach: Werke, ed. Bach-Gesellschaft, i–xlvii (Leipzig, 1851–99/R1947) [BG]

J. S. Bach: Neue Ausgabe sämtlicher Werke (Neue Bach-Ausgabe), ed. Johann-Sebastian-Bach-Institut, Göttingen, and Bach-Archiv, Leipzig, ser. I–VIII (Kassel and Basle, 1954–) [vols. in square brackets are in preparation] [NBA; CC = Critical Commentary]

Catalogues: W. Schmieder: Thematisch-systematisches Verzeichnis der musikalischen Werke Johann Sebastian Bachs: Bach-Werke-Verzeichnis (Leipzig, 1950, 3/1966, rev., enlarged edn. in preparation) [BWV; A = Anhang]

W. Neumann: Handbuch der Kantaten Johann Sebastian Bachs (Leipzig, 1947, rev. 4/1977) [Neumann follows Schmieder but lists a larger number of cantatas than bwv1950. Neumann's numbers are shown below for incomplete and lost compositions only] [N]

Numbers in the right-hand column denote references in the text.

• – another version

CHURCH CANTATAS

Advent I = 1st Sunday in Advent; Trinity/Easter I = 1st Sunday after Trinity/Easter, etc; most texts are compilations including at least one chorale; only single text sources given; where the text is entirely or mainly based on that of a chorale, its author's name is given in parentheses

BWV	Title (text/librettist)	Occasion: 1st perf.	Scoring	BG	NBA	
						84, 124–33
1	Wie schön leuchtet der Morgenstern, chorale (P. Nicolai)	Annunciation: 25 March 1725	S, T, B, 4vv, 2 hn, 2 ob da caccia, 2 vn, str, bc	i, 1	[I/xxviii]	130
2	Ach Gott, vom Himmel sieh darein, chorale (M. Luther)	Trinity II; 18 June 1724	A, T, B, 4vv, 4 trbn, 2 ob, str, bc	i, 55	I/xvi, 83	130
3	Ach Gott, wie manches Herzleid, chorale (M. Möller)	Epiphany II; 14 Jan 1725	S, A, T, B, 4vv, hn, trbn, 2 ob d'amore, str, bc	i, 75	I/v, 191	130
4	Christ lag in Todes Banden, chorale (Luther)	Easter; probably by 1708	S, A, T, B, 4vv, cornett, 3 trbn, str, bc	i, 97	[I/ix]	57, 124, 130, 131
5	Wo soll ich fliehen hin, chorale (J. Heermann)	Trinity XIX; 15 Oct 1724	S, A, T, B, 4vv, tpt, tpt da tirarsi, 2 ob, str, bc	i, 127	[I/xxiv]	130
6	Bleib bei uns, denn es will Abend werden	Easter Monday; 2 April 1725	S, A, T, B, 4vv, 2 ob, ob da caccia, vc piccolo, str, bc	i, 153	I/x, 45	130
7	Christ unser Herr zum Jordan kam, chorale (Luther)	St John; 24 June 1724	A, T, B, 4vv, 2 ob d'amore, str, bc	i, 179	I/xxix, 27	130, 137
8	Liebster Gott, wann werd ich sterben?, chorale (C. Neumann)	Trinity XVI; 24 Sept 1724	S, A, T, B, 4vv, hn, fl, 2 ob d'amore, str, bc	i, 213	I/xxiii, 107, 165	130
9	Es ist das Heil uns kommen her, chorale (P. Speratus)	Trinity VI; c1732–5	S, A, T, B, 4vv, fl, ob d'amore, str, bc	i, 245	[I/xvii]	97

10	Meine Seel erhebt den Herren (*Luke* i.46–55)	Visitation; 2 July 1724	S, A, T, B, 4vv, tpt, 2 ob, str, bc	i, 277	[I/xxviii]	130
12	Weinen, Klagen, Sorgen, Zagen (S. Franck)	Easter III; 22 April 1714	A, T, B, 4vv, tpt, ob, str, bc incl. bn	ii, 61	[I/xi]	126, 139
13	Meine Seufzer, meine Tränen (G. C. Lehms)	Epiphany II; 20 Jan 1726	S, A, T, B, 4vv, 2 rec, ob da caccia, str, bc	ii, 81	I/v, 231	131
14	Wär Gott nicht mit uns diese Zeit, chorale (Luther)	Epiphany IV; 30 Jan 1735	S, T, B, 4vv, hn/tpt, 2 ob, str, bc	ii, 101	[I/vi]	97
16	Herr Gott, dich loben wir (Lehms)	New Year; 1 Jan 1726	A, T, B, 4vv, hn, 2 ob, ob da caccia, str, bc	ii, 175	I/iv, 105	131
17	Wer Dank opfert, der preiset mich (?C. Helm)	Trinity XIV; 22 Sept 1726	S, A, T, B, 4vv, 2 ob ?d'amore, str, bc	ii, 201	I/xxi, 149	131, 139
18	Gleichwie der Regen und Schnee vom Himmel fällt (E. Neumeister)	Sexagesima; ? 24 Feb 1715 or ? 1713–14	S, T, B, 4vv, 4 va, bc incl. bn [2 rec added 1724]	ii, 229	I/vii, 109	65, 126
19	Es erhub sich ein Streit (after Picander)	St Michael; 29 Sept 1726	S, T, B, 4vv, 3 tpt, timp, 2 ob, 2 ob d'amore, taille, str, bc	ii, 255	I/xxx, 57	
20	O Ewigkeit, du Donnerwort, chorale (J. Rist)	Trinity I; 11 June 1724	A, T, B, 4vv, tpt da tirarsi, 3 ob, str, bc	ii, 293	I/xv, 135	130
21	Ich hatte viel Bekümmernis (?Franck)	Trinity III; 17 June 1714 [part earlier]	S, T, B, 4vv, 3 tpt, timp, 4 trbn, ob, str, bc incl. bn [4 trbn added 1723]	v/1, 1	I/xvi, 111	65, 125, 126
22	Jesus nahm zu sich die Zwölfe	Quinquagesima; 7 Feb 1723	A, T, B, 4vv, ob, str, bc	v/1, 67	[I/viii]	80, 129
23	Du wahrer Gott und Davids Sohn	Quinquagesima; 7 Feb 1723	S, A, T, 4vv, 2 ob d'amore, cornett, 3 trbn, str, bc; *c1730: 2 ob, str, bc	v/1, 95	[I/viii]	80, 129
24	Ein ungefärbt Gemüte (Neumeister)	Trinity IV; 20 June 1723	A, T, B, 4vv, tpt da tirarsi, 2 ob, 2 ob d'amore, str, bc	v/1, 127	[I/xvii]	129
25	Es ist nicht Gesundes an meinem Leibe	Trinity XIV; 29 Aug 1723	S, T, B, 4vv, cornett, 3 trbn, 3 rec, 2 ob ?d'amore, str, bc	v/1, 155	I/xxi, 81	87, 129
26	Ach wie flüchtig, ach wie nichtig, chorale (M. Franck)	Trinity XXIV; 19 Nov 1724	S, A, T, B, 4vv, hn, fl, 3 ob, str, bc	v/1, 191	I/xxvii, 31	130
27	Wer weiss, wie nahe mir mein Ende?, chorales (Neumeister; 2 chorales from Dresden Gesangbuch)	Trinity XVI; 6 Oct 1726	S, A, T, B, 4vv, hn, 2 ob, ob da caccia, org obbl, str, bc	v/1, 219	I/xxiii, 223	
28	Gottlob! nun geht das Jahr zu Ende (Neumeister)	Christmas I; 30 Dec 1725	S, A, T, B, 4vv, cornett, 3 trbn, 2 ob, taille, str, bc	v/1, 247	[I/iii]	131
29	Wir danken dir, Gott, wir danken dir	inauguration of town council; 27 Aug 1731	S, A, T, B, 4vv, 3 tpt, timp, 2 ob, org obbl, str, bc	v/1, 275	[I/xxxii]	97, *138*, 139
30	Freue dich, erlöste Schar (adapted ?Picander from 30a)	St John; 24 June 1738 or later	S, A, T, B, 4vv, 2 fl, 2 ob, ob d'amore, str, bc	v/1, 323	I/xxix, 61	
31	Der Himmel lacht! die Erde jubilieret (Franck)	Easter; 21 April 1715	S, T, B, 5vv, 3 tpt, timp, 3 ob, str, bc [taille added 1724]	vii, 3	[I/ix]	126
32	Liebster Jesu, mein Verlangen, dialogue (Lehms)	Epiphany I; 13 Jan 1726	S, B, 4vv, ob, str, bc	vii, 55	I/v, 145	131

BWV	Title (text/librettist)	Occasion; 1st perf.	Scoring	BG	NBA	
33	Allein zu dir, Herr Jesu Christ, chorale	Trinity XIII; 3 Sept 1724	A, T, B, 4vv, 2 ob, str, bc	vii, 83	I/xxi, 25	130
34	O ewiges Feuer, O Ursprung der Liebe (adapted from 34a)	Whit Sunday; early 1740s	A, T, B, 4vv, 3 tpt, timp, 2 fl, 2 ob, str, bc	vii, 117	I/xiii, 131	
34a	O ewiges Feuer, O Ursprung der Liebe	wedding; ? 6 March 1726	S, A, T, B, 4vv, 3 tpt, timp, 2 fl, 2 ob, str, bc	xli, 117	I/xxxiii, 29	
35	Geist und Seele wird verwirret (Lehms) [partly adapted from lost ob conc., cf 1059]	Trinity XII; 8 Sept 1726	A, 2 ob, taille, org obbl, str, bc	vii, 173	[I/xx]	131, 157
36	Schwingt freudig euch empor (adapted ?Picander from 36c)	Advent I; 2 Dec 1731	S, A, T, B, 4vv, 2 ob d'amore, str, bc	vii, 223	I/i, 19, 43	130
37	Wer da gläubet und getauft wird	Ascension; 18 May 1724	S, A, T, B, 4vv, 2 ob d'amore, str, bc	vii, 261	I/xii, 81	129
38	Aus tiefer Not schrei ich zu dir, chorale (Luther)	Trinity XXI; 29 Oct 1724	S, A, T, B, 4vv, 4 trbn, 2 ob, str, bc	vii, 285	[I/xxv]	130
39	Brich dem Hungrigen dein Brot (?Helm)	Trinity I; 23 June 1726	S, A, B, 4vv, 2 rec, 2 ob, str, bc	vii, 303	I/xv, 181	131
40	Dazu ist erschienen der Sohn Gottes	2nd day of Christmas; 26 Dec 1723	A, T, B, 4vv, 2 hn, 2 ob, str, bc	vii, 351	[I/iii]	129, 139
41	Jesu, nun sei gepreiset, chorale (J. Herman)	New Year; 1 Jan 1725	S, A, T, B, 4vv, 3 tpt, timp, 3 ob, vc piccolo, str, bc	x, 3	I/iv, 39	130
42	Am Abend aber desselbigen Sabbats	Easter I; 8 April 1725	S, A, T, B, 4vv, 2 ob, str, bc incl. bn	x, 65	[I/xi]	155
43	Gott fähret auf mit Jauchzen (?Helm)	Ascension; 30 May 1726	S, A, T, B, 4vv, 3 tpt, timp, 2 ob, str, bc [later without tpts]	x, 95	I/xii, 135	131
44	Sie werden euch in den Bann tun	Ascension I; 21 May 1724	S, A, T, B, 4vv, 2 ob, str, bc	x, 129	I/xii, 167	129
45	Es ist dir gesagt, Mensch, was gut ist (?Helm)	Trinity VIII; 11 Aug 1726	A, T, B, 4vv, 2 fl, 2 ob, str, bc	x, 153	I/xviii, 199	131
46	Schauet doch und sehet	Trinity X; 1 Aug 1723	A, T, B, 4vv, 2 rec, str, bc [tpt/hn da tirarsi, 2 taille added later]	x, 189	[I/xix]	131, 157
47	Wer sich selbst erhöhet (J. F. Helbig)	Trinity XVII; 13 Oct 1726	S, B, 4vv, 2 ob, org obbl, str, bc	x, 241	I/xxiii, 321	129
48	Ich elender Mensch, wer wird mich erlösen	Trinity XIX; 3 Oct 1723	A, T, 4vv, tpt da tirarsi, 2 ob, str, bc	x, 277	[I/xxiv]	
49	Ich geh und suche mit Verlangen, dialogue [sinfonia adapted from lost conc. 1053]	Trinity XX; 3 Nov 1726	S, B, ob d'amore, org obbl, vc piccolo, str, bc	x, 301	[I/xxv]	131, 157
50	Nun ist das Heil und die Kraft (Revelation xii.10) [movt of inc. or lost cantata]	St Michael	8vv, 3 tpt, timp, 3 ob, str, bc	x, 343	I/xxx, 143	
51	Jauchzet Gott in allen Landen!	Trinity XV; ? 17 Sept 1730	S, tpt, str, bc [2 tpt, timp added by W. F. Bach]	xii/2, 3	[I/xxii]	97
52	Falsche Welt, dir trau ich nicht	Trinity XXIII; 24 Nov 1726	S, 4vv, 2 hn, 3 ob, str, bc	xii/2, 27	[I/xxvi]	
54	Widerstehe doch der Sünde (Lehms)	Oculi or Trinity VII; 4 March or 15 July 1714	A, str, bc	xii/2, 61	I/xviii, 3	126, 134, 137

No.	Title	Occasion; date	Scoring	NBA	BG	pp.
55	Ich armer Mensch, ich Sündenknecht	Trinity XXII; 17 Nov 1726	T, 4vv, fl, ob d'amore, str, bc	[I/xxvi]	xii/2, 75	
56	Ich will den Kreuzstab gerne tragen	Trinity XIX; 27 Oct 1726	B, 4vv, 2 ob, taille, str, bc	[I/xxiv]	xii/2, 89	
57	Selig ist der Mann, dialogue (Lehms)	2nd day of Christmas; 26 Dec 1725	S, B, 4vv, 2 ob, taille, str, bc	[I/iii]	xii/2, 107	131
58	Ach Gott, wie manches Herzeleid, dialogue	New Year I; 5 Jan 1727	S, B, 2 ob, taille, str, bc	I/iv, 219	xii/2, 135	
59	Wer mich liebet, der wird mein Wort halten (Neumeister)	Whit Sunday; 16 May 1723 or 28 May 1724	S, B, 4vv, 2 tpt, timp, str, bc	I/xiii, 67	xii/2, 153	80, 86
60	O Ewigkeit, du Donnerwort, dialogue (Neumeister)	Trinity XXIV; 7 Nov 1723	A, T, B, 4vv, hn, 2 ob d'amore, str, bc	I/xxvii, 3	xii/2, 171	129
61	Nun komm, der Heiden Heiland (Neumeister)	Advent I; 2 Dec 1714	S, T, B, 4vv, str, bc	I/i, 3	xvi, 3	126
62	Nun komm, der Heiden Heiland, chorale (Luther)	Advent I; 3 Dec 1724	S, A, T, B, 4vv, hn, 2 ob, str, bc	I/i, 77	xvi, 21	130
63	Christen, ätzet diesen Tag (?N. Heineccius)	Christmas; 1713–15, ?lost earlier version	S, A, T, B, 4vv, 4 tpt, timp, 3 ob, str, bc [org obbl added after c1729]	I/ii, 3	xvi, 53	65, 88
64	Sehet, welch eine Liebe (Knauer)	3rd day of Christmas; 27 Dec 1723	S, A, B, 4vv, cornett, 3 trbn, ob d'amore, str, bc	[I/iii]	xvi, 113	129
65	Sie werden aus Saba alle kommen	Epiphany; 6 Jan 1724	T, B, 4vv, 2 hn, 2 rec, 2 ob da caccia, str, bc	I/v, 3	xvi, 135	129
66	Erfreut euch, ihr Herzen, dialogue [adapted from 66a]	Easter Monday; 10 April 1724	A, T, B, 4vv, tpt, 2 ob, bn, str, bc	I/x, 3	xvi, 169	
67	Halt im Gedächtnis Jesum Christ	Easter I; 16 April 1724	A, T, B, 4vv, hn, fl, 2 ob d'amore, str, bc	I/xi, 3	xvi, 217	129, 135
68	Also hat Gott die Welt geliebt (M. von Ziegler)	Whit Monday; 21 May 1725	S, B, 4vv, hn, cornett, 3 trbn, 2 ob, taille, vc piccolo, str, bc	I/xiv, 33	xvi, 249	130
69	Lobe den Herrn, meine Seele (partly Knauer) [adapted from 69a]	inauguration of town council; 1742–8	S, A, T, B, 4vv, 3 tpt, timp, 3 ob, ob d'amore, str, bc	[I/xxxii]	xvi, 283	
69a	Lobe den Herrn, meine Seele (Knauer)	Trinity XII; 15 Aug 1723	S, A, T, B, 4vv, 3 tpt, timp, rec, 3 ob, ob da caccia, str, bc	I/xx	xvi, 379	129
70	Wachet! betet! betet! wachet! (partly Franck) [adapted from 70a]	Trinity XXVI; 21 Nov 1723	S, A, T, B, 4vv, tpt, ob, str, bc incl. bn	I/xxvii, 109	xvi, 329	
70a	Wachet! betet! betet! wachet! (Franck) [composed 1716, probably not perf. in this version, lost]	Advent II	—	I/xxvii, CC	—	67, 126
71	Gott ist mein König	inauguration of Mühlhausen town council; 4 Feb 1708	S, A, T, B, 4vv, 3 tpt, timp; 2 rec, vc; 2 ob; str, bc incl. org obbl, bn	[I/xxxii]	xviii, 3	58, 116, 124
72	Alles nur nach Gottes Willen (Franck)	Epiphany III; 27 Jan 1726	S, A, B, 4vv, 2 ob, str, bc	[I/vi]	xviii, 57	131, 139
73	Herr, wie du willt, so schicks mit mir	Epiphany III; 23 Jan 1724	S, T, B, 4vv, hn, 2 ob, str, bc [later version, 1730s, with org obbl instead of hn]	[I/vi]	xviii, 87	129
74	Wer mich liebet, der wird mein Wort halten (Ziegler) [partly adapted from 59]	Whit Sunday; 20 May 1725	S, A, T, B, 4vv, 3 tpt, timp, 2 ob, ob da caccia, str, bc	I/xiii, 85	xviii, 107	130

BWV	Title (text/librettist)	Occasion; 1st perf.	Scoring	BG	NBA	
75	Die Elenden sollen essen	Trinity I; 30 May 1723	S, A, T, B, 4vv, tpt, 2 ob, ob d'amore, str, bc incl. bn	xviii, 149	I/xv, 87	80, 85, 129
76	Die Himmel erzählen die Ehre Gottes	Trinity II; 6 June 1723	S, A, T, B, 4vv, tpt, 2 ob, ob d'amore, va da gamba, str, bc	xviii, 191	I/xvi, 3	85, 129, 159
77	Du sollt Gott, deinen Herren, lieben (Knauer)	Trinity XIII; 22 Aug 1723	S, A, T, B, 4vv, tpt da tirarsi, 2 ob, str, bc	xviii, 235	I/xxi, 3	129
78	Jesu, der du meine Seele, chorale (Rist)	Trinity XIV; 10 Sept 1724	S, A, T, B, 4vv, hn, fl, 2 ob, str, bc	xviii, 257	I/xxi, 117	130
79	Gott der Herr ist Sonn und Schild	Reformation Festival; 31 Oct 1725	S, A, B, 4vv, 2 hn, timp, 2 fl, 2 ob, str, bc	xviii, 289	[I/xxxi]	139
80	Ein Feste Burg ist unser Gott (Franck) [adapted from 80a]	Reformation Festival; before 1744	S, A, T, B, 4vv, 2 ob, taille, str, bc [3 tpt, timp added by W. F. Bach]	xviii, 319, 381	[I/xxxi]	126
80a	Alles, was von Gott geboren (Franck) [music lost]	Lent III; 1715		—	[I/viii, CC]	
80b	Ein feste Burg ist unser Gott (Franck)	31 Oct 1723	autograph frag., movts 1–2	—	[I/vi]	129
81	Jesus schläft, was soll ich hoffen?	Epiphany IV; 30 Jan 1724	A, T, B, 4vv, 2 rec, 2 ob d'amore, str, bc	xx/1, 3	[I/vi]	129
82	Ich habe genung	Purification; 2 Feb 1727	B, ob, str, bc; other versions for S/A with altered ww	xx/1, 27	[I/xxviii]	129
83	Erfreute Zeit im neuen Bunde	Purification; 2 Feb 1724	A, T, B, 4vv, 2 hn, 2 ob, str, bc	xx/1, 53	[I/xxviii]	129
84	Ich bin vergnügt mit meinem Glücke (Picander)	Septuagesima; 9 Feb 1727	S, 4vv, ob, str, bc	xx/1, 79	I/vii, 23	90, 91
85	Ich bin ein guter Hirt	Easter II; 15 April 1725	S, A, T, B, 4vv, 2 ob, vc piccolo, str, bc	xx/1, 101	[I/xi]	130
86	Wahrlich, wahrlich, ich sage euch	Easter V; 14 May 1724	S, A, T, B, 4vv, 2 ob d'amore, str, bc	xx/1, 121	I/xii, 47	129
87	Bisher habt ihr nichts gebeten (Ziegler)	Easter V; 6 May 1725	A, T, B, 4vv, 2 ob, 2 ob da caccia, str, bc	xx/1, 137	I/xii, 63	130
88	Siehe, ich will viel Fischer aussenden	Trinity V; 21 July 1726	S, A, T, B, 4vv, 2 hn, 2 ob d'amore, taille, str, bc	xx/1, 155	[I/xvii]	131
89	Was soll ich aus dir machen, Ephraim?	Trinity XXII; 24 Oct 1723	S, A, B, 4vv, hn, 2 ob, str, bc	xx/1, 181	[I/xxvi]	129
90	Es reisset euch ein schrecklich Ende	Trinity XXV; 14 Nov 1723	A, T, B, 4vv, tpt, str, bc	xx/1, 197	I/xxvii, 61	129
91	Gelobet seist du, Jesu Christ, chorale (Luther)	Christmas; 25 Dec 1724	S, A, T, B, 4vv, 2 hn, timp, 3 ob, str, bc incl. bn	xxii, 3	I/ii, 133	130
92	Ich hab in Gottes Herz und Sinn, chorale (P. Gerhardt)	Septuagesima; 28 Jan 1725	S, A, T, B, 4vv, 2 ob d'amore, str, bc	xxii, 35	I/vii, 43	130
93	Wer nur den lieben Gott lässt walten, chorale (G. Neumark)	Trinity V; 9 July 1724	S, A, T, B, 4vv, 2 ob, str, bc	xxii, 71	[I/xvii]	130
94	Was frag ich nach der Welt, chorale (G. M. Pfefferkorn)	Trinity IX; 6 Aug 1724	S, A, T, B, 4vv, fl, 2 ob, ob d'amore, str, bc	xxii, 97	[I/xix]	130
95	Christus, der ist mein Leben, stanzas from 3 chorales	Trinity XVI; 12 Sept 1723	S, T, B, 4vv, hn, 2 ob, ob d'amore, str, bc	xxii, 131	I/xxiii, 67	129

No.	Title	Occasion; date	Scoring			
	..., ... selige Gottessohn, chorale (E. Kreuziger)	Trinity XVIII; 8 Oct 1724	S, A, T, B, 4vv, hn, trbn, rec [4th fl], fl, 2 ob, vn piccolo, str, bc	xxii, 157	[I/xxiv]	130
97	In allen meinen Taten, chorale (P. Fleming)	1734	S, A, T, B, 4vv, 2 ob, str, bc	xxii, 187	[I/xxxiv]	97, 131
98	Was Gott tut, das ist wohlgetan	Trinity XXI; 10 Nov 1726	S, A, T, B, 4vv, ob, ob d'amore, taille, str, bc	xxii, 233	[I/xxv]	130
99	Was Gott tut, das ist wohlgetan, chorale (P. Rodigast)	Trinity XV; 17 Sept 1724	S, A, T, B, 4vv, hn, fl, ob d'amore, str, bc	xxii, 253	[I/xxii]	130
100	Was Gott tut, das ist wohlgetan, chorale (Rodigast)	after 1732, by c1735	S, A, T, B, 4vv, 2 hn, timp, fl, ob d'amore, str, bc	xxii, 279	[I/xxii]	97, 131
101	Nimm von uns, Herr, du treuer Gott, chorale (Möller)	Trinity X; 13 Aug 1724	S, A, T, B, 4vv, cornett, 3 trbn, fl, 2 ob, ob da caccia, str, bc	xxiii, 3	[I/xix]	130
102	Herr, deine Augen sehen nach dem Glauben	Trinity X; 25 Aug 1726	A, T, B, 4vv, fl, 2 ob, str, bc	xxiii, 35	[I/xix]	131, 139
103	Ihr werdet weinen und heulen (Ziegler)	Easter III; 22 April 1725	A, T, 4vv, tpt, rec [4th fl], 2 ob d'amore, str, bc	xxiii, 69	[I/xi]	130
104	Du Hirte Israel, höre	Easter II; 23 April 1724	T, B, 4vv, 2 ob, ob da caccia, 2 ob d'amore, str, bc	xxiii, 97	[I/xi]	129
105	Herr, gehe nicht ins Gericht	Trinity IX; 25 July 1723	S, A, T, B, 4vv, hn, 2 ob, str, bc	xxiii, 119	[I/xix]	129
106	Gottes Zeit ist die allerbeste Zeit (Actus tragicus)	funeral; probably by 1708	S, A, T, B, 4vv, 2 rec, 2 va da gamba, bc	xxiii, 149	[I/xxxiv]	57, 124, 125
107	Was willst du dich betrüben, chorale (Heermann)	Trinity VII; 23 July 1724	S, T, B, 4vv, hn, 2 fl, 2 ob d'amore, str, bc	xxiii, 181	I/xviii, 57	130
108	Es ist euch gut, dass ich hingehe (Ziegler)	Easter IV; 29 April 1725	A, T, B, 4vv, 2 ob d'amore, str, bc	xxiii, 205	I/xii, 19	130
109	Ich glaube, lieber Herr, hilf meinem Unglauben!	Trinity XXI; 17 Oct 1723	A, T, 4vv, hn, 2 ob, str, bc	xxiii, 233	[I/xxv]	129
110	Unser Mund sei voll Lachens [cf 1069] (Lehms)	Christmas; 25 Dec 1725	S, A, T, B, 4vv, 3 tpt, timp, 2 fl, 3 ob, ob d'amore, ob da caccia, str, bc incl. bn	xxiii, 265	I/ii, 73	131, 158
111	Was mein Gott will, das g'scheh allzeit, chorale (A. von Brandenburg)	Epiphany III; 21 Jan 1725	S, A, T, B, 4vv, 2 ob, str, bc	xxiv, 3	[I/vi]	130
112	Der Herr ist mein getreuer Hirt, chorale (W. Meuslin)	Easter II; 8 April 1731	S, A, T, B, 4vv, 2 hn, 2 ob d'amore, str, bc	xxiv, 31	[I/xi]	131
113	Herr Jesu Christ, du höchstes Gut, chorale (B. Ringwaldt)	Trinity XI; 20 Aug 1724	S, A, T, B, 4vv, fl, 2 ob d'amore, str, bc	xxiv, 51	[I/xx]	130
114	Ach, lieben Christen, seid getrost, chorale (J. Gigas)	Trinity XVII; 1 Oct 1724	S, A, T, B, 4vv, hn, fl, 2 ob, str, bc	xxiv, 83	I/xxiii, 289	130
115	Mache dich, mein Geist, bereit, chorale (J. B. Freystein)	Trinity XXII; 5 Nov 1724	S, A, T, B, 4vv, hn, fl, ob d'amore, vc piccolo, str, bc	xxiv, 111	[I/xxvi]	130
116	Du Friedefürst, Herr Jesu Christ, chorale (J. Ebert)	Trinity XXV; 26 Nov 1724	S, A, T, B, 4vv, hn, 2 ob d'amore, str, bc	xxiv, 135	[I/xxvii, 81]	130

BWV	Title (text/librettist)	Occasion: 1st perf.	Scoring	BG	NBA	
117	Sei Lob und Ehr dem höchsten Gut, chorale (J. J. Schütz)	c1728-31	A, T, B, 4vv, 2 fl, 2 ob d'amore, str, bc	xxiv, 161	[I/xxxiv]	97, 131
119	Preise, Jerusalem, den Herrn	inauguration of town council; 30 Aug 1723	S, A, T, B, 4vv, 4 tpt, timp, 2 rec, 3 ob, 2 ob da caccia, str, bc	xxiv, 195	[I/xxxii]	86, 129
120	Gott, man lobet dich in der Stille (Picander)	inauguration of town council; ? 29 Aug 1729	S, A, T, B, 4vv, 3 tpt, timp, 2 ob d'amore, str, bc	xxiv, 249	[I/xxxii]	72, 139
120a	Herr Gott, Beherrscher aller Dinge [adapted from 120, partly lost]	wedding; ?1729	S, A, T, B, 4vv, 3 tpt, timp, 2 ob, 2 ob d'amore, org obbl, str, bc	xii, 149	I/xxxiii, 77	131
120b	Gott, man lobet dich in der Stille (Picander) [adapted from 120, music lost]	2nd day of 200th anniversary of Augsburg Confession, 26 June 1730	—	—	—	97
121	Christum wir sollen loben schon, chorale (Luther)	2nd day of Christmas; 26 Dec 1724	S, A, T, B, 4vv, cornett, 3 trbn, ob d'amore, str, bc	xxvi, 3	[I/iii]	130
122	Das neugeborne Kindelein, chorale (C. Schneegass)	Christmas I; 31 Dec 1724	S, A, T, B, 4vv, 3 rec, 2 ob, taille, str, bc	xxvi, 23	[I/iii]	130
123	Liebster Immanuel, Herzog der Frommen, chorale (A. Fritsch)	Epiphany; 6 Jan 1725	A, T, B, 4vv, 2 fl, 2 ob d'amore, str, bc	xxvi, 43	I/v, 49	130
124	Meinen Jesum lass ich nicht, chorale (C. Keymann)	Epiphany I; 7 Jan 1725	S, A, T, B, 4vv, tpt da tirarsi, ob d'amore, str, bc	xxvi, 63	I/v, 117	130
125	Mit Fried und Freud ich fahr dahin, chorale (Luther)	Purification; 2 Feb 1725	A, T, B, 4vv, hn, fl, ob, ob d'amore, str, bc	xxvi, 85	[I/xxviii]	130
126	Erhalt uns, Herr, bei dienem Wort, chorale (Luther)	Sexagesima; 4 Feb 1725	A, T, B, 4vv, tpt, 2 ob, str, bc	xxvi, 113	I/vii, 157	130
127	Herr Jesu Christ, wahr' Mensch und Gott, chorale (P. Eber)	Quinquagesima; 11 Feb 1725	S, T, B, 4vv, tpt, 2 rec, 2 ob, str, bc	xxvi, 135	[I/viii]	130
128	Auf Christi Himmelfahrt allein (Ziegler)	Ascension; 10 May 1725	A, T, B, 4vv, tpt, 2 hn, 2 ob d'amore, taille, str, bc	xxvi, 163	I/xii, 103	130
129	Gelobet sei der Herr, mein Gott, chorale (J. Olearius)	Trinity or Reformation; 16 June or 31 Oct 1726	S, A, B, 4vv, 3 tpt, timp, fl, 2 ob, ob d'amore, str, bc	xxvi, 187	I/xv, 39	
130	Herr Gott, dich loben alle wir, chorale (Eber)	St Michael; 29 Sept 1724	S, A, T, B, 4vv, 3 tpt, timp, fl, 3 ob, str, bc	xxvi, 233	I/xxx, 3	130
131	Aus der Tiefen rufe ich, Herr, zu dir	1707	S, A, T, B, 4vv, ob, bn, vn, 2 va, bc incl. bn	xxviii, 3	[I/xxxiv]	57, 124
132	Bereitet die Wege, bereitet die Bahn! (Franck)	Advent IV; 22 Dec 1715	S, A, T, B, 4vv, ob, str, bc	xxviii, 35	I/i, 101	126
133	Ich freue mich in dir, chorale (K. Ziegler)	3rd day of Christmas; 27 Dec 1724	S, A, T, B, 4vv, cornett, 2 ob d'amore, str, bc	xxviii, 53	[I/iii]	130
134	Ein Herz, das seinen Jesum lebend weiss [adapted from 134a]	Easter Tuesday; 11 April 1724	A, T, 4vv, 2 ob, str, bc	xxviii, 83, 287	I/x, 71	130

No.	Title	Occasion; date	Scoring	BG	NBA	Bibl.
135	Ach Herr, mich armen Sünder, chorale (Schneegass)	Trinity III; 25 June 1724	A, T, B, 4vv, cornett, trbn, 2 ob, str, bc	xxviii, 121	I/xvi, 199	130
136	Erforsche mich, Gott, und erfahre mein Herz	Trinity VIII; 18 July 1723	A, T, B, 4vv, hn, 2 ob d'amore, str, bc	xxviii, 139	I/xviii, 131	129, 139
137	Lobe den Herren, den mächtigen König der Ehren, chorale (J. Neander)	Trinity XII; 19 Aug 1725	S, A, T, B, 4vv, 3 tpt, timp, 2 ob, str, bc	xxviii, 167	[I/xx]	131
138	Warum betrübst du dich, mein Herz?, chorale (anon.)	Trinity XV; 5 Sept 1723	S, A, T, B, 4vv, 2 ob d'amore, str, bc	xxviii, 199	[I/xxii]	87, 129, 139
139	Wohl dem, der sich auf seinen Gott, chorale (J. C. Rüben)	Trinity XXIII; 12 Nov 1724	S, A, T, B, 4vv, 2 ob d'amore, str, bc	xxviii, 225	[I/xxvi]	130
140	Wachet auf, ruft uns die Stimme, chorale (Nicolai)	Trinity XXVII; 25 Nov 1731	S, T, B, 4vv, hn, 2 ob, taille, vn piccolo, str, bc	xxviii, 251	I/xxvii, 151	97
144	Nimm, was dein ist, und gehe hin	Septuagesima; 6 Feb 1724	S, A, T, 4vv, 2 ob, ob d'amore, str, bc	xxx, 77	I/vii, 3	129
145	Ich lebe, mein Herze, zu deinem Ergötzen (Picander)	Easter Tuesday; ?1729	S, T, B, 4vv, tpt, fl, 2 ob d'amore, str, bc	xxx, 95	I/x, 113	91
146	Wir müssen durch viel Trübsal [partly adapted from lost vn conc.; cf 1052]	Easter III; ? 18 April 1728	S, A, T, B, 4vv, fl, 2 ob, 2 ob d'amore, taille, org obbl, str, bc	xxx, 125	[I/xi]	131
147	Herz und Mund und Tat und Leben (partly Franck) [adapted from 147a]	Visitation; 2 July 1723	S, A, T, B, 4vv, tpt, 2 ob, ob d'amore, 2 ob da caccia, str, bc incl. bn	xxx, 193	[I/xxviii]	
147a	Herz und Mund und Tat und Leben (Franck) [composed 1716, probably not perf. in this version, lost]	Advent IV	—	—	I/i, CC	67, 126
148	Bringet dem Herrn Ehre seines Namens (after Picander)	Trinity XVII; ? 19 Sept 1723	A, T, 4vv, tpt, ob, ob d'amore, ob da caccia, str, bc	xxx, 237	I/xxiii, 255	129
149	Man singet mit Freuden vom Sieg (Picander)	St Michael; ? 29 Sept 1728 or ? 1729	S, A, T, B, 4vv, 3 tpt, timp, 3 ob, bn, str, bc	xxx, 263	I/xxx, 99	91
150	Nach dir, Herr, verlanget mich [? inc.]	c1708–9	S, A, T, B, 4vv, bn, 2 vn, bc	xxx, 303	[I/xlij]	64, 124
151	Süsser Trost, mein Jesus kömmt (Lehms)	3rd day of Christmas; 27 Dec 1725	S, A, T, B, 4vv, fl, str, bc [ob d'amore added c1727]	xxxii, 3	[I/iii]	131
152	Tritt auf die Glaubensbahn (Franck)	Christmas I; 30 Dec 1714	S, B, rec, ob, va d'amore, va da gamba, bc	xxxii, 19	[I/iii]	126
153	Schau, lieber Gott, wie meine Feind	New Year I; 2 Jan 1724	A, T, B, 4vv, str, bc	xxxii, 43	I/iv, 201	129
154	Mein liebster Jesus ist verloren	Epiphany I; 9 Jan 1724	A, T, B, 4vv, 2 ob d'amore, str, bc	xxxii, 61	I/v, 91	129
155	Mein Gott, wie lang, ach lange (Franck)	Epiphany II; 19 Jan 1716	S, A, T, B, 4vv, bn, str, bc	xxxii, 85	I/v, 175	126
156	Ich steh mit einem Fuss im Grabe (Picander) [sinfonia adapted from lost ob conc.; cf 1056]	Epiphany III; ? 23 Jan 1729	A, T, B, 4vv, ob, str, bc	xxxii, 99	I/vi	91, 131
157	Ich lasse dich nicht, du segnest mich denn (Picander)	Purification; ? 2 Feb 1728 or later	T, B, 4vv, fl, ob d'amore, str, bc	xxxii, 117	[I/xxxiv]	
158	Der Friede sei mit dir (? partly Franck) [inc.]	Easter Tuesday, Purification; after 1723	B, 4vv, ob, vn, bc	xxxii, 143	I/x, 131	

BWV	Title (text/librettist)	Occasion; 1st perf.	Scoring	BG	NBA	
159	Sehet, wir gehn hinauf gen Jerusalem (Picander)	Estomihi; ? 27 Feb 1729	A, T, B, 4vv, ob, str, bc incl. bn	xxxii, 157	[I/viii]	91, 131
161	Komm, du süsse Todesstunde (Franck)	Trinity XVI; 6 Oct 1715	A, T, 4vv, 2 rec, org obbl, str, bc	xxxiii, 3	I/xxiii, 35	126
162	Ach! ich sehe, jetzt, da ich zur Hochzeit gehe (Franck)	Trinity XX; 3 Nov 1715	S, A, T, B, 4vv, tpt da tirarsi, str, bc incl. bn	xxxiii, 31	[I/xxv]	126
163	Nur jedem das Seine (Franck)	Trinity XXIII; 24 Nov 1715	S, A, T, B, 4vv, str, bc	xxxiii, 49	[I/xxvi]	126
164	Ihr, die ihr euch von Christo nennet (Franck)	Trinity XIII; 26 Aug 1725	S, A, T, B, 4vv, 2 fl, 2 ob, str, bc	xxxiii, 67	I/xxi, 59	126
165	O heiliges Geist- und Wasserbad (Franck)	Trinity; 16 June 1715	S, A, T, B, 4vv, str, bc incl. bn	xxxiii, 91	I/xv, 3	126
166	Wo gehest du hin?	Easter IV; 7 May 1724	A, T, B, 4vv, ob, str, bc	xxxiii, 107	I/xii, 3	129
167	Ihr Menschen, rühmet Gottes Liebe	St John; 24 June 1723	S, A, T, B, 4vv, tpt da tirarsi, ob, ob da caccia, str, bc	xxxiii, 125	I/xxix, 3	129
168	Tue Rechnung! Donnerwort (Franck)	Trinity IX; 29 July 1725	S, A, T, B, 4vv, 2 ob d'amore, str, bc	xxxiii, 149	[I/xix]	131, 157
169	Gott soll allein mein Herze haben [partly adapted from lost conc.; cf 1053]	Trinity XVIII; 20 Oct 1726	A, 4vv, 2 ob d'amore, taille, org obbl, str, bc	xxxiii, 169	[I/xxiv]	131, 157
170	Vergnügte Ruh', beliebte Seelenlust (Lehms)	Trinity VI; 28 July 1726	A, ob d'amore, org obbl, str, bc	xxxiii, 195	[I/xvii]	131
171	Gott, wie dein Name, so ist auch dein Ruhm (Picander)	New Year; 1 Jan ?1729	S, A, T, B, 4vv, 3 tpt, timp, 2 ob, str, bc	xxxv, 3	I/iv, 133	91, 139
172	Erschallet, ihr Lieder (?Franck)	Whit Sunday; 20 May 1714	S, A, T, B, 4vv, 3 tpt, timp, ob, str, bc incl. bn	xxxv, 37	I/xiii, 3	126
173	Erhöhtes Fleisch und Blut [adapted from 173a]	Whit Monday; ? 29 May 1724	S, A, T, B, 4vv, 2 fl, str, bc	xxxv, 73	I/xiv, 3	*128*
174	Ich liebe den Höchsten von ganzem Gemüte (Picander)	Whit Monday; 6 June 1729	A, T, B, 4vv, 2 hn, 2 ob, taille, str, bc	xxxv, 105	I/xiv, 65	91, 93, 131
175	Er rufet seinen Schafen mit Namen (M. von Ziegler)	Whit Tuesday; 22 May 1725	A, T, B, 4vv, 2 tpt, 3 rec, vc piccolo, str, bc	xxxv, 161	I/xiv, 149	130
176	Es is ein trotzig, und verzagt Ding (M. von Ziegler)	Trinity; 27 May 1725	S, A, B, 4vv, 2 ob, ob da caccia, str, bc	xxxv, 181	I/xv, 19	130
177	Ich ruf zu dir, Herr Jesu Christ, chorale (J. Agricola)	Trinity IV; 6 July 1732	S, A, T, 4vv, 2 ob, taille, bn, str, bc	xxxv, 201	[I/xvii]	97, 131
178	Wo Gott der Herr nicht bei uns hält, chorale (J. Jonas)	Trinity VIII; 30 July 1724	A, T, B, 4vv, hn, 2 ob, 2 ob d'amore, str, bc	xxxv, 237	I/xviii, 161	130
179	Siehe zu, dass deine Gottesfurcht	Trinity XI; 8 Aug 1723	S, T, B, 4vv, 2 ob, 2 ob da caccia, str, bc	xxxv, 275	[I/xx]	129, 139
180	Schmücke dich, o liebe Seele, chorale (J. Franck)	Trinity XX; 22 Oct 1724	S, A, T, B, 4vv, 2 rec, fl, ob, ob da caccia, vc piccolo, str, bc	xxxv, 295	[I/xxv]	130

181	Leichgesinnte Flattergeister [? incl. earlier material]	Sexagesima; 13 Feb 1724	S, A, T, B, 4vv, tpt, str, bc [fl, ob added later]	xxxvii, 3	I/vii, 135	129
182	Himmelskönig, sei willkommen (?Franck)	Palm Sunday; 25 March 1714	A, T, B, 4vv, rec, str, bc	xxxvii, 23	[I/viii]	65, 126
183	Sie werden euch in den Bann tun (Ziegler)	Ascension I; 13 May 1725	S, A, T, B, 4vv, 2 ob d'amore, 2 ob da caccia, vc piccolo, str, bc	xxxvii, 61	I/xii, 189	130
184	Erwünschtes Freudenlicht [adapted from 184a]	Whit Tuesday; 30 May 1724	S, A, T, 4vv, 2 fl, str, bc	xxxvii, 77	I/xiv, 121	72
185	Barmherziges Herze der ewigen Liebe (Franck)	Trinity IV; 14 July 1715	S, A, T, B, 4vv, ob, str, bc incl. bn [later version with tpt da tirarsi instead of ob]	xxxvii, 103	[I/xvii]	126
186	Ärgre dich, o Seele, nicht (partly Franck) [adapted from 186a]	Trinity VII; 11 July 1723	S, A, T, B, 4vv, 2 ob, taille, str, bc	xxxvii, 121	I/xviii, 17	
186a	Ärgre dich, o Seele, nicht (Franck) [composed 1716, probably not perf. in this version, lost]	Advent III	—	—	I/i, CC	67, 126
187	Es wartet alles auf dich	Trinity VII; 4 Aug 1726	S, A, B, 4vv, 2 ob, str, bc	xxxvii, 157	I/xviii, 93	131, 139
188	Ich habe meine Zuversicht (Picander) [sinfonia adapted from lost vn conc.; cf 1052]	Trinity XXI; Oct ?1728	S, A, T, B, 4vv, 2 ob, taille, org obbl, str, bc incl. bn	xxxvii, 195	[I/xxv]	91, 131
190	Singet dem Herrn ein neues Lied! [partly lost]	New Year; 1 Jan 1724	A, T, B, 4vv, 3 tpt, timp, 3 ob, ob d'amore, bn, str, bc	xxxvii, 229	I/iv, 3	129
190a	Singet dem Herrn ein neues Lied! [adapted from 190, lost]	200th anniversary of Augsburg Confession, 1730	—	—	—	97
191	Gloria in excelsis Deo [adapted from Mass 232]	Christmas; after 1740	S, T, 5vv, 3 tpt, timp, 2 fl, 2 ob, str, bc	xli, 3	I/ii, 173	139
192	Nun danket alle Gott, chorale	1730	S, B, 4vv, 2 fl, 2 ob, str, bc	xli, 67	[I/xxxiv]	97, 131
193	Ihr Tore zu Zion [partly lost]	inauguration of town council; 25 Aug 1727	S, A, 4vv, 2 ob, str, bc	xli, 93	[I/xxxii]	
194	Höchsterwünschtes Freudenfest [adapted from 194a]	consecration of Störmthal church and org; 2 Nov 1723	S, T, B, 4vv, 3 ob, str, bc incl. bn	xxix, 101	I/xv, CC	72, 87, 129
195	Dem Gerechten muss das Licht	wedding; after 1737	S, B, 4vv, 3 tpt, timp, 2 fm, 2 fl, 2 ob, 2 ob d'amore, str, bc	xiii/1, 3	I/xxxiii, 17	97, 107
196	Der Herr denket an uns (Ps cxv)	wedding; ?1708	S, T, B, 4vv, str, bc	xiii/1, 73	I/xxxiii, 3	58, 124
197	Gott ist unsre Zuversicht [partly based on 197a]	wedding; 1739-42	S, A, B, 4vv, 3 tpt, timp, 2 ob, 2 ob d'amore, str, bc incl. bn	xiii/1, 97	I/xxxiii, 119	97, 107
197a	Ehre sei Gott in der Höhe (Picander) [partly lost]	Christmas; c1728	A, B, 4vv, 2 fl, ob d'amore, vc/bn, str, bc	xli, 109	I/ii, 65	91
199	Mein Herze schwimmt im Blut (Lehms)	Trinity XI; 12 Aug 1714	S, ob, str, bc	—	[I/xx]	126
200	Bekennen will ich seinen Namen [frag. of lost cantata]	Purification; ?c1742	A, 2 vn, bc incl. bn	—	[I/xxviii]	97, 107

Lost or incomplete

BWV; N	Title (librettist)	Occasion; 1st perf.	Remarks	BG	NBA, CC	
223; xix	Meine Seele soll Gott loben	—	only incipit extant	—	I/iv, CC; [I/xxxiv, CC]	58
244a	Klagt, Kinder, klagt es aller Welt (Picander)	funeral of Prince Leopold of Anhalt-Cöthen; 24 March 1729	music lost, text partly same as St Matthew Passion (244), and Trauer Ode (198)	—	[I/xxxiv, CC]	137
A1; xvii	Gesegnet ist die Zuversicht (?Neumeister)	Trinity VII	cited in Breitkopf catalogue, 1770; lost	—	I/xviii, CC	
A2; xxix	[untexted frag.]	Trinity XIX; 1729	6-bar frag. in autograph of 226	—	—	
A3; xi	Gott, gib dein Gerichte dem Könige (Picander)	change of town council; 28 Aug 1730	only text extant	—	[I/xxxii, CC]	
A4; xvia	Wünschet Jerusalem Glück (Picander)	change of town council; 26 Aug 1726 or 30 Aug 1727	only text extant	—	[I/xxxii, CC]	
A4a; xvib	Wünschet Jerusalem Glück (Picander)	3rd day of 200th anniversary of Augsburg Confession, 27 June 1730	only text extant	—	[I/xxiv, CC]	97
A5; xiii	Lobet den Herrn, alle seine Heerscharen (C. F. Hunold)	birthday of Prince Leopold of Anhalt-Cöthen; 10 Dec 1718	only text extant	—	I/xxxv, CC	71, 127
A14; xiv	Sein Segen fliesst daher wie ein Strom	wedding; 12 Feb 1725	only text extant	—	I/xxxiii, CC	
A15; xxi	Siehe, der Hüter Israel	degree ceremony, Leipzig; 1723–49	cited in Breitkopf catalogue, 1761; lost	—	[I/xxxiv, CC]	
A17; xx	Mein Gott, nimm die gerechte Seele	funeral	cited in Breitkopf catalogue, 1761; lost	—	[I/xxxiv, CC]	
—; v	Herrscher des Himmels, König der Ehren	change of town council; 29 Aug 1740	last chorus adapted from 208, otherwise lost	—	[I/xxxii, CC]	
—; vi	Ich bin ein Pilgrim auf der Welt (Picander)	Easter Monday; ? 18 April 1729	only frag. of 4th movt extant	—	I/xxxiii, CC	
—	Ihr wallenden Wolken	New Year	cited in Forkel: *Nachlassverzeichnis*, 1819; lost	—	I/iv, CC	
—	Leb ich oder leb ich nicht (Franck)	Easter IV; 19 May 1715 ? Ascension I	music lost	—	—	
—;	Sie werden euch in den Bann tun		6-bar sketch in autograph score of 79	—	—	
xxxiii	[title unknown]	change of Mühlhausen town council; 1709	lost	—	[I/xxxii, CC]	
xxiv xxviii	[title unknown]	Trinity VI	autograph title: 'Concerto à 4 Voci e 4 stromenti'; in MS of music by			

—; XXXI	[title unknown]	St Michael	14-bar sketch for opening of cantata autograph score of 201	—	—	
—; XXXII	[title unknown]	Easter I	7-bar sketch in autograph score of 103	—	—	
1045; XXX	[title unknown]	c1742	autograph frag.: 'Concerto à 4 voci'	—	—	

Doubtful and spurious

BWV	Title	Occasion	Notes	BG	NBA	
15	Denn du wirst meine Seele	Easter	by J. L. Bach	ii, 135	I/xxxix, 53	42, 118
53	Schlage doch, gewünschte Stunde (?Franck)	funeral	by M. Hoffmann	xii/2, 53	—	118
141	Das ist je gewisslich wahr (Helbig)	Advent III	by G. P. Telemann	xxx, 3	—	118
142	Uns ist ein Kind geboren (Neumeister)	Christmas	? by J. Kuhnau	xxx, 19	—	65
143	Lobe den Herrn, meine Seele	New Year	probably spurious	xxx, 45	I/iv, 167	
160	Ich weiss, dass mein Erlöser lebt (Neumeister)	Easter	by Telemann	xxxii, 171	—	
189	Meine Seele rühmt und preist	?Visitation	probably by M. Hoffmann	xxxvii, 215	—	118
217	Gedenke, Herr, wie uns gehet	Epiphany I	spurious	xli, 207	—	
218	Gott der Hoffnung erfülle euch (Neumeister)	Whit Sunday	by Telemann	xli, 223	—	
219	Siehe, es hat überwunden der Löwe	St Michael	by Telemann	xli, 239	—	
220	Lobt ihn mit Herz und Munde	St John	spurious	xli, 259	—	
221	Wer sucht die Pracht, wer wünscht den Glanz		spurious	—	—	
222	Mein Odem ist schwach		by (10) J. E. Bach	—	—	
A16	Schliesset die Gruft! ihr Trauerglocken (B. Hoffmann)	funeral; 9 Nov 1735	lost, doubtful	—	—	
—	Siehe, eine Jungfrau ist schwanger	Annunciation; 25 March 1724	only text extant, 1724; probably by J. S. Bach	—	—	

SECULAR CANTATAS

BWV	Title (librettist)	Occasion; date	Scoring	BG	NBA	
30a	Angenehmes Wiederau, freue dich (Picander)	for J. C. von Hennicke; 28 Sept 1737	S, A, T, B, 4vv, 3 tpt, timp, 2 fl, 2 ob, ob d'amore, str, bc	v/1, 399; xxxiv, 325	I/xxxix, 53	102, 133
36a	Steigt freudig in die Luft (Picander) [music lost, arr. from 36c]	birthday of wife of Prince Leopold of Anhalt-Cöthen; 30 Nov 1726 or ?1725	—	—	I/i, CC; I/xxxv, CC	71, 133
36b	Die Freude reget sich (?Picander)	for member of Rivinus family; ?1735	S, A, T, 4vv, fl, ob d'amore, str, bc	xxxiv, 41	I/xxxviii, 257	133

BWV	Title (librettist)	Occasion; date	Scoring	BG	NBA	
36c	Schwingt freudig euch empor (?Picander)	birthday; 1725	S, T, B, 4vv, ob d'amore, va d'amore, str, bc	xxxiv, 41	I/xxxii, 3	71, 89, 133
66a	Der Himmel dacht auf Anhalts Ruhm und Glück (C. F. Hunold), serenata [music lost]	birthday of Prince Leopold of Anhalt-Cöthen; 10 Dec 1718	—	—	I/xxxv, CC	71
134a	Die Zeit, die Tag und Jahre macht (Hunold)	New Year; 1 Jan 1719	A, T, 4vv, 2 ob, str, bc	xxix, 209	I/xxxv, 51	71
173a	Durchlauchtster Leopold, serenata	birthday of Prince Leopold of Anhalt-Cöthen; ?c1722	S, B, 2 fl, bn, str, bc	xxxiv, 3	I/xxxv, 97	71, 128
184a	[some music preserved in 184, text lost, ? = x8]	?New Year; ?1722-3	—	—	I/xiv, CC; I/xxxv, CC	
193a	Ihr Häuser des Himmels, ihr scheinenden Lichter (Picander), dramma per musica [music lost]	name day of August II; 3 Aug 1727	—	—	I/xxxvi, CC	
194a	[some music preserved in 194, text lost]	for court of Anhalt-Cöthen; before 1723	—	—	I/xxxv, CC	
198	Trauer Ode: Lass, Fürstin, lass noch einen Strahl (J. C. Gottsched)	memorial service for Electress Christiane Eberhardine; 17 Oct 1727	S, A, T, B, 4vv, 2 fl, 2 ob d'amore, 2 va da gamba, 2 lutes, str, bc	xiii/3, 3	I/xxxviii, 181	91, 133, 134, 137
201	Der Streit zwischen Phoebus und Pan: Geschwinde, ihr wirbeln den Winde (Picander), dramma per musica	?1729	S, A, T, T, B, B, 6vv, 3 tpt, timp, 2 fl, 2 ob, ob d'amore, str, bc	xi/2, 3	I/xl, 119	110
202	Weichet nur, betrübte Schatten	wedding; ?1718-23	S, ob, str, bc	xi/2, 75	I/xl, 3	133
203	Amore traditore [not fully authenticated]	—	B, hpd obbl	xi/2, 93	[I/xli]	133
204	Ich bin in mir vergnügt (Hunold)	1726-7	S, fl, 2 ob, str, bc	xi/2, 105	I/xl, 81	133
205	Der zufriedengestellte Äolus: Zerreisset, zerspringet, zertrümmert die Gruft (Picander), dramma per musica	name day of Dr A. F. Müller; 3 Aug 1725	S, A, T, B, 4vv, 3 tpt, timp, 2 fl, 2 ob, ob d'amore, va d'amore, va da gamba, str, bc	xi/2, 139	I/xxxviii, 3	89, 133
205a	Blast Lärmen, ihr Feinde! [adapted from 205; music lost]	coronation of August III; 19 Feb 1734	—	—	I/xxxvii, CC	99
206	Schleicht, spielende Wellen, dramma per musica	birthday and name day of August III; ? 7 Oct 1736	S, A, T, B, 4vv, 3 tpt, timp, 3 fl, 2 ob, 2 ob d'amore, str, bc	xx/2, 3	I/xxxvi, 159	102, 133
207	Vereinigte Zwietracht der wechselnden Saiten, dramma per musica	installation of Professor Gottlieb Kortte; c11 Dec 1726	S, A, T, B, 4vv, 3 tpt, timp, 2 fl, 2 ob d'amore, ob da caccia, str, bc	xx/2, 73	I/xxxviii, 99	90, 133
207a	Auf, schmetternde Töne, dramma per musica	name day of August III; ? 3 Aug 1735	S, A, T, B, 4vv, 3 tpt, timp, 2 fl, 2 ob d'amore, ob da caccia, str, bc	xx/2, 141; xxxiv, 345	I/xxxvii, 3	133

BWV, N	Title (librettist)	Occasion; 1st perf.	Remarks	BG	NBA	
208	Was mir behagt, ist nur die muntre Jagd! (Franck)	birthday of Duke Christian of Saxe-Weissenfels; 1713	S, S, T, B, 2 hn, 2 rec, 2 ob, ob da caccia, bn, str, bc	xxix, 3	I/xxxix, 3	63, 64, 66, 125, 156
208a	Was mir behagt, ist nur die muntre Jagd! [after Franck] [music lost]	name day of August III; 1740-42		—	I/xxxvii, CC	
209	Non sa che sia dolore	departure of scholar (?J. M. Gesner); ?1734	S, fl, str, bc	xxix, 45	[I/xlii]	133
210	O holder Tag, erwünschte Zeit	wedding; ? 3 April 1742	S, fl, ob d'amore, str, bc	xxix, 69	I/xl, 37	133
210a	O angenehme Melodei [music lost, mostly =210]	for Joachim Friedrich, Graf von Flemming; 11 Oct 1740	S, fl, ob d'amore, str, bc	xxix, 245	I/xxxix, 143	133
211	Schweigt stille, plaudert nicht (Coffee Cantata) (Picander)	c1734-5	S, T, B, fl, str, bc	xxix, 141	I/xl, 195	124, 133
212	Mer hahn en neue Oberkeet (Peasant Cantata) (Picander)	manorial accession celebration for C. H. von Dieskau; 30 Aug 1742	S, B, hn, fl, str, bc	xxix, 175	I/xxxix, 153	106, 121, 124, 133
213	Hercules auf dem Scheidewege: Lasst uns sorgen, lasst uns wachen (Picander), dramma per musica	birthday of Prince Friedrich Christian; 5 Sept 1733	S, A, T, B, 4vv, 2 hn, 2 ob, ob d'amore, str, bc	xxxiv, 121	I/xxxvi, 3	99, 100, 133, 134
214	Tönet, ihr Pauken! Erschallet, Trompeten!, dramma per musica	birthday of Electress Maria Josepha; 8 Dec 1733	S, A, T, B, 4vv, 3 tpt, timp, 2 fl, 2 ob, ob d'amore, str, bc	xxxiv, 177	I/xxxvi, 91	99, 100, 133, 134
215	Preise dein Glücke, gesegnetes Sachsen (J. C. Clauder), dramma per musica	anniversary of election of August III as King of Poland; 5 Oct 1734	S, T, B, 8vv, 3 tpt, timp, 2 fl, 2 ob, 2 ob d'amore, str, bc incl. bn	xxxiv, 245	I/xxxvii, 87	99, 100, 133, 134
216	Vergnügte Pleissenstadt (Picander) [only vv extant]	wedding; 5 Feb 1728	S, A, fl, str, bc	—	I/xl, 23	133
216a	Erwählte Pleissenstadt [music lost]	for Leipzig city council; after 1728		—	I/xxxix, CC	
249a	Entfliehet, verschwindet, entweichet, ihr Sorgen (Picander) [music lost, but most in 249]	birthday of Duke Christian of Saxe-Weissenfels; 23 Feb 1725	S, A, T, B, 3 tpt, timp, 2 rec, fl, 2 ob, ob d'amore, str, bc	—	I/xxxv, CC	88, 89, 133, 134
249b	Die Feier des Genius: Verjaget, zerstreuet, zerrüttet, ihr Sterne (Picander), dramma per musica [music lost]	birthday of Joachim Friedrich, Graf von Flemming; 25 Aug 1726		—	I/xxxix, CC	133

Lost

BWV, N	Title (librettist)	Occasion; 1st perf.	Remarks	BG	NBA	
A6; ix	Dich loben die lieblichen Strahlen (Hunold)	New Year; 1 Jan 1720	only text extant	—	I/xxxv	71

BWV: N	Title (librettist)	Occasion; 1st perf.	Remarks	BG	NBA	
A7; XII	Heut ist gewiss ein guter Tag (Hunold)	birthday of Prince Leopold of Anhalt-Cöthen; ? 10 Dec 1720	only text extant	—	I/xxxv	71
A8	[title unknown]	New Year; 1 Jan 1723	lost; ? = 184a	—	I/xxxv	71
A9; X	Entfernet euch, ihr heitern Sterne (C. F. Haupt)	birthday visit of August III; 12 May 1727	only text extant	—	I/xxxvi	
A10; VII	So kämpfet nur, ihr muntern Töne (Picander)	birthday of Joachim Friedrich, Graf von Flemming; 25 Aug 1731	only text extant	—	I/xxxix, CC	
A11; II	Es lebe der König, der Vater im Lande (Picander)	name day of August II; 3 Aug 1732	only text extant	—	I/xxxvi	140
A12; IV	Frohes Volk, vergnügte Sachsen (Picander) [adapted from A18]	name day of August III; 3 Aug 1733	only text extant	—	I/xxxvi	99
A13; XV	Willkommen! Ihr herrschenden Götter (Gottsched)	king's visit and marriage of Princess Maria Amalia; 28 April 1738	only text extant	—	I/xxxvii	102, 121, 133
A18; III	Froher Tag, verlangte Stunden (J. H. Winckler)	opening of Thomasschule after renovation; 5 June 1732	only text extant	—	I/xxxix, CC	98, 133, 134, 139
A19; VIII	Thomana sass annoch betrübt (J. A. Landvoigt)	in honour of new Rektor of Thomasschule J. A. Ernesti; 21 Nov 1734	only text extant	—	I/xxxix, CC	100, 133
A20	Latin ode [title unknown]	birthday of Duke Friedrich II of Saxe-Gotha; 9 Aug 1723	lost	—	I/xxxviii	86
—; 1	Auf! süss entzückende Gewalt (Gottsched)	wedding; 27 Nov 1725	only text extant	—	I/xl	

MASSES, MAGNIFICAT SETTINGS, ETC

BWV	Title	Remarks	Scoring	BG	NBA	
	[Mass in B minor]:	assembled c1747–9				137–40
232	Missa (Kyrie, Gloria)	ded. new Elector of Saxony, Friedrich August II, 1733; Gratias agimus from 29, 1731; Qui tollis from 46, 1723	2 S, A, T, B, 5vv, 3 tpt, timp, hn, 2 fl, 2 ob, 2 ob d'amore, 2 bn, str, bc	vi	II/i	97, 104, 107, 139, 170, 171, 172, 176, 177 98, 99, 121, 139, 140

				NBA	BG	
Symbolum Nicenum (Credo)		added to autograph score c1714–9; Patrem omnipotentem from 171, ?1729; Crucifixus from 12, 1714; Et exspecto from 120, 1728–9	S, A, B, 5vv, 3 tpt, timp, 2 fl, 2 ob, 2 ob d'amore, str, bc			107, 123, 139, 173
Sanctus		1st perf. Christmas Day 1724; added to autograph score c1747–9	6vv, 3 tpt, timp, 3 ob, str, bc			139, 140
Osanna, Benedictus, Agnus Dei et Dona nobis pacem		added to autograph score c1747–9; Osanna from a9, 1727, and A11, 1732; Agnus Dei from 11, 1735; Dona nobis pacem from 29, 1731 (cf Gratias agimus, above)	A, T, 8vv, 3 tpt, timp, 2 fl, 2 ob, str, bc			140
4 missae breves:		probably late 1730s; mostly adaptations of cantata movts				97
233	F	from 11, 40, 102, A18	S, A, B, 4vv, 2 hn, 2 ob, 2 bn, str, bc	II/ii, 199	viii, 3	139
233a	Kyrie, F	orig. Kyrie of 233	5vv, bc	II/ii, 287		137
234	A	from 67, 79, 136, 179	S, A, B, 4vv, 2 fl, str, bc	II/ii, 3	viii, 53	104, 139
235	g	from 72, 102, 187	A, T, B, 4vv, 2 ob, str, bc	II/ii, 129	viii, 101	139
236	G	from 17, 79, 138, 179	S, A, T, B, 4vv, 2 ob, str, bc	II/ii, 63	viii, 157	104, 139
	5 settings of Sanctus:	except 238, all probably arrs. of music by other composers				139
237	C	perf. 1723	4vv, 3 tpt, timp, 2 ob, str, bc	II/ii, 313	xi/1, 69	139
238	D	perf. ?Christmas Day 1723 or ?1724	4vv, cornett, str, bc	II/ii, 327	xi/1, 81	88, 139
239	d	perf. 1735–46	4vv, str, bc	[II/ix]	xi/1, 89	
240	G	perf. 1735–46	4vv, 2 ob, str, bc	[II/ix]	xi/1, 95	
241	D	arr. from piece by J. C. Kerll inserted in Mass, c, by ?J. L. Krebs	8vv, 2 ob d'amore, bn, 2 str, bc	[II/ix]	xli, 177	137, 139
242	Christe eleison	perf. c1740; inserted in Mass, F, by G. B. Bassani	S, A, bc	II/ii, 297	xli,197	137
1083	Credo		4vv, bc	II/ii, CC		
243a	Magnificat, Eb	perf. Christmas Day 1723; incl. 4 Christmas texts: Vom Himmel hoch; Freut euch und jubiliert; Gloria in excelsis; Virga Jesse floruit	2 S, A, T, B, 5vv, 3 tpt, timp, 2 rec, 2 ob, str, bc	II/iii, 3	—	88, 137, 171
243	Magnificat, D	rev. of above, c1728–31; without Christmas texts	2 S, A, T, B, 5vv, 3 tpt, timp, 2 fl, 2 ob, 2 ob d'amore, str, bc	II/iii, 67	xi/1, 3	137, 176
—	Suscepit Israel	after 1742, from Magnificat, C, by Caldara with addl 2 ?vn pts	4vv, 2 ?vn, bc	—		137, 164
PASSIONS, ORATORIOS						133–7
244b	Passio secundum Matthaeum (St Matthew Passion) (Picander)	perf. Good Friday, 11 April 1727 and/or Good Friday 1728/1729	scoring similar to 244, but with only 1 bc group	II/va (facs.)	—	86, 90, 92, 96, 119, 131, 134, 135, 136

BWV	Title	Remarks	Scoring	BG	NBA	
244	Passio secundum Matthaeum (S Matthew Passion) (Picander)	perf. Good Friday, 30 March 1736, incl. 2 org; also perf. late 1740s	S in ripieno; chorus I: S, A, T, B, 4vv, 2 rec, 2 fl, 2 ob, 2 ob d'amore, 2 ob da caccia, va da gamba, str, bc; chorus II: S, A, T, B, 4vv, 2 fl, 2 ob, 2 ob d'amore, va da gamba, str, bc [bc incl. bassono grosso, late 1740s]	iv, 1	II/v	101, 107, 170, 171, 176f
245	Passio secundum Joannem (St John Passion) (anon. compilation from B. H. Brockes and others)	perf. Good Friday, 7 April 1724; 30 March 1725 with 5 nos. replaced (see NBA II/iv, suppl. ii); c1730 and late 1740s with further revs.	S, A, T, B, 4vv, 2 fl, 2 ob, 2 ob d'amore, 2 ob da caccia, 2 va d'amore, va da gamba, lute/org/hpd, str, bc [bc incl. bassono grosso in late 1740s]	xii/1, 3	II/iv	88, 107, 134, 135, 136, 171
247	Passio secundum Marcum (St Mark Passion) (Picander)	perf. Good Friday, 23 March 1731; lost except for 1 movt rev. in 248 and 7 movts in orig. form in 198 and 54; see NBA II/v, CC, SBA	—	—	—	97, 134, 137, 143
248	Oratorium ... Die heilige Weynacht (Christmas Oratorio) (?Picander):	in 6 pts. for feastdays Christmas to Epiphany 1734–5; pts. of nos.1–5 adapted from secular cantatas 213–15, most of no.6 from lost church cantata 248a		v/2	II/vi	97, 133, 134, 137
	Jauchzet, frohlocket, auf preiset die Tage	perf. Christmas Day 1734	A, T, B, 4vv, 3 tpt, timp, 2 fl, 2 ob, 2 ob d'amore, str, bc			
	Und es waren Hirten in derselben Gegend	perf. 26 Dec 1734	A, T, B, 4vv, 2 fl, 2 ob d'amore, 2 ob da caccia, str, bc			
	Herrscher des Himmels, erhöre das Lallen	perf. 27 Dec 1734	S, A, T, B, 4vv, 3 tpt, timp, 2 fl, 2 ob, 2 ob d'amore, str, bc			
	Fallt mit Danken, fallt mit Loben	perf. 1 Jan 1735	S, T, B, 4vv, 2 hn, 2 ob, str, bc			
	Ehre sei dir, Gott, gesungen	perf. 2 Jan 1735	S, A, T, B, 4vv, 2 ob d'amore, str, bc			
	Herr, wenn die stolzen Feinde schnauben	perf. Epiphany, 6 Jan 1735	S, A, T, B, 4vv, 3 tpt, timp, 2 ob, 2 ob d'amore, str, bc			
249	Oratorium Festo Paschali: Kommt, eilet und laufet (Easter Oratorio) (?Picander)	perf. Easter, 1 April 1725 as cantata; rev. as oratorio 1732–5	S, A, T, B, 4vv, 3 tpt, timp, 2 rec, fl, 2 ob d'amore, str, bc	xxi/3	II/vii	89, 101, 130, 133, 134
11	Oratorium Festo Ascensionis Christi: Lobet Gott in seinen	perf. Ascension, 19 May 1735	S, A, T, B, 4vv, 3 tpt, timp, 2 fl, 2 ob, str, bc	ii, 1	II/viii	101, 133, 134, 139, 140

Spurious

BWV	Title		BG	NBA	
246	Passio secundum Lucam (St Luke Passion)		xlv/2	—	134

MOTETS

Texts of 225–8 are compilations, incl. chorale; other texts and librettist given in parentheses

140-42, 171

BWV	Title	Occasion; date	Scoring	BG	NBA	
225	Singet dem Herrn ein neues Lied	1726–7	8vv	xxxix, 5	III/i, 3	142
226	Der Geist hilft unser Schwachheit auf	funeral of J. H. Ernesti; 20 Oct 1729	8vv, 2 ob, taille, bn, str, bc	xxxix, 41	III/i, 39	96, 140, 141
227	Jesu, meine Freude	?memorial service for Johanna Maria Kees; ?18 July 1723	5vv	xxxix, 61	III/i, 77	86, 141, 175
228	Fürchte dich nicht	?memorial service for Frau Stadthauptmann Winckler; ?4 Feb 1726	8vv	xxxix, 87	III/i, 107	141
229	Komm, Jesu, komm! (P. Thymich)	memorial service or funeral; c1725–1749	8vv	xxxix, 109	III/i, 127	140, 141
230	Lobet den Herrn alle Heiden (Ps cxvii)	? funeral or memorial service, Leipzig; ?1720s	4vv, org	xxxix, 129	III/i, 149	142
118	O Jesu Christ, mein Lebens Licht (2 versions), chorale	burial or memorial service; 1st version 1736–7, 2nd version (118b) c1745–9	4vv, 2 hn, cornett, 3 trbn; *4vv, 2 hn, str, bc; 2 ob, ob da caccia and bn, ad lib	xxiv, 185	III/i, 163 171; I/xxxiii, CC	141, 142
—	Tilge, Höchster, mein Sünden (Ps ii) [arr. from Pergolesi: Stabat mater]	1744–8	S. A. str. bc	—	II/ii, CC	104, 142, 164

Doubtful

BWV	Title	Occasion; date	Scoring	BG	NBA	
—	Der Gerechte kommt um (Isaiah lvii.1–2) [reworking of J. Kuhnau: Tristis est anima mea; ed. in SBA]	by c1740, ?c1730	5vv, 2 ob, str, bc	—	—	

CHORALES, SACRED SONGS, ARIAS

BWV

Wedding chorales, 4vv, 2 hn, ob, ob d'amore, str, bc; by c1740, BG 143

250 [Vor der Trauung]: Was Gott tut das ist wohlgetan
251 [Nach der Trauung]: Sei Lob und Ehr' dem höchsten Gut
252 [Nach dem Segen]: Nun danket alle Gott

BWV

Chorales, 4vv, from Joh. Seb. Bachs vierstimmige Choral-gesänge, ed. J. P. Kirnberger and C. P. E. Bach, i–iv (Leipzig, 1784–7) [excluding those within larger works]; BG xxxix, 177; NBA [III/ii]: 142-4

253 Ach bleib' bei uns, Herr Jesu Christ

501 So giebst du nun, mein Jesu, gute Nacht
502 So wünsch' ich mir zu guter Letzt
503 Steh' ich bei meinem Gott
504 Vergiss mein nicht, dass ich dein nicht
505 Vergiss mein nicht, vergiss mein nicht [melody by Bach]   143
506 Was bist du doch, o Seele, so betrübet
507 Wo ist mein Schäflein, das ich liebe

Pieces in Clavierbüchlein, ii, for Anna Magdalena Bach; BG xxix, 289; NBA V/iv, 91:

511 Gib dich zufrieden, chorale, g [*512]
512 Gib dich zufrieden, chorale, e [arr. of 511]
513 O Ewigkeit, du Donnerwort, chorale [from 397]
515[b] So oft ich meine Tobackspfeife, aria, g (bass by Bach)
518 Willst du dein Herz mir schenken, aria ('Aria di Giovanni')

524 Quodlibet, SATB, bc, frag., for wedding, Mühlhausen, late Oct   20, 143
1707

Doubtful and spurious

Pieces in Clavierbüchlein, ii, for Anna Magdalena Bach; BG   143
xxix, 309; NBA V/iv, 102:

508 Bist du bei mir, aria (? by G. H. Stölzel)
509 Gedenke doch, mein Geist, aria (anon.)
510 Gib dich zufrieden, chorale, F (anon. bass added)
514 Schaffs mit mir, Gott, chorale (anon.)
515[a] So oft ich meine Tobackspfeife, aria, d (anon., ?by Gottfried Heinrich Bach)
516 Warum betrübst du dich, aria (anon.)
517 Wie wohl ist mir, o Freund der Seelen (anon.)

Sacred songs, 5 for lv, bc (probably spurious); NBA [III/iii]:

519 Hier lieg' ich nun
520 Das walt' mein Gott
521 Gott mein Herz dir Dank
522 Meine Seele, lass es gehen
523 Ich gnüge mich an meinem Stande

119, 144–8, 171

ORGAN
(independent of chorales)

BWV	Title	Remarks	BG	NBA	
525-30	6 sonatas (E♭, c, d, e, C, G)	Leipzig, c1727; no.3: cf 1044; no.4 arr. from 76	xv, 3–66	[IV/vii]	159, 174
531	Prelude and fugue, C	? before 1707	xv, 81	IV/v, 3	
532	Prelude and fugue, D	before 1712–13; *fugue, 532a	xv, 88	IV/v, 58; IV/v, 95	146, 148
533	Prelude and fugue, e	? by 1707; *533a	xv, 100	IV/v, 90; IV/vi, 106	
534	Prelude and fugue, f	?Weimar, 1712–17	xv, 104	IV/v, 130	146
535	Prelude and fugue, g	?Weimar, 1708–17; 535a, before 1707, frag.	xv, 112	IV/v, 157; IV/vi, 109	145
536	Prelude and fugue, A	1708–23; *536a, before 1708	xv, 120	IV/vi, 180; IV/vi, 114	146
537	Fantasia and fugue, c	?Leipzig, after 1723	xv, 129	IV/v, 47	
538	Toccata and fugue, 'Dorian', d	1712–23	xv, 136	IV/v, 76	
539	Prelude and fugue, d	c1720–25; fugue adapted from vn sonata, 1001	xv, 148	IV/v, 70	98
540	Toccata and fugue, F	?Weimar, after 1712	xv, 154	IV/v, 112	
541	Prelude and fugue, G	?Weimar, after 1712; rev. after 1742	xv, 169	IV/v, 146	

BWV	Title	Remarks	BG	NBA	
542	Fantasia and fugue, g	fugue: Weimar, after 1712; fantasia: Weimar, ? before 1712	xv, 177	IV/v, 167	74, 147
543	Prelude and fugue, a	Leipzig, after 1723; *543a; fugue: cf 944	xv, 189	IV/v, 186; IV/vi, 121	
544	Prelude and fugue, b	Leipzig, 1727–31	xv, 199	IV/v, 198	116
545	Prelude and fugue, C	Weimar, 1712–17; *545a, ? before 1708	xv, 212	IV/v, 10; IV/vi, 77	
546	Prelude and fugue, c	Leipzig, 1723–9	xv, 218	IV/v, 35	
547	Prelude and fugue, C	by c1725, probably c1719	xv, 228	IV/v, 20	
548	Prelude and fugue, e	Leipzig, 1725–8	xv, 236	IV/v, 94	147
549	Prelude and fugue, c	Leipzig, after 1723; *549a, before 1707	xxxviii, 3	IV/v, 30; IV/vi, 101	
550	Prelude and fugue, G	by 1712	xxxviii, 9	IV/v, 138	108
551	Prelude and fugue, a	by 1707	xxxviii, 17	IV/vi, 63	108, 147, 175
552	Prelude and fugue, 'St Anne', Eb	in Clavier-Übung, iii, (Leipzig, 1739), see 669–89	iii, 173, 254	IV/iv, 2	108
562	Fantasia and fugue, c	fantasia: Leipzig, c1730; fugue: Leipzig, ? c1740–45	xxxviii, 64, 209	IV/vi, 54, 105	108
563	Fantasia, b	before 1707	xxxviii, 59	IV/vi, 68	108
564	Toccata, adagio and fugue, C	Weimar, ? 1712–17	xv, 253	IV/vi, 3	108, 146
565	Toccata and fugue, d	?pre-Weimar, before 1708	xv, 267	IV/v, 31	108
566	Prelude and fugue, E	?pre-Weimar, before 1708	xv, 276	IV/iv, 40	108
568	Prelude, G	?pre-Weimar, before 1708	xxxviii, 85	IV/vi, 51	108
569	Prelude, a	?pre-Weimar, before 1708	xxxviii, 89	IV/vi, 59	
570	Fantasia, C	? before 1707	xxxviii, 62	IV/vi, 16	
572	Fantasia, G	? by c1712	xxxviii, 75	[IV/vii]	145
573	Fantasia, C	Cöthen, c1722; frag. in Clavierbüchlein, i, for Anna Magdalena Bach	xxxviii, 209	IV/vi, 18	147
574	Fugue on theme by Legrenzi, c	?pre-Weimar; *574a–b, ? spurious; ?pre-Weimar; *574a–b	xxxviii, 94, 205	IV/vi, 19, 82, 88	145, 159
575	Fugue, c	?Weimar, 1708–17	xxxviii, 101	IV/vi, 26	
578	Fugue, g	? before 1707	xxxviii, 116	IV/vi, 55	145, 159
579	Fugue on theme by Corelli, b	?pre-Weimar	xxxviii, 121	IV/vi, 71	146
582	Passacaglia, c	?1708–12, or later	xv, 289	[IV/vii]	
583	Trio, d	by Telemann, transcr. org by Bach	xxxviii, 143	[IV/vii]	
586	Trio, G	transcr. from Couperin: Les nations	—	IV/viii, 78	
587	Aria, F	Weimar, c1715	xxxviii, 222	IV/viii, 82	
588	Canzona, d	pre-Weimar	xxxviii, 126	[IV/vii]	145
590	Pastorale, F	Weimar, c1713–14; arrs. of works by other composers	xxxviii, 135	[IV/vii]	145
	6 concertos:				
592	G	arr. of conc. by Duke Johann Ernst of Saxe-	xxxviii, 149;	IV/viii, 56	

593	a	arr. of Vivaldi op.3 no.8 = rv522	xxxviii, 158	[IV/viii]	146
594	C	arr. of Vivaldi op.7/ii no.5 = rv208	xxxviii, 171	IV/viii, 30	
595	d	arr. of conc. by Duke Johann Ernst of Saxe-Weimar	xxxviii, 196	IV/viii, 65	
596	d	arr. of Vivaldi op.3 no.11 = rv565	—	IV/viii, 3	
597	E♭	arr. of conc. by unknown composer	—	[IV]	
598	Pedal-Exercitium	improvisation by Bach, recorded by C. A. Thieme, or ? frag. not for org	xxxviii, 210	[IV/vii]	146
802–5	4 duettos (e, F, G, a)	in Clavier-Übung, iii (Leipzig 1739); probably not for org; see also 552, 669–89	iii, 242–51	IV/iv, 92–102	147
1027a	Trio, G	transcr. from last movt of va da gamba sonata, 1027	—	—	

Doubtful and spurious

131a	Fugue, g	spurious adaptation from cantata, 131	xxxviii, 217	—	118
553–60	[8 short preludes and fugues] (C, d, e, F, G, g, a, B♭)	probably spurious: ? by J. T. Krebs	xxxviii, 23	[IV/ix]	
561	Fantasia and fugue, a	spurious	xxxviii, 48	—	
567	Prelude, C	by J. L. Krebs	xxxviii, 84	—	
571	Fantasia, G	spurious	xxxviii, 67	—	
576	Fugue, G	spurious	xxxviii, 106	—	
577	Fugue, G	spurious	xxxviii, 111	—	
580	Fugue, D	spurious	xxxviii, 215	—	
581	Fugue, G	spurious	—	—	
584	Trio, g	probably spurious	xxxviii, 219	IV/viii, 73	
585	Trio, c	by J. F. Fasch	xxxviii, 131	[IV/vii]	
589	Allabreve, D	doubtful	xxxviii, 225	[IV/ix]	145
591	Kleines harmonisches Labyrinth	probably spurious; ? by J. D. Heinichen			

Das Orgel-Büchlein:

(based on chorales)

Weimar

599	Nun komm' der Heiden Heiland	Advent 1714–Whitsuntide 1715	xxv/2, 3	[IV/i]	69, 78, 122, 252, 146, 147, 160, 165
600	Gott, durch deine Güte	Advent 1714–Whitsuntide 1715	xxv/2, 4	[IV/i]	
601	Herr Christ, der ein'ge Gottes-Sohn	by Advent 1713–Whitsuntide 1714	xxv/2, 5	[IV/i]	
602	Lob sei dem allmächtigen Gott	by Advent 1714–Whitsuntide 1715	xxv/2, 6	[IV/i]	147
603	Puer natus in Bethlehem	Advent 1713–Whitsuntide 1714	xxv/2, 7	[IV/i]	
604	Gelobet seist du, Jesu Christ	Advent 1713–Whitsuntide 1714	xxv/2, 8	[IV/i]	
605	Der Tag, der ist so freudenreich	by Advent 1713–Whitsuntide 1714	xxv/2, 9	[IV/i]	
606	Vom Himmel hoch, da komm' ich her	by Advent 1713–Whitsuntide 1714	xxv/2, 10	[IV/i]	78
607	Vom Himmel kam der Engel Schar	Advent 1714–Whitsuntide 1715	xxv/2, 12	[IV/i]	
608	In dulci jubilo	Advent 1713–Whitsuntide ?1714	xxv/2, 13	[IV/i]	
609	Lobt Gott, ihr Christen, allzugleich	Advent 1713–Whitsuntide 1714	xxv/2, 14	[IV/i]	147
610	Jesu, meine Freude	Advent 1713–Whitsuntide 1714	xxv/2, 14	[IV/i]	
611	Christum wir sollen loben schon	Christmas 1715–Passiontide 1716	xxv/2, 15	[IV/i]	

BWV	Title	Remarks	BG	NBA	
612	Wir Christenleut'	Advent 1714–Whitsuntide 1715	xxv/2, 16	[IV/i]	
613	Helft mir Gottes Güte preisen	c1740 or later	xxv/2, 18	[IV/i]	147
614	Das alte Jahr vergangen ist	by Advent 1713–Whitsuntide 1715	xxv/2, 19	[IV/i]	
615	In dir ist Freude	by Christmas 1715–Passiontide 1716	xxv/2, 20	[IV/i]	147
616	Mit Fried' und Freud' ich fahr dahin	by Advent 1714–Whitsuntide 1715	xxv/2, 24	[IV/i]	
617	Herr Gott, nun schleuss den Himmel auf	by Advent 1714–Whitsuntide 1715	xxv/2, 26	[IV/i]	
618	O Lamm Gottes unschuldig	by Advent 1714–Whitsuntide 1715	xxv/2, 28	[IV/i]	
619	Christe, du Lamm Gottes	by Advent 1714–Whitsuntide 1715	xxv/2, 30	[IV/i]	
620a	Christus, der uns selig macht	by Advent 1714–Whitsuntide 1715	xxv/2, 149	[IV/i]	
620	Christus, der uns selig macht	rev. of 620a, c1740 or later	xxv/2, 30	[IV/i]	
621	Da Jesus an dem Kreuze stund'	by Advent 1713–Whitsuntide 1714	xxv/2, 32	[IV/i]	
622	O Mensch, bewein' dein' Sünde gross	Advent 1713–Whitsuntide 1714	xxv/2, 33	[IV/i]	147
623	Wir danken dir, Herr Jesu Christ	by Christmas 1715–Passiontide 1716	xxv/2, 35	[IV/i]	
624	Hilf Gott, das mir's gelinge	by Christmas 1715–Passiontide 1716	xxv/2, 36	[IV/i]	
625	Christ lag in Todesbanden	by Advent 1713–Whitsuntide 1714	xxv/2, 38	[IV/i]	
626	Jesus Christus, unser Heiland	by Advent 1713–Whitsuntide 1714	xxv/2, 39	[IV/i]	
627	Christ ist erstanden	Advent 1713–Whitsuntide 1714	xxv/2, 40	[IV/i]	147
628	Erstanden ist der heil'ge Christ	Advent 1714–Whitsuntide 1715	xxv/2, 44	[IV/i]	
629	Erschienen ist der herrliche Tag	Advent 1714–Whitsuntide 1715	xxv/2, 45	[IV/i]	
630a	Heut' triumphieret Gottes Sohn	before 630	—	[IV/i]	
630	Heut' triumphieret Gottes Sohn	by Advent 1714–Whitsuntide 1715	xxv/2, 46	[IV/i]	147
631a	Komm, Gott Schöpfer, heiliger Geist	Advent 1713–Whitsuntide 1714	xxv/2, 150	[IV/i]	
631	Komm, Gott Schöpfer, heiliger Geist	rev. of 631a, c1740 or later	xxv/2, 47	[IV/i]	
632	Herr Jesu Christ, dich zu uns wend'	by 1715	xxv/2, 48	[IV/i]	
633	Liebster Jesu, wir sind hier	1715	xxv/2, 49	[IV/i]	
634	Liebster Jesu, wir sind hier	by 1715	xxv/2, 50	[IV/i]	
635	Dies sind die heil'gen zehn Gebot'	1715	xxv/2, 50	[IV/i]	
636	Vater unser im Himmelreich	1715	xxv/2, 52	[IV/i]	
637	Durch Adams Fall ist ganz verderbt	1714	xxv/2, 53	[IV/i]	
638	Es ist das Heil uns kommen her	by 1714	xxv/2, 54	[IV/i]	
639	Ich ruf' zu dir, Herr Jesu Christ	by 1714	xxv/2, 55	[IV/i]	147
640	In dich hab' ich gehoffet, Herr	by 1714	xxv/2, 56	[IV/i]	108
641	Wenn wir in höchsten Nöten sein	1714	xxv/2, 57	[IV/i]	
642	Wer nun den lieben Gott lässt walten	by 1714	xxv/2, 58	[IV/i]	
643	Alle Menschen müssen sterben	1714	xxv/2, 59	[IV/i]	147
644	Ach wie nichtig, ach wie flüchtig	by 1714	xxv/2, 60	[IV/i]	147
—	O Trauerigkeit, o Herzeleid	c1740 or later; frag.	—		
	Sechs Choräle ['Schübler' chorales]:	(Zella, c1748–9), transcr. of cantata movts pubd by Schübler			
645	Wachet auf, ruft uns die Stimme	from 140, movt 4	xxv/2, 63	[IV/i]	108, 116, 148

BWV	Title	Remarks	BG	NBA
677	Fughetta super Allein Gott in der Höh sei Ehr	manuals only	iii, 205	IV/iv, 41ᵛ
678	Dies sind die heilgen zehen Gebot	c.f. in canon	iii, 206	IV/iv, 42
679	Fughetta super Dies sind die heiligen zehen Gebot	manuals only	iii, 210	IV/iv, 49
680	Wir gläuben all an einen Gott	organo pleno	iii, 212	IV/iv, 52
681	Fughetta super Wir gläuben all an einen Gott	manuals only	iii, 216	IV/iv, 57
682	Vater unser im Himmelreich	c.f. in canon	iii, 217	IV/iv, 58
683	Vater unser im Himmelreich	alio modo, manuals only	iii, 223	IV/iv, 66
684	Christ, unser Herr, zum Jordan kam	c.f. in pedal	iii, 224	IV/iv, 68
685	Christ, unser Herr, zum Jordan kam	alio modo, manuals only	iii, 228	IV/iv, 73
686	Aus tiefer Not schrei ich zu dir	a 6, organo pleno, pedal doppio	iii, 229	IV/iv, 74
687	Aus tiefer Not schrei ich zu dir	a 4, alio modo, manuals only	iii, 232	IV/iv, 78
688	Jesus Christus, unser Heiland, der von uns den Zorn Gottes wandt	c.f. in pedal	iii, 234	IV/iv, 81
689	Fuga super Jesus Christus unser Heiland	a 4, manuals only	iii, 239	IV/iv, 89
690	Wer nur den lieben Gott lässt walten	manuals only; ?Weimar, 1708–17	xl, 3	IV/iii, 98
691	Wer nur den lieben Gott lässt walten	manuals only; autograph in Clavier-Büchlein for W. F. Bach; early 1720	xl, 4	IV/iii, 98
694	Wo soll ich fliehen hin	2 kbd, pedal; before 1708; cf 646	xl, 6	IV/iii, 103
695	Fantasia super Christ lag in Todes Banden	manuals only; ?Weimar, 1708–17; cf 695a	xl, 10	IV/iii, 20
696	Christum wir sollen loben schon	fughetta, manuals only; ? 1739–42	xl, 13	IV/iii, 23
697	Gelobet seist du, Jesu Christ	fughetta, manuals only; ? 1739–42	xl, 14	IV/iii, 32
698	Herr Christ, der einig Gottes Sohn	fughetta, manuals only; ? 1739–42	xl, 15	IV/iii, 35
699	Nun komm, der Heiden Heiland	fughetta, manuals only; ? 1739–42	xl, 16	IV/iii, 73
700	Vom Himmel hoch, da komm ich her	before 1708, rev. 1740s	xl, 17	IV/iii, 92
701	Vom Himmel hoch, da komm ich her	fughetta, manuals only; ? 1739–42	xl, 19	IV/iii, 96
703	Gottes Sohn ist kommen	fughetta, manuals only; ? 1739–42	xl, 21	IV/iii, 34
704	Lob sei dem allmächtigen Gott	fughetta, manuals only; ? 1739–42	xl, 22	IV/iii, 62
706	Liebster Jesu, wir sind hier	Weimar, 1708–17; cf 706ii [alio modo]	xl, 25	IV/iii, 59
709	Herr Jesu Christ, dich zu uns wend	2 kbd, pedal; ?Weimar, 1708–17	xl, 30	IV/iii, 43
710	Wir Christenleut habn jetzund Freud	2 kbd, pedal; ?Weimar, 1708–17	xl, 32	IV/iii, 100
711	Allein Gott in der Höh sei Ehr	bicinium; ?Weimar, 1708–17; rev. 1740s	xl, 34	IV/iii, 11
712	In dich hab ich gehoffet, Herr	manuals only; ?Weimar, 1708–17 or ?later	xl, 36	IV/iii, 48
713	Fantasia super Jesu, meine Freude	manuals only; ?Weimar, 1708–17; cf 713a	xl, 38	IV/iii, 54
714	Ach Gott und Herr	per canonem; ?Weimar, 1708–17	xl, 43	IV/iii, 3
715	Allein Gott in der Höh sei Ehr	Arnstadt, 1703–8, or Weimar, 1708–17	xl, 44	IV/iii, 14
717	Allein Gott in der Höh sei Ehr	manuals only; ?Weimar, 1708–17	xl, 47	IV/iii, 8
718	Christ lag in Todes Banden	2 kbd, pedal; before 1708	xl, 52	IV/iii, 16
720	Ein feste Burg ist unser Gott	3 kbd, pedal; Weimar, 1709	xl, 57	IV/iii, 24
721	Erbarm dich mein, o Herre Gott	manuals only; ?Weimar, 1708–17	xl, 60	IV/iii, 28

BWV	Title	Notes			
		Arnstadt, 1705–6, or Weimar, 1708–17; sketch, 722a	xl, 62, 158	IV/iii, 30–1	145
724	Gott, durch deine Güte (Gottes Sohn ist kommen)	before 1708; alternative title in BWV, BG a 5; ?Weimar, 1708–17	xl, 65	IV/iii, 33	
725	Herr Gott, dich loben wir	?Weimar, 1708–17	xl, 66	IV/iii, 36	
726	Herr Jesu Christ, dich zu uns wend	?Weimar, 1708–17	xl, 72	IV/iii, 45	
727	Herzlich tut mich verlangen	2 kbd, pedal; ?Weimar, 1708–17	xl, 73	IV/iii, 46	
728	Jesus, meine Zuversicht	manuals only; ?Weimar, 1708–17; autograph in Clavierbüchlein, i, for Anna Magdalena Bach	xl, 74	IV/iii, 58	
729	In dulci jubilo	?Weimar, 1708–17; sketch, 729a	xl, 74, 158	IV/iii, 52, 50	
730	Liebster Jesu, wir sind hier	?Weimar, 1708–17	xl, 76	IV/iii, 60	
731	Liebster Jesu, wir sind hier	2 kbd, pedal; ?Weimar, 1712–17	xl, 77	IV/iii, 61	
732	Lobt Gott, ihr Christen, allzugleich	Arnstadt, 1703–8, or Weimar, 1708–17; sketch, 732a	xl, 78, 159	IV/iii, 63–4	145
733	Meine Seele erhebet den Herren (Fuge über das Magnificat)	organo pleno; ?Weimar, 1708–17	xl, 79	IV/iii, 65	
734	Nun freut euch, lieben Christen gmein	manuals only; c.f. in tenor; ?Weimar, 1708–17; cf 734a	xl, 160	IV/iii, 70	
—	O Lamm Gottes, unschuldig	manuals only; ?Weimar, 1708–17	xl, 86, 161	IV/iii, 74	
735	Fantasia super Valet will ich dir geben	with pedal obbl; Leipzig, after 1723; *735a; Weimar, 1708–17		IV/iii, 77, 81	
736	Valet will ich dir geben	c.f. in pedal; ?Weimar, 1708–17	xl, 90	IV/iii, 84	
737	Vater unser im Himmelreich	manuals only; ?Weimar, 1708–17	xl, 96	IV/iii, 90	
738	Vom Himmel hoch, da komm ich her	?Weimar, 1708–17; sketch, 738a	xl, 97, 159	IV/iii, 94	
739	Wie schön leucht't uns der Morgenstern	Arnstadt, 1705–6	xl, 99	[IV/ix]	118, 145
741	Ach Gott vom Himmel sieh darein	organo pleno; before 1708, rev. 1740s	xl, 167	IV/iii, 4	
753	Jesu, meine Freude	frag.; autograph in Clavier-Büchlein for W. F. Bach	xl, 163	V/v	
764	Wie schön leuchtet uns der Morgenstern	frag.; Arnstadt, 1705–6	xl, 164	[IV/ix]	145
	Partite diverse:				
766	Christ, der du bist der helle Tag	chorale variations, completed by c1715, ? begun c1704	xl, 107	[IV/j]	
767	O Gott, du frommer Gott		xl, 114	[IV/j]	
768	Sei gegrüsset, Jesu gütig	much rev. later	xl, 122	[IV/j]	
	Doubtful and spurious				
691a	Wer nur den lieben Gott lässt walten	*691; doubtful	xl, 151	[IV/ix]	
692	Ach Gott und Herr	by J. G. Walther; *692a	xl, 4, 152	[IV/ix]	
693	Ach Gott und Herr	by J. G. Walther	xl, 5	—	
695a	Fantasia super Christ lag in Todes Banden	c.f. in pedal; *695; doubtful	xl, 153	—	
702	Das Jesulein soll doch mein Trost	fughetta; doubtful	xl, 20	[IV/ix]	
705	Durch Adam's Fall ist ganz verderbt	doubtful	xl, 23	[IV/ix]	
707	Ich hab' mein' Sach' Gott heimgestellt	doubtful; ? based on extemporization or a pupil's exercise	xl, 26	[IV/ix]	
708	Ich hab' mein' Sach' Gott heimgestellt	doubtful; *708a. doubtful	xl, 30, 152	[IV/ix]	

BWV	Title	Remarks	BG	NBA	
713a	Fantasia super Jesu, meine Freude	c.f. in pedal; *713; doubtful	xl, 155	—	
716	Fuga super Allein Gott in der Höh sei Ehr	doubtful	xl, 45	[IV/ix]	
719	Der Tag, der ist so freudenreich	doubtful	xl, 55	[IV/ix]	
723	Gelobet seist du, Jesu Christ	doubtful	xl, 63	[IV/ix]	
734a	Nun freut euch, lieben Christen gmein	c.f. in pedal; *734; doubtful	xl, 84	—	
740	Wir glauben all' an einen Gott, Vater	doubtful	xl, 103	[IV/ix]	
742	Ach Herr, mich armen Sünder	spurious	—	—	
743	Ach, was ist doch unser Leben	spurious	—	—	
744	Auf meinen lieben Gott	? by J. L. Krebs	xl, 170	—	
745	Aus der Tiefe rufe ich	? by (2) J. C. Bach	xl, 171	—	
746	Christ ist erstanden	? by J. C. F. Fischer	xl, 173	—	
747	Christus, der uns selig macht	spurious	—	—	
748	Gott der Vater wohn' uns bei	? by (2) J. C. Bach or J. G. Walther; *748a	xl, 177	—	
749	Herr Jesu Christ, dich zu uns wend'	spurious	—	—	
750	Herr Jesu Christ, mein's Lebens Licht	spurious	—	—	
751	In dulci jubilo	spurious	—	—	
752	Jesu, der du meine Seele	spurious	—	—	
754	Liebster Jesu, wir sind hier	spurious	—	—	
755	Nun freut euch, lieben Christen	spurious	—	—	
756	Nun ruhen alle Wälder	spurious	—	—	
757	O Herre Gott, din göttlich's Wort	doubtful	xl, 179	—	
758	O Vater, allmächtiger Gott	by G. A. Homilius	xl, 181	—	
759	Schmücke dich, o liebe Seele	by G. Böhm	xl, 183	—	
760	Vater unser im Himmelreich	by Böhm	xl, 184	—	
761	Vater unser im Himmelreich	spurious	—	—	
762	Vater unser im Himmelreich	spurious	—	—	
763	Wie schön leuchtet der Morgenstern	spurious	—	—	
765	Wir glauben all' an einen Gott	spurious	—	—	
770	Ach, was soll ich Sünder machen?	chorale variations; doubtful	xl, 189	—	
771	Allein Gott in der Höh sei Ehr'	chorale variations; nos.3, 8 (?all) by A. N. Vetter	xl, 195	—	148–54

OTHER KEYBOARD

BWV	Title	Remarks	BG	NBA	
772–86	15 Inventions (C, c, D, d, Eb, E, e, F, f, G, g, A, a, Bb, b)	Cöthen, 1723; *Clavier-Büchlein for W. F. Bach; 772: *772a	iii, 1	V/iii	79, 123, 149, 152, 165, 252
787–801	15 Sinfonias (C, c, D, d, Eb, E, e, F, f, G, g, A, a, Bb, b)	Cöthen, 1723; *Clavier-Büchlein for W. F. Bach	iii, 19	V/iii	79, 149, 152
		... 1774.5	xtv/1 3	V/vii	149 152

BWV	Title	Remarks	BG	NBA	Page refs
812–17	6 [French] Suites (d, c, b, Eb, G, E)	nos.1–5: orig. versions in Clavierbüchlein, i, for Anna Magdalena Bach; no.6 by c1724; later modified	xiv/1, 89	V/viii	152
	Clavier-Übung [i] bestehend in Präludien, Allemanden, Couranten, Sarabanden, Giguen, Menuetten, und anderen Galanterien:	partitas pubd singly (Leipzig, 1726–31) and as op.1 (Leipzig, 1731); nos.3, 6: *Clavierbüchlein, ii, for Anna Magdalena Bach; no.6 of 1019, 2nd version modified			
825–30	6 Partitas (Bb, c, a, D, G, e)		iii, 46	V/i	50, 61, 90, 97, 152, 252
831	Ouvertüre [Partita] nach französischer Art, b	in Clavier-Übung, ii (Leipzig, 1735); see also 971; *831a, c, Leipzig, by 1733	iii, 154	V/ii, 20	101, 153
846–69	Das wohltemperirte Clavier, oder Praeludia, und Fugen durch alle Tone und Semitonia [i] [The Well-tempered Clavier]: 24 Preludes and fugues (C, c, C#, c#, D, d, Eb, eb/d#, E, e, F, f, F#, f#, G, g, Ab, g#, A, a, Bb, bb, B, b)	Cöthen, 1722; some preludes: *Clavier-Büchlein for W. F. Bach	xiv	[V/vi]	77, 149, 162, 165, 169, 171, 173, 174, 175, 176, 238, 239, 252
870–93	[Das wohltemperirte Clavier, ii]: 24 Preludes and fugues (C, c, C#, c#, D, d, Eb, eb/d#, E, e, F, f, F#, f#, G, g, Ab, g#, A, a, Bb, bb, B, b)	Leipzig, 1738–42; some pieces earlier, 1720s	xiv	[V/vi]	102, 150–51, 153, 162, 165, 169, 171, 173, 174, 175, 176, 252
971	Concerto nach italiänischen Gusto [Italian Concerto]	in Clavier-Übung, ii (Leipzig, 1735)	iii, 139	V/ii, 3	101, 104, 153
988	Aria mit [30] verschiedenen Veraenderungen [Goldberg Variations]	Clavier-Übung, [iv] (Nuremberg, 1741–2)	iii, 263	V/ii, 69	106, 109, 121, 123, 153, 161, 255
	Miscellaneous suites and suite movts:				
818	Suite, a	Cöthen, c1722	xxxvi, 3	V/viii, 129	
819	Suite, Eb	Cöthen, c1722; 819a, Allemande, Leipzig, ? 1730s	xxxvi, 8	V/viii, 136	
820	Ouverture, F	Weimar, 1708–14 or earlier	xxxvi, 14	V/x, 43	
821	Suite, Bb	Weimar, 1708–14; probably authentic	xlii, 213	[V]	
822	Suite, g	?arr. of work by another composer	—	V/x, 68	
823	Suite, f	frag.; Weimar, 1708–14	xxxvi, 229	V/x, 50	
832	Partie, A	Weimar, 1708–14	xlii, 255	V/x, 54	
836–7	2 allemandes, g (1 inc.)	c1720–22; from Clavier-Büchlein for W. F. Bach; ? by W. F. Bach assisted by J. S. Bach	xiv/1, 214–15	V/v, 8–10	
841–3	3 minuets, G, g, G	c1720: from Clavier-Büchlein for W. F. Bach	xxxvi, 209–10	V/v, 16–18	
	Miscellaneous preludes, fugues, fantasias, toccatas:				
894	Prelude and fugue, a	Weimar, 1708–17; cf 1044	xxxvi, 91	[V/ix]	
896	Prelude and fugue, A	Weimar, c1709; fugue only in edn.; prelude ed. in BJb, ix (1912), suppl.	xxxvi, 157	[V/ix]	158
900	Prelude and fughetta, e	Cöthen, c1720	xxxvi, 108	[V/ix]	
901	Prelude and fughetta, F	fughetta = early version of 886	xxxvi, 112	[V/ix]	
902	Prelude and fughetta, G	fughetta = early version of 884; alternative prelude, 902a	xxxvi, 114, 220	[V/ix]	

BWV	Title	Remarks	BG	NBA	
903	Chromatic fantasia and fugue, d	Cöthen, c1720; rev. Leipzig, c1730; *903a by 1723	xxxvi, 71, 219	[V/ix]	149, 174
904	Fantasia and fugue, a	Leipzig, c1725	xxxvi, 81	[V/ix]	
906	Fantasia and fugue, c	Leipzig, c1738; fugue inc.	xxxvi, 145, 238	[V/ix]	148
910	Toccata, f♯	c1710	iii, 311	[V/ix]	
911	Toccata, c	c1710	iii, 322	[V/ix]	148
912	Toccata, D	Weimar, c1710	xxxvi, 26	[V/ix]	
913	Toccata, d	before 1708	xxxvi, 36	[V/ix]	
914	Toccata, e	before 1708	xxxvi, 47	[V/ix]	
915	Toccata, g	before 1708	xxxvi, 54	[V/ix]	
916	Toccata, G	Weimar, c1710	xxxvi, 63	[V/ix]	
917	Fantasia, g	?Weimar, before 1710	xxxvi, 143	[V/xii]	
919	Fantasia, c	?Weimar, after 1712	xxxvi, 152	[V/xii]	
944	Fugue, a	?Weimar, early version of org fugue 543	iii, 334	[V/ix]	
946	Fugue on theme by Albinoni, C	c1708	xxxvi, 159	[V/ix]	
950	Fugue on theme by Albinoni, A	Weimar, c1710	xxxvi, 173	[V/ix]	
951	Fugue on theme by Albinoni, b	Weimar, c1710; *951a of earlier date	xxxvi, 178, 221	[V/ix]	
953	Fugue, C	c1723; from Clavier-Büchlein for W. F. Bach	xxxvi, 186	V/v, 46	51
954	Fugue, B♭	arr. of fugue from J. A. Reincken: Hortus musicus	xlii, 50	[V/xi]	
955	Fugue, B♭	arr. of org fugue, G, by J. C. Erselius	xlii, 55	[V/xi]	
958	Fugue, a	Weimar, c1710	xlii, 205	[V/ix]	
959	Fugue, a	?Weimar, after 1712	xlii, 208	[V/xii]	
961	Fughetta, c		xxxvi, 154	[V/xii]	
	Pieces from Clavier-Büchlein for W. F. Bach:	?Cöthen, 1720–; incl. also 836–7, 841–3, 924a–5, 931–2, 953, 994; see 691, 753, 772ff, 846ff	xxxvi, 118	V/v	72, 77, 149, 238
924	Praeambulum, C	cf 924a			
926	Prelude, d				
927	Praeambulum, F				
928	Prelude, F				
929	Trio, g	inserted in Partita, g, by G. H. Stölzel			
930	Praeambulum, g				
	Clavierbüchlein, i, for Anna Magdalena Bach	Cöthen, 1722–5; see 573, 728, 812–16, 841, 991	xliii/2, 3	V/iv, 3	77, 149
	Clavierbüchlein, ii, for Anna Magdalena Bach	Leipzig, 1725; incl. 82 (recit, aria), 299, 508–18, 691, 812–13, 827, 830, 846 (prelude), 988 (aria); see A113–32, A183	xliii/2, 6	V/iv, 47	88, 90, 152, 253
933–8	[6 little preludes] (C, c, d, D, E, e)		xxxvi, 128	[V/ix]	
939–43	5 Preludes (C, d, e, a, C)		xxxvi, 119	[V/ix]	
	Sonatas, variations, capriccios, etc:				
963	Sonata, D	c1704	xxxvi, 19	V/x, 32	
965	Sonata, a	arr. of sonata from J. A. Reincken: Hortus musicus	xlii, 29	[V/xi]	51

BWV	Title	Notes			
966	Sonata, C	arr. of part of sonata from Reincken: Hortus musicus	xlii, 42	[V/xi]	51
967	Sonata, a	by 1715; arr. of 1st movt of anon. chamber sonata	xiv/1, 168	[V/xi]	
989	Aria variata, a	Weimar, before 1714; incl. 10 variations	xxxvi, 203	V/x, 21	148
991	Air with variations, c	frag.; in Clavierbüchlein, i, for Anna Magdalena Bach	xliii/2, 4	V/iv, 40	
992	Capriccio sopra la lontananza del suo fratello dilettissimo [Capriccio on the Departure of his Most Beloved Brother], Bb	?1703, 1704 or 1706	xxxvi, 190	V/x, 3	14, 53, 120, 148
993	Capriccio, E	c1704	xxxvi, 197	V/x, 12	149
994	Applicatio, C	Feb 1720; 1st entry in Clavier-Büchlein for W. F. Bach	xxxvi, 237	V/v, 4	149
	16 Concertos:	Weimar, 1713–16; arrs. of works by other composers			149
972	D	from Vivaldi op.3 no.9 = rv230	xlii, 59	[V/xi]	
973	G	from Vivaldi op.7/ii no.2 = rv299	xlii, 66	[V/xi]	
974	d	from ob conc. by A. Marcello	xlii, 73	[V/xi]	
975	g	from Vivaldi op.4 no.6 = rv316	xlii, 80	[V/xi]	
976	C	from Vivaldi op.3 no.12 = rv265	xlii, 87	[V/xi]	
977	C	source unknown	xlii, 96	[V/xi]	
978	F	from Vivaldi op.3 no.3 = rv310	xlii, 101	[V/xi]	
979	b	source unknown	xlii, 108	[V/xi]	
980	G	from Vivaldi op.4 no.1 = rv381	xlii, 119	[V/xi]	
981	c	arr. of B. Marcello op.1 no.2	xlii, 127	[V/xi]	
982	Bb	from conc. by Duke Johann Ernst of Saxe-Weimar	xlii, 135	[V/xi]	
983	g	source unknown	xlii, 142	[V/xi]	
984	C	from conc. by Duke Johann Ernst of Saxe-Weimar	xlii, 148	[V/xi]	
985	g	from vn conc. by Telemann	xlii, 155	[V/xi]	
986	G	source unknown	xlii, 161	[V/xi]	
987	d	from conc. by Duke Johann Ernst of Saxe-Weimar	xlii, 165	[V/xi]	
Doubtful and spurious					
824	Suite, A	frag.; by Telemann	xxxvi, 231	—	
833	Prelude and partita, F	? by B. Pasquini	—	V/x, 60	
834	Allemande, c	spurious	xlii, 259	[V/xii]	118
835	Allemande, a	by Kirnberger	xlii, 267	—	118
838	Allemande and courante, A	by C. Graupner	xlii, 265	[V/xii]	118
839	Sarabande, g	spurious		[V]	118
840	Courante, G	by Telemann		—	
844	Scherzo, d	by W. F. Bach; arr., 844a	xlii, 220, 281	—	
845	Gigue, f	spurious	xlii, 263	—	
895	Prelude and fugue, a	doubtful; ? by J. P. Kellner or one of his pupils	xxxvi, 104	[V/xii]	
897	Prelude and fugue, a	prelude, at least, by C. H. Dretzel	xlii, 173	[V/xii]	

BWV	Title	Remarks	BG	NBA	
898	Prelude and fugue, Bb	doubtful	—	[V/xii]	
899	Prelude and fughetta, d	doubtful	—	[V/xii]	
905	Fantasia and fugue, d	probably spurious	xlii, 179	[V/xii]	
907	Fantasia and fughetta, Bb	? by G. Kirchhoff	xlii, 268	[V/xii]	
908	Fantasia and fughetta, D	? by G. Kirchhoff	xlii, 272	[V/xii]	
909	Concerto and fugue, c	doubtful	xlii, 190	[V/xii]	
918	Fantasia on a rondo, c	doubtful	xxxvi, 148	[V/xii]	
920	Fantasia, g	doubtful	xlii, 183	[V/xii]	
921	Prelude [Fantasia], c	doubtful	xxxvi, 136	[V/xii]	
922	Prelude [Fantasia], a	doubtful	xxxvi, 138	[V/xii]	
923	Prelude, b	also attrib. W. H. Pachelbel; spurious arr., 923a	xlii, 211	[V/xii]	
945	Fugue, e	spurious	xxxvi, 155	[V/xii]	
947	Fugue, a	doubtful	xxxvi, 161	[V/xii]	
948	Fugue, d	doubtful	xxxvi, 164	[V/xii]	
949	Fugue, A	doubtful	xxxvi, 169	[V/xii]	
952	Fugue, C	doubtful	xxxvi, 184	[V/xii]	
956	Fugue, e	doubtful	xlii, 200	[V/xii]	
957	Fugue, G	doubtful	xlii, 203	[V/xii]	
960	Fugue, e	inc.; spurious	xlii, 276	[V/xii]	
962	Fugato, e	by Albrechtsberger	xlii, 198	—	118
	Pieces from Clavier-Büchlein for W. F. Bach:	Cöthen, 1720–			
924a	Prelude, C	1725/6; reworking of 924; ? by W. F. Bach	xxxvi, 221	V/v, 41	
925	Prelude, D	1725/6; ? by W. F. Bach	xxxvi, 121	V/v, 42	
931	Prelude, a	spurious	xxxvi, 237	V/v, 45	
932	Prelude, e	1725/6; ? by W. F. Bach	xxxvi, 238	V/v, 44	
964	Sonata, d	arr. of vn sonata 1003; ? by W. F. Bach	xlii, 3	—	
968	Adagio, G	arr. of vn sonata 1005, movt 1; ? by W. F. Bach	xlii, 27	—	
969	Andante, g	spurious	xlii, 218	[V/xii]	
970	Presto, d	by W. F. Bach	—	[V/xii]	
990	Sarabande con partite, C	spurious	xlii, 221	[V/xii]	118
	Clavierbüchlein, ii, for Anna Magdalena Bach [only anon. pieces listed]:	Leipzig, 1725–; also incl. 5 pieces by C. P. E. Bach (A122–5, 129), 1 by F. Couperin (A183), 1 by Böhm (without no.); remainder anon., ? by J. S. Bach and/or Bach's sons	xliii/2, 25	V/iv, 47	

Minuet, F (A113); Minuet, G (A114); Minuet, g (A115); Minuet, G (A116); Polonaise, F (A117a, 117b); Minuet, Bb (A118); Polonaise, g (A119); Minuet, a (A120); Minuet, c (A121); Musette, D (A126);

March, Eb (A127); [Polonaise], d (A128);
Polonaise, G (A130); [untitled], F (A131);
Minuet, d (A132)

LUTE

154-5

BWV	Title, scoring	Remarks	BG	NBA	
995	Suite, g	Leipzig, 1727–31; arr. of vc suite 1011	—	V/x, 81	
996	Suite, e	Weimar, c1708–17 (or earlier); orig. in d	xlv/1, 149	V/x, 94	
997	Partita, c	Leipzig, 1737–41; orig. in different key	xlv/1, 156	V/x, 102	
998	Prelude, fugue and allegro, Eb	Leipzig, early to mid-1740s	xlv/1, 141	V/x, 114	
999	Prelude, c	Cöthen, c1720	xxxvi, 119	V/x, 122	107
1000	Fugue, g	?Leipzig, c1725; arr. of fugue from vn sonata 1001	—	V/x, 124	
1006a	Partita. E: see 1006	unplayable on lute; ? for lute-harpsichord	—	V/x, 134	

CHAMBER

BWV	Title, scoring	Remarks	BG	NBA	
1001–6	Sonatas and partitas, solo vn:	Cöthen, 1720; 1006 arr. lute = 1006a (BG xiii, 16)	xxvii/1, 3	VI/i, 3	119, 159–60
	Sonata no.1, g; Partita no.1, b; Sonata no.2, a; Partita no.2, d; Sonata no.3, C; Partita no.3, E				74, 138, 154, 160, 165, 171
1014–19	6 sonatas, vn, hpd:	Cöthen, 1717–23; earlier version of no.5 (Adagio only) = 1018a (BG ix, 250; NBA VI/i, 195); 1st version of no.6 incl. 1019a (BG ix, 252; NBA VI/i, 197); 3 versions of 1019 [9 movts], 2nd version related to 830	ix, 69	VI/i, 83	159, 171, 175
	no.1, b; no.2, A; no.3, E; no.4, c; no.5, f; no.6, G				
	Miscellaneous vn pieces:				
1021	Sonata, G, vn, bc	?Cöthen, before 1720	xliii/1, 31	VI/i, 65	159
1023	Sonata, e, vn, bc	Weimar, 1714–17	xxvii/1, 59	VI/i, 73	159
1007–12	6 suites, solo vc (G, d, C, Eb, c, D)	Cöthen, c1720	ix, 175	[VI/ii]	154, 160, 171
1027–9	3 sonatas. hpd, va da gamba (G, D, g)	c1720–39		[VI/ii]	
	Miscellaneous fl pieces:				
1013	Partita, a, fl	? early 1720s	—	VI/iii, 3	159
1026	Fugue, g, vn, hpd	Weimar, c1712	xliii/1, 39	[VI/iv]	160
1030	Sonata, b, fl, hpd	?Leipzig, 1738; earlier version, g, ?rec, ?c1730	ix, 3	VI/iii, 33, 89	94, 159

BWV	Title, scoring	Remarks	BG	NBA	
1031	Sonata, E♭, fl, hpd	Leipzig, before 9 Sept 1734	ix, 22	[VI]/iv	118, 159
1032	Sonata, A, fl, hpd	Leipzig, ? late 1724; 1st movt inc.; 1032a, C, rec, hpd, c1731	ix, 245, 32	VI/iii, 54	159
1033	Sonata, C, fl	probably for unacc. fl [hpd added later by pupil]	xliii/1, 3	[VI]/iv	159
1034	Sonata, e, fl, bc	?Cöthen, 1717–20	xliii/1, 9	VI/iii, 11	159
1035	Sonata, E, fl, bc	Leipzig or Potsdam, ? July–Aug 1741	xliii/1, 21	VI/iii, 23	159
	Trio sonatas:				
1039	Sonata, G, 2 fl, bc	Cöthen, c1720; cf 1027	ix, 260	VI/iii, 71	94, 159
Doubtful and spurious					
1020	Sonata, g, vn, hpd	? by C. P. E. Bach	ix, 274	[VI]/iv	160
1022	Sonata, F, vn, hpd	arr. of 1038; ? by one of Bach's sons or pupils	—	[VI]/iv	
1024	Sonata, c, vn, bc	? by J. G. Pisendel	ix, 43	[VI]/iv	
1025	Suite, A, vn, hpd	? by W. F. Bach	ix, 231	[VI]/iv	
1037	Sonata, C, 2 vn, hpd	? by J. G. Goldberg	—	[VI]/iv	118
1036	Sonata, d, 2 vn, hpd	probably spurious	ix, 221	[VI]/iv	
1038	Sonata, G, fl, vn, bc	constructed on bass of 1021; probably by one of Bach's sons or pupils; cf 1022	ix, 221	[VI]/iv	
1040	Trio, F, vn, ob, bc	early 1713; movt based on material from Cantata 208, ? perf. with cantata; later used in Cantata 68	xxix, 250	I/xxxv, 47	159

ORCHESTRAL

(where applicable, scoring given as concertino/solo: ripieno)

155–8

BWV	Title, key	Scoring	Remarks	BG	NBA	
1041	Concerto, a	vn; str, bc	Cöthen, 1717–23; cf 1058	xxi/1, 3	[VII]/iii	157
1042	Concerto, E	vn; str, bc	Cöthen, 1717–23; cf 1054	xxi/1, 21	[VII]/iii	157
1043	Concerto, d	2 vn; str, bc	Cöthen, 1717–23; cf 1062	xxi/1, 41	[VII]/iii	157
1044	Concerto, a	fl, vn, hpd; str, bc	Leipzig, ?after 1730; movts adapted from prelude and fugue 894 and trio sonata 527	xvii, 223	[VII]/iii	158
1045	Concerto movt, D	vn; 3 tpt, timp, 2 ob, str, bc	frag.; intended as opening sinfonia for church cantata	xxi/1, 65	—	
	Brandenburg Concertos:		Weimar, Cöthen, before 1720–21; autograph MS ded. Christian Ludwig, Margrave of Brandenburg, 24 March 1721			74, 155, 156, 157

1046	no.1, F	2 hn, ob, vn piccolo; 2 ob, bn, str, bc	?Cöthen, by 24 March 1721	xix, 3	VII/ii, 3	156
1046a	Sinfonia, F	2 hn, 3 ob, bn, str, bc	*1046; formerly 1071; also used in 52	xxxi/1, 96	VII/ii, 225	156
1047	no.2, F	tpt, rec, ob, vn; str, bc	by 24 March 1721	xix, 33	VII/ii, 43	93, 156
1048	no.3, G	3 vn, 3 va, 3 vc, bc	by 24 March 1721	xix, 59	VII/ii, 73	156, 157
1049	no.4, G	fl, vn, 2 rec; str, bc	by 24 March 1721; cf 1057	xix, 85	VII/ii, 99	157, 158
1050	no.5, D	fl, vn, hpd; str, bc	by 24 March 1721; *1050a	xix, 127	VII/ii, 145, appx	156
1051	no.6, Bb	2 va, 2 va da gamba, vc, bc	by 24 March 1721	xix, 167	VII/ii, 197	158
	Harpsichord concertos:		Leipzig, c1738-9; mostly transcrs. of vn concs.; some orig./transcrs. also used in church cantatas			
1052	d	hpd; str, bc	from lost vn conc. reconstructed in NBA VII/vii	xvii, 3	[VII/iv]	95, 105, 156, 157, 176
1053	E	hpd; str, bc	from lost ?ob conc.; see NBA VII/vii, CC	xvii, 45	[VII/iv]	95, 105, 157
1054	D	hpd; str, bc	from 1042	xvii, 81	[VII/iv]	95, 105
1055	A	hpd; str, bc	from lost ob d'amore conc. reconstructed in NBA VII/vii	xvii, 109	[VII/iv]	95, 105, 157
1056	f	hpd; str, bc	outer movts from lost ob conc. in g reconstructed in NBA VII/vii	xvii, 135	[VII/iv]	95, 105, 157
1057	F	hpd, 2 rec; str, bc	from 1049	xvii, 153	[VII/iv]	95, 105
1058	g	hpd; str, bc	from 1041	xvii, 199	[VII/iv]	95, 105
1059	d	hpd, ob; str, bc	inc.; from lost ob conc., see NBA VII/vii, CC	xvii, p.xx	[VII/iv]	157
1060	c	2 hpd; str, bc	from lost ob and vn conc. reconstructed in NBA VII/vii	xxi/2, 3	[VII/v]	157
1061	C	2 hpd; str, bc	orig. for 2 hpd, ? without acc.	xxi/2, 39	[VII/v]	
1062	c	2 hpd; str, bc	from 1043	xxi/2, 83	[VII/v]	
1063	d	3 hpd; str, bc	source unknown, see NBA VII/vii, CC	xxxi/3, 3	VII/vi, 3	157
1064	C	3 hpd; str, bc	from lost 3 vn conc. in D reconstructed in NBA VII/vii	xxxi/3, 53	VII/vi, 57	157
1065	a	4 hpd; str, bc	from Vivaldi op.3 no.10 = RV580	xliii/1, 71	VII/vi, 117	94
	4 orchestral suites:					
1066	C	2 ob, bn, str, bc	late Cöthen or early Leipzig, by 1724-5	xxxi/1, 3	VII/i, 3	157
1067	b	fl; str, bc	Leipzig, c1738-9	xxxi/1, 24	VII/i, 27	158
1068	D	3 tpt, timp, 2 ob, str, bc	Leipzig, c1729-31	xxxi/1, 40	VII/i, 49, 119	158
1069	D	3 tpt, timp, 3 ob, bn, str, bc	orig. without tpt, timp; tpt, timp added in arr. for Christmas Cantata 110, 1725; later version c1729	xxxi/1, 66	VII/i, 81	157, 158
1070	Overture, g	str, bc	spurious	xlv/1, 190	—	118
1071	Sinfonia: see 1046a					

160-63, 165

BWV	Title, scoring	Remarks	BG	NBA	
769	Einige [5] canonische Veränderungen über das Weynacht Lied, Vom Himmel hoch da komm ich her, org	written on becoming member of Mizler's Societät der Musicalischen Wissenschaften, June 1747 (Nuremberg, 1748); autograph version 769a, chronology of versions uncertain, several pubd in puzzle form	xl, 137	IV/ii, 197, 98	109, 116, 148, 153, 162
1079	Musikalisches Opfer [fl, 2 vn, bc, kbd]	May–July 1747 (Leipzig, 1747); 2 Ricercars, a 3, a 6; 10 canons; sonata, fl, vn, bc; insts not fully specified	xxxi/2	VIII/i, 12	107, 109, 116, 121, 153, 160, 162, 242, 263
1080	Die Kunst der Fuge [kbd]	Leipzig, c1740–45, autograph, D-B P200, rev., enlarged (Leipzig, 1751, 2/1752); series of fugues (contrapuncti), mostly a 4, on same theme; for contents see Wolff (1975)	xxv/1	[VIII/ii]	110, 116, 153, 162, 263
1072	Canon trias harmonica	a 8, in contrary motion; in F. W. Marpurg: Abhandlung von der Fuge, ii (Berlin, 1754)	xlv, 131	VII/i, 3, 6	161
1073	Canon a 4 perpetuus	Weimar, 2 Aug 1713	xlv, 132	VII/i, 3, 6	161
1074	Canon a 4	Leipzig, 1727; completely invertible puzzle canon; ded. L. F. Hudemann; solution in J. Mattheson: Der volkommene Capellmeister (Hamburg, 1739/R1954)	xlv, 134	VII/i, 3, 7	116, 161
1075	Canon a 2 perpetuus	Leipzig, 10 Jan 1734; ded. J. M. Gesner	—	VIII/i, 3, 7	161
1076	Canon triplex a 6	3 simultaneous canons a 2, each in contrary motion; written for Haussmann portrait; 1087 incl. earlier version	xlv, 138	VIII/i, 3, 8	*112*, 115, 116, 161
1077	Canone doppio sopr'il soggetto	2 simultaneous canons a 2, each in contrary motion; Leipzig, 15 Oct 1747; ded. J. G. Fulde; 1087 incl. earlier version	—	VIII/i, 4, 8	161
1078	Canon super fa mi a 7 post tempus musicum	Leipzig, 1 March 1749; ded. 'Schmidt' (alias Benjamin Faber)	xlv, 136	VIII/i, 4, 9	161
1086	Canon concordia discors	a 2, in contrary motion; Leipzig, ?1731	—	VIII/i, 4, 10	161
1087	[14] Verschiedene Canones	14 puzzle canons (some solved) on first 8 notes of aria ground of 988; autograph, 1742–6, in Bach's copy of 988; incl. earlier versions of 1076–7	—	V/ii, 119	106, 161, 162

BIBLIOGRAPHY

CATALOGUES, BIBLIOGRAPHIES, TEXTUAL CRITICISM ETC

Prefaces to *J. S. Bach: Werke*, ed. Bach-Gesellschaft (Leipzig, 1851–99/*R*1947) [BG]

A. Dörffel: *Thematisches Verzeichnis der Instrumentalwerke von Joh. Seb. Bach* (Leipzig, 1867, 2/1882)

H. Kretzschmar: *Johann Sebastian Bachs Handschrift in zeitlich geordneten Nachbildungen*, BG, xliv (1895)

——: *Verzeichnis sämtlicher Werke und der einzelnen Sätze aus Werken Johann Sebastian Bachs*, BG, xlvi (1899)

M. Seiffert: 'Neue Bach-Funde', *JbMP 1904*, 15

Bach-Jahrbuch (BJb) (1904–)

M. Schneider: 'Verzeichnis der bisher erschienenen Literatur über Johann Sebastian Bach', *BJb*, ii (1905), 76–110

——: 'Verzeichnis der bis zum Jahre 1851 gedruckten (und der geschrieben im Handel gewesenen) Werke von Johann Sebastian Bach', *BJb*, iii (1906), 84–113

M. Seiffert: 'Zur Kritik der Gesamtausgabe von Bachs Werken', *BJb*, iii (1906), 79

M. Schneider: 'Neues Material zum Verzeichnis der bisher erschienenen Literatur über Johann Sebastian Bach', *BJb*, vii (1910), 133

J. Schreyer: *Beiträge zur Bach-Kritik*, i (Dresden, 1910); ii (Leipzig, 1912)

G. Frotscher: 'Übersicht über die wichtigsten im Zeitschriften erschienenen Aufsätze über Seb. Bach aus den Jahren 1915–1918', *BJb*, xv (1918), 151

R. Schwartz: 'Die Bach-Handschriften der Musikbibliothek Peters', *JbMP 1919*, 56

H. Tessmer: 'Joh. Sebastian Bach im öffentlichen Schrifttum seiner Zeit', *Neue Musik-Zeitung*, xl (1919), 127–215

A. Landau: 'Übersicht über die Bach-Literatur in Zeitschriften vom 1. Januar 1928 bis zum 30. Juni 1930', *BJb*, xxvii (1930), 132

——: 'Übersicht über die Bach-Literatur in Zeitschriften vom 1. Juli 1930 bis zum 1. Juli 1931', *BJb*, xxix (1932), 146

G. Kinsky: *Die Originalausgaben der Werke Johann Sebastian Bachs* (Vienna, 1937/*R*1968)

H. Miesner: 'Philipp Emanuel Bachs musikalischer Nachlass: vollständiger, dem Original entsprechender Neudruck des Nachlassverzeichnisses von 1790', *BJb*, xxxv (1938), 103; xxxvi (1939), 81; xxxvii (1940–48), 161

L. E. R. Picken: 'Bach Quotations from the Eighteenth Century', *MR*, v (1944), 83

W. Neumann: *Handbuch der Kantaten Johann Sebastian Bachs* (Leipzig, 1947, rev. 4/1977)

W. Schmieder: 'Die Handschriften Johann Sebastian Bachs', *Bach-Gedenkschrift 1950*, ed. K. Matthaei (Zurich, 1950), 190

——: *Thematisch-systematisches Verzeichnis der musikalischen Werke Johann Sebastian Bachs: Bach-Werke-Verzeichnis* (Leipzig, 1950, 3/1966, rev., enlarged edn. in preparation)

Die wissenschaftliche Bachtagung der Gesellschaft für Musikforschung: Leipzig 1950

W. Schmieder: 'Das Bachschrifttum 1945–1952', *BJb*, xl (1953), 119–68

Critical Commentaries to *J. S. Bach: Neue Ausgabe sämtlicher Werke* (*Neue Bach-Ausgabe*), ed. Johann-Sebastian-Bach-Institut, Göttingen, and Bach-Archiv, Leipzig (Kassel and Basle, 1954–)

P. Kast: *Die Bach-Handschriften der Berliner Staatsbibliothek*, Tübinger Bach-Studien, ii–iii (Trossingen, 1958)

W. Schmieder: 'Das Bachschrifttum 1953–1957', *BJb*, xlv (1958), 127

S. W. Kenney, ed.: *Catalog of the Emilie and Karl Riemenschneider Memorial Bach Library* (New York and London, 1960)

G. von Dadelsen: 'Originale Daten auf den Handschriften J. S. Bachs', *Hans Albrecht in memoriam* (Kassel, 1962), 116

M. McAll, ed.: *Melodic Index to the Works of Johann Sebastian Bach* (New York, 1962)

P. Krause, ed.: *Handschriften der Werke Johann Sebastian Bachs in der Musikbibliothek der Stadt Leipzig* (Leipzig, 1964)

W. Blankenburg: 'Zwölf Jahre Bachforschung', *AcM*, xxxvii (1965), 95–158

F. Blume: 'Der gegenwärtige Stand der Bachforschung', *NRMI*, iii (1969), 381

M. Geck, ed.: *Bach-Interpretationen* (Göttingen, 1969)

H. Zietz: *Quellenkritische Untersuchungen an den Bach-Handschriften P 801, P 802 und P 803 aus dem Krebsschen Nachlass unter Berücksichtigung der Choralbearbeitungen des jungen Bach* (Hamburg, 1969)

K. Engler: *Georg Poelchau und seine Musikaliensammlung: ein Beitrag zur Überlieferung Bachscher Musik im 19. Jahrhundert* (diss., U. of Tübingen, 1970)

P. Krause, ed.: *Originalausgaben und ältere Drucke der Werke Johann Sebastian Bachs in der Musikbibliothek der Stadt Leipzig* (Leipzig, 1970)

Y. Kobayashi: 'Zu einem neu entdeckten Autograph Bachs: Choral Aus der Tiefen', *BJb*, lvii (1971), 5

W. Hobohm: 'Neue "Texte zur Leipziger Kirchen-Music" ', *BJb*, lix (1973), 5

Bibliography

Y. Kobayashi: *Franz Hauser und seine Bach-Handschriftensammlung* (diss., U. of Göttingen, 1973)

R. Nestle: 'Das Bachschrifttum 1963–1967', *BJb*, lix (1973), 91

I. S. Duyzenkunst and K. Vellekoop, eds.: *Bachboek* (Utrecht, 1975)

Wissenschaftliche Bach-Konferenz: Leipzig 1975

R. Nestle: 'Das Bachschrifttum 1968–1972', *BJb*, lxii (1976), 95

H.-J. Schulze: *Katalog der Sammlung Manfred Gorke: Bachiana und andere Handschriften und Drucke des 18. und frühen 19. Jahrhunderts* (Leipzig, 1977)

——: *Studien zur Bach-Überlieferung im 18. Jahrhundert* (diss., U. of Rostock, 1977)

Bachforschung und Bachinterpretation heute: Bachfest-Symposium: Marburg 1978

W. Blankenburg: 'Die Bachforschung seit etwa 1965', *AcM*, l (1978), 93–153; liv (1982), 162–207; lv (1983), 1–58

W. Neumann: *Aufgaben und Probleme der heutigen Bachforschung* (Berlin, 1979)

R. Nestle: 'Das Bachschrifttum 1973–1977', *BJb*, lxvi (1980), 87–152

R. Wade, ed.: *The Catalog of Carl Philipp Emanuel Bach's Estate: a Facsimile of the Edition by Schniebes, Hamburg, 1790* (New York, 1981) [with annotations]

Katalog der Sammlung A. van Hoboken, i: *Johann Sebastian Bach* (Tutzing, 1982)

SOURCE MATERIAL: DOCUMENTS, LETTERS ETC

Ursprung der musikalisch-Bachischen Familie, genealogy, first draft, 1735, by J. S. Bach, in *Bach-Urkunden*, Veröffentlichungen der Neuer Bach-Gesellschaft, xvii/3, ed. M. Schneider (Leipzig, 1917), and in C. S. Terry: *The Origin of the Family of Bach Musicians* (London, 1929)

L. C. Mizler: *Neu eröffnete musikalische Bibliothek* (Leipzig, 1736–54)

J. A. Scheibe: *Der critische Musikus* (Leipzig, 1745/*R*1970)

J. F. Agricola and C. P. E. Bach: Obituary in L. Mizler: *Neu eröffnete musikalische Bibliothek*, iv/1 (Leipzig, 1754); repr. in *BJb*, xvii (1920), 11

E. Müller von Asow: *Johann Sebastian Bach: gesammelte Briefe* (Regensburg, 1938, 2/1950)

H. T. David and A. Mendel: *The Bach Reader: a Life of Johann Sebastian Bach in Letters and Documents* (New York, 1945, rev. 2/1966)

W. Neumann, ed.: *Facsimile-Reihe Bachser Werke und Schriftstücke* (Leipzig, 1954–)

H. Besch: 'Eine Auktions-Quittung J. S. Bachs', *Festschrift für Friedrich Smend* (Berlin, 1963), 74

217

W. Neumann and H.-J. Schulze, eds.: *Schriftstücke von der Hand Johann Sebastian Bachs*, Bach-Dokumente, i (Leipzig, 1963; Fr. trans., 1976)

H.-J. Schulze: 'Beiträge zur Bach-Quellenforschung', *GfMKB, Leipzig 1966*, 269

———: *Fremdschriftliche und gedruckte Dokumente zur Lebensgeschichte Johann Sebastian Bachs 1685–1750*, Bach-Dokumente, ii (Leipzig, 1969)

A. Dürr: 'Zur Chronologie der Handschrift Johann Christoph Altnickols und Johann Friedrich Agricolas', *BJb*, lvi (1970), 44

H.-J. Schulze, ed.: *Dokumente zum Nachwirken Johann Sebastian Bachs 1750–1800*, Bach-Dokumente, iii (Leipzig, 1972)

'Johann Sebastian Bach: Studies of the Sources', *Studies in Renaissance and Baroque Music in Honor of Arthur Mendel* (Kassel and Hackensack, 1974), 231–300 [contributions by P. Brainard, A. Dürr, G. Herz, E. May and C. Wolff]

H.-J. Schulze: 'Wie enstand die Bach-Sammlung Mempell-Preller?', *BJb*, lx (1974), 104

K.-H. Köhler: 'Die Bach-Sammlung der Deutschen Staatsbibliothek – Überlieferung und Bedeutung', *Bach-Studien*, v (1975), 139

W. Neumann, ed.: *Bilddokumente zur Lebensgeschichte Johann Sebastian Bachs*, Bach-Dokumente, iv (Leipzig, 1978)

H.-J. Schulze: 'Das Stück in Goldpapier: Ermittlungen zu einigen Bach-Abschriften des frühen 18. Jahrhunderts', *BJb*, lxiv (1978), 19

Y. Kobayashi: 'Neuerkenntnisse zu einigen Bach-Quellen an Handschriftkundlicher Untersuchungen', *BJb*, lxiv (1978), 43

H.-J. Schulze: 'Ein "Dresdner Menuett" im zweiten Klavierbüchlein der Anna Magdalena Bach: nebst Hinweisen zur Überlieferung einiger Kammermusikwerke Bachs', *BJb*, lxv (1979), 45

H. Stiehl: 'Taufzettel für Bachs Kinder: ein Dokumentenfund', *BJb*, lxv (1979), 7

G. Butler: 'Leipziger Stecher in Bachs Originaldrucken', *BJb*, lxvi (1980), 9

W. Plath: 'Zum Schicksal der Andre-Gerberschen Musikbibliothek', *Festschrift für Alfred Dürr* (Kassel, 1983), 209

G. Herz: *Bach Sources in America* (Kassel, in preparation)

ICONOGRAPHY

E. Vogel: 'Bach-Porträts', *JbMP 1896*, 11

M. Schneider: 'Verzeichnis von Bildnissen Bachs', *BJb*, ii (1905), 109

A. Kurzwelly: 'Neues über das Bachbildnis der Thomasschule und andere Bildnisse Johann Sebastian Bachs', *BJb*, xi (1914), 1–37

J. Müller: 'Bach Portraits', *MQ*, xxi (1935), 155

G. Herz: 'A "New" Bach Portrait', *MQ*, xxix (1943), 225

Bibliography

K. Geiringer: *The Lost Portrait of J. S. Bach* (New York, 1950)

H. Raupach: *Das wahre Bildnis J. S. Bachs* (Wolfenbüttel, 1950)

F. Smend: *J. S. Bach bei seinem Namen gerufen* (Kassel, 1950)

H. Besseler: *Fünf echte Bildnisse Johann Sebastian Bachs* (Kassel, 1956)

H. O. R. van Tuyll van Serooskerken: *Probleme des Bachporträts* (Bilthoven, 1956)

C. Freyse: *Bachs Antlitz* (Eisenach, 1964)

H. Börsch-Supan: 'Gruppenbild mit Musikern: ein Gemälde von Balthasar Denner und das Problem der Bach-Ikonographie', *Kunst und Antiquitäten*, iii (1982), 22

M. Staehelin: 'Zu einer umstrittenen Bach-Porträtzeichnung des 18. Jahrhunderts', *Festschrift für Alfred Dürr* (Kassel, 1983), 260

BIOGRAPHY, LIFE AND WORKS

J. N. Forkel: *Über Johann Sebastian Bachs Leben, Kunst und Kunstwerke* (Leipzig, 1802/*R*1966; Eng. trans., 1820/*R* in *The Bach Reader: a Life of Johann Sebastian Bach in Letters and Documents*, ed. H. T. David and A. Mendel (New York, 1945, rev. 2/1966); also *R*1974)

C. L. Hilgenfeldt: *Johann Sebastian Bach's Leben, Wirken und Werke: ein Beitrag zur Kunstgeschichte des achtzehnten Jahrhunderts* (Leipzig, 1850/*R*1965)

C. H. Bitter: *Johann Sebastian Bach* (Berlin, 1865, enlarged 2/1881/*R*1978)

P. Spitta: *Johann Sebastian Bach* (Leipzig, 1873–80/*R*1964, 5/1962; Eng. trans., 1884–5/*R*1951)

A. Schweitzer: *J. S. Bach, le musicien-poète* (Paris, 1905; Eng. trans., 1911/*R*1967)

A. Pirro: *Johann-Sebastian Bach* (Paris, 1906; Eng. trans., 1958)

P. Wolfrum: *Johann Sebastian Bach*, i (Berlin, 1906, 2/1910); ii (Leipzig, 1910)

C. H. H. Parry: *Johann Sebastian Bach* (London, 1909, 2/1934/*R*1968)

J. Tiersot: *J.-S. Bach* (Paris, 1912, 2/1934)

C. S. Terry: *Bach: a Biography* (London, 1928; Ger. trans., rev., 1929)

H. J. Moser: *J. S. Bach* (Berlin, 1935, 2/1943)

J. Müller-Blattau: *Johann Sebastian Bach* (Leipzig, 1935)

W. Gurlitt: *Johann Sebastian Bach: der Meister und sein Werk* (Berlin, 1936, rev., enlarged 2/1947; Eng. trans., 1957)

W. Cart: *J. S. Bach: 1685–1750* (Lausanne, 1946)

A. E. Cherbuliez: *Johann Sebastian Bach: sein Leben und sein Werk* (Olten, 1946, 2/1947)

E. M. and S. Grew: *Bach* (London, 1947/*R*1965)

H. Engel: *Johann Sebastian Bach* (Berlin, 1950)

W. Neumann: *Auf den Lebenswegen Johann Sebastian Bachs* (Berlin, 1953)

——: *Bach: eine Bildbiographie* (Munich, 1960; Eng. trans., 1961)

E. Buchet, ed.: *Jean-Sébastien Bach: l'oeuvre et la vie* (Paris, 1963)

K. Geiringer: *Johann Sebastian Bach: the Culmination of an Era* (New York, 1966; Ger. edn., rev., enlarged, 1978)

E. Buchet: *Jean-Sébastien Bach, après deux siècles d'études et de témoignages* (Paris, 1968)

Kalendarium zur Lebensgeschichte J. S. Bachs, ed. Bach-Archiv, Leipzig (Leipzig, 1970, rev. 2/1979)

B. Schwendowius and W. Dömling, eds.: *Johann Sebastian Bach: Zeit, Leben, Wirken* (Kassel, 1976; Eng. trans., 1978)

W. Siegmund-Schulze: *Johann Sebastian Bach* (Leipzig, 1976)

H.-J. Schulze: 'Über die "unvermeidlichen Lücken" in Bachs Lebensbeschreibung', *Bachforschung und Bachinterpretation heute: Bachfest-Symposium: Marburg 1978*, 32

C. Wolff: 'Probleme und Neuansätze der Bach-Biographik', *Bachforschung und Bachinterpretation heute: Bachfest-Symposium: Marburg 1978*, 21

T. Wilhelmi: 'Bachs Bibliothek', *BJb*, lxv (1979), 107

A. Basso: *Frau Musika: la vita e le opere di J. S. Bach* (Turin, 1979–)

P. Buscarolli: *La nuova immagine di J. S. Bach* (Milan, 1982)

F. Otterbach: *Johann Sebastian Bach: Leben und Werk* (Stuttgart, 1982)

M. Boyd: *Bach* (London, 1983)

BIOGRAPHY: SPECIAL STUDIES

C. Scherer: 'Joh. Seb. Bachs Aufenthalt in Kassel', *MMg*, xxv (1893), 129

B. F. Richter: 'Stadtpfeifer und Alumnen der Thomasschule in Leipzig zu Bachs Zeit', *BJb*, iv (1907), 32–78

K. Pottgiesser: 'Die Briefentwürfe des Johann Elias Bach', *Die Musik*, xii/2 (1912–13), 3

B. F. Richter: 'Johann Sebastian Bach im Gottesdienst der Thomaner', *BJb*, xii (1915), 1–38

C. Freyse: *Eisenacher Dokumente um Sebastian Bach* (Leipzig, 1933)

——: 'Das Bach-Haus zu Eisenach', *BJb*, xxxvi (1939), 66; xxxvii (1940–48), 152

G. Herz: 'Bach's Religion', *JRBM*, i (1946), 124

G. Fock: *Der junge Bach in Lüneburg* (Hamburg, 1950)

F. Wiegand: *J. S. Bach und seine Verwandten in Arnstadt* (Arnstadt, 1950)

F. Smend: *Bach in Köthen* (Berlin, 1951)

H. Löffler: 'Die Schüler Joh. Seb. Bachs', *BJb*, xl (1953), 5

Bibliography

K. Geiringer: *The Bach Family: Seven Generations of Creative Genius* (New York, 1954)

W. Neumann: 'Das "Bachische Collegium Musicum" ', *BJb*, xlvii (1960), 5

F. Blume: 'Outlines of a New Picture of Bach', *ML*, xliv (1963), 214

P. M. Young: *The Bachs, 1500–1850* (London, 1970)

I. Ahlgrimm: 'Von Reisen, Kirchererbsen und Fischbeinröcken', *Bach-Studien*, v (1975), 155

R. Eller: 'Gedanken über Bachs Leipziger Schaffensjahre', *Bach-Studien*, v (1975), 7

W. Schrammek: 'Johann Sebastian Bach, Gottfried Silbermann und die französische Orgelkunst', *Bach-Studien*, v (1975), 93

H.-J. Schulze: 'Johann Sebastian Bach und Georg Gottfried Wagner – neue Dokumente', *Bach-Studien*, v (1975), 147

E. Zavarský: 'J. S. Bachs Entwurf für den Umbau der Orgel in der Kirche Divi Blasii und das Klangideal der Zeit', *Bach-Studien*, v (1975), 83

A. Glöckner: 'Johann Sebastian Bachs Aufführungen zeitgenössischer Passionsmusiken', *BJb*, lxiii (1977), 75–119

A. Dürr: 'Heinrich Nicolaus Gerber als Schüler Bachs', *BJb*, lxiv (1978), 7

C. Wolff: 'Bachs Leipziger Kantoratsprobe und die Aufführungsgeschichte der Kantate BWV 23', *BJb*, lxiv (1978), 78

A. Plichta: 'J. S. Bach und J. A. von Questenberg', *BJb*, lxvii (1981)

Festschrift für Alfred Dürr (Kassel, 1983) [contributions by W. Felix, H. Heussner, W. Neumann, W. H. Scheide, H.-J. Schulze and E. Zavarsky]

U. Siegele: 'Bachs Stellung in der Leipziger Kulturpolitik seiner Zeit', *BJb*, lxix (1983)

WORKS: GENERAL

A. Pirro: *L'esthétique de Jean-Sébastien Bach* (Paris, 1907)

R. Oppel: 'Beziehungen Bachs zu Vorgängern und Nachfolgern', *BJb*, xxii (1925), 11

F. Jöde: *Die Kunst Bachs* (Wolfenbüttel, 1926)

F. Rochlitz: *Wege zu Bach* (Augsburg, 1926)

C. S. Terry: *The Music of Bach: an Introduction* (London, 1933)

A. E. F. Dickinson: *The Art of J. S. Bach* (London, 1935, rev., enlarged 2/1950)

G. Herz: *Joh. Seb. Bach im Zeitalter des Rationalismus und der Frühromantik* (Kassel, 1935)

G. Frotscher: *J. S. Bach und die Musik des 17. Jahrhunderts* (Wädenswil, 1939)

A. Schering: *Johann Sebastian Bach und das Musikleben Leipzigs im 18. Jahrhundert* (Leipzig, 1941)

W. Blankenburg: *Die innere Einheit von Bachs Werk* (diss., U. of Göttingen, 1942)

L. Schrade: 'Bach: the Conflict between the Sacred and the Secular', *Journal of the History of Ideas*, vii (1946), 151–94

F. Blume: *Johann Sebastian Bach im Wandel der Geschichte* (Kassel, 1947; Eng. trans., 1950 as *Two Centuries of Bach*)

M. Dehnert: *Das Weltbild J. S. Bachs* (Leipzig, 1948, 2/1949)

W. Blankenburg: 'Bach geistlich und weltlich', *Musik und Kirche*, xx (1950)

K. Geiringer: 'Artistic Interrelations of the Bachs', *MQ*, xxxvi (1950), 363

R. Petzoldt and L. Weinhold: *Johann Sebastian Bach: das Schaffen des Meisters in Spiegel einer Stadt* (Leipzig, 1950)

R. Steglich: *Wege zu Bach* (Regensburg, 1950)

W. Vetter: *Der Kapellmeister Bach: Versuch einer Deutung* (Potsdam, 1950)

H. Besseler: 'Bach und das Mittelalter', *Die wissenschaftliche Bachtagung der Gesellschaft für Musikforschung: Leipzig 1950*, 108

A. T. Davison: *Bach and Handel: the Consummation of the Baroque in Music* (Cambridge, Mass., 1951)

F. Hamel: *J. S. Bach: geistige Welt* (Göttingen, 1951)

A. Salazar: *Juan Sebastian Bach: un esayo* (Mexico City, 1951)

P. Hindemith: *Johann Sebastian Bach: Heritage and Obligation* (New Haven, 1952)

H. Besseler: 'Bach als Wegbereiter', *AMw*, xii (1955), 1–39

F. Blume: 'Bach in the Romantic Era', *MQ*, l (1964), 290

F. Neumann: *Ornamentation in Baroque and Post-Baroque Music with Special Emphasis on J. S. Bach* (Princeton, 1978)

U. Siegele: *Bachs theologische Formbegriff und das Duett F-Dur* (Stuttgart, 1978)

J. Jersild: 'Die Harmonik J. S. Bachs: eine funktionanalytische Studie', *BJb*, lxvi (1980), 53

W. Mellers: *Bach and the Dance of God* (London, 1980)

R. Szeskus, ed.: 'Johann Sebastian Bach und die Aufklärung', *Bach-Studien*, vii (1982)

C. Wolff: '"Die sonderbaren Vollkommenheiten des Herrn Hof Compositeurs": Versuch über die Eigenart der Bachschen Musik', *Festschrift für Alfred Dürr* (Kassel, 1983), 356

WORKS: SPECIAL STUDIES

E. Dannreuther: 'Die Verzierungen in den Werken von J. S. Bach', *BJb*, vi (1909), 41–101

K. Grunsky: 'Bachs Bearbeitungen und Umarbeitungen eigener und fremder Werke', *BJb*, ix (1912), 61

Bibliography

M. Schneider: 'Der Generalbass Joh. Seb. Bachs', *JbMP 1914–15*

E. Kurth: *Grundlagen des linearen Kontrapunkts: Einführung in Stil und Technik von Bachs melodischer Polyphonie* (Berne, 1917, 4/1946)

R. Oppel: 'Zur Fugentechnik Bachs', *BJb*, xviii (1921), 9–48

A. Schering: 'Über Bachs Parodieverfahren', *BJb*, xviii (1921), 49–95

J. Müller: 'Motivsprache und Stilart des jungen Bach', *BJb*, xix (1922), 38–70

A. Schering: 'Bach und das Symbol, insbesondere die Symbolik seines Kanons', *BJb*, xxii (1925), 40

M.-A. Souchay: 'Das Thema in der Fuge Bachs', *BJb*, xxiv (1927), 1–102; xxvii (1930), 1–48

A. Schering: 'Bach und das Symbol, ii: Das "Figürliche" und "Metaphorische" ', *BJb*, xxv (1928), 119

W. Danckert: *Beiträge zur Bachkritik* (Kassel, 1934)

G. Schünemann: 'Bachs Verbesserungen und Entwürft', *BJb*, xxxii (1935), 1–32

A. Schering: 'Bach und das Symbol, iii: Psychologische Grundlegung des Symbolbegriffs aus Christian Wolffs "Psychologia empirica" ', *BJb*, xxxiv (1937), 83

W. Emery: 'Bach's Symbolic Language', *ML*, xxx (1949), 345
——: *Bach's Ornaments* (London, 1953)

F. Rothschild: *The Lost Tradition in Music: Rhythm and Tempo in J. S. Bach's Time* (London, 1953)

K. Geiringer: *Symbolism in the Music of Bach* (Washington, DC, 1955)

A. Mendel: 'On the Pitches in Use in Bach's Time', *MQ*, xli (1955), 332, 466

A. Dürr: 'Gedanken zu J. S. Bachs Umarbeitungen eigener Werke', *BJb*, xliii (1956), 93

B. Paumgartner: 'Johann Sebastian Bach, Mozart und die Wiener Klassik', *BJb*, xliii (1956), 5

G. von Dadelsen: *Bemerkungen zur Handschrift Johann Sebastian Bachs, seiner Familie und seines Kreises*, Tübinger Bach-Studien, i (Trossingen, 1957)
——: *Beiträge zur Chronologie der Werke Johann Sebastian Bachs*, Tübinger Bach-Studien, iv–v (Trossingen, 1958)

A. Mendel: 'Recent Developments in Bach Chronology', *MQ*, xlvi (1960), 283

R. Steglich: 'Johann Sebastian Bach über sich selbst und im Urteil der Mit- und Nachwelt', *Festschrift Hans Engel* (Kassel, 1964), 393

W. Blankenburg: 'Zwölf Jahre Bachforschung', *AcM*, xxxvii (1965), 95ff

F. Neumann: 'A New Look at Bach's Ornamentation', *ML*, xlvi (1965), 4, 126

N. Carrell: *Bach the Borrower* (London, 1967)

223

A. Dürr: 'Neues über Bachs Pergolesi-Bearbeitung', *BJb*, liv (1968), 89

C. Wolff: *Der stile antico in der Musik Johann Sebastian Bachs* (Wiesbaden, 1968)

D. Gojowy: 'Wie entstand Hans Georg Nägelis Bach-Sammlung? Dokumente zur Bach-Renaissance im 19. Jahrhundert', *BJb*, lvi (1970), 66

R. L. Marshall: 'How J. S. Bach Composed Four-part Chorales', *MQ*, lvi (1970), 198

W. Emery: 'Is your Bach Playing Authentic?', *MT*, cxii (1971), 483, 697, 796

M. Geck: 'Bachs Probestück', *Quellenstudien zur Musik: Wolfgang Schmieder zum 70. Geburtstag* (Frankfurt am Main, 1972), 55

R. Stephan: 'J. S. Bach und das Problem des musikalischen Zyklus', *BJb*, lix (1973), 39

'Johann Sebastian Bach: Approaches to Analysis and Interpretation', *Studies in Renaissance and Baroque Music in Honor of Arthur Mendel* (Kassel and Hackensack, 1974), 139–230 [contributions by W. Blankenburg, E. T. Cone, W. Emery, R. L. Marshall, F. Neumann, N. Rubin and W. H. Scheide]

W. Emery: 'A Note on Bach's Use of Triplets', *Bach-Studien*, v (1975), 109

H. Eppstein: 'Zum Formproblem bei J. S. Bach', *Bach-Studien*, v (1975), 29

H. Grüss: 'Tempofragen der Bachzeit', *Bach-Studien*, v (1975), 73

U. Siegele: *Kompositionsweise und Bearbeitungstechnik in der Instrumentalmusik Johann Sebastian Bachs* (Stuttgart, 1975)

R. L. Marshall: 'Bach the Progressive: Observations on his Later Works', *MQ*, lxii (1976), 313

L. Dreyfus: 'J. S. Bach's Experiment in Accompaniment: Tacet Indications in Organ Parts', *JAMS*, xxxii (1979), 321

U. Prinz: *Studien zum Instrumentarium J. S. Bachs mit besonderer Berücksichtigung der Kantaten* (diss., U. of Tübingen, 1979)

Z. P. Ambrose: '"Weinen, Klagen, Sorgen, Zagen" und die antike Redekunst', *BJb*, lxvi (1980), 35

L. Dreyfus: *Basso Continuo Practice in the Vocal Works of J. S. Bach: a Study of the Original Performance Parts* (diss., Columbia U., 1980)

R. L. Marshall: 'Editore traditore: ein weiterer "Fall Rust"', *Festschrift für Alfred Dürr* (Kassel, 1983), 183

VOCAL WORKS

R. Rolland: *Bachs Matthäuspassion* (1905)

B. F. Richter: 'Über die Schicksale der Thomasschule zu Leipzig angehörenden Kantaten Joh. Seb. Bachs', *BJb*, iii (1906), 43–73

——: 'Über Seb. Bachs Kantaten mit obligater Orgel', *BJb*, v (1908), 49

Bibliography

W. Voigt: 'Zu Bachs Weihnachtsoratorium, Teil 1 bis 3', *BJb*, v (1908), 1–48

A. Heuss: *Bachs Matthäuspassion* (Leipzig, 1909)

R. Wustmann: 'Bachs Matthäuspassion, erster Theil', *BJb*, vi (1909), 129

——: 'Sebastian Bachs Kirchenkantatentexte', *BJb*, vii (1910), 45

B. F. Richter: 'Über die Motetten Seb. Bachs', *BJb*, ix (1912), 1–32

L. Wolff: *J. Sebastian Bachs Kirchenkantaten* (Leipzig, 1913)

R. Wustmann: *Joh. Seb. Bachs Kantatentexte* (Leipzig, 1913, 2/1967)

C. S. Terry: *Bach's Chorales* (Cambridge, 1915–21)

W. Voigt: *Die Kirchenkantaten Johann Sebastian Bachs* (Stuttgart, 1918, 2/1928)

W. Werker: *Die Matthäuspassion* (Leipzig, 1923)

C. S. Terry: *Bach's B minor Mass* (Oxford, 1924)

H. J. Moser: 'Aus Joh. Seb. Bachs Kantatenwelt', *Die Musik*, xvii (1924–5), 721

F. W. Franke: *Bachs Kirchen-Kantaten* (Leipzig, 1925)

C. S. Terry: *Bach: the Cantatas and Oratorios* (London, 1925/*R*1972)

W. G. Whittaker: *Fugitive Notes on certain Cantatas and the Motets of J. S. Bach* (Oxford, 1925)

F. Smend: 'Die Johannes-Passion von Bach', *BJb*, xxiii (1926), 105

C. S. Terry: *Johann Sebastian Bach: Cantata Texts, Sacred and Secular* (London, 1926/*R*1964)

F. Smend: 'Bachs Matthäus-Passion', *BJb*, xxv (1928), 1–95

C. S. Terry: *Bach: the Passions* (London, 1928)

H. Abert: *Bachs Matthäuspassion* (Halle, 1929)

F. Atkins: *Bach's Passions* (London, 1929)

K. Ziebler: *Das Symbol in der Kirchenmusik Bachs* (Kassel, 1930)

F. Blume: *Die evangelische Kirchenmusik*, HMw, x (1931, rev. 2/1965 as *Geschichte der evangelischen Kirchenmusik*; Eng. trans., enlarged, 1974, as *Protestant Church Music: a History*)

H. Sirp: 'Die Thematic der Kirchenkantaten J. S. Bachs in ihren Beziehungen zum protestantischen Kirchenlied', *BJb*, xxviii (1931), 1–50; xxix (1932), 51–118

R. Gerber: 'Über Geist und Weisen von Bachs h-moll-Messe', *BJb*, xxix (1932), 119

W. Lütge: 'Bachs Motette, Jesu meine Freude', *Musik und Kirche*, iv (1932), 97

C. S. Terry: 'The Spurious Bach "Lukas-Passion" ', *ML*, xiv (1932), 207

K. Ziebler: 'Aufbau und Gliederung der Matthäuspassion von Johann Sebastian Bach', *Musik und Kirche*, iv (1932), 145

A. Schering: 'Kleine Bachstudien', *BJb*, xxx (1933), 30–70

C. O. Dreger: 'Die Vokalthematic Johann Sebastian Bachs: dargestellt an den Arien der Kirchenkantaten', *BJb*, xxxi (1934), 1–62

W. Lütge: 'Das architektonische Prinzip der Matthäuspassion J. S.

Bachs', *Zeitschrift für Ästhetik und allgemeine Kunstwissenschaft*, xxx (1936), 65

A. Schering: *Johann Sebastian Bachs Leipziger Kirchenmusik* (Leipzig, 1936, 2/1954)

——: 'Die Hohe Messe in h-moll', *BJb*, xxxiii (1936), 1–30

E. Thiele: *Die Chorfugen J. S. Bachs* (Berne, 1936)

M. Jansen: 'Bachs Zahlensymbolik, an seinen Passionen untersucht', *BJb*, xxxiv (1937), 96

F. Smend: 'Bachs h-moll-Messe: Entstehung, Überlieferung, Bedeutung', *BJb*, xxxiv (1937), 1–58

W. Neumann: *J. S. Bach's Chorfuge* (Leipzig, 1938)

A. Schering: 'Zur Markus-Passion und zur "vierten" Passion', *BJb*, xxxvi (1939), 1–32

F. Smend: 'Bachs Markus-Passion', *BJb*, xxxvii (1940–48), 1–35

A. Schering: *Über Kantaten Johann Sebastian Bachs* (Leipzig, 1942, 3/1950)

F. Smend: 'Neue Bach-Funde', *AMf*, vii (1942), 1

H. S. Drinker: *Texts of Choral Works of J. S. Bach in English Translation* (New York, 1942–3)

W. Neumann: *Handbuch der Kantaten Johann Sebastian Bachs* (Leipzig, 1947, rev. 3/1967, 4/1971)

F. Smend: *Joh. Seb. Bach: Kirchen-Kantaten* (Berlin, 1947–9, 3/1966)

A. Dürr: 'Zu den verschollenen Passionen Bachs', *BJb*, xxxviii (1949–50), 81

W. Blankenburg: *Einführung in Bachs h-moll Messe* (Kassel, 1950, rev. 3/1973)

A. Dürr: 'Zur Aufführungspraxis der vor-Leipziger Kirchenkantaten J. S. Bachs', *Musik und Kirche*, xx (1950)

——: 'Über Kantatenformen in den geistlichen Dichtungen Salomon Francks', *Mf*, iii (1950), 18

I. F. Finlay: *J. S. Bachs weltliche Kantaten* (Göttingen, 1950)

——: 'Bach's Secular Cantata Texts', *ML*, xxxi (1950), 189

R. Gerber: 'Über Formstrukturen in Bachs Motetten', *Mf*, iii (1950), 177

A. Mendel: 'On the Keyboard Accompaniments to Bach's Leipzig Church Music', *MQ*, xxxvi (1950), 339

A. Schmitz: *Die Bildlichkeit der wortgebundenen Musik J. S. Bachs* (Mainz, 1950)

F. Smend: 'Bachs Himmelfahrts-Oratorium', *Bach-Gedenkschrift 1950*, ed. K. Matthaei (Zurich, 1950), 42

A. Dürr: *Studien über die frühen Kantaten J. S. Bachs* (Leipzig, 1951, rev. 2/1977)

——: 'Zur Echtheit einiger Bach zugeschriebener Kantaten', *BJb*, xxxix (1951–2), 30

Bibliography

W. H. Scheide: *J. S. Bach as a Biblical Interpreter* (Princeton, 1952)

W. Serauky: 'Die "Johannes-Passion" von Joh. Seb. Bach und ihr Vorbild', *BJb*, xli (1954), 29

F. Hudson and A. Dürr: 'An Investigation into the Authenticity of Bach's "Kleine Magnificat" ', *ML*, xxxvi (1955), 233

W. Neumann, ed.: *Johann Sebastian Bach: sämtliche Kantatentexte* (Leipzig, 1956, 2/1967)

L. F. Tagliavini: *Studi sui testi delle cantate sacre di J. S. Bach* (Padua, 1956)

A. Dürr: 'Zur Chronologie der Leipziger Vokalwerke J. S. Bachs', *BJb*, xliv (1957), 5–162; pubd separately, rev. (Kassel, 1976)

B. Smallman: *The Background of Passion Music: J. S. Bach and his Predecessors* (London, 1957, rev., enlarged, 2/1970)

H. Melchert: *Das Rezitativ der Kirchenkantaten J. S. Bach* (diss., U. of Frankfurt am Main, 1958; extract in *BJb*, xlv (1958), 5–83)

W. H. Scheide: 'Johann Sebastian Bachs Sammlung von Kantaten seines Vetters Johann Ludwig Bach', *BJb*, xlvi (1959), 52–94; xlviii (1961), 5; xlix (1962), 5

W. G. Whittaker: *The Cantatas of Johann Sebastian Bach* (London, 1959, 2/1964)

P. Mies: *Die geistlichen Kantaten Johann Sebastian Bachs und der Hörer von heute* (Wiesbaden, 1959–64)

K. Ameln: 'Zur Entstehungsgeschichte der Motette "Singet dem Herrn ein neues Lied" von J. S. Bach (BWV 225)', *BJb*, xlviii (1961), 25

J. C. F. Day: *The Literary Background to Bach's Cantatas* (London, 1961)

U. Siegele: 'Bemerkungen zu Bachs Motetten', *BJb*, xlix (1962), 33

J. Chailley: *Les Passions de J.-S. Bach* (Paris, 1963)

A. Mendel: 'Traces of the Pre-history of Bach's St John and St Matthew Passions', *Festschrift Otto Erich Deutsch* (Kassel, 1963), 31

A. Dürr: 'Beobachtungen am Autograph der Matthäus-Passion', *BJb*, l (1963–4), 47

D. Gojowy: 'Zur Frage der Köthener Trauermusik und der Matthäuspassion', *BJb*, li (1965), 87–134

W. Neumann: 'Über Ausmass und Wesen des Bachschen Parodieverfahrens', *BJb*, li (1965), 63

R. Bullivant: 'Zum Problem der Begleitung der Bachschen Motetten', *BJb*, lii (1966), 59

F. Smend: 'Zu den ältesten Sammlungen der vierstimmigen Choräle J. S. Bachs', *BJb*, lii (1966), 5

J. A. Westrup: *Bach Cantatas* (London, 1966)

F. Zander: *Die Dichter der Kantatentexte Johann Sebastian Bachs: Untersuchungen zu ihrer Bestimmung* (diss., U. of Cologne, 1966;

extract in *BJb*, liv (1968), 9–64)

P. Mies: *Die weltlichen Kantaten Johann Sebastian Bachs und der Hörer von heute* (Wiesbaden, 1966–7)

M. Geck: 'Zur Echtheit der Bach-Motette "Lobet den Herrn, alle Heiden" ', *BJb*, liii (1967), 57

——: *Die Wiederentdeckung der Matthäuspassion im 19. Jahrhundert* (Regensburg, 1967)

P. Brainard: 'Bach's Parody Procedure and the St Matthew Passion', *JAMS*, xxii (1969), 241

G. Herz: 'BWV131: Bach's First Cantata', *Studies in Eighteenth-century Music: a Tribute to Karl Geiringer* (New York and London, 1970), 272

H. Schmalfuss: 'Johann Sebastian Bachs "Actus tragicus" (BWV106): ein Beitrag zu seiner Entstehungsgeschichte', *BJb*, lvi (1970), 36

A. Dürr: *Die Kantaten von Johann Sebastian Bach* (Kassel, 1971)

R. Leavis: 'Bach's Setting of Psalm CXLII (BWV230)', *ML*, lii (1971), 19

R. L. Marshall: *The Compositional Process of J. S. Bach: a Study of the Autograph Scores of the Vocal Works* (Princeton, 1972)

W. Neumann: 'Johann Sebastian Bachs "Rittergutskantaten" BWV30a und 212', *BJb*, lviii (1972), 76

A. Robertson: *The Church Cantatas of J. S. Bach* (London, 1972)

R. Gerlach: 'Besetzung und Instrumentation der Kirchenkantaten J. S. Bach und ihre Bedingungen', *BJb*, lix (1973), 53

G. Herz: 'Der lombardische Rhythmus im "Domine Deus" der h-Moll-Messe J. S. Bachs', *BJb*, lx (1974), 90

F. Krummacher: 'Textauslegung und Satzstruktur in J. S. Bachs Motetten', *BJb*, lx (1974), 5–43

A. Dürr: 'Bachs Kantatentexte: Probleme und Aufgaben der Forschung', *Bach-Studien*, v (1975), 49

M. Geck: 'Zur Datierung, Verwendung und Aufführungspraxis von Bachs Motetten', *Bach-Studien*, v (1975), 63

A. Glöckner: 'Bach and the Passion Music of his Contemporaries', *MT*, cxvi (1975), 613

D. Gojowy: 'Ein Zwölftonfeld bei J. S. Bach? Beobachtungen am Rezitativ BWV 167, Satz 2, Takte 13–19', *Bach-Studien*, v (1975), 43

K. Häfner: 'Der Picander Jahrgang', *BJb*, lxi (1975), 70

A. Mendel: 'Meliora ac Melioranda in the Two Versions of BWV 245/1', *Bach-Studien*, v (1975), 113

E. Platen: 'Zur Echtheit einiger Choralsätze Johann Sebastian Bachs', *BJb*, lxi (1975), 50

J. Rifkin: 'The Chronology of Bach's Saint Matthew Passion', *MQ*, lxi (1975), 360

Bibliography

W. H. Scheide: 'The "Concertato" Violin in BWV139', *Bach-Studien*, v (1975), 123

W. Neumann, ed.: *Sämtliche von J. S. Bach vertonte Texte* (Leipzig, 1974)

W. Schrammek: 'Fragen des Orgelgebrauchs in Bachs Aufführungen der Matthäus-Passion', *BJb*, lxi (1975), 114

W. Blankenburg: 'Eine neue Textquelle zu sieben Kantaten Johann Sebastian Bachs und achtzehn Kantaten Johann Ludwig Bachs', *BJb*, lxiii (1977), 7

H. E. Smither: *A History of the Oratorio*, ii (Chapel Hill, 1977), 154ff

E. Axmacher: 'Ein Quellenfund zum Text der Matthäus-Passion', *BJb*, lxiv (1978), 181

P. Brainard: 'Über Fehler und Korrekturen der Textunterlage in den Vokalwerken J. S. Bachs', *BJb*, lxiv (1978), 113

G. Herz: 'Der lombardische Rhythmus in Bachs Vokalschaffen', *BJb*, lxiv (1978), 148–80

U. Siegele: 'Bachs Endzweck einer regulierten und Entwurf einer wohlbestallten Kirchenmusik', *Festschrift G. von Dadelsen* (Stuttgart, 1978), 313–51

P. Steinitz: *Bach's Passions* (London, 1979)

G. J. Buelow: 'Symbol and Structure in the "Kyrie" of Bach's B minor Mass', *Essays on Bach and Other Matters: a Tribute to Gerhard Herz* (Louisville, Ken., 1981), 21

E. Chafe: 'Key Structure and Tonal Allegory in the Passions of J. S. Bach: an Introduction', *CMc*, xxxi (1981), 39

H. K. Krausse: 'Eine unbekannte Textquelle Bachs', *BJb*, lxvii (1981)

F. Krummacher: 'Mehrchörigkeit und thematischer Satz bei Johann Sebastian Bach', *Schütz-Jb*, iii (1981), 39

A. Mann: 'Bach's A major Mass: a Nativity Mass?', *Essays on Bach and Other Matters: a Tribute to Gerhard Herz* (Louisville, Ken., 1981), 43

E. Chafe: 'J. S. Bach's *St Matthew Passion*: Aspects of Planning, Structure, and Chronology', *JAMS*, xxxv (1982), 49–114

K. Hofmann: 'Bachs Kantate "Ich lasse dich nicht, du segnest mich denn" BWV 157', *BJb*, lxviii (1982)

J. Rifkin: 'Bach's Chorus: a preliminary Report', *MT*, cxxiii (1982), 747 [see also *MT*, cxxiv (1983), 19, 161]

W. H. Scheide: '"Nun ist das Heil und die Kraft" BWV 50: Doppelchörigkeit, Datierung und Bestimmung', *BJb*, lxviii (1982)

C. Wolff: 'Bach's Cantata "Ein feste Burg": History and Performance Practice', *American Choral Review*, xxiv (1982)

R. L. Marshall: 'Bach's Chorus; a Reply to Joshua Rifkin', *MT*, cxxiv (1983), 19

H.-J. Schulze: '"150 Stück von den Bachischen Erben": Zur

Überlieferung der vierstimmigen Choräle J. S. Bachs', *BJb*, lxix (1983)

G. Wachowski: 'Die vierstimmigen Choräle J. S. Bachs: Untersuchungen zu den Druckausgaben von 1765 bis 1932 und zur Frage der Authentizität', *BJb*, lxix (1983)

Festschrift für Alfred Dürr (Kassel, 1983) [contributions by E. Axmacher, W. Blankenburg, P. Brainard, W. Gerstenberg, G. von Dadelsen, K. Hofmann, U. Meyer, J. Stalmann, L. and R. Steiger and G. Stiller]

INSTRUMENTAL WORKS

H. Riemann: *Katechismus der Fugenkomposition*, iii (Leipzig, 1894, 2/1906)

A. Pirro: *L'orgue de Jean-Sébastien Bach* (Paris, 1895; Eng. trans., 1902/*R*1978)

M. Seiffert: *Geschichte der Klaviermusik* (Leipzig, 1899)

A. Schering: *Geschichte des Instrumentalkonzerts* (Leipzig, 1905, 2/1927/*R*1965)

R. Oppel: 'Die neuen deutschen Ausgaben der zwei- und dreistimmigen Inventionen', *BJb*, iv (1907), 89

R. Buchmayer: 'Cembalo oder Pianoforte?', *BJb*, v (1908), 64–93

J. A. Fuller Maitland: 'The Toccatas of Bach', *SIMG*, xiv (1912–13), 578

A. Aber: 'Studien zu J. S. Bachs Klavierkonzerten', *BJb*, x (1913), 5

H. Luedtke: 'Seb. Bachs Choralvorspiele', *BJb*, xv (1918), 1–96

A. Halm: 'Über J. S. Bachs Konzertform', *BJb*, xvi (1919), 1–44

H. Luedtke: 'Zur Entstehung des Orgelbüchleins (1717)', *BJb*, xvi (1919), 62

A. Moser: 'Zu Joh. Seb. Bachs Sonaten und Partiten für Violine allein', *BJb*, xvii (1920), 30–65

H. Grace: *The Organ Works of Bach* (London, 1922)

W. Werker: *Studien über die Symmetrie im Bau der Fugen und die motivische Zusammengehörigkeit der Präludien und Fugen des Wohltemperierten Klaviers von J. S. Bach* (Leipzig, 1922)

W. Fischer: 'Zur Chronologie der Klaviersuiten J. S. Bachs', *Kongressbericht: Basel 1924*

W. Graeser: 'Bachs "Kunst der Fuge" ', *BJb*, xxi (1924), 1–104

J. A. Fuller Maitland: *The '48': Bach's Wohltemperirtes Clavier* (London, 1925)

——: *The Keyboard Suites of J. S. Bach* (London, 1925)

H. David: 'Die Gestalt von Bachs Chromatischer Fantasie', *BJb*, xxiii (1926), 23–67

H. Rietsch: 'Zur "Kunst der Fuge" von J. S. Bach', *BJb*, xxiii (1926), 1

K. A. Rosenthal: 'Über Sonatenvorformen in den Instrumental-

Bibliography

werken Joh. Seb. Bachs,' *BJb*, xxiii (1926), 68

F. Blume: 'Eine unbekannte Violinsonate von J. S. Bach', *BJb*, xxv (1928), 96

G. Oberst: 'J. S. Bachs englische und französische Suiten', *Gedenkschrift für Hermann Abert* (Halle, 1928)

P. Wackernagel: *Bachs Brandenburgische Konzerte* (Berlin, 1928)

F. Dietrich: 'J. S. Bachs Orgelchoral und seine geschichtlichen Wurzeln', *BJb*, xxvi (1929), 1–89

J. A. Fuller Maitland: *Bach's 'Brandenburg' Concertos* (London, 1929, 2/1945)

K. Hasse: 'Die Instrumentation J. S. Bachs', *BJb*, xxvi (1929), 90–141

A. E. Hull: *Bach's Organ Works* (London, 1929)

R. Sietz: *Die Orgelkompositionen des Schülerkreises um Bach* (diss., U. of Göttingen, 1930)

F. Dietrich: 'Analogieformen in Bachs Tokkaten und Präludien für die Orgel', *BJb*, xxviii (1931), 51

H. Neemann: 'J. S. Bachs Lautenkompositionen', *BJb*, xxviii (1931), 72

E. Schwebsch: *J. S. Bach und die Kunst der Fuge* (Stuttgart, 1931, 2/1955)

D. F. Tovey: *A Companion to the Art of Fugue* (London, 1931)

W. Krüger: 'Das Concerto grosso Joh. Seb. Bachs', *BJb*, xxix (1932), 1–50

C. S. Terry: *Bach's Orchestra* (London, 1932, 2/1958)

W. Ehmann: 'Der 3. Teil der Klavier-Übung', *Musik und Kirche*, v (1933)

L. Landshoff: *Revisionsbericht zur Urtextausgabe von J. S. Bachs Inventionen und Sinfonien* (Leipzig, 1933)

F. Smend: 'Bachs Kanonwerk über "Vom Himmel hoch da komm ich her" ', *BJb*, xxx (1933), 1–30

H. Klotz: *Über die Orgelkunst der Gotik, der Renaissance und des Barock* (Kassel, 1934)

W. Menke: *History of the Trumpet of Bach and Handel* (London, 1934)

H. E. Huggler: *J. S. Bachs Orgelbüchlein* (diss., U. of Berne, 1935)

G. Frotscher: *Geschichte des Orgel-Spiels und der Orgel-Komposition* (Berlin, 1935–6, enlarged 3/1966)

H. Keller: 'Unechte Orgelwerke Bachs', *BJb*, xxxiv (1937), 59

C. Gray: *The 48 Preludes and Fugues of J. S. Bach* (London, 1938)

H. Husmann: 'Die "Kunst der Fuge" als Klavierwerk: Besetzung und Anordnung', *BJb*, xxv (1938), 1–61

H. J. Moser: 'J. S. Bachs sechs Sonaten für Cembalo und Violine', *ZfM*, cv (1938), 1220

B. Martin: 'Praktische Anwendung der im Studium der *Kunst der Fuge*

von J. S. Bach gewonnenen Erkenntnisse vom perspektivischen (dreidimensionalen) Raum auf die Komposition einer Fuge', *BJb*, xxxvii (1940–48), 56

——: 'Zwei Durchformungsmodi der Tripelfuge zum Fragment aus der *Kunst der Fuge* von Johann Sebastian Bach', *BJb*, xxxvii (1940–48), 36

——: *Untersuchungen zur Struktur der Kunst der Fuge* (Regensburg, 1941)

S. Taylor: *The Chorale Preludes of J. S. Bach* (London, 1942)

H. T. David: *J. S. Bach's Musical Offering: History, Interpretation and Analysis* (New York, 1945/*R*1972)

W. Apel: *Masters of the Keyboard* (Cambridge, Mass., 1947)

J. M. Barbour: 'Bach and "The Art of Temperament" ', *MQ*, xxxiii (1947), 64

F. Florand: *Jean-Sébastien Bach: l'oeuvre d'orgue* (Paris, 1947)

N. Dufourcq: *Le clavecin* (Paris, 1949)

H. Keller: *Die Orgelwerke Bachs: ein Beitrag zu ihrer Geschichte, Form, Deutung und Wiedergabe* (Leipzig, 1948; Eng. trans., 1967)

N. Dufourcq: *Le clavecin* (Paris, 1949)

F. Germani: *Guida illustrativa alle composizioni per organo di J. S. Bach* (Rome, 1949)

K. Ehricht: 'Die zyklische Gestalt und die Aufführungsmöglichkeit des III. Teiles der Klavierübung von Johann Sebastian Bach', *BJb*, xxxviii (1949–50), 40

H. Keller: *Die Klavierwerke Bachs* (Leipzig, 1950)

H. Klotz: 'Bachs Orgeln und seine Orgelmusik', *Mf*, iii (1950), 200

K. Matthaei: 'Johann Sebastian Bachs Orgel', *Bach-Gedenkschrift 1950*, ed. K. Matthaei (Zurich, 1950), 118–149

A. Riemenschneider: *The Use of the Flutes in the Works of J. S. Bach* (Washington, DC, 1950)

H. Shanet: 'Why did J. S. Bach Transpose his Arrangements?', *MQ*, xxxvi (1950), 180

P. Aldrich: *Ornamentation in J. S. Bach's Organ Works* (New York, 1951)

W. David: *Johann Sebastian Bachs Orgeln* (Berlin, 1951)

W. Kaegi: *Die simultane Denkweise in J. S. Bachs Inventionen, Sinfonien und Fugen* (Basle, 1951)

W. Emery: 'The London Autograph of the "Forty-eight" ', *ML*, xxxiv (1953), 106

——: *Notes on Bach's Organ Works: a Companion to the Revised Edition* (London, 1953–7)

W. Schrammek: 'Die musikgeschichtliche Stellung der Orgeltrio sonaten von Joh. Seb. Bach', *BJb*, xli (1954), 7

A. E. F. Dickinson: *Bach's Fugal Works* (London, 1956)

Bibliography

L. Czaczkes: *Analyse des Wohltemperierten Klaviers* (Vienna, 1956–65)

J. N. David: *Die zweistimmigen Inventionen von Johann Sebastian Bach* (Göttingen, 1957)

G. Hausswald: 'Zur Stilistik von J. S. Bachs Sonaten und Partiten für Violine allein', *AMw*, xiv (1957), 304

K.-H. Köhler: 'Zur Problematik der Violinsonaten mit obligatem Cembalo', *BJb*, xlv (1958), 114

J. N. David: *Die dreistimmigen Inventionen von Johann Sebastian Bach* (Göttingen, 1959)

E. Bodky: *The Interpretation of Bach's Keyboard Works* (Cambridge, Mass., 1960)

R. Donington: *Tempo and Rhythm in Bach's Organ Music* (London, 1960)

C. Dahlhaus: 'Bach und der "lineare Kontrapunkt" ', *BJb*, xlix (1962), 58

J. N. David: *Das wohltemperierte Klavier* (Göttingen, 1962)

N. Carrell: *Bach's Brandenburg Concertos* (London, 1963)

G. von Dadelsen: 'Zur Entstehung des Bachschen Orgelbüchleins', *Festschrift Friedrich Blume* (Kassel, 1963), 74

G. Friedemann: *Bach zeichnet das Kreuz* (Pinneberg, 1963)

P. F. Williams: 'J. S. Bach and English Organ Music', *ML*, xliv (1963), 140

H. Eppstein: 'Zur Problematik von J. S. Bachs Sonate für Violine und Cembalo G dur (BWV 1019)', *AMw*, xxi (1964), 217

H. Keller: *Das Wohltemperierte Klavier von Johann Sebastian Bach: Werk und Wiedergabe* (Kassel, 1965)

E. Arfken: 'Zur Entstehungsgeschichte des Orgelbüchleins', *BJb*, lii (1966), 41

H. Eppstein: 'Studien über J. S. Bach's Sonaten für ein Melodieinstrument und obligates Cembalo', *Acta Universitatis uppsalensis*, new ser., ii (1966)

E. Franke: 'Themenmodelle in Bachs Klaviersuiten', *BJb*, lii (1966), 72

H. Ferguson: 'Bach's "Lauten Werck" ', *ML*, xlviii (1967), 259

H.-J. Schulze: 'Johann Sebastian Bachs Kanonwidmungen', *BJb*, liii (1967), 82

C. Wolff: 'Der Terminus "Ricercar" in Bachs Musikalischem Opfer', *BJb*, liii (1967), 70

C. Albrecht: 'J. S. Bachs "Clavier Übung dritter Theil": Versuch einer Deutung', *BJb*, lv (1969), 46

F.-P. Constantini: 'Zur Typusgeschichte von J. S. Bachs Wohltemperiertem Klavier', *BJb*, lv (1969), 31

H. Eppstein: 'Grundzüge in J. S. Bachs Sonatenschaffen', *BJb*, lv (1969), 5

C. Wolff: 'Ordnungsprinzipien in den Originaldrucken Bachscher

Werke', *Bach-Interpretationen*, ed. M. Geck (Göttingen, 1969)

T. Göllner: 'J. S. Bach and the Tradition of Keyboard Transcriptions', *Studies in Eighteenth-century Music: a Tribute to Karl Geiringer* (New York and London, 1970), 253

H. G. Klein: *Der Einfluss der Vivaldischen Konzertform im Instrumentalwerk Johann Sebastian Bach* (Strasbourg, 1970)

C. Wolff: 'New Research on Bach's Musical Offering', *MQ*, lvii (1971), 379–408

J. Chailley: *L'Art de la fugue de J.-S. Bach* (Paris, 1971–2)

L. Hoffmann-Erbrecht: 'Johann Sebastian Bach als Schöpfer des Klavier Konzerts', *Quellenstudien zur Musik: Wolfgang Schmieder zum 70. Geburtstag* (Frankfurt am Main, 1972), 69

P. Schmiedel: 'Zum Gebrauch des Cembalos und des Klaviers bei der heutigen Interpretation Bachscher Werke', *BJb*, lviii (1972), 95

S. Vogelsänger: 'Zur Herkunft der kontrapunktischen Motive in J. S. Bachs "Orgelbüchlein" (BWV599–644)', *BJb*, lviii (1972), 118

C. Wolff: 'Überlegungen zum "Thema Regium" ', *BJb*, lix (1973), 33

H.-J. Schulze: 'Johann Sebastian Bachs Konzertbearbeitungen nach Vivaldi und anderen – Studien- oder Auftragswerke?', *DJbM*, xviii (1973–7), 80

H. Hering: 'Spielerische Elemente in J. S. Bachs Klaviermusik', *BJb*, lx (1974), 44

E. D. May: *Breitkopf's Role in the Transmission of J. S. Bach's Organ Chorales* (diss., Princeton U., 1974)

——: 'Eine neue Quelle für J. S. Bachs einzeln überlieferte Orgelchoräle', *BJb*, lx (1974), 98

U. Meyer: 'Zur Einordnung von J. S. Bachs einzeln überlieferten Orgelchorälen', *BJb*, lx (1974), 75

W. Breig: 'Bachs Goldberg-Variationen als zyklisches Werk', *AMw*, xxxii (1975), 243

A. Dürr: 'Zur Entstehungsgeschichte des 5. Brandenburgischen Konzerts', *BJb*, lxi (1975), 63

H. Eichberg: 'Unechtes unter Johann Sebastian Bachs Klavierwerken', *BJb*, lxi (1975), 7–49

C. Wolff and others: 'Bach's "Art of Fugue": an Examination of the Sources', *CMc* (1975), no.19, p.47

W. Breig: 'Bachs Violinkonzert d-Moll: Studien zu seiner Gestalt und Entstehungsgeschichte', *BJb*, lxii (1976), 7

H. Eppstein: 'Chronologieprobleme in Johann Sebastian Bachs Suiten für Soloinstrument', *BJb*, lxii (1976), 35–57

N. Kenyon: 'A Newly Discovered Group of Canons by Bach', *MT*, cxvii (1976), 391

H. Schmidt: 'Bach's C major Orchestral Suite: a New Look at Possible Origins', *ML*, lvii (1976), 152

H.-J. Schulze: 'Melodiezitate und Mehrtextigkeit in der Bauernkantate

und in den Goldberg-Variationen', *BJb*, lxii (1976), 58

C. Wolff: 'Bach's *Handexemplar* of the Goldberg Variations: a New Source', *JAMS*, xxix (1976), 224

A. Burguéte: 'Die Lautenkompositionen Johann Sebastian Bachs', *BJb*, lxiii (1977), 26

W. Kolneder: *Die Kunst der Fuge: Mythen des 20. Jahrhunderts* (Wilhelmshaven, 1977)

C. Wolff: 'Bachs Handexemplar der Schübler-Choräle', *BJb*, lxiii (1977), 120

W. Breig: 'Zu Bachs Umarbeitungsverfahren in den "Achtzehn Chorälen"', *Festschrift G. von Dadelsen* (Stuttgart, 1978), 33

A. Dürr: 'Tastenumfang und Chronologie in Bachs Klavierwerken', *Festschrift G. von Dadelsen* (Stuttgart, 1978), 73

T. Harmon: *The Registration of J. S. Bach's Organ Works* (Buren, 1978)

D. Kilian: 'Über einige neue Aspekte zur Quellenüberlieferung von Klavier- und Orgelwerken Johann Sebastian Bachs', *BJb*, lxiv (1978), 61

S. Schmalzriedt: 'Über Zwischenspiele in den Fugen des "Wohltemperierten Klaviers"', *Festschrift G. von Dadelsen* (Stuttgart, 1978), 284

W. Breig: 'Bachs Cembalokonzert-Fragment in d-Moll BWV 1059', *BJb*, lxv (1979), 29

R. Leavis: 'Zur Frage der Authentizität von Bachs Violinkonzert d-Moll', *BJb*, lxv (1979), 19

R. L. Marshall: 'J. S. Bachs Compositions for Solo Flute', *JAMS*, xxxii (1979), 463–98

J. O'Donnell: 'The French Style and the Overtures of Bach', *Early Music*, vii (1979), 190, 336

G. Wagner: 'Concerto-Elemente in Bachs zweistimmigen Inventionen', *BJb*, lxv (1979), 37

W. Wiemer: 'Johann Heinrich Schübler, der Stecher der Kunst der Fuge', *BJb*, lxv (1979), 75

C. Wolff: 'Textkritische Bemerkungen zum Originaldruck der Bachschen Partiten', *BJb*, lxv (1979), 65

E. Bergel: *J. S. Bach – Die Kunst der Fuge: ihre geistige Grundlage im Zeichen der thematischen Bipolarität* (Bonn, 1980)

U. Kirkendale: 'The Source for Bach's Musical Offering', *JAMS*, xxxiii (1980), 88–141

K.-J. Sachs: 'Die "Anleitung . . . , auff allerhand Arth einen Choral durchzuführen", als Paradigma der Lehre und der Satzkunst Johann Sebastian Bachs', *AMw*, xxxvii (1980), 135

G. B. Stauffer: *The Organ Preludes of Johann Sebastian Bach* (Ann Arbor, 1980)

P. Williams: *The Organ Music of J. S. Bach* (Cambridge, 1980–83)

P. Ansehl, K. Heller and H.-J. Schulze, eds.: 'Beiträge zum Konzertschaffen J. S. Bachs', *Bach-Studien*, vi (1981)

E. S. Derr: 'The Two-Part Inventions: Bach's Composers' Vademecum', *Music Theory Spectrum*, iii (1981), 26

H. Vogt: *Johann Sebastian Bachs Kammermusik* (Stuttgart, 1981)

P. Williams: 'BWV565: A Toccata in D minor for Organ by J. S. Bach?', *Early Music*, ix (1981), 330

C. Wolff: 'Zur Entstehungsgeschichte von Bachs Kunst der Fuge', *Almanach der Bachwoche: Ansbach 1981*, 77

H. Schieckel: 'Johann Sebastian Bachs Auflösung eines Kanons von Teodoro Riccio', *BJb*, lxviii (1982)

P. Williams: 'J. S. Bach – Orgelsachverständiger unter dem Einfluss A. Werckmeisters?', *BJb*, lxviii (1982)

——: 'The Musical Aims of J. S. Bach's "Clavierübung III"', *Source Materials and the Interpretation of Music: a memorial Volume to Thurston Dart* (London, 1982), 259

D. Kilian: 'Zu einem Bachschen Tabulaturautograph', *Festschrift für Alfred Dürr* (Kassel, 1983), 161

REPUTATION, REVIVAL

J. F. Reichardt: 'Johann Sebastian Bach', *Musikalisches Kunstmagazin*, iv (1782), 196; repr. in Schulze (1972), 357ff

J. A. Hiller: 'Bach (Johann Sebastian)', *Lebensbeschreibungen berühmter Musikgelehrten und Tonkünstler neuerer Zeit* (Leipzig, 1784), i, 9; repr. in Schulze (1972), 395ff

[C. P. E. Bach]: comparison between Bach and Handel, *Allgemeine deutsche Bibliothek*, lxxxi (1788), 295; repr. in Schulze (1972), 437ff

J. N. Forkel: *Über Johann Sebastian Bachs Leben, Kunst, und Kunstwerke* (Leipzig, 1802; Eng. trans. in David and Mendel)

A. F. C. Kollman: 'Of John Sebastian Bach and his Works', *Quarterly Musical Register*, ii (1812), 105

M. Mason: announcement of plans for opera season, *Harmonicon*, x (1832), 29

E. Wesley, ed.: *Letters of Samuel Wesley to Mr. Jacobs* (London, 1875)

M. Schneider: 'Verzeichnis der bis zum Jahre 1851 gedruckten (und der geschriebenen im Handel gewesenen) Werke von Johann Sebastian Bach', *BJb*, iii (1906), 84–113

J. R. Sterndale Bennett: *The Life of Sterndale Bennett* (Cambridge, 1907), 202ff, 232ff

G. Schünemann: 'Die Bachpflege der Berliner Singakademie', *BJb*, xxv (1928), 138–71

G. Herz: *Bach im Zeitalter des Rationalismus und der Frühromantik* (Kassel, 1934)

L. Schrade: 'J. S. Bach und die deutsche Nation: Versuch einer

Bibliography

Deutung der frühen Bachbewegung', *Deutsche Vierteljahrsschrift für Litteraturwissenschaft und Geistesgeschichte*, xv (1937), 220–52

L. E. R. Picken: 'Bach Quotations from the 18th Century', *MR*, v (1944), 83

H. T. David and A. Mendel: *The Bach Reader: a Life of Johann Sebastian Bach in Letters and Documents* (New York, 1945, rev. 2/1966)

F. Blume: *Johann Sebastian Bach im Wandel der Geschichte* (Kassel, 1946, Eng. trans., 1950, as *Two Centuries of Bach*)

G. Osthoff: *Untersuchungen zur Bach-Auffassung im 19. Jahrhundert* (diss., U. of Cologne, 1950)

H. Redlich: 'The Bach Revival in England (1750–1850)', *HMYB*, vii (1952), 274, 287

W. Emery: 'The London Autograph of "The Forty-eight"', *ML*, xxxiv (1953), 114

D. Mintz: 'Some Aspects of the Revival of Bach', *MQ*, lx (1954), 201

G. Feder: *Bachs Werke in ihren Bearbeitungen 1750–1950* (diss., U. of Kiel, 1955)

M. Ruhnke: 'Moritz Hauptmann und die Wiederbelebung der Musik J. S. Bachs', *Festschrift Friedrich Blume* (Kassel, 1963), 305

M. Geck: *Die Wiederentdeckung der Matthäuspassion im 19. Jahrhundert* (Regensburg, 1967)

S. Grossman-Vendrey: *Felix-Mendelssohn-Bartholdy und die Musik der Vergangenheit* (Regensburg, 1969)

W. Wiora, ed.: *Die Ausbreitung des Historismus über die Musik* (Regensburg, 1969)

K. Engler: *Ein Beitrag zur Überlieferung Bachscher Musik im 19. Jahrhundert*, (diss., U. of Tübingen, 1970)

L. Plantinga: 'Clementi, Virtuosity, and the "German Manner"', *JAMS*, xxv (1972), 303

H.-J. Schulze, ed.: *Bach-Dokumente*, iii: *Dokumente zum Nachwirken Johann Sebastian Bachs 1750–1800* (Kassel, 1972)

C. Dahlhaus: 'Zur Entstehung der romantischen Bach-Deutung', *BJb*, lxiv (1978), 192

K. Heller and F. K. Griepenkerl: 'Aus unveröffentlichten Briefen des Bach-Sammlers und -Editors', *BJb*, lxiv (1978), 211

R. Stephan: 'Zum Thema "Schönberg und Bach"', *BJb*, lxiv (1978), 232

G. Wagner: 'J. A. Scheibe – J. S. Bach: Versuch einer Wertung', *BJb*, lxviii (1982)

M. Zenck: 'Studien der Bach-Deutung in der Musikkritik, Musikästhetik und Musikgeschichtsschreibung zwischen 1750 und 1800', *BJb*, lxviii (1982)

Festschrift für Alfred Dürr (Kassel, 1983) [contributions by G. Feder, A. Mann and L. F. Tagliavini]

CHAPTER EIGHT

Wilhelm Friedemann Bach (45)

ı Life

Wilhelm Friedemann, known as the 'Halle Bach', was
the eldest son of (7) Johann Sebastian (24) and Maria
Barbara Bach. Born in Weimar on 22 November 1710,
he was a greatly gifted composer who did not fully set
aside his background of contrapuntal training in favour
of the new styles of the mid-18th century. He led an
unstable life and never quite developed his full creative
potential.

His first academic studies were at the Lateinschule in
Cöthen. In early 1720 Sebastian began a 'Clavier-
Büchlein vor Wilhelm Friedemann Bach' that was to be
used for Bach's other children and pupils as well. The
'Clavier-Büchlein' abandons the beginner's realm in its
first few pages and becomes a compendium of preludes,
inventions, dances and similar works, including a
foretaste of *Das wohltemperirte Clavier*; its contents no
doubt reflect young Friedemann's rapid progress as a
keyboard player. The year 1720 also brought the death
of Maria Barbara; that unhappy event, followed a year
and a half later by Sebastian's marriage to Anna
Magdalena, may have had a bearing on Friedemann's
later difficulties in life.

When the family moved to Leipzig in 1723, the 13-
year-old Friedemann (like the nine-year-old Emanuel)
was enrolled in the Thomasschule; and for the first
Christmas in their new home Sebastian presented to his

238

beloved 'Friede' a certificate showing his registration for eventual matriculation at the university. Friedemann's academic success was not allowed to interfere with his musical education, which must have been uniquely thorough and systematic: book 1 of the '48', for instance, was composed with the 12-year-old Friedemann in mind. Nor did Sebastian permit too much keyboard specialization; in 1726 Friedemann was sent to Merseburg to study the violin with J. G. Graun for almost a year. It is plain that Friedemann was Sebastian's favourite child.

In 1729 Friedemann graduated from the Thomasschule, and his outstanding career as a scholar continued for four more years at the University of Leipzig, where he studied mathematics, philosophy and law. It was also during 1729 that he visited Handel in Halle with an invitation to the Bach home in Leipzig, which Handel was unable to accept. By that time Friedemann, like Emanuel, was regularly working as Sebastian's assistant in such tasks as private instruction (one of his pupils was Christoph Nichelmann), the conducting of rehearsals and music copying; when the opportunity to become organist at the Dresden Sophienkirche presented itself in 1733, he was able, as a finished musician, to win the trials for the post easily, earning the warmest commendation from Pantaleon Hebenstreit, vice-Kapellmeister at the Dresden court. Friedemann had been present at Sebastian's recital on the Silbermann organ in the Sophienkirche two years earlier, and had visited Dresden with Sebastian on other occasions. Sebastian's reputation obviously helped his candidature.

The new position was a part-time one and his pay was modest, but Friedemann did have time to pursue other interests in Dresden: composition, further study in

mathematics, the operas and ballets presented at the brilliant Dresden court, the friendship of such musicians as Hebenstreit, Sylvius Weiss, J. G. Goldberg (his pupil), J. A. Hasse, Faustina Bordoni Hasse and P. G. Buffardin. Entrée to the music of the court was made possible to him through Count Keyserlingk, Sebastian's patron. His opulent surroundings in Dresden, the prodigality and luxuriousness of the court, must have contrasted sharply with the austerity of the Bach home and St Thomas's; it must also have been disturbing for him to realize that the combined salary of the Hasses was more than 16 times that paid to his father. As a Protestant organist, moreover, he gradually came to realize that in this Catholic city where opera reigned supreme, both his religion and his music would always make him something of an outsider. In 1742 the organist's position at the Frauenkirche in Dresden (considerably more important in Protestant circles than his part-time appointment at the Sophienkirche) became vacant; it constituted a natural step up for him. But he failed to secure it, and the post went to G. A. Homilius. In 1746 he had better luck, thanks to Sebastian's influence: his application for the important position of organist at the Liebfrauenkirche in Halle (which Sebastian himself had reluctantly rejected 32 years earlier) was enough to give him the post without even a trial performance.

In his new occupation, as a successor in the Liebfrauenkirche of such eminent figures as Scheidt and Zachow, Friedemann might well have made a distinguished career. By this time he was widely regarded as the best organist in Germany, and the last survivor of the Baroque organ tradition – though this recognition

240

9. *Wilhelm Friedemann Bach: portrait (2nd half of the 18th century) by Wilhelm Weitsch*

came primarily through his improvisations, not through his performances of works composed by or in the style of his father. In addition to his duties as organist he was in charge of the productions of music, involving

orchestra, in the three principal churches of Halle. He began his stay there with a performance of his first cantata, *Wer mich liebet*. But Halle was under the rule of Pietism in its most doctrinaire form, and Friedemann, coming from 13 years in liberal Dresden, was incapable of being an earnest and sober Pietist. To make matters worse, his free-thinking tendencies were abetted by the presence of Christian Wolff in Halle University. Wolff, once banished from Halle for his reputation as a philosopher–mathematician of the Enlightenment, had now been restored by Frederick the Great; and Friedemann's young mind, like many others of his time, was irresistibly attracted to Wolff's rationalistic system. It was hardly an appropriate mode of thought for a Lutheran church organist, least of all a son of J. S. Bach. After Friedemann accompanied Sebastian on his famous visit to Frederick's court in 1747 (the visit that produced the *Musical Offering*), at the height of that enlightened despot's brilliant patronage of a music far removed from his own, his surroundings in Halle no doubt seemed drab by comparison. A second trip to Berlin took place in 1750, after Sebastian's death, when he delivered young Johann Christian to Emanuel's care; that time he overstayed his leave and earned a reprimand from his Halle employers.

Without Sebastian's steadying influence, and in spite of marriage at the age of 41 (only one of his children, a daughter, survived infancy), Friedemann was unable to settle down happily in Halle. He repeatedly left town to apply for other posts, to the displeasure of his superiors, who were none too tolerant to begin with. When the Seven Years War began, in 1756, Halle became an open city, subject to exploitation and outrageous taxation by

occupying troops of one side or another. Friedemann and his family suffered like all Halle residents, and in 1761 he did not hesitate to ask the church elders to produce, from their exhausted treasury, a rise in salary for him. The elders' refusal was vituperative, even threatening.

In 1762 a change of fortune seemed imminent: the court of Darmstadt offered him the post of Kapellmeister, an important and well-salaried position which had fallen vacant on the death of Christoph Graupner. He accepted; yet, incredibly, through circumstances that are obscure, the position slipped through his fingers. He delayed moving his belongings, even though moving expenses were offered. The official decree naming him as Kapellmeister awaited him in Darmstadt, yet he insisted that it be sent to him in Halle. The details are unknown, but evidently his behaviour in general was inappropriate. Eventually the Darmstadt court gave him only the title, without the position. He went back to his uncomfortable relation with his Halle superiors, and finally, on 12 May 1764, he unceremoniously walked away from his job without notice. There were no prospects of further employment, and this was indeed the last formal post he would occupy.

Friedemann remained in Halle until 1770, earning his living mainly as a teacher; his distant relative Johann Christian Bach (*77*) (1743–1814), F. W. Rust and J. S. Petri were among his pupils. In 1770 his wife's property in Halle was sold, and the family moved to Brunswick. There he began those occupational vacillations that were to be the point of departure for the characterizations of him (especially the grossly inaccurate and unfair accounts by Marpurg, Reichardt and Rochlitz) as an ec-

centric, giving organ recitals, composing, applying here and there in vain for permanent employment. He also received some money from the sale of manuscripts of his father's music, especially autographs, of which he was the chief owner. Friedemann was a shockingly poor custodian of this treasure, much of which has never been found; even Forkel, who befriended him around this time, was unable to account for the loss.

By 1774 he found himself in Berlin, where his prospects looked better. His power as an organ virtuoso was especially appreciated, and he was strongly favoured by Princess Anna Amalia, sister of Frederick the Great. Among his Berlin pupils was Sara Levy, Mendelssohn's great-aunt. J. P. Kirnberger, Anna Amalia's court composer and a former pupil of Sebastian, offered his friendship to Friedemann, who reciprocated by trying to discredit Kirnberger at court so that Kirnberger's position might be offered to him. His plan backfired, and he had to look elsewhere in Berlin for favour.

Hardened now in his aloofness, his unwillingness to see through the eyes of others, and his inability to pursue a task to its end, the aging composer remained in Berlin for ten years, in poverty and ill-health, gradually retreating from reality. An opera, *Lausus und Lydie*, was begun but left unfinished. He was reduced to claiming some music by Sebastian as his own, and on at least one occasion he signed his father's name to his own work. He died of a pulmonary disease on 1 July 1784, leaving his widow and daughter in dire poverty. Proceeds from a Berlin performance of Handel's *Messiah* in 1785 were donated to them.

II Works

In spite of such aids as the Falck thematic catalogue and the Kast study on Bach family manuscripts, many of Wilhelm Friedemann's compositions cannot yet be either positively identified or dated. But the general outline is clear enough: while living at home (before 1733) he wrote only a few pieces, mainly for keyboard; at Dresden (1733–46) he largely concentrated on instrumental works; at Halle (1746–70), while continuing to compose in instrumental genres, he produced some two dozen church cantatas, which are almost the whole body of his vocal compositions; and at Brunswick and Berlin (1771–84), aside from the abortive attempt at an opera, what little he composed was primarily for keyboard or chamber groups.

Of the four Bach sons who became well known as composers, Friedemann, the oldest, seems to have been the one least interested in reconciling his training under Sebastian with the new styles. Rather than forging the old and new into a unique blend, as Emanuel did, or turning wholeheartedly to the new, like Johann Christian, Friedemann shifted back and forth throughout his career between old and new, from work to work and even within single works.

It is often a very attractive vacillation. In the brilliant *Concerto â duoi cembali concertati* for two unaccompanied harpsichords (F10), composed early in the Dresden period, the last movement follows the ritornello procedure characteristic of Baroque concertos, with the 'orchestral' and 'solo' parts carried on by the two harpsichords; yet the first movement, not concerto-like at all, is actually a sonata movement in clear sonata form.

Similarly, the important Sinfonia in F (F67), also from the Dresden years, straddles two eras by managing to be both a sinfonia and an orchestral suite. The double-dotted French overture that is its first movement is repeatedly shattered by sudden harmonic and metrical shifts in *empfindsamer Stil*; if initially disturbing, these surprising changes of *Affekt* soon seem charming, and even well integrated. The second movement is an Andante, beautiful but indistinguishable in style from hundreds of other Baroque andantes. The third movement, an Italianate Allegro in duple time, presents Classical-sounding antecedent and consequent phrases in a clear though truncated sonata form. That is not the end of the so-called 'Sinfonia': the final movement is made up of a pair of *abwechselnde Menuetten* whose serene cantilena is quite specifically Handelian. Four superb flute duets composed in Dresden (F54, 55, 57, 59) are quite conservative, especially in their adherence to imitative polyphony. The 12 equally superb keyboard polonaises (F12), composed in the Halle period and particularly esteemed in the 19th century, are paramount among the intensely expressive works that cause some scholars to classify Friedemann Bach as a proto-Romantic composer. And by the end of his career Friedemann was hardly closer to the dominant musical language of the Classical era than he had been while still under his father's tutelage. During the Berlin years he dedicated excellent works in sharply opposed styles to Princess Amalia: on the one hand, a keyboard sonata in D (F4) with a 'Mozartian' first movement; on the other, a set of eight keyboard fugues (F31).

This mixture of old and new was not always so successful, of course. The cantatas, sublime moments

246

notwithstanding, follow too slavishly in Sebastian's foot-
steps, too often consist of parodies and borrowings from
earlier works rather than original composition, and too
seldom adopt the new homophonic textures. The keyboard sonatas sometimes present nearly insoluble problems of performance in their sudden changes of tempo
or texture in the *empfindsamer Stil*. Some important
forms, such as rondo and variation, are neglected. He
composed not a single known lied. There are evidences
of indolence or expediency even in Friedemann's prime
years, and of failing inspiration towards the end of his
career.

Yet Friedemann's great gifts remain evident in an
outpouring of rich melody, a harmonic palette more
varied and more daring than that of most of his contemporaries, a consistent deepening of homophonic texture
by means of effortless counterpoint and, above all, a
highly personal style of emotional expression. 'The cultivated musician who chooses the esoteric, precious
music of Friedemann in place of the lighter, more
popular, standardized music of Christian is akin to the
literate who chooses Sterne's *Sentimental Journey* or
one of Klopstock's followers in place of the more
pedestrian writings of a C. F. Nicolai' (Newman).

WORKS

Principal MS sources are *D-B, Bds*; there is a catalogue in Falck [F], with corrections in Blume and
Kast.
Edition: *W. F. Bach: Complete Works for Organ*, ed. E. P. Biggs and G. Weston (New York, 1947)
[CW]

KEYBOARD
(*for hpd unless otherwise stated*)

F
1   Sonata (C), *c*1745, 2 versions; 1 ed. E. Pauer, Alte Meister, xxiv (Leipzig, 1875), 1 ed. in NM,
      clvi (1941)
2   Sonata (C), *c*1778 [movts 2–3 rev. in F15]; ed. in NM, clvi (1941)
3   Sonata I (D), as Sei sonate (Dresden, 1745) [according to Falck, F5–9 were intended to form
      remainder of set]; ed. in NM, lxxviii (1930)

4	Sonata (D), *c*1778; ed. in NM, lxxviii (1930)
5	Sonate pour le clavecin (E♭) (Dresden, 1748); ed. in NM, lxxviii (1930)
6–9	Sonatas (F, G, A, B♭), ? all complete by 1745, F6 in 3 versions; F6 ed. in NM, clvi (1941), F7–9 ed. in NM, lxiii (1930)
10	Concerto â duoi cembali concertati (F), 2 hpd, *c*1773; ed. J. Brahms as Sonate für 2 Klavier (Leipzig, 1864/R1966), ed. in *J. S. Bach: Werke*, xliii [attrib. J. S. Bach], ed. H. Brandts Buys (London, 1953)
11	Sonata (D), 2 kbd, lost
—	6 sonatas, *D-Bds*, cited by Kast; ed. in SBA
12	12 polonaises (C, c, D, d, E♭, e♭, E, e, F, f, G, g), *c*1765, ed. in Le trésor des pianistes, x (Paris, *c*1865), ed. W. Niemann (Leipzig, 1914), F. Wührer (Vienna, 1949), 6 ed. in Hausmusik, xcviii (Vienna, 1951)
13	Polonaise (C), *c*1765
—	28 polonaises, *Bds*, cited by Kast
14–23	10 fantasias (C, c, c, D, d, d, e, e, G, a), F20 from 1770, F15–16 from 1784 [cf F2], some others from Dresden, 1733–46: F14 ed. L. Hoffmann-Erbrecht (Lippstadt, 1963)
—	Fantasia (c), *Bds*, cited by Kast; ed. in SBA
24	Suite (g); ed. H. Riemann (Leipzig, 1893)
25–30	Various short pieces, most ? before 1733; selections ed. H. Riemann (Leipzig, *c*1890), and as Leichte Spielstücke (Zurich, 1971)
—	2 minuets, *Bds*, cited by Kast
31	VIII Fugen (C, c, D, d, E♭, e, B♭, f) (Berlin, 1778); ed. in Le trésor des pianistes, x (Paris, *c*1865), ed. as Huit fugues (Paris, 1959)
32–4	3 fugues (C, F, B♭), all ? before 1735 [F34 arr. of fugue in ov. to Handel's Esther]
35–7	3 fugues (C, F, g), org, F35 frag., F36 a triple fugue composed in Halle; ed. in CW, ed. T. Fedtke, *W. F. Bach: Orgelwerke* (Frankfurt am Main, 1968)
—	3 fugues, *Bds*, cited by Kast
38/1	7 chorale-preludes, org; ed. in CW, ed. T. Fedtke, *W. F. Bach: Orgelwerke* (Frankfurt am Main, 1968)
38/2	Trio on 'Allein Gott in der Höh', org, lost
39	Canons and studies, org
40	Concerto (G), ? before 1735 [cf F97]; ed. L. Hoffmann-Erbrecht (Lippstadt, 1960)
—	Praeludium (c), cited by Blume
—	March (E♭), cited by Blume
—	Scherzo (d); ed. in *J. S. Bach: Werke*, xlii [also attrib. J. S. Bach, BWV844]
—	Presto (d) [attrib. J. S. Bach, BWV970]
—	18 pieces for musical clock; no.1 = F22, no.3 = F62, no.6 = F12/7, no.18 from F6, F13; attrib. J. S. Bach, BWV Anh.133–50, ed. A. Klughardt (Leipzig, 1897) [see E. Simon: *Mechanische Musikinstrumente früherer Zeiten und ihre Musik* (Wiesbaden, 1960), 50]

Doubtful: sonatas (C, E♭ [although autograph], F, G [1 movt]); fugue (c), ed. in CW; 2 allemandes (g) (1 inc.), from Clavier-Büchlein for W. F. Bach, ed. in *J. S. Bach: Werke*, xlv [attrib. J. S. Bach, BWV836–7]; 3 preludes (C, D, e), 1725/6, from Clavier-Büchlein for W. F. Bach, ed. in *J. S. Bach: Werke*, xxxvi [attrib. J. S. Bach, BWV924a, 925, 932]; Sonata (d), Adagio (G), ed. in *J. S. Bach: Werke*, xlii [attrib. J. S. Bach, BWV964, 968]

Spurious: sonatas (c, D, E♭, e); polonaises (F, G); divertimento (a); fantasia (F); sonata (A), 2 kbd, after Couperin

CONCERTOS

(for hpd and orch unless otherwise stated)

41	Conc. (D), ? Dresden, 1733–46; ed. H. Riemann (Leipzig, 1897)
42	Conc. (E♭), inc., 1750s [rev. as introduction to F88]
43	Conc. (e), ? before 1767; ed. H. Riemann (Leipzig, *c*1880), ed. W. Upmeyer (Berlin, 1931)
44	Conc. (F), Dresden, 1733–46; ed. H. Riemann (Leipzig, 1894)
45	Conc. (a), date controversial [see Geiringer, p.326]; ed. H. Riemann (Leipzig, 1897)
46	Conc. (E♭), 2 hpd; ed. H. Riemann (Leipzig, 1894)
—	Conc. (f), cited by Kast; ed. W. Smigelski (Hamburg, 1959)

Doubtful: Conc. (g); Concert (f), ?*c*1753, B [attrib. W. F. Bach; attrib. C. P. E. Bach, H486]

Works

Spurious: Conc. (c) [? by Kirnberger]; Conc. (d), org [arr. by J. S. Bach, BWV596, of Vivaldi's Vn Conc., op.3 no.11]

CHAMBER AND ORCHESTRAL

47–9	4 trio sonatas (D, D, a [frag.], B♭), 2 fl, bc, ? before 1762; ed. L. Schittler (Munich, 1910/*Rc*1960)
50	Trio sonata (B♭), 2 vn, bc, ? before 1768, ed. H. Brandts Buys (Amsterdam, n.d.) [attrib. C. P. E. Bach, H597]
51–3	3 sonatas (F, a, D), fl, bc, cited in Breitkopf catalogues 1761, 1763, lost
54–9	6 duets (e, E♭, E♭, F, f, G), 2 fl, F54–5, 57, 59 composed in Dresden, 1733–46, F56, 58 after 1770; ed. K. Walter (Wiesbaden, 1969)
60–62	3 duets (C, G, g), 2 va, after 1770; ed. K. Haas (London, 1953)
63	Sinfonia (C), 1733–46
64	Sinfonia (D), 1746–64 [used as introduction to F85]; ed. W. Lebermann (Mainz, 1971)
65	Sinfonia (d), 2 fl, str; ed. L. Schittler (Munich, 1910), ed. W. Lebermann (Mainz, 1971)
66	Sinfonia ['Ricercata'] (d) [anon. arr. *c*1800 of 2 of W. F. Bach's choral fugues incl. as add to MS containing fugues F31/8, 31/5, 37]
67–71	Sinfonias (F, G, G, A, B♭), 1733–46; F67 ed. M. Schneider (Leipzig, 1954)
—	Sinfonia (a), 1758, cited by Blume

Doubtful: Trio (B), vn, hpd, ed. L. Schittler (Munich, 1910/*Rc*1960); trio (c), va, hpd, ed. Y. Pessl (London, 1947)

Spurious: Sonata (G), 2 fl, va; sonata (C), 2 fl, bc; sonata (F), (vn/fl, hpd)/(vn, fl, bc)

CHURCH CANTATAS
(for 4vv, insts, 1746–64)

72	Wer mich liebet, 1746
73	Der Herr zu deiner Rechten, 1747
74	Wir sind Gottes Werke, 1748
75	Gott fähret auf, 1748
76	Wohl dem, der den Herrn fürchtet
77	Vergnügte Ruh [partly parody of J. S. Bach's cantatas BWV170, 147]
78	Heilig, heilig ist Gott, *c*1748, ed. A. Schering (Leipzig, 1922); later adapted as Lobet Gott, unsern Herrn Zebaoth, ed. in SBA
80	Lasset uns ablegen, 1749
81	Der Herr wird mit Gerechtigkeit, before 1756
82	Wie schön leucht uns [partly parody]
83	Erzittert und fallet; ed. in SBA
84	Dienet dem Herrn, 1755, 'W.F.' changed to 'J.S.' Bach on MS, but by Friedemann
85	Dies ist der Tag, da Jesu Leidenskraft [cf F64]; ed. L. Nowak (Leipzig, 1937), ed. in SBA
86	Der Höchste erhöret, 1756 [partly parody]
87	Verhängnis, dein Wüten, after 1756 [partly parody]
88	Ertönet, ihr seligen Völker [partly parody; cf F42]
89	Es ist eine Stimme eines Predigers
91	Wo geht die Lebensreise hin
92	O Wunder, wer kann dieses fassen
93	Ach, dass dir den Himmel zerreissest
96	Heraus, verblendeter Hochmut, ? composed at Brunswick [partly parody]
101–5	only printed texts extant: Wertes Zion, sei getrost, 1756 [? by J. S. Bach]; Blast Lärmen, ihr Feinde, 1756 [? borrowed from J. S. Bach's cantata BWV205a]; Blast Lärmen, 1757 [mostly a parody of the preceding]; Ja, ja, es hat mein Gott, 1757; Halleluja, wohl diesem Volk, 1757; Viele sind berufen, 1757; Lobe den Herrn in seinem Heiligtum, 1762; Gott, ist unsere Zuversicht und Stärke, 1762
—	Man singet mit Freuden, 1756 [parody of J. S. Bach's cantata BWV149], cited by Blume
—	Es ist das Heil uns kommen her [parody of J. S. Bach's cantata BWV9], cited by Blume
—	Gaudete omnes populi [partly parody of J. S. Bach's cantata BWV80], cited by Blume
—	Nimm von uns, Herr [parody of J. S. Bach's cantata BWV101], cited by Blume
—	Church cantata for Easter 1747

Spurious: Jesu, deine Passion, *D-Bds*

OTHER SACRED

98	Deutsche Messe [partly parody]
99	Amen–Alleluja [parody]
100	Kyrie, 'W.F.' changed to 'J.S.' on MS, authorship uncertain

SECULAR CANTATAS

| 90 | O Himmel, schöne, for birthday of Frederick the Great, 1758 [partly parody]; sinfonia ed. E. Prieger (Cologne, *c*1910) |
| 95 | Auf, Christen, posaunt, for celebration of end of Seven Years War, 1763 [partly parody] |

OTHER VOCAL

79	… Gnade finden, aria, frag.
94	Zerbrecht, zerreist, aria, S, hn obbl [? cantata frag.]; ed. L. Schittler (Munich, 1910)
97	Herz, mein Herz, sei ruhig, 'Cantilena nuptiarum consolatoria', 1774–84 [parody of Andante from F40)
106	Lausus und Lydie (opera, C. M. Plümicke, after Marmontel), inc., 1778–9, lost

Spurious: Kein Hälmlein wächst auf Erden (lied, E. Brachvogel), 19th-century falsification, music by Brachvogel and Emil Bach

WRITING

Abhandlung vom harmonischen Dreiklang, begun *c*1754, advertised in Leipzig newspapers in 1758 for Easter fair 1759, unpubd, lost

BIBLIOGRAPHY

F. Chrysander: 'Johann Sebastian Bach und sein Sohn Friedemann Bach in Halle', *Jb für musikalische Wissenschaft,* ii (Leipzig, 1863–7), 235

C. H. Bitter: *Carl Philipp Emanuel und Wilhelm Friedemann Bach und deren Brüder* (Berlin, 1868)

W. Nagel: 'W. Fr. Bachs Berufung nach Darmstadt', *SIMG,* i (1899–1900), 290

K. Zehler: 'W. Fr. Bach und seine hallische Wirksamkeit', *BJb,* vii (1910), 103–32

M. Falck: *Wilhelm Friedemann Bach* (Leipzig, 1913, 2/1919)

H. Miesner: 'Portraits aus dem Kreise Ph. E. und W. Fr. Bachs', *Musik und Bild: Festschrift Max Seiffert* (Kassel, 1938), 101

F. Blume: 'Bach, Wilhelm Friedemann', *MGG*

P. Kast: *Die BAch-Handschriften der Berliner Staatsbibliothek,* Tübinger Bach-Studien, ii–iii (Trossingen, 1958)

W. S. Newman: *The Sonata in the Classic Era* (Chapel Hill, 1963, rev. 2/1972)

W. Braun: 'Material zu Wilhelm Friedemann Bachs Kantatenaufführungen in Halle (1746–1764)', *Mf,* xviii (1965), 267

H.-J. Schulze: 'Eine "Drama per Musica" als Kirchenmusik: zu Wilhelm Friedemann Bachs Aufführungen der Huldigungskantate BWV205a', *BJb,* lxi (1975), 133

CHAPTER NINE

Carl Philipp Emanuel Bach (46)

1 The early years

Carl Philipp Emanuel, the most famous and most prolific of the sons of (7) Johann Sebastian Bach (24), was born at Weimar on 8 March 1714. He could claim descent from musicians – and indeed from Bachs – on both sides of his family. His godfathers were Telemann and the Weissenfels court musician A. I. Weldig. Emanuel was three years old (Wilhelm Friedemann was seven) when the family moved to Cöthen, seven when Sebastian married Anna Magdalena after Maria Barbara's premature death, nine when Sebastian became Kantor of the Leipzig Thomasschule. In Cöthen, Sebastian sent the children to the Lutheran seminary rather than to the better-equipped Calvinist school; in Leipzig, Emanuel and Friedemann were of course among the 'Scholaren' at the Thomasschule that Sebastian had to oversee.

Emanuel makes it clear in his little autobiographical sketch that he never had any music teacher besides his father. There is no evidence that he seriously studied any instrument except the keyboard; by the age of 11, according to Schubarth, he could play Sebastian's keyboard pieces at sight. Throughout his career he was hardly to travel at all in an age when travel, especially to Italy, was considered an important part of a young German musician's training. All this might have resulted in a certain narrowness of musical outlook,

251

even in a man whose teacher was the author of such pedagogical works as the Inventions, the *Orgelbüchlein*, the *Clavier-Übung* and *Das wohltemperirte Clavier*; but quite the opposite was the case: Sebastian's penetrating and lifelong study of Italian and French music, the frequent visits to the Bach home of distinguished musicians from various parts of Europe, and the performance of many styles, genres and nationalities of music, instrumental and vocal, sacred and secular, undoubtedly gave the young Emanuel a rare breadth of musical experience. The only major genre of music relatively closed to him as a boy was opera (though he no doubt had some slight experience of opera, probably mainly Hasse's, in nearby Dresden).

Emanuel also received a sound general education at the Thomasschule, in spite of its decline under J. H. Ernesti; whatever its faults, and whatever Sebastian's difficulties in it, the school was to remain important enough, thanks in part to its proximity to and its connections with the great University of Leipzig, to attract such outstanding rector–scholars as J. M. Gesner and J. A. Ernesti. From the Thomasschule to the University of Leipzig was a predictable step for a superior student. Emanuel matriculated at the university on 1 October 1731 to study law, though still living with his parents, still acting as a most important musical assistant to Sebastian, and even applying unsuccessfully in 1733 for a position as organist at Naumburg. Not so predictable was his move to the University of Frankfurt an der Oder, again as a law student, where he matriculated on 9 September 1734 and remained, according to the autobiographical sketch, until the end of the academic year in 1738, supporting himself in this musically arid town

mostly by giving keyboard lessons and by composing for or directing public concerts and ceremonies such as the dedication of a church renovation, the production by students of congratulatory cantatas for visiting royalty etc.

The years 1731–8 also mark the real beginning of his composing career. In 1730–31, under Sebastian's supervision, he composed his first known works: the two marches and two polonaises (BWV Anh.122–5, H1) that Sebastian added as nos.16–19 to Anna Magdalena's second *Clavierbüchlein*, and a little one-page minuet 'with hand crossings' (W111, H1·5) that Emanuel engraved with his own hands. By 1734, as further products of his apprenticeship with his father, he completed five keyboard sonatas, seven trios, solos for oboe and flute, a keyboard suite, two harpsichord concertos and six keyboard sonatinas; by 1738, now on his own as a composer, he added about a dozen more such instrumental works to this list.

Thus the objective evidence is that until his 24th year Emanuel Bach energetically pursued both an unusually extensive university training, lasting almost seven years, and a thoroughly professional career in music. Whether he intended his lifetime career to be legal or musical is a question that has been much discussed by scholars; but his actions seem to indicate that he simply wanted to keep his options open as long as possible, and that he was guided and encouraged in that by Sebastian. Regarding his study of law, it should be understood that a 'law' curriculum in European universities was one of the most ordinary approaches to a university (meaning liberal, not vocational) education, and did not necessarily lead to the practice of law. Handel, Mattheson,

J. F. Agricola, Schütz, Kuhnau and many other German musicians studied law. Some, like J. D. Heinichen (a product of the University of Leipzig), actually practised law in an incidental fashion while concentrating on music; others, like C. G. Krause (a product of the University of Frankfurt an der Oder), had distinguished legal careers while also making significant achievements in music.

Sebastian Bach was determined that, if possible, his sons would have the university education he lacked; he wanted them to be able to rise above the petty indignities that he had to suffer throughout his career. Friedemann, then Emanuel, and then Johann Christoph Friedrich were enrolled by Sebastian at the University of Leipzig, all as students of law (Friedemann also studied mathematics and philosophy). Of these three, Emanuel was the one who perceived most clearly the value of a liberal education as a defence against 18th-century society's evaluation of ordinary musicians as ignorant servants, an evaluation richly articulated by his father's superiors, especially J. A. Ernesti, for all the Bach family to hear. For the rest of his life Emanuel generally preferred the company of literati to that of musicians; he would be able to show his literacy and intellectual discipline in an epoch-making *Essay*; and in financial matters he would become quite lawyer-like, keeping scrupulous account books and unapologetically billing his patrons for services rendered. If this sounds rather dull (and dullness is indeed his chief characteristic in letter after letter dealing primarily with money), it should be balanced against his considerable breadth of interest, his keen enjoyment of good company, and his reputation as a ready wit, especially as a punster, from boyhood until old age.

254

'When I finished my academic year in 1738 and went to Berlin', he said in the autobiographical sketch, 'I was given a very advantageous opportunity to guide a young gentleman in foreign travel; an unexpected and gracious summons to Ruppin from the then crown prince of Prussia, now king, caused me to break off plans for my journey'. The 'young gentleman' whom Emanuel was about to accompany as tutor on the traditional grand tour (in this case to Austria, Italy, France and England) was Count Heinrich Christian Keyserlingk, son of the Russian ambassador to Dresden, Count Hermann Keyserlingk, for whom Sebastian had composed the Goldberg Variations. Count Hermann had been a friend of Sebastian for some years. Here was a chance for foreign travel, of the kind that Emanuel would later regret not having experienced; but an offer from the 26-year-old crown prince, the future Frederick II of Prussia, represented an opportunity not to be refused – even though Frederick, in these last two years at Ruppin and Rheinsberg before he became king, would pursue music as he pursued literature and philosophy: rather clandestinely, on borrowed money, under the disapproval of his father.

Some 17 musicians, devoted primarily to chamber music in which Frederick took a leading part as flautist, were already in Frederick's employ when Emanuel was engaged, including J. J. Quantz, C. H. and J. G. Graun, and Franz and Johann Benda. Several interesting anecdotes notwithstanding, it is not known exactly why Frederick chose Emanuel to be his harpsichordist; it seems likely that the royal flautist must have heard of him through Quantz or the Grauns, all of whom came from Saxony and knew the Bachs (Wilhelm

10. *Flute concert at Sans Souci: painting (1852) by Adolf Menzel; Frederick the Great plays the flute, Carl Philipp Emanuel Bach is at the keyboard, and Quantz stands on the extreme right*

Friedemann, at the age of 15, had been under J. G. Graun's tutelage for almost a year). Frederick might also have been favourably impressed by Emanuel's production, by 1738, of no less than ten chamber works involving the flute. It is even possible that Emanuel laid the groundwork for his new position while still in Frankfurt: among the Prussian royalty musically honoured there in 1737 was Margrave Friedrich Wilhelm, then a student at the university; perhaps Friedrich Wilhelm had brought favourable word of Emanuel back to Berlin (presuming Emanuel was involved in this little congratulatory cantata, of which only the text survives). Whatever prompted Frederick's interest in Emanuel, the unofficial nature of the musical establishment at Ruppin and Rheinsberg prevented the regularization of the appointment until after Frederick's accession to the throne in 1740. Emanuel's salary was among the lowest paid to the musicians: a budget-list of 1744–5 in Frederick's hand shows it to be 300 thalers, as against 2000 each for Quantz and C. H. Graun, 1200 for J. G. Graun and 800 for Franz Benda. In the same season, the leading castrato received 3000 thalers.

II Berlin

Emanuel was in the service of Frederick the Great for nearly 30 years. He writes proudly in the autobiographical sketch that in 1740 he 'had the honour of accompanying in Charlottenburg, alone at the harpsichord, the first flute solo played by Frederick as king'. His basic role at court, as accompanist in the royal chamber music, did not change. It is charmingly illustrated in Menzel's famous and historically meticulous painting, now in the Neue Nationalgalerie, Berlin, of a

257

candlelit musical evening in the splendid rococo music room of Sans Souci (see fig.10): Frederick is soloist; C. H. Graun, as director of the Opera, stands to one side as an observer, amid members of the royal family, cabinet ministers and visiting intellectuals; Emanuel and a few other musicians provide the accompaniment; and Quantz stands by to supervise the performance. What the painting could not show is that at various times the 'accompanist' had to fulfil the roles of soloist, teacher, coach, transposer, Kapellmeister, composer and arranger. These chamber-music evenings usually took place at least three times a week; Emanuel alternated every four weeks with a second harpsichordist (from 1741, C. F. Schale; 1744–56, J. S. Bach's pupil Christoph Nichelmann; from 1756, C. F. C. Fasch).

Being in close company with Frederick the Great – a monarch whose quite good if not completely professional flute playing was his way of resting from the prosecution of unprecedented social reforms and international warfare – and working daily with musicians of considerable distinction must have been immensely stimulating at first to the young Emanuel. The sections on accompaniment in his *Versuch über die wahre Art das Clavier zu spielen*, or *Essay on the True Art of Playing Keyboard Instruments*, among the most important such writings ever published, were largely an outgrowth of his work as Frederick's accompanist. He was on hand at precisely the right time to witness Frederick's personal establishment of the great Berlin Opera, which opened its doors in 1742. As the Italian singers, French dancers, extra instrumentalists and all the other ingredients of *opera seria* poured into Berlin,

as Emanuel heard the operas of Hasse and C. H. Graun, in many cases for the first time, the dramatic style crept into his compositions. He never composed an opera – Johann Christian was the only Bach son young enough to escape totally the Protestant-organist syndrome so antithetic to that genre – but instead he channelled his dramatic impulse into instrumental works, beginning with the Prussian Sonatas dedicated to Frederick in 1743 and the Württemberg Sonatas dedicated to his pupil the Duke Carl Eugen of Württemberg in 1744. This dramatic impulse, which was to take many forms, continued to influence his style.

Yet the flowering of music under Frederick the Great was not without its disadvantages, the most discouraging of which was Frederick's arch-conservative musical taste. Almost no operas but those of Graun and Hasse were heard at the opera house. It became apparent that staple fare at the chamber-music soirées would be the flute concertos of Quantz, played in rotation or interspersed with compositions by Frederick himself, with Frederick as soloist. Quantz, the only member of the ensemble privileged to compliment the king with an occasional, judicious 'bravo', received bonuses for making new flutes and writing new compositions to supplement his salary (already enormous for an instrumental musician); he eventually composed about 300 flute concertos for Frederick's exclusive use. Another important member of the chamber group, Franz Benda, writing his autobiography in 1763, stated proudly that by that date he had accompanied 'our truly great Frederick' in flute concertos 'at least ten thousand times'. That kind of statistic held little appeal for Emanuel. Emanuel's

works were seldom heard; his true importance was never understood by the king; and his independence of mind offended a monarch who was accustomed to obedience in artistic matters as in civil and political ones. The other accompanists could readily accommodate themselves to Frederick's free rhythms, his occasional missed notes, his narrow musical outlook; for Emanuel it was not so easy, and Frederick knew it.

Emanuel's application for a Kantorate in Zittau in 1753 attests to his dissatisfaction with his Berlin position. In 1755 his salary was still 300 thalers, while that paid to J. F. Agricola and Christoph Nichelmann, both his pupils, was raised above his own; only after he threatened to resign was his pay increased to 500 thalers. In the same year he applied unsuccessfully for the post of Thomaskantor in Leipzig, just vacated by Gottlob Harrer, his father's successor. From 1756 to 1763 the Seven Years War caused the curtailment of all music in Berlin. In 1758 a Russian attack on the city made it necessary for Emanuel and his family to move for some months to Zerbst. During the war all court employees were paid in paper money whose severe depreciation more than offset Emanuel's increase in salary. At the end of the war, in 1762–3, his salary was still 500 thalers. Frederick, fighting for Prussia's existence, rapidly lost interest in his musical establishment, and in the postwar years this interest returned only in the most attenuated form.

Berlin offered compensations to a court musician. Emanuel had time for a substantial amount of teaching, both within the court and privately. His most important pupil was his own young half-brother, Johann Christian,

who lived in Emanuel's home from Sebastian's death in 1750 to 1754. Other notable pupils were J. A. P. Schulz and F. W. Rust. There was also time for composing and writing on a very large scale, as the list of works below testifies. His most influential compositions in the Berlin years were the solo keyboard pieces making up W48 and 49 (H24–9 and H30–34, 36; the Prussian and Württemberg sonatas), W50 (H126, 136–40, 'Sonatas with Varied Repeats'), parts of W62 and 65, W63 (H70–75, the 'sample pieces' published with the *Essay*), W67 (H300) and the *Essay* itself. The first part of the *Essay* appeared in 1753, a year after Quantz's book on playing the flute. It established Emanuel's reputation as the leading keyboard teacher of his time. The main causes of its inception were Emanuel's desire for a creative outlet outside court circles, and the theorizing–explaining atmosphere of mid-18th-century Berlin, the city that Frederick had made into a centre of Enlightenment thought. Quantz, Marpurg, Kirnberger, Sulzer, Agricola, Krause and other treatise-writing members of the rather pedantic 'Berlin School' exercised a not altogether wholesome influence on Emanuel; but in his great *Essay* he produced the best kind of treatise, permanently valuable not only for its broad and practical approach but also in the clarity of its language and organization.

Although he undoubtedly respected his fellow Berlin musicians, Emanuel's best friends were from literary and commercial circles: the poets Lessing, Ramler and Gleim; the banking family of Itzig, including Sara Levy, Mendelssohn's great-aunt, whose assiduously collected library of Bach family music became a major

source of Bachiana; and the hard-working burghers and officials among whom he could escape from court protocol at the Berlin Monday Club, and whose wives he honoured in little Frenchified musical portraits for the keyboard.

In 1744 he married Johanna Maria Dannemann, daughter of a wine merchant. Of their two sons and one daughter, none was a musician. Johann August [?Adam] (1745–89) became a lawyer. The second son, born in 1748, was named Johann Sebastian after his grandfather; he was a painter of some accomplishment, a pupil of A. F. Oeser, but his promising career was cut short by his death in Rome in 1778 after a prolonged illness. His medical expenses were high during more than five months of intense suffering and, as Emanuel described it, 'three of the most frightful life-and-death operations'. A letter from Emanuel to Forkel, in which as much sorrow seems to be expressed over the expense as over the suffering, has often been cited as an example of Emanuel's miserliness; but a reading of the entire letter shows that Emanuel is asking Forkel's assistance towards the quick publication of a new set of sonatas as a means of dealing with a real financial crisis. The daughter, Anna Carolina Philippina (1747–1804), never married and, as neither of the sons had children, Emanuel's branch of the family died out in 1804.

In his household Emanuel continued the tradition of hospitality that he had known in his parents' home. Baldassare Galuppi was one of his visitors; Schulz and Fasch were among the young musicians for whom his house became a haven while they established themselves in Berlin. Sebastian visited him in 1741; a second visit

in 1747, during which he met Frederick the Great, was the occasion of his composition of the *Musical Offering*.

On Sebastian's death in 1750, Emanuel came into possession of about a third of Sebastian's musical estate, along with the 'Alt-Bachisches Archiv' of music, portraits and documents from earlier generations of Bachs. Emanuel has often been criticized for offering for sale in September 1756, after the outbreak of the Seven Years War, one of the most valuable parts of this legacy, the copper engraving plates of the *Art of Fugue*, from which only 30 copies had been printed; but, without attempting to excuse any mercenary attitude on his part, it should be understood that his aim was further publication of the work, and that the 60-odd plates were a heavy mass to move should evacuation of Berlin become necessary. Emanuel was, in fact, an honourable and effective guardian of Sebastian's music and other Bach family treasures important to Bach research; most of the Bachiana now extant were owned by him. Perhaps less defensible is his treatment of his stepmother after Sebastian's death: for nearly ten years, until her own 'alms-woman's' funeral in 1760, Anna Magdalena subsisted mainly on charity. Yet Emanuel's letters do show that he, probably alone among the Bach sons, regularly sent her money, despite geographic separation and the difficulty of communication in wartime. In any case, Sebastian's sons were sadly distant from one another, and not only geographically (except for a little friendly business communication between Emanuel and Johann Christoph Friedrich, his half-brother in Bückeburg).

When the Seven Years War ended in 1763 and it

became apparent that Frederick was not going to compensate his musicians for their losses, Emanuel made his resentment known and intensified his search for new career opportunities. For many years Emanuel had engaged in correspondence of almost a filial character with his godfather, Telemann, in Hamburg, exchanging music, discussing aspects of Emanuel's duties at court and Telemann's position as Kantor and music director in Hamburg. Telemann's death in June 1767 opened up a possible avenue of escape. Emanuel's competitors for the vacated post were well-known musicians – his brother J. C. F. Bach, H. F. Raupach and J. H. Rolle; but after five months of deliberation Emanuel was chosen. Telemann, before his death, had probably suggested Emanuel as his replacement, and Emanuel's candidature was helped by the recommendation of G. M. Telemann, grandson of the deceased. Procuring his release from the king, who was displeased with his attitude, proved difficult; only after repeated requests and a trumped-up plea of ill-health was it granted. After all those years, and in spite of the antipathy between the two men, Frederick obviously continued to value his harpsichordist. Emanuel's health was probably satisfactory throughout his long life, except for severe attacks of gout and a tremor of the hands, both of which appeared fairly early in life. On his departure the king's sister Anna Amalia, who had been his friend (though not closely associated with him) and to whom in 1760 he had dedicated his first collection of 'Sonatas with Varied Repeats' w50 (H126, 136–40), named him her Kapellmeister *von Haus aus*. In March 1768, at the age of 54, the most famous keyboard player and teacher in Europe assumed his new position in Hamburg, being

formally installed on 19 April with an elaborate ceremony, according to the local custom, during which he delivered an inaugural speech, 'de nobilissimo artis musicae fine'.

III Hamburg

Emanuel's duties in the new post were similar to those of his father in Leipzig: to act as Kantor of the Johanneum (the Lateinschule) and director of music in the five principal churches. According to church and city regulations more than a century old at the time of his arrival in Hamburg, the position required that the Kantor teach both musical and non-musical subjects in the Johanneum; but Telemann had been permitted to relinquish the teaching of non-musical subjects, and Emanuel was allowed the additional privilege of paying a helper to teach music in the school. Still, the workload was enormous: to provide about 200 musical performances (including 10 Passions within 13 days) yearly among the five churches, as well as sacred music in the school, funeral music, cantatas for the inaugurations of an endless procession of new pastors, congratulatory cantatas or musical celebrations for various new city officials, music for school plays and even for public examinations at the school, birthday cantatas for prominent citizens, music for visiting royalty, etc. Like his predecessor Telemann, he naturally sought suitable music wherever he could find it to supplement his own compositions, often manufacturing an 'inaugural music' here or a Passion there out of bits and pieces of his own and others' works. After 20 years of such demands on Emanuel and the students and town musicians under his directorship in Hamburg, it is no wonder that after his

death the 'Report concerning the New Arrangement of Church Music' of 1789–90 recommended halving the yearly number of performances of concerted music in the five churches, both to improve the quality of the performances and to spare the performers who, according to the report, were often overwhelmed with work.

The bright side was that Emanuel throve on all this activity. Although his basic salary was a fairly modest 600 Hamburg marks (a rector was paid 1000), there were extra fees attached to most of his duties outside the school and churches, and he found himself rather well off financially. The many administrative tasks required by his position – recruitment and payment of performers and copyists, keeping expense accounts etc – were handled by him with easy competence. Life in the free Hanseatic city-state of Hamburg, completely under the influence of commercial enterprises, was informal, busy and cheerful, a welcome change from court life. Emanuel found himself very much at home, even though Hamburg could not compare with Berlin in musical sophistication. As in Berlin, his closest friends were not musicians but poets, writers, professors, burghers and intellectuals who, like him, had been attracted by the freedom and openness of Hamburg; he was particularly close to Professor J. G. Büsch, the famous writer on mercantile topics. In his attractive home, decorated with portraits of more than 150 well-known musicians, Bach entertained Lessing (now living in Hamburg), Klopstock, J. H. Voss, Gerstenberg and the preacher–teacher Sturm, all poets whose verses he set to music; the historian C. D. Ebeling, one of the translators of Burney's *Present State of Music in Germany* into

11. *Carl Philipp Emanuel Bach* (centre), *Pastor Sturm* (right)
and the artist Andreas Stöttrup: pen and ink drawing with wash
(1784) by Andreas Stöttrup

German; the publisher J. J. C. Bode; and the philosopher J. A. H. Reimarus.

A visit to Emanuel's home in 1773 was the source of Burney's famous description, in his *Present State of Music*, of Emanuel's rapturous improvisation at the clavichord:

After dinner, which was elegantly served, and chearfully eaten, I prevailed upon him to sit down again to a clavichord, and he played, with little intermission, till near eleven o'clock at night. During this time, he grew so animated and possessed, that he not only played, but looked like one inspired. His eyes were fixed, his under lip fell, and drops of effervesence distilled from his countenance. He said, if he were to be set to work frequently, in this manner, he should grow young again.

Among other musical visitors were J. F. Reichardt and Antonio Lotti. Gottfried van Swieten, while Austrian ambassador to the Prussian court, went from Berlin to Hamburg expressly to meet Emanuel, who wrote the six symphonies of W182 (H657–62) for him, and dedicated to him the third collection of keyboard pieces 'für Kenner und Liebhaber' ('for connoisseurs and amateurs'). Van Swieten's presentation in his Viennese concerts of music by Emanuel and especially Sebastian Bach was a source of inspiration to Mozart. Through repute and correspondence, Emanuel's circle of influence steadily widened. Diderot, seeking music for his harpsichord-playing daughter, wrote to him with a request for manuscripts of keyboard sonatas. Haydn had discovered one or two sets of his keyboard music (probably the Prussian and Württemberg sonatas) years earlier, and later testified that he was unable to leave the keyboard until he had played through them all. C. G. Neefe, Beethoven's teacher in Bonn, was one of the most dedicated and voluble admirers of Emanuel's music and

his *Essay*, both of which were basic to his teaching of Beethoven. Emanuel's communication with Klopstock, Claudius and Gerstenberg, dealing with the aesthetic boundary between word and note (a popular concern of the 'Sturm und Drang' generation of poets), casts light on the *empfindsamer Stil* in his instrumental works, as does his learned and detailed announcement, in the *Hamburger unpartheiischer Correspondent*, of the first volume of Forkel's history of music.

As the only musician of major stature in a city built on free enterprise, Emanuel found many opportunities to exercise his entrepreneurial talents. Only a few weeks after his inauguration ceremony he announced in the *Hamburger unpartheiischer Correspondent*, 'with the permission of high authority', a concert series 'at which, along with a variety of vocal pieces and other musical things, he will be heard in harpsichord concertos. The start will be at five-thirty. Price of tickets, two marks'. In some of these concerts he directed performances of choral and dramatic works by such composers as C. H. Graun, Hasse, Telemann, Jommelli, Haydn, Handel, Gluck and J. S. Bach, as well as his own music. After a few seasons he discontinued such productions because of too much competition from (as one journalist put it) 'clubs, assemblies, lotteries, picnics, balls and banquets'. Other ventures were more successful: his teaching (F. J. Hérold, Niels Schiørring, Baron von Grotthus, Dussek and N. J. Hüllmandel were among his Hamburg pupils); his *Musikalisches Vielerley* of 1770, which was a serially issued compilation designed for the popular market and consisting of keyboard pieces, arias and songs with keyboard accompaniment, and chamber music, mostly by such former Berlin colleagues as J. G.

Graun, C. F. C. Fasch and Kirnberger, in addition to pieces of his own; his personal management of the sale of the librettos of his church music, in the matter-of-fact mixing of commerce and religion that was characteristic of Hamburg; and his actions as his own publisher and advertiser. The announcement in the *Correspondent* for 20 October 1773 of his forthcoming settings of the Cramer Psalms w196 (H733) is typical in giving the names of his selling agents in a far-flung, and alphabetically arranged, list of cities: Berlin, Brunswick, Bückeburg, Celle, Copenhagen, Dresden, Eisenach, Göttingen, Gotha, Hamburg (not himself, but no less than three other persons), Hanover, Leipzig, Ludwigslust, Parchim, (St) Petersburg, Riga, Schleswig, Stettin and Weimar. Later this kind of list would be extended to include such capitals as Moscow, Vienna, Warsaw, London, Prague and Stockholm. The market for the bulk of his published works, both popular ('für Liebhaber') and serious ('für Kenner'), was always reasonably satisfying.

In the Hamburg period, the last 20 years of his life, Emanuel was required to represent himself as a composer of church music; in all his Berlin years his only important church work was the excellent *Magnificat* of 1749. As a result of the demand for sheer quantity, much of his church music that was not for publication – for example, every one of the 21 Passions listed in the *Verzeichniss des musikalischen Nachlasses* – is a mixture of original works and portions of works by such composers as Sebastian Bach, (2) Johann Christoph Bach and Telemann, often with new instrumental parts added to the borrowed sections. Yet in his day the mixing of church styles was not the

musical sin it became in the 19th and 20th centuries, and his own parts of these works were usually composed with great care. No apologia needs to be offered concerning the published church works; throughout, they are superior creations from a church-music era hardly noted for superiority. Many non-liturgical choruses, songs, arias and cantatas composed by Emanuel in this period were works of high reputation. But the habit of casting his finest thoughts in instrumental terms was too firmly established. Above everything else in importance are the six keyboard collections of sonatas, rondos and fantasias 'für Kenner und Liebhaber' (w55–9, 61), begun in Berlin and continuing to appear almost up to the end of his life, written to please himself in spite of criticism over their difficulty and declining numbers of subscribers. Nearly as important are ten symphonies (w182–3; h657–66), 12 keyboard concertos (w41–7; h408, 469–79) and certain chamber works (w79, 89–91, 93–5; h522–35, 537–9).

Throughout his career it seems that it was necessary for Emanuel to observe two standards in his compositions, his own and those of his present patron or public; even the titles of his compositions reflect this duality. Articulate and idealistic, he nevertheless liked the practical more than the theoretical (e.g. in his *Essay*), making music more than discussing it. Nothing illustrates his practical turn of mind better than the list of works below: its most striking characteristic is the number of arrangements, alternative versions, revisions and variants it contains. If a piece did not suit it was re-tailored.

His criticisms of shallow music critics seem strikingly modern, and in his insistence on craftsmanship

along with originality even in the most 'popular' composition he rose above the weaknesses of the post-Baroque age. In his edition (with Kirnberger) of Sebastian's chorales, in his long correspondence with Forkel as preparation for Forkel's essay on Sebastian, and in the detailed and telling comparison of Sebastian's music with Handel's that he sent anonymously in 1788 to the editor of the *Allgemeine deutsche Bibliothek*, he showed himself increasingly aware of his father's greatness. He was far from being the counterpoint-hater Burney opportunely described him to be.

Emanuel died on 14 December 1788 of an acute 'chest ailment'. In 1795, when Haydn, returning to Vienna from London, stopped at the Bach household hoping to meet Emanuel, he found only the daughter surviving. The family, except for the son who died in Rome, are buried in the vault of St Michael's Church in Hamburg (the grave was discovered by Heinrich Miesner in 1925). Emanuel's wife and daughter were apparently well enough provided for after his death, and were able to derive income from the sale of his works along with his rich collection of other Bachiana, all listed with considerable thoroughness (though in some parts misleadingly) in the *Verzeichniss des musikalischen Nachlasses des verstorbenen Capellmeisters Carl Philipp Emanuel Bach*, published under the guidance of his widow in Hamburg in 1790. Although the collection of portraits of musicians was scattered, most of the music was acquired by Georg Pölchau, later librarian of the Berlin Singakademie. The bulk of the Pölchau collection, together with several other Berlin collections rich in autographs and manuscript copies of Emanuel's music, is now in the two divisions of the Berlin

Staatsbibliothek (see Kast). Another extensive, but curiously unrelated, collection of Emanuel's music, in clear manuscript copies (with very few autographs), was made by a remarkably assiduous admirer, the Schwerin court organist J. J. H. Westphal (apparently unrelated to the Hamburg publisher J. C. Westphal). This collection was assembled almost under Emanuel's supervision – that is, in a correspondence with Westphal during the last few years of Emanuel's life. It was acquired virtually intact, along with Westphal's meticulous thematic catalogue of it, by F. J. Fétis, and purchased from the Fétis estate in 1871 by the Belgian government. It is now divided between the Conservatory and the Royal Library in Brussels, and has been augmented through the purchase of important items from the libraries of other admirers of Emanuel Bach, such as the 19th-century physician Richard Wagener.

The *Thematisches Verzeichnis* of 1905, made by Alfred Wotquenne of the Brussels Conservatory, is essentially little more than a copy of the Westphal catalogue. It provides incipits of first movements only, and does not describe or give locations of sources. Titles in the Wotquenne catalogue are frequently Westphal's rather than the composer's, attached as part of the categorizing process.

IV Keyboard music

Solo keyboard music was central to Emanuel's long career, and remained so even when he was most pressed with commitments involving other media. The clavichord – specifically, the large instrument built to his exacting requirements – remained his most personal mode of expression, although he composed more and

more for the piano in the last two decades of his life. His advocacy of the clavichord persisted in spite of the fact that the instrument had never been widely accepted outside Germany and was being speedily forgotten even there, just as he brought it to the artistic peak of its existence. Any study of the *empfindsamer* ('highly sensitive') *Stil*, of which he was the chief exponent, must begin with an understanding (or better, a reconstruction) of the best traditions of 18th-century clavichord playing, and by extension, of 18th-century piano playing. The fantasias above all, but also most of the rondos and about a third of the sonatas, often demand alternations of mood so abrupt as to be difficult to perform on the relatively impersonal modern piano (especially in a large hall), and nearly unperformable altogether on the harpsichord: sudden remote modulations, startling departures from supposedly cursive statements, melodies shaped like the pitch patterns of emotional speech, painstakingly exact dynamic indications depicting an orator's emphases, rhythms imitating an actor's hesitations and changes of pace. The source of these features was the French-created atmosphere of rapprochement between music and literature then penetrating northern Europe, especially among 'Sturm und Drang' poets, many of whom were Emanuel's friends. Emanuel's own part in this rapprochement took place, not in the seemingly more suitable genres of song or opera, but in the realm of pure instrumental music; and his goal, conscious or unconscious, was to speak emotively without using words.

Played properly on the clavichord or early piano, or even on the modern piano in relatively intimate surroundings, such passages can be made to sound not only

original and forceful, but also coherent; for these are not the meanderings of a dilettante. Even in the most *empfindsam* work there is never a moment when the hand of the consummate craftsman is not in evidence. Emanuel's famous complaints about the shallowness and faddishness of other composers, especially composers in the *galant* style, have to be taken seriously today, just as they were, because of his formidable reputation, in his own. The fantasias, even when they are so 'free' as to be partly or wholly without bar-lines, are usually in clear tripartite or rondo-like forms, and their harmonic progressions, daring in microcosm, fall obediently under the rule in the *Essay* that the principal tonality be impressed upon the memory of the listener.

Most of his keyboard works are in a more conservative idiom, however, and many of these, such as the 'Easy Keyboard Sonatas' w53 (H162–3, 180–83) and the sonatas 'for ladies' w54 (H184–5, 204–7), are frankly written for the popular market. Before 1740 Emanuel showed his heavy indebtedness to Sebastian in this genre, and throughout his career he perpetuated the brilliant harpsichord idiom of Domenico Scarlatti. His keyboard sonatas are usually in three movements, quick–slow–quick. Slow movements are generally through-composed, and outer movements are in binary form with a recapitulation in the second half, marking him as one of the scores of composers already using sonata form. That is only an incidental aspect of his style.

The keyboard works show that his gradual (though never total) abandonment of contrapuntal and continuous-expansion techniques was not matched by a corresponding adoption of the regular phraseology and slow

harmonic rhythm of the Classical style. Instead, he pursued the *empfindsam* mode on the one hand, and on the other created a kind of motivic variation that must be considered a cornerstone of his style. This technique appears in many different guises. In his sonata-form recapitulations the opening theme is usually given a new twist as soon as it reappears. In the rondos of the 'Kenner und Liebhaber' series the rondo theme is subjected to every imaginable reshaping; in any restatement literal repetition seems to be abhorrent, and is endured only briefly, for establishing formal signposts. Emanuel's many revisions of sonatas nearly always involve reshapings of motif or melody, but not alteration of form. On the other hand, the urge for varied restatement sometimes has formal consequences, as in the varied repetitions of entire movements in the sonatinas for harpsichord and orchestra, or in the first movement of a sonata of 1758 or later (W65/32; H135), which consists of six statements of one musical sentence, the last five being variants of the first. The idea of varied restatement is raised to a formal principle in the 'Amalian' sonatas 'with altered repeats' W50 (H126, 136–40; 1760) as well as in the single-movement 'Short and Easy Keyboard Pieces' W113–14 (H193–203, 1766; H228–38, 1768), where the repeats of binary form are a point of departure for written-out varied repetitions in place of the traditional improvisation of varied repetitions. Curiously, none of those procedures resulted in important development sections in his sonata forms; his kind of 'development' is present in nearly all parts of the movement. Having satisfied his desire for variation in this all-pervading way, he wrote only a few traditional sets of variations, and these, along with his

numerous minuets, polonaises, *solfeggi* and other single-movement keyboard pieces, were designed primarily to fill pages in the popular collections of the time.

v **Orchestral and chamber music**

If the relatively inaccessible medium of the clavichord impedes our understanding of the solo keyboard works, no such impediment exists for the keyboard concertos. There he is seen as a harpsichord virtuoso, not improvising rapturously at home for a Burney or a Reichardt, but performing brilliant, fiery compositions on the concert stage for a large audience. Emanuel and Johann Christian form perhaps the chief link between the harpsichord concertos of their father (who virtually created the genre) and the piano concertos of Mozart. Not surprisingly, Emanuel's concertos are a blend of the Bach–Vivaldi type of ritornello procedure with the principles of sonata form, yet they should be regarded not as leading to Mozart but as the finished and sophisticated apex of the north German concerto style. Their standard movement plan is quick–slow–quick. They show a fine balance between soloist and orchestra, with each having opportunity to sound assertive. These more public works are painted with a broader brush than are the compositions for keyboard alone. They are much more homophonic and slower in harmonic rhythm, often with long stretches of repeated notes in the bass. Whereas sequences are fairly rare in the music for keyboard alone, here they are too frequent; they seem to be the standard mode of transition from one key to another, usually via a circle-of-5ths progression, with arrival at the desired key often being announced by a harmonic

side-slip. Yet the tutti and solo themes are delightfully flamboyant, the opportunities for virtuoso display are abundant, and the slow movements are elegiac poems of considerable beauty. As the list of works below shows, the ten concertos for non-keyboard solo instruments are all alternative versions of keyboard concertos; these are in no way inferior to their keyboard counterparts, and the adaptation ensures that each is eminently idiomatic to its solo instrument.

Apparently alone among north German composers of his time, Emanuel wrote 'sonatinas' for a solo harpsichord (two require two solo harpsichords) with orchestra. Because of the concertato and often quite virtuoso nature of their harpsichord parts, they are categorized in the list below as 'miniature concertos', for want of a better term and in spite of their often inflated proportions. Clearly experimental works, they resemble not only the concerto but also the suite, in their general adherence to a single key throughout, with fluctuations between major and minor modes; the Viennese divertimento, in having two to ten sections or movements, and in the lightness or even triviality of their musical content; and the sonata in their use of diminutive binary and sonata forms (hence the term 'sonatina'). Of the 12 such sonatinas that are indisputably genuine, not counting versions with altered instrumentation, four are played through without pause, and six are stretched out by repetitions of previous sections or movements, with the repetitions usually consisting of 'varied repeats'. The most extreme use of this technique is in w97 (H450), whose plan can be expressed as $ABA^1B^1A^2CDC^1EC^2$. This is music for light entertainment only.

Emanuel's chamber music reliably depicts his conser-

vative side from the very beginning to the very end of his career, and it may be taken as illustrative of the whole development of north German chamber music between the late Baroque and high Classical eras: he gradually learnt to prefer written-out keyboard accompaniments to the continuo, he helped preside over the disappearance (by about 1756 in his own works) of the trio sonata, he adopted the clarinet and the piano, and in his best chamber works he slowly abandoned Baroque contrapuntal–canonic texture in favour not of *galant* simplicity but of equal importance among non-imitative parts.

It is important to single out his chamber works that have a leading or concertante, rather than accompanying, keyboard part, as (following Sebastian's lead) he was among the first to make keyboard players leaders rather than followers in all kinds of instrumental ensembles. Still, his chamber music remains comparatively conservative, no doubt largely because of the reactionary taste of his royal patron in Berlin. He returned again and again to canonic entries at the beginnings of movements or sections. The solo sonata with continuo accompaniment was never completely given up. The genre of the string quartet was ignored. The movement plans of the ensemble sonatas show no clear preference for the quick–slow–quick pattern. Except for an abortive experiment with programme music in a trio sonata of 1749 (W161/1; H579) and an accompanied version (W80; H536) of his 'Empfindungen' fantasia W67 (H300), there is little evidence of the *empfindsamer Stil*. In chamber music, as elsewhere, this keen businessman turned out a steady stream of readily marketable, but nevertheless delightful, single-

279

12. Autograph MS of the opening of C. P. E. Bach's 'Clavier-Fantasie mit Begleitung einer Violine, C. P. E. Bachs Empfindungen' in F♯ minor, composed 1787

movement trifles for small instrumental ensembles: minuets, polonaises, marches, 'little pieces', 'little sonatas', even pieces for mechanical instruments. Not until the accompanied sonatas of 1775–7 (W89–91; H522–34) and the quartets (not trios) of 1788 (W93–5; H537–9) is there a clear turn to the Classical style; in the former, the accompanying instruments – essential, not optional – are insistently independent, and in the latter the Beethovenian piano quartet is adumbrated.

In considering the symphonies the *empfindsamer Stil* is met again. Except perhaps the first four, these are not 'easy pre-Classical symphonies'. They bear little resemblance to the *galant* and sometimes watery symphonies of Johann Christian Bach and his stylistic contemporaries except in their quick–slow–quick movement plan. Not one of them begins with a triad in three hammer-strokes. Most are based on the idea that the day of the Italian opera sinfonia is past, and that a symphony, in order to stand alone, must sound arresting and audacious in its first movement, meditatively beautiful in its second and cheerful or innocent in its third. Most of the audacities are tonal. The first movement of W182/3 (H659) begins with five bars of diatonic broken triads in C, which come to rest on a unison A♭; the 'recapitulation' consists only of those same five bars, stopping this time on a B♭, which begins (without pause) the Adagio second movement, whose key is E. The first movement of W183/1 (H663) so successfully avoids perfect cadences that it is not solidly in any key at all until bar 115, shortly before the recapitulation begins. The themes in all movements of the symphonies, but especially the first movements, are wide-ranging and compelling, one theme being derived from another in a modification of Baroque continuous-

expansion technique; there is seldom a feeling of real thematic contrast. The texture is homophonic except for the tossing of motifs back and forth. Emanuel's handling of the orchestral instruments is remarkably sensitive and individual, especially in the profoundly poetical slow movements; the woodwind are handled with great mastery, and solo passages and chamber-music combinations are woven into the orchestral fabric with a sophistication hardly surpassed in the 18th century. Some formal and expressive devices almost become trademarks: sudden interruptions of forward movement and changes in tempo or dynamics; the connection of movements without pause, often by a transition whose modulatory purpose is perhaps too obvious; the truncated or aborted recapitulation; the statement of intact themes on so many tonal levels that the perception of principal and subsidiary key areas is blurred; and the comparative conservatism of third movements, which often sound a bit anti-climactic. It needs to be emphasized, even when notions about evolution in musical form are suffering the disrepute they deserve, that Emanuel's use of formal patterns must be assessed in its own terms rather than in the terms of later musical eras: truncated recapitulations and the blurring of key areas, for instance, may well be cause for admiration in the contexts where they occur.

VI Vocal music

Emanuel wrote about 300 songs (lieder, Oden, Gesänge, Psalmen) with keyboard accompaniment. Most are miniatures in comparison to the standard repertory, and are strophic, with all strophes (sometimes over 24) sung to the same music (on average about 20 bars in length)

and simple in musical design and texture. Comparing them with 19th-century lieder on a qualitative basis would be illogical since, like most of the songs of Emanuel's contemporaries, they were intended to heighten awareness of the poem rather than to draw attention to the music for its own sake. Goethe's complaint about the too-sensitive, and hence smothering, musical expression of every line of a poem in through-composed songs could never have been levelled against Emanuel's songs as a group.

Once the genre is understood, it is seen at its highest level in Emanuel's works. The typical texture is three parts, fully written out, with the voice line doubling the upper part. The harmony is often so thin that one is tempted to fill it out, especially on short acquaintance with a work (modern editors have too frequently succumbed to this temptation). The restraint and dignity of the settings – especially of the sacred poems, which make up about two-thirds of the total – are Classical in the best sense rather than merely simple; Emanuel generally escaped the dryness characteristic of the 'ode manufacturers' of his time, notably through sensitive portrayal of general emotional atmosphere and carefully wrought melodic interchanges (subtle effects which many modern editors have obscured by being too heavy-handed with additions to the harmony). The sacred texts, most of which are by Gellert, Cramer or Sturm, are universal in their appeal, expressing hope, thanks, joy and reassurance, frequently a bit tedious (especially after a dozen verses) but seldom doctrinaire or in bad taste. The secular songs celebrate nature, mythology, romantic love, fellowship, the drinking of good German wine and the rewards of virtue.

The huge demand for choral music during Emanuel's Hamburg years affected him in several striking ways. It came just when the long and tragic decline of Lutheran church music was beginning and when constant novelty was more highly valued than quality and tradition; small wonder that as an enemy of superficiality he found such a demand uninspiring. And it was surely obvious to Emanuel that the height of that fading tradition had been most fully embodied in the church music of his father. Thus, on the one hand, he found it practical to use pastiches of his own church music with that of other composers; on the other, in the published choral works, he successfully came to grips with a problem that defeated many lesser choral composers of his time, doing so not so much through the aid of his family inheritance as in spite of it. The problem may be simply described as the necessity of building one's own structure in the presence of a venerable and imposing edifice. For Emanuel, solving the problem was primarily a matter of rejection, substitution and modification.

The technique most often rejected was counterpoint. Even the *Magnificat* of 1749, which shows Sebastian's influence on nearly every page, contains only one contrapuntal movement, the 'Sicut erat in principio' (a fugue whose theme has often been compared with that of the Kyrie in the Mozart Requiem); in the other movements counterpoint appears only in briefly canonic treatments of new lines of text. Among substitutes for contrapuntal interest are chromaticism, as in the first movement of the totally homophonic oratorio *Die Israeliten in der Wüste* of 1769, or in the continual reharmonizations of a single motif that comprise the

Zwey Litaneyen of 1786 in their entirety; remarkably colourful orchestration, as in the accompanied recitatives of the *Auferstehung und Himmelfahrt Jesu* (1777–80); and minute attention to dynamic levels, as in a 'Halleluja' duet celebrating dawn in the *Morgengesang am Schöpfungsfeste* (1783), where continually rising groups of three quavers – miniature sunrises – are individually marked 'piano–crescendo'. Modification of his artistic inheritance takes place in such procedures as simplification of ritornello procedure, where the orchestra presents a systematically returning statement that serves both as ritornello and as accompaniment to broad chordal statements by the chorus (e.g. the opening of the *Magnificat*); returning in homophonic garb to the ancient practice of writing for antiphonally opposed choirs of voices and instruments (the *Heilig* of 1778); following his famous inclination towards written-out varied repeats, as in the dramatic aria 'Donnre nur ein Wort der Macht' of *Die letzten Leiden des Erlösers* (1770), where the normal plan of the da capo aria is expanded to $ABA^1B^1A^2$; featuring a distinctive and un-interrupted instrumental figure or countermelody that runs like a single, bright thread through the fabric of an entire movement, sometimes for the sake of musical unity alone (as in the opening movement of the *Magnificat*) and sometimes for the most unmistakable and non-mystical kind of tone-painting (as in the chorus of thanks in the *Israeliten*, where a constantly flowing violin figure represents the water coming out of the rock that Moses struck). The texts and the music of the choral works generally stop short of the sentimentality then rife in Lutheran church music. At its best, and

especially in *Morgengesang*, *Israeliten*, *Heilig* and *Auferstehung*, this music has a power and a universal appeal that point clearly towards Beethoven.

VII The Essay

Emanuel's *Essay on the True Art of Playing Keyboard Instruments* is recognized as probably the most important practical treatise on music written in the 18th century. More widely owned and studied today than any of his compositions, it is a standard guide to 18th-century keyboard fingering, ornamentation, aesthetic outlook, continuo playing and improvisation. It led the way towards the acceptance of the modern standards of keyboard fingering (especially the use of the thumb) that had been inaugurated by his father and was to form a basis of 19th-century keyboard virtuosity. It stated the rules of embellishment in a clear and authoritative way at a time when scores of other treatises were compounding the confusion. (If, for instance, performers of today dutifully begin trills on the upper auxiliary note and give appoggiaturas the right duration – yet start both before the beat – it is their fault, not Emanuel's; if they take every word he wrote as unalterable gospel, on the other hand, it might well be Emanuel's fault for writing so clearly and convincingly.) While requiring technical mastery of the performer in no uncertain terms, Emanuel warned against empty virtuosity. Unlike the many inept discussions of continuo playing then being published (and which should probably never be resurrected), the *Essay* leads the reader steadily and clearly through mountains of detail on harmony at the keyboard. In the chapter on accompaniment it shows how, for the sake of

spontaneity, the accompanist's written music may be considered only an outline to be filled in or even changed during performance. And in the remarkable chapter on improvisation Emanuel demonstrated that, in his own time at least, inspiration had to be harnessed to the intellect and the improviser had to know exactly where he was going, even when, as in his own case, 'his eyes were fixed, his under lip fell, and drops of effervescence distilled from his countenance'.

Catalogues: Verzeichniss des musikalischen nachlasses ... Carl Philipp Emanuel Bach (Hamburg, 1790) [NV]
  A. Wotquenne: Thematisches Verzeichnis der Werke von Carl Philipp Emanuel Bach (1714–1788) (Leipzig, 1905/R1964) [W]
  E. Helm: A New Thematic Catalog of the Works of Carl Philipp Emanuel Bach (in preparation) [H]

Principal MS sources are A-Wgm, B-Bc, Br, D-B, Bds, F-Pc, GB-Lbm (for full information see H); individual MSS listed below contain versions different from the better-known form of a work. Nos. quoted refer to H unless otherwise indicated.

* – alternative version   † – partial alternative version

Numbers in the right-hand column denote references in the text.

SOLO KEYBOARD	273–7

Editions: Le trésor de pianistes (Paris, 1861–72): H2, 5, 15, 21, 24–34, 36, 38–41, 47, 51, 55, 58–60, 66, 68, 68, 71–5, 78, 84, 105, 116–19, 121, 130–32, 173–4, 176–9, 186–7, 189, 192, 208, 211–13, 244, 246–7, 267, 269, 274, 276, 280, 282–3, 298, 375 [T]

  C. P. E. Bach: Die Sechs Sammlungen von Sonaten, freien Fantasien und Rondos für Kenner und Liebhaber, ed. C. Krebs (Leipzig, 1895, rev. 2/1953 by L. Hoffmann-Erbrecht) [K]

  C. P. E. Bach: Klavierwerke, ed. H. Schenker (Vienna, 1902–3): H130, 173, 186–7, 188 (inc.), 208, 243–4, 245 (inc.), 246–7, 268, 282 (inc.) [S]

  C. P. E. Bach: Ausgewählte Kompositionen, ed. H. Riemann (Leipzig, n.d.): H29, 37, 51, 75, 89–90, 94–5, 173, 220, 234, 265, 291 [R]

  C. P. E. Bach: Kleine Stücke für Klavier, ed. O. Vrieslander (Hanover, 1930): H54, 144, 146, 148–9, 166, 168, 170, 214–16, 218, 220–24, 241, 292–7 [VK]

  C. P. E. Bach: Vier leichte Sonaten, ed. O. Vrieslander (Hanover, 1932): H21, 42, 56, 143 [VL]

  C. P. E. Bach: Sonaten und Stücke, ed. K. Herrmann (Leipzig, 1938): H94, 126–8, 153, 158, 263, 280, 288, 311, 338 [HS]

  C. P. E. Bach: Leichte Tänze und Stücke für Klavier, ed. K. Herrmann (Hamburg, 1949): H65, 91–2, 96–8, 122, 145, 147, 165, 169, 310, 320, 325 [HL]

  C. P. E. Bach: Six Sonatas for Keyboard, ed. P. Friedheim (New York, 1967): H18, 46, 57, 119, 142, 182 [F]

  C. P. E. Bach: 43 Keyboard Sonatas, ed. D. M. Berg (in preparation): H23, 32-5, 36–7, 39–41, 46–7, 50–51, 53, 56–7, 59–60, 78, 83, 105–6, 116, 118–19, 121, 129, 131–2, 135, 143, 150, 156–7, 174, 176–7, 189, 210–11, 213, 240, 248, 280 [B]

Sei sonate ... che all'augusta maesta di Federico II rè di Prussia (Nuremberg, 1742 or 1743): H24–9; w48 [1742]   259, 261, 268

Sei sonate ... dedicate all'altezza serenissima di Carlo Eugenio duca di Wirtemberg (Nuremberg, 1744): H30–31, 33, 32, 34, 36; w49 [1744]   259, 261, 268

Sechs Sonaten ... mit veränderten Reprisen (Berlin, 1760), ded. to Princess Amalia of Prussia: H136–9, 126, 140; w50 [1760]

Fortsetzung von Sechs Sonaten (Berlin, 1761): H150–51, 127–8, 141, 62; w51 [1761¹]

Musikalisches Allerley (Berlin, 1761): H2, 40, 63, 66, 69, 109–13, 123, 155, 773–4 [1761²]

Musikalisches Mancherley (Berlin, 1762–3): H59, 77, 81, 92–5, 118–20, 171–2, 340–41, 562, 584, 590, 601 [1762]

Zweyte Fortsetzung von sechs Sonaten (Berlin, 1763): H50, 142, 158, 37, 161, 129; w52 [1763]

Clavierstücke verschiedener Art (Berlin, 1765): H190, 144, 165, 145, 166, 693, 179, 146, 167, 147, 168, 694, 191, 695, 148, 169–70, 149, 101:5; w112 [1765]

Kurze und leichte Clavierstücke mit veränderten Reprisen und beygefügter Fingersetzung für Anfänger (Berlin, 1766): H193–203; w113 [1766¹]

Sechs leichte Clavier-Sonaten (Leipzig, 1766): H162, 180–82, 163, 183; w53 [1766²]

Six sonates, op.1 (Paris, before 1768): H55, 19, 56, 67, 18, 48, 54 [54 not indicated in the title] [1768¹]

Kurze und leichte Clavierstücke mit veränderten Reprisen und beygefügter Fingersetzung, ii (Berlin, 1768): H228–38; w114 [1768²]

Six sonates ... à l'usage des dames (Amsterdam, 1770): H204–5, 184, 206, 185, 207; w54 [1770¹]   269

Musikalisches Vielerley, ed. C. P. E. Bach (Hamburg, 1770): H69, 155, 210, 214–25, 227, 240–41, 376, 598, 698 [1770²]

H	W	
58-61	62/9-10; 65/24-5	4 sonatas, F, C, d, C, 1749, 58 in Oeuvres mêlées (Nuremberg, 1755-65), 59 (1762); 58-60 ed. in T, 59-60 ed. in B
62	51/6	Sonata, G, 1750 (1761²)
63	62/11	Sonata, G, 1750 (1761²); variant, D-B
64	65/26	Sonata, G, 1750
65	118/5	Allegretto con VI variazioni, C, 1750; ed. in HL
66	62/12	Sonata, e, 1751 (1761²); ed. in T
67-8	62/13; 65/27	2 sonatas, D, g, 1752, 67 in Raccolta delle più nuove composizioni (Leipzig, 1756) and (1768); 68 ed. in T
69	118/1	24 Veränderungen über das Lied: Ich schlief, da träumte mir, F, 1752, variations 1-17 (1761²), variations 18-24 (1770²); also as Canzonette with [15] variations (London, ?c1765); as Was helfen mir tausend Ducaten, with 15 variations, DS
70-75	63/1-6; 202/M without text	18 Probestücke in 6 Sonaten, C, d, A, b, E♭, f, 1753; bound with exx. for Versuch, i [see 868]; cf 377 [*640]; 71-5 ed. in T, 75 ed. in R — 261
76	119/1	Duo in contrap. ad, 8, 11 & 12 mit Anmerkungen, a, by 1754, in F. W. Marpurg: Abhandlung von der Fuge (Berlin, 1754), 'Anmerkungen' [? by Marpurg]
77-8	62/14; 65/28	2 sonatas, G, E♭, 1754, 77 (1762); 78 ed. in T, B
79	117/17	La Borchward, polonoise, G, 1754
80	117/18	La Pott, minuet, C, 1754, in Raccolta delle più nuove composizioni (Leipzig, 1756); cf 480
81	117/26	La Boehmer, D, 1754 (1762); as Murqui, A-Wgm
82	117/37	La Gause, F, 1754; cf 480
83	65/29	Sonata, E, 1755; ed. in B
84-7	70/3-6 [265]	4 org sonatas, F, a, D, g, 1755 (1790); 84 ed. in T
89-90	117/19-20	La Gleim, rondeau, a; La Bergius, B♭: 1755, in Raccolta delle più nuove composizioni (Leipzig, 1756); ed. in R
91	117/21	La Prinzette, F, 1755, in Raccolta delle più nuove composizioni (Leipzig, 1757); ed. in HL
92-5	117/23-5, 27	L'Herrmann, g; La Buchholz, d; La Stahl, d; L'Aly Rupalich, C,1755 (1762); 92 ed. in HL, 94-5 ed. in R, 94 ed. in HS
96-8	117/34-5, 39	La Philippine, A; La Gabriel, C; La Caroline, a: 1755; ed. in HL
99	119/2	Fuga a, 2, d, 1755, in F. W. Marpurg: Fugen-Sammlung, i (Berlin, 1758) and (n.d.); ed. in Barford
100	119/3	Fuga 3, F, 1755, in Tonstücke . . . vom Herrn C. P. E. Bach und andern classischen Musikern (Berlin, 1762, 2/1774 as C. P. E. Bachs, Nichelmanns and Handels Sonaten und Fugen) and (n.d.)
101, 101-5, 102	119/4-6 [119/5 = 112/19]	Fuga a 3 mit Anmerkungen, A; Fuga a 3, g; Fuga a 4, org, mit Anmerkungen, E♭; 1755; 101 in Raccolta delle più nuove composizioni (Leipzig, 1757); 101, 102 in F. W. Marpurg: Clavierstücke mit einem practischen Unterricht (Berlin, 1762-3); 101-5 (1765); 101-2 (n.d.); 101, 102 ed. in Barford
103	119/7	Fantasia e fuga a 4, c, 1755; Fuga (n.d.)
104	122/2	Sinfonia, F, ?1755 or later, in F. W. Marpurg: Raccolta delle megliore sinfonie (Leipzig, 1761-2) [*650]
105-6	62/15; 65/30	2 sonatas, d, e, 1756, 105 in Raccolta delle più nuove composizioni (Leipzig, 1757); 105 ed. in T, both ed. in B
107	70/7 [265]	Preludio, org, D, 1756 (1790)
108	116/18	Andantino, F, 1756, in F. W. Marpurg: Kritische Briefe über die Tonkunst (Berlin, 1760)

H	Wq	Work	refs
109	117/28	La complaisante, Bb, 1756 (1761¹) [*456]	
110–13	117/30–33	Les langueurs tendres, c; L'irrésolue, G; La journalière, c; La capricieuse, e: 1756 (1761²); 110 also as La memoire raisonée (1761²) [*507, *585]	
114	117/36	La Louise, D, 1756 [*507, *585]	
115	122/3	Sinfonia, D, 1756 or later, lost [*652, *653]	
116–20	62/16–19; 62/20	5 sonatas, Bb, E, g, G, C, 1757, 116–17 in Oeuvres mêlées (Nuremberg, 1755–65), 118–20 (1762); 119, cf 50; 116–19 ed. in T, 119 ed. in F, 116, 118–19 ed. in B	
121	65/31 [266]	Sonata, c, 1757 (1792); ed. in T, B	
122	117/22	L'Auguste, polonoise, F, 1757, in Raccolta delle più nuove composizioni (Leipzig, 1757); ed. in HL	
123	117/29	La Xénophon La Sybille, C♯, 1757 (1761²) [*455]	
124–5	117/38, 40	L'Ernestine, D; La Sophie, aria, Bb; 1757 [*685]	
126	50/5	Sonata, Bb, 1758 (1760); ed. in HS	261, 264, 276
127–9	51/3–4; 52/6	3 sonatas, c, d, e, 1758, 127–8 (1761¹), 129 (1763); 127–8 ed. in HS, 129 ed. in B	
130	55/2	Sonata, F, 1758 (1779); ed. in T, K, S	
131–2	62/21–2	2 sonatas, a, b, 1758, 131 in Oeuvres mêlées (Nuremberg, 1755–65), 132 in Collection récréative (Nuremberg, 1760–61); ed. in T, B	261, 264, 276
133–4	70/1; 70/2 [265]	2 sonatas, A, Bb, org, 1758, 134 (1790) and in III sonates … par Mrs. C. P. E. Bach, C. S. Binder e C. Fasch (Nuremberg, n.d.), cf 135	
135	65/32	Sonata, A, 1758 or later; rev. of 133; orig. version, D-B; ed. in B	276
136–40	50/1–4, 6	5 sonatas, F, G, a, d, c, 1759 (1760); 136 ed. in H. Fischer, Die Sonate (Berlin, 1937); cf 334	
141–2	51/5; 52/2	2 sonatas, F, d, 1759, 141 (1761¹), 142 (1763); 142 ed. in F	
143	65/33	Sonata, a, 1759, KVu; ed. in VL, B	
144–9	112/2, 4, 8, 10, 15, 18 [117/8, 5, 9, 6, 10, 7]	Fantasia, D; Solfeggio, C; Fantasia, Bb; Solfeggio, C; Fantasia, F; Solfeggio, G: 1759 (1765); 144, 146, 148–9 ed. in VK, 145, 147 ed. in HL	
150–52	51/1–2; 65/34	3 sonatas, C, Bb, Bb, 1760, 150–51 (1761¹); cf 156–7; 150 ed. in B	
153	116/21	Allegro, C, 1760; ed. in HS	
154	116/22	Polonoise, g, 1760 [*168]	
155	118/2	Clavierstück mit [22] Veränderungen, A, 1760 [? only variations 13–14, 17–22 by C. P. E. Bach, others by [J. A.] Steffan, C. Fasch]; theme and variations 1–17 (1761²); theme and variations 18–22 (1770¹)	
156–7	65/35–6	2 sonatas, C, 1760 or later, revs. of 150; ed. in B	
158	52/3	Sonata, g, 1761 (1763); ed. in HS	
159	116/15	Minuet, C, ? by 1762 [*601]	
160	117/14	Fantasia, D, by 1762, pubd in Versuch, ii [see 870]	
161–3	52/5; 53/1, 5	3 sonatas, E, C, C, 1762, 161 (1763), 162–3 (1766?)	275
164	68	Veränderungen und Auszierungen über einige meiner Sonaten, completed 1762 or later, autograph, D-Bds	
165–70	112/3, 5, 9, 11, 16–17 [116/9–14]	Minuet, D: Alla polacca, a; Minuet, D: Alla polacca, g; Minuet, A; Alla polacca, D: 1762–5 (1765) [*154, *602–5]; 165, 169 ed. in HL, 166, 168, 170 ed. in VK	
171–2	116/1–2	Minuet, Polonoise, Eb, by 1763 (1762)	
173	57/6	Sonata, f, 1763 (1781) and (Berlin, n.d.); ed. in T, K, S, R	
174–8	65/37–41	5 sonatas, A, Bb, e, D, C, 1763; 174, 176–8 ed. in T; 174, 176–7 ed. in B	
179	112/7	Sonata, d, 1763 (1765); ed. in T	
180–83	53/2–4, 6	4 sonatas, Bb, a, b, F, 1764 (1766?); 182 ed. in F	
184–5	54/3, 5	2 sonatas, d, D, 1765 (1770¹); ed. K. Johnen (Frankfurt am Main, 1950)	275
186–7	55/4, 6	2 sonatas, A, G, 1765 (1779); ed. in T, K, S	
188–9	58/4; 65/42	2 sonatas, e, Eb, 1765, 188 (1783); 188 ed. in K, S (inc.); 189 ed. in T, B	275
190	112/1	Concerto, hpd solo, C, 1765 (1765)	
191	112/13 [122/4]	Sinfonia, hpd solo, G, 1765 (1765) [*655]	
192	65/43	Sonata, A, 1765–6; ed. in T	
193–203	113/1–11	Allegro, G; Arioso, a; Fantasia, d; Minuet,	276

No.	Source	Title / description
231-4	59/1, 3-4, 6	2 sonatas, e, b♭; Rondo, c; Fantasia, C: 1784 (1785), 282 (1791); ed. in K, 282 ed. in S (inc.), 282-3 ed. in T
285	—	Fughetta on the name 'C. Filippo E. Bach' [C–F–E–B–A–C–H], F, 1784; pubd in Bitter, ii, 303-4; cf 867
286-91	61/2, 5, 1, 3, 4, 6	2 sonatas, D, G; Rondo, E♭; Fantasia B♭; Rondo, d; Fantasia, C: 1785-6 (1787), 288, 290 (1791); ed. in K, 288 ed. in HS, 291 ed. in R
292-7	63/7-12	VI sonatine nuove, G, E, D, B♭, F, d, 1786, pubd in 868 (2/1787), also pubd as 2 sonatas of 3 movts (Leipzig, 1786); ed. in VK, ed. L. Hoffmann-Erbrecht (Leipzig, 1957)
298-9	65/49-50	2 sonatas, E♭, G, 1786 [*517, *633]; 298 ed. in T
300	67	Freie Fantasie fürs Clavier, f♯, 1787 [*536]; ed. A. Kreutz (Mainz, 1950) — 261, 279
301-9	116/19-20, 29-35	Allegretto, F; Allegro D; Minuet, G; Minuet, G; Minuet, F; Minuet, F; Minuet, D; Polonoise, A; Minuet, D [*622-7, *635, *638]; cf 258
310-14	116/36-40	Allegro di molto, A; Allegro, E; Allegro, B♭; Presto, a; Minuet, D [*635]; 310 ed. in HL, 311 ed. in HS
315-18	116/41-4	4 polonoises, F, A, B♭, E♭ [*635]
319-22	116/45-8	2 marches, F, D; 2 minuets, C, G [*635, *637]; 320 ed. in HL
323-31	116/49-57	Polonoise, D; Langsam und traurig, a; Allegro, C; Allegro ma non troppo, E♭; Allegro, C; Allegro, G; Allegro, E♭; Allegro, D; Allegretto grazioso, C [*612, *615, *617-19, *620/1, *632, *634-5]; 325 ed. in HL
333	—	La Juliane, F
334	—	Variations C, ? late work [*138, variant of 3rd movt]
336	—	5 Chorâle mit ausgesetzten Mittelstimmen, kbd, no text: O Gott du frommer Gott, Ich bin ja Herr in deiner Macht, Jesus meine Zuversicht, Wer nur den Lieben Gott, Komm heiliger Geist; cited in NV 64, 2 in D-B: see W, p.96
		Chorale: Wo Gott zum Haus nicht gibt, a 4, bc, Bds

possibly authentic

No.	Source	Title / description
337	—	2 unattrib. single movts ['Allegro'], A, G, ?1755, in F. W. Marpurg: Anleitung zum Clavierspielen (Berlin, 1755); in B-Bc as by C. P. E. Bach; ? same as Zwey Allegro in NV 11; ed. in HS
338	116/16-17	Fantasia, E♭, c1755 or later; in D-Bds unattrib.
339	—	Garten-Sonata, D, by 1762; unattrib. in (1762); attrib. C. P. E. Bach in GOI
340	—	Sonata, e, by 1762; unattrib. in (1762); attrib. C. P. E. Bach in B
341	—	Polonoise, G, 1768 or later
341-5	—	Sinfonia per il clavicembalo, B♭, ?1786, LEm
342	—	2 sonatas, C, c, A-Wn, D-B
343-4	—	Sonata, D, n.d. B, Bds, USSR-KAu
346	—	Sonata, E♭, D-B
347	—	Solo, F, B
348	—	2 sonatas, c, B♭, GOI
350-51	—	Sonata [Suite], B♭, KII
352	—	5 sonatas, C, F, G, G, B♭, USSR-KAu
353-6, 358	—	Fantasia e fuga, d, B-Bc
359	—	Fuga, C, ? by 1767, D-B
360	—	Arioso con variazioni, A, GOI (as Sonata), KII, Mbs
361	—	Alla Pol[acca] con variatio, G; Giga con variazioni, F; Minuetto, D: US-Wc
362-4	—	Adagio, per il organo a 2 claviere e pedal, d, D-B
364-5	—	1 untitled, a, frag.: Menueten zum Tantzen, D, frag.; Polonoise, D; Polonoise, D; Polonoise, A; Larghetto, G
365-9	—	La Walhauer, A, GOI
370	—	

doubtful or spurious

H	W	
371	—	Chorale: Ach Gott und Herr, kbd, c1732, autograph, B [chorale from cantata bwv48]
372	—	VI Sonaten, Bb, G, d, F, G, D, by 1757, GOI [G. Benda: 6 Sonate (Berlin, 1757)]
373	—	Sonata, F, by 1764, B, kbd pt. of accompanied sonata op.2 no.1 [r313/1] by J. C. Bach
374	—	Fugue, Bb, B, not in NV
375	—	Polonise, Eb, c1765, GOI [by W. F. Bach, f12]; ed. in T
376	—	Clavier-Sonate, C, by 1770 (1770²), B [described by C. P. E. Bach in the print as by J. C. F. Bach, HW XI/2, cf DDT, lvi (1917), xiii]
377	—	5., 4., 6. Sonate, E, b, c, c1770, GOI [no.4 = 73, nos.5–6 by J. C. Bach, op.5 nos.5–6, r338/1]
378	—	Sonata: Concerto, A, c1771, GOI [anon. kbd arr. of conc. ? by J. C. Bach, r297/4; *379, *489-5]
379	—	A Favourite Concerto, A, kbd, c1771 [? by J. C. Bach (London, c1775); *378, *489-5]
380	—	Due Sonate . . . del Sigi. Daniele Turck, La troisi – La quartiem Mons. P. E. Bach, Bb, by 1776, GOI [nos.3-4 also by Türk]
381	272	La Bataille de Bergen, F, c1778 (Worms, n.d.), also as La Bataille de Rosbach; in S-Skma, US-Wc, attrib. J. C. Bach [r343/7] and Graun; cf Jacobi (1790)
382	—	A Favourite Overture of Sig. Bach of Berlin, D, c1785 (London, c1785) [pf arr. of sym. by J. C. Bach, r277/4]
383	—	Sonata, e, USSR-KAu, 1 movt uncertainly attrib. W. F. Bach in D-B
383-5	—	Sonata, F, A-Wn, D-B, attrib. J. E. Bach in Oeuvres mêlées (Nuremberg, 1755-65), v
383-6	—	Sonata, a, B, USSR-KAu [by J. C. Bach, r358/4]

H	W	
384	—	Parthia, C, D-B
384-5	—	Sonata, A, US-Bp
385-90	—	VI petites pièces arrangées pour le piano forte: Le Travagant, G; Le Caressant – Le Contente, C; Le petit maître, F; Le Flegmatique – En Colère, Bb; Le Moribant, d: Il est vive, D: D-B
		And.te ed Allegro, B
391	—	Fuga, C, ?1764; not in NV [F-Pc attrib. C. P. E. Bach, D-B attrib. J. S. Bach (cf bwv Anh.90)]
392	—	Fuga, c, in bwv575 as by J. S. Bach
393	—	Fuga, D, D-Bds
393-5	—	Fuga [Sopra il nome di Bach], C, A-Wgm, Wn [in bwv Anh.108 as doubtful work of J. S. Bach]
394	—	2 chorales: Allein Gott in der Höh, Vater unser im Himmelreich, kbd, D-B
395-6	—	Menuetto mit V Variazionen, Eb, KII
398	—	Tempo di men[uetto]-variation, A; 2 works in 1 movt: B
399-401	—	
402	—	1 untitled, a, frag. [by Kirnberger]

277-8

CONCERTOS AND SONATINAS

Concertos, hpd/org, vns, insts (London, c1753): H414, 429, 417 [1153]; H421, 444, 428 [1760]
A Second Set of Three Concertos, org/hpd, insts (London, c1760); H421, 444, 428 [1760]

H	W	
403	1	Conc., a, hpd, str, 1733, lost, 1744; in D-B, misattrib. J. S. Bach
404	2	Conc., Eb, hpd, str, 1734, lost, rev. 1743 as op.2 (Paris, n.d.)
405	3	Conc., G, hpd, str, 1737, lost, rev. 1745
406	4	Conc., G, hpd, str, 1738
407	5	Conc., c, hpd, str, 1739, lost, rev. 1762
408	46	Conc. doppio, F, 2 hpd, 2 hn, str, 1740; 2nd version, B, with hns ad lib — 271
409-10	6-7	2 concs., g, A, hpd, str, 1740
411-13	8-10	3 concs., A, G, Bb, hpd, str, 1741-2

No.	Pages	Description
414	11	Conc., D, hpd, str, 1743 (Nuremberg, 1745), and (1753) also with added 2 tpt, timp ad lib, B-Bc
415-17	12-14	3 concs., F, D, E, hpd, str, 1744, 417 (1753) and (Berlin, 1760); for fl conc. version of 417 see Newman (1965); 417 also with added 2 hn
418-21	15-18	4 concs., e, G, d, D, hpd, str, 1745, 421 (1760); another version of 419, ?1738, US-BE
427	23	Conc., d, hpd, str, 1748; ed. in DDT, xxix-xxx (1906/R)
428	24	Conc., e, hpd, str, 1748 (1760); ? earlier version, BE
429	25	Conc., Bb, hpd, str, 1749 (Nuremberg, 1752) and (1753); arr. 2 hpd, D-Dlb
430-32	26; 166; 170	Conc., a, hpd, str, 1750; versions for fl, str, ?1750, and for vc, str, ?1750; 432 orig. version, autograph, B
433	27	Conc., D, hpd, str, with 2 ob, 2 tpt/hn, 2 fl ad lib, timp ad lib, 1750: 2nd version, NV 31, for str, 2 hn
434-6	28; 167; 171	Conc., Bb, hpd, str, 1751; versions for fl, str, 1751, and for vc, str, ?1751; cf Newman (1965)
437-9	29; 168; 172	Conc., A, hpd, str, 1753; versions for fl, str, ?1753, and for vc, str, ?1753
440-43	30-33	4 concs., b, c, g, F, hpd, 2 vn, b, 1753-5, 441, autograph, B: 442 with opt. 2 fl
444-5	34; 169	Conc., G, org/hpd, str, 1755, 444 (1760); version for fl, str, ?1755 or later; cf NV 32
446	35	Conc., Eb, org/hpd, 2 hn, str, 1759; ? orig. for org, cf NV 33; also without hns
447-8	36-7	Conc., Bb, hpd, str, 1762; conc., c, hpd, 2 hn, str, 1762; 448, Bds, with added 2 hn
449-52	96-9	4 sonatinas, D, G, G, F, hpd, 2 fl, 2 hn, str, 1762; 2nd version of 449, LEm; †600/1, 4, 11 (276, 278)
453	109	Sonatina ... con 18 stromenti, D, 2 hpd, 2 fl, 2 ob, bn, 2 hn, 3 tpt, timp, 2 vn, va, vc, vle, 1762; variant, B [*481] (276, 278)
454	38	Conc., F, hpd, str, 2 fl ad lib, 1763 (276, 278)
455-7	100; 102-3	3 sonatinas, E, D, C, hpd, 2 fl, 2 hn, str, 1763; †109, †123, †600/7 (276, 278)
458	106	Sonatina I, C, hpd, 2 fl, str, 1763 (Berlin, 1764); cf 460 (276, 278)
459	110	Sonatina, Bb, 2 hpd, 2 fl, 2 hn, str, 1763; also for pf, hpd, SWV, and for 1 kbd, LEm (276, 278)
460	101	Sonatina, C, hpd, 2 fl, 2 hn, str, 1763 or later; rev. of 458
461-4	107-8; 104-5	Sonatinas II, III, F, Eb; 2 sonatinas, F, Eb; hpd, 2 fl, str, 1764-5, 463-4 [revs. of 461-2] also 2 hn, 461 (Berlin, 1764) [see Newman, (1965)], 462 (Berlin, 1766) (276, 278)
465-8	39; 164; 40; 165	Conc., Bb, hpd, str, 1765, version for ob, str, ?1765; Conc., Eb, hpd, str, 1765, version for ob, str, ?1765; ob concs..., ? orig. versions, see autographs, Bds
469	41	Conc., Eb, hpd, 2 fl, 2 hn, str, 1769 (271)
470	42	Conc., F, hpd, 2 hn, str, 1770 [*242] (271)
471-6	43/1-6	Sei concerti, F, D, Eb, c, G, C, hpd, str, with 2 hn, 2 fl ad lib, 1771 (Hamburg, 1772) (271)
477-8	44-5	2 concs., G, D, hpd, 2 hn, vn, va, b, 1778 (271)
479	47	Conc. doppio, Eb, hpd, pf, 2 fl, 2 hn, str, 1788 (271)
479-5	[bwv1052a]	Conc., d, hpd, str, c1732-4, B; ?arr. or recomposition by C. P. E. Bach of (lost) vn conc., d, by J. S. Bach
479-6	—	Conc., fl, str, ?1747; ? orig. version of 425, B, Bds [? by F. Benda]

possibly authentic

No.	Pages	Description
480	—	Sonatina III, D, hpd, 2 fl, str, 1758 or later, LEm; combination of 80, 82, 600/9 and 12
481	—	Sonatina, D, hpd, 2 fl, str, c1762, B [*453]
483	—	2 concs., g, e, US-Wc
484-5	—	11 fl concs., ? before 1768, formerly Berlin, Singakademie, now lost
485-5	—	

doubtful or spurious

H	W		Pages
486	—	Concert, f, hpd, insts, ?c1753, D-B [? by J. C. Bach, r301/4, rev. C. P. E. Bach]; B [attrib. W. F. Bach]; attrib. C. P. E. Bach, ed. W. Szarvady (Leipzig, c1900)	
487	—	Conc., d, hpd, insts, c1759, B [by C. Nichelmann]	
488-9	—	2 concs., Bb, G, hpd, insts, by 1763, CS-Bm [by J. C. Bach, r292/1, 7]	
489·5	—	Conc., c, hpd, orch, by 1768, private collection of E. Bücken, A-Wn (film) [378-9]	
490	—	Sonatina, C, glass harmonica, 2 vn, vc, 1775 or later, CS-Pnm; combination of movts from 522, 524	
491	—	Conc., C, hpd, insts, by 1777, Bm [by J. C. Bach, r295/1]	
492	—	Sonatina, C, glass harmonica, str, by 1777, Pnm; arr. of variations selected from 259	
493-4	—	2 concs., Eb, Bb, hpd, insts, by 1780, 493, D-GOl, 494, W-Rtl [both by J. C. Bach] r294/5, 3]	
495	—	Conc., Eb, hpd, str, B	
496	—	Conc., f, hpd, insts, GOl [by G. Benda]	
497	—	Conc., Bb, hpd, insts, B [by C. Nichelmann]	
498-500	—	3 concs., C, b, F, hpd, insts, CS-Bm, D-DS [? by J. C. Bach]	
500-1	—	Conc., D, hpd, str, private collection of E. N. Kulukundis	
501	—	Conc., D, vn/va/4 viols, pf/orch; [? by member of the Casadesus family, c1905]	

CHAMBER MUSIC WITH OBBLIGATO KEYBOARD

H	W		Pages
			279-81
502	71	Sonata, D, hpd, vn, 1731, rev. 1746	
503	72	Duetto, d, hpd, vn, 1731, rev. 1747; also as sonata, fl, vn, bc, US-Wc [*596]	
504	73	Duetto, C, hpd, vn, ?1745 or later [*573]	
505	83	Sonata, D, hpd, fl, ?1747 or later [*575]	
506	84	Duetto, E, hpd, fl, ?1749 or later [*580]	
507	74	Sonata o vero sinfonia, D, hpd, vn, 1754 [*585; †114]; attrib. J. S. Bach in D-B [*585]	

H	W		Pages
508-9	85-6	2 sonatas, G, hpd, fl, 1754-5 [*581, *583, *586]	
510	88	Sonata, g, hpd, va da gamba, 1759	
511-14	75-8	4 sonatas, F, b, Bb, c, hpd, vn, 1763	
515	87	Sonata, C, hpd, fl, 1766	
516-21	92	Sechs kleine Sonaten, Eb, Eb, Eb, Bb, Eb, Bb, hpd, cl, bn, after 1767 [*251, *254, *299, *610, *613-14, *629-31, *633, *635]	
522-4	90	[3] Claviersonaten, i, a, G, C, hpd, vn, vc, 1775 (Leipzig, 1776) [†490]	271, 281
525-30	89	Six Sonatas, Bb, C, A, Eb, e, D, hpd/pf, vn, vc, 1775-6 (London, 1776)	271, 281
531-4	91	[4] Claviersonaten, ii, e, D, F, C, hpd, vn, vc, 1777 (Leipzig, 1777); 534 variations on 249; cf 259	271, 281
535	79	Arioso con variazioni, A, hpd, vn, 1781	271
536	80	Clavier-Fantasie mit Begleitung (C. P. E. Bachs Empfindungen), f#, hpd, vn, 1787 [*300]; sketches in 867	279, 280
537-9	93-5	3 quartets, a, D, G, hpd, fl, va, [vc], 1788; listed as qts in NV 51, 537-8 also entitled Trio; kbd pt. incl. indications for vc, formerly Berlin, Singakademie, now lost, [cf Schmid, 139]	271, 281
540	—	[Sonata], E, kbd, melody inst, B-Bc, frag.	
541	—	[Sonata], G, kbd, va [modern copy listed in Katalog der bedeutenden Musiksammlung ... Erich Prieger ... Versteigerung, iii (Cologne, 1924), no.186; ? in private collection]	

possibly authentic

H	W		Pages
542	—	Sonata, A, hpd, vn, ?1731 or 1747, D-B [*570]	
542·5	—	Sonata, g, hpd, vn, by c1734, A-Wgm, attrib. C. P. E. Bach in Breitkopf Catalogue, 1763, but ? disowned by him [cf Bitter, i, 338]; listed in bwv1020 as doubtful work by J. S. Bach [? recomposition by C. P. E. Bach of bwv1031]	

Wq	H	Description
		[...], b), hpd, vn, ?1755, US-Wc [*567–?]
544	—	Sonata, E, hpd, vn, D-DS

doubtful or spurious

Wq	H	Description
546-7	—	2 sonatas, C, G, kbd, vn, c1773, RH [now housed at MÜu; by J. C. Bach, op.i0 nos.2–3, τ322/1]

SOLO SONATAS FOR WIND AND STRINGS   279-81

Wq	H	Description
548	134	Sonata, G, fl, bc, by ?1735
549	135	Solo, g, ob, bc, by ?1735
550-56	123-9	7 sonatas, G, e, Bb, D, G, a, D, fl, bc, 1735–40; ed. K. Walther (Kassel and Frankfurt, 1936–58)
557	138	Solo, g, vc, bc, 1740, rev. 1769, lost
558-9	136-7	2 solos, C, D, va da gamba, bc, 1745–6
560-61	130-31	2 sonatas, Bb, D, fl, bc, 1746–7
562	132	Sonata, a, fl, 1747 (Berlin, 1763) and in Musikalisches Mancherley (Berlin, 1762–3)
563	139	Solo, G, harp, 1762
564	133	Sonata, G, fl, bc, 1786
564-5	[bwv1033]	Sonata, C, fl, bc, ?c1731, D-B [partly autograph]; ? recomposition by C. P. E. Bach of lost Sonata for solo fl by J. S. Bach

possibly authentic

Wq	H	Description
565	—	2 sonatas, G, b, fl, bc, by 1763, collab. C. Schaffrath [listed in Katalog der bedeutenden Musiksammlung ... Erich Prieger ... Versteigerung, iii (Cologne, 1924), no.353; ? in private collection]

TRIO SONATAS   279-81

Wq	H	Description
566	—	Trio ... mit Johann Sebastian Bach gemeinschaftlich verfertigt, vn, va, bc, by ?1731, lost; title in NV 65 [cf Bitter, ii, 307]
567-71	143-7	5 sonatas, b, e, d, A, C, fl, vn, bc, 1731, rev. 1747, 569 similar to trio sonata listed as doubtful work of J. S. Bach (bwv1036), ? composed jointly by J. S. and C. P. E. Bach [*542]
572-5	148-51	4 sonatas, a, C, G, D, fl, vn, bc, 572, 1735, rev. 1747, 573–5, 1745–7 [*504–5]; 575 ed. in SBA
576-7	154-5	2 sonatas, F, e, 2 vn, bc, 1747; 576 incl. in doubtful works of J. S. Bach (bwv Anh.186)
578-9	161/2, 1	Sonata, Bb, fl and vn/fl/vn, bc, 1748; Sonata, c, 2 vn/vn, bc, 1749: pubd as Zwey Trio (Nuremberg, 1751); 579 ed. in SBA
580-81	162; 152	Trio, E, 2 fl, bc, 1749; trio, G, fl, vn, bc, 1754 [*506, *508, *583]
582	156	Sinfonia, a, 2 vn, bc, 1754
583-4	157-8	2 sonatas, G, Bb, 2 vn, bc, 1754, 584 (Berlin, 1763), also in Musikalisches Mancherley (Berlin, 1762–3) [*508, *581]
585	—	Sinfonia a 3 voce, D, 2 vn, bc, ?1754, D-B, US-Wc [for autograph, cf M. Pincherle, Cent raretés musicales (Paris, 1966)] [*114, *507]
586	153	Sonata, G, fl, vn, bc, 1755 [*509]
587-9	159; 163	Sonata, Bb, 2 vn, bc, 1755; versions as trio, F, va, b rec, bc, 1755, and trio, bn, b rec, bc, ?1775 [*543]; 587 listed as doubtful work of J. S. Bach
590	160	Sonata, F, 2 vn, bc, 1756, variant in Musikalisches Mancherley (Berlin, 1762–3)

possibly authentic

Wq	H	Description
591	—	Sonata, E, 2 vn, bc, ? before 1768, US-Wc
592	—	Sonata, c, fl/vn, vn, bc, D-HVs
593	—	Sonata, Eb, fl, vn, bc, formerly Berlin, Singakademie, now lost

doubtful or spurious

Wq	H	Description
595	—	Sonata, G, fl, vn, 1735 [listed in Bitter, i, 27, ii, 326, but not found]
596	—	Sonata, d, fl, vn, bc, ?1747, US-Wc [*503]
597	—	Trio, F, fl, vn, bc, ? before 1768, attrib. C. P. E. Bach, Wc; doubtfully attrib. J. C.

279

H	W	
		Bach as Sonata, r332/1, fl, hpd, *D-B*; doubtfully attrib. W. F. Bach, *Bds*; ed. H. Brandt Buys as Trio, 2 vn, bc; attrib. W. F. Bach F50 (Amsterdam, n.d.); ed. K. Marguerre as Sonata, attrib. J. C. Bach (Celle, 1960)

OTHER CHAMBER

H	W	(279–81 / 269)	
598	140	269	Duetto, e, fl, vn, 1748, in *Musikalisches Vielerley* (Hamburg, 1770); ed. W. Stephan (Kassel, 1928), J. Marx (New York, 1948)
599	141		Duetto, d, 2 vn, 1752, lost
600	81		Zwölf kleine Stücke mit 2 und 3 Stimmen, 2 fl/2 vn, hpd, 1758 (Berlin, 1758) [*450, *456, *480]; ed. F. Oberdörffer (Berlin, 1934), K. Walther (Frankfurt am Main, 1971)
601	192		Zwey Menuetten, C, 2 fl, 2 bn, 3 tpt, timp, 2 vn, bc, by 1762, in *Musikalisches Mancherley* (Berlin, 1762–3) [*159]
602–3	189/1–2		2 minuets, D, 2 fl, 2 cl, 2 vn, bc, ?c1765 [*165, *167]
604–5	190/1, 3		Polonoise, D, 2 cl, 2 vn, bc; Polonoise, a, 2 vn, bc, ?c1765 [*166, *170]
606–9	189/8; 190/2, 4–5		Minuet, D, 2 fl, 2 cl, 2 hn, 2 vn, bc; Polonoise, G, 2 vn, bc; Polonoise, C, 2 vn, bc; ?c1766 [*214–15, *217, *219]
610–13	115/1–4		4 kleine Duetten, Bb, F, a, Eb, 2 hpd, ? after 1767 [*251, *324, *518, *614, *620, *635]
614–19	185/1–6		VI Märsche, D, C, F, G, Eb, D, 2 ob, 2 cl, bn, 2 hn, after 1767 [*252, *254, *327–330, *518, *613]
620	186		2 kleine Stücke, C, F, 2 cl, bn, 2 hn, after 1767, lost [*250, *324, *611–12, *635]; with 2 ob in NV 52
621	188		Marcia ... für die Arche, C, 3 tpt, timp, after 1767

H	W	
622	189/3	Minuet, G, 2 fl, bn, 2 hn, 2 vn, bc, ? before 1768 [*303]
623–6	189/4–7	4 minuets, G, C, F, D, 2 fl, 2 hn, 2 vn, bc, ? before 1768 [*258, *304–7, *635]
627	190/6	Polonoise, A, 2 vn, bc, ? before 1768 [*308]
628	82	Zwölf 2- und 3-stimmige kleine Stücke, 2 fl/2 vn, hpd, 1769 (Hamburg, 1770)
629–34	184/1–6	VI sonate, D, F, G, Eb, A, C, 2 fl, 2 cl, bn, 2 hn, 1775 [*299, *326, *331, *516–17, *519–20]; ed. J. Lorenz (Milan, 1939), K. Janetzky (London, 1958)
635	193	[30] Stücke für Spieluhren, auch Dreh-Orgeln, no.2, 1775 or later [*251, *257–8, *305–6, *310–25, *521, *610, *612, *620, *624–5, *636–7]; 1 ed. in E. Simon: *Mechanischer Musikinstrumente früherer Zeiten und ihre Musik* (Wiesbaden, 1960)
636	142	Duett, C, 2 cl [*635/26–7]
637	187	2 Märsche, F, D, 2 ob, bn, 2 hn [*319–20, *635]
638	191	Zwo abwechselnde Menuetten, D, 2 fl, 2 ob, 2 hn, 3 tpt, timp, str, bc [*309]

possibly authentic

H	W	
639	—	Fantasia sopra Jesu meines Lebens Leben, ob, 3 insts, ? before 1735, *D-B*

doubtful or spurious

H	W	
640	—	Sonata, C, harmonica, vc, 1753 or later, *CS-Pnm* [*74–5]
641	—	3 trios, d, Eb, G, 2 vn, va, c1765, *A-M* [by J. C. Bach r315/10, r315/4, r315/7]
642	—	Quintette, C, fl, ob, vn, va, vc, c1772, *CS-Bm* [by J. C. Bach r303/1]
643	—	III sonate, D, G, C, fl, vn, *A-Wn* [? by J. C. Bach r337/1]
644–5	—	2 divertimentos, D, G, fl, vn, va, vc, *PL-WRu*
646	—	Frühlings Erwachen, 2 vn, pf, ? 19th century
647	—	Adagio, str, ? 1904

SYMPHONIES

			281–2
648	173	Sinfonie, G, str, 1741 [*45]	
649	174	Sinfonia, C, 2 fl, 2 hn, str, 1755, also without hns/fls	
650	175	Sinfonia, F, 2 fl, 2 bn, 2 hn, str, 1755 [*104]; wind pts. opt.	
651	176	Sinfonia, D, 2 fl, 2 ob, 2 hn, 3 tpt, timp, str, 1755; wind and timp pts. opt.	
652	177	Sinfonia, e, str, 1756 (Nuremberg, 1759) [*115, *653], ed. K. Geiringer, *Music of the Bach Family: an Anthology* (Cambridge, Mass., 1955)	
653	178	Sinfonia, e, 2 fl, 2 ob, 2 hn, str, ? 1756 [*115, *652]	
654–6	179–81	3 sinfonias, Eb, G, F, 2 ob, 2 hn, str, 1757–62 [*191, *227]; wind pts. opt.	
657–62	182	Set sinfonie, G, Bb, C, A, b, E, str, 1773: for G. van Swieten	268, 271, 281
663–6	183	[4] Orchester-Sinfonien mit 12 obligaten Stimmen, D, Eb, F, G, 2 fl, 2 ob, bn, 2 hn, 2 vn, va, vc, db, 1775–6 (Leipzig, 1780); ed. in EDM, 1st ser., xviii (1942/R)	271, 281
667	—	Sinfonia, G, str, ?1750–51, *D-B*; probably collab. Prince Ferdinand Philipp von Lobkowitz [cf NV 65 and Suchalla, 128ff]	

doubtful or spurious

668	—	Numerous further syms., divertimentos attrib. C. P. E. Bach ('Bach', 'Baach', 'Pach' etc), *A-M, Gd, B-Bc, CH-E, CS-Bm, D-LEm, Rtt, PL-Wn*; none is authentic, mostly by J. C. Bach

WORKS FOR SOLO VOICE

(with kbd acc. unless otherwise stated)

Oden mit Melodien (Berlin, 1762): H677, 670, 679, 673–4, 680, 678, 683, 681, 671, 675, 672, 682, 676, 684, 689–92, 687 [1762]

Neue Lieder-Melodien nebst einer Kantate zum singen beym Klavier (Lübeck, 1789): H745, 755–7, 748, 702, 758, 703, 734, 700, 704–5, 740, 747, 706, 759, 707, 760, 708, 701, 741, 735 [1789]

669	211	3 arias: Edle Freiheit, Götterglück; Himmels Tochter, Ruh der Seelen; Reiche bis zum Wolkensitze: T, str, bc, ? by 1738
670–72	199/2, 10, 12	3 songs: Schäferlied (M. von Ziegler), 1741; Der Zufrieden (Stahl), 1743; Die verliebte Verzweiflung (Steinhauer), 1743: (1762) and in Sammlung verschiedener und auserlesener Oden (Halle, 1737–43)
673–5	199/4–5, 11	3 songs: Die Küsse (N. D. Giseke); Trinklied (J. W. L. Gleim); Amint (E. von Kleist): 1750–53 (1762) and in Oden mit Melodien, i (Berlin, 1753), 673–5 in Lieder der Deutschen mit Melodien (Berlin, 1767–8)
676	199/14	Die märkische Helene (G. E. Lessing), 1754 (1762) and in F. W. Marpurg *Historisch-kritische Beyträge*, i/1 (1754)
677–8	199/1, 7	2 songs: Die sächsische Helene (Gleim); Dorinde (Gleim): 1754 or 1755 (1762) and in Oden mit Melodien, ii (Berlin, 1755) and Lieder der Deutschen mit Melodien (Berlin, 1767–8)
679–80	199/3, 6	2 songs: Lied eines jungen Mägdchens (Fräulein von H [?Lessing]); Der Morgen (F. von Hagedorn): 1756 (1762), 679 in Berlinische Oden und Lieder (Leipzig, 1756), 680 in F. W. Marpurg: Neue Lieder zum singen beym Claviere (1756)
681–4	199/9, 13, 8, 15	4 songs: Die Biene (Lessing); Die Küsse (Lessing); Der Stoiker; Serin: 1756–7 (1762) and in Berlinische Oden und Lieder (Leipzig, 1756)

282–3

Editions: *Geistliche Lieder*, ed. K. H. Bitter (Berlin, 1867): H686, 696, 733, 749, 752 [B]

Fünfundzwanzig ausgewählte geistliche Lieder, ed. J. Dittberner (Leipzig, 1917): H686, 696, 733, 749, 752 [D]

H	W	
685	—	La Sophie, aria, 1757, autograph, D-B [125 with added text]
686	194	[55] Geistliche Oden und Lieder mit Melodien (C. F. Gellert), 1757 (Berlin, 1758/R1973) [*790, *794, *800, *826, *836]; 5 nos. in Lieder und Arien aus Sophiens Reise (Leipzig, 1779), 9 nos. in Fünfzig und sechs neue Melodien (Memmingen, 1780), no.1 in Musikalische Blumenlese (Zürich, 1786); various songs ed. in B, D
687	199/20	Herausforderungslied vor der Schlacht bey Rosbach (Gleim), 1758 (1762)
688	202/A	Freude, du Lust der Götter und Menschen (C. M. Wieland), 1760, in Drey verschiedene Versuche eines einfachen Gesanges für den Hexameter (Berlin, 1760) [*723]
689-92	199/16-19	4 songs: Auf den Namenstag der Mademoiselle S.; Der Traum; Die Tugend (A. von Haller); Doris (von Haller): 1761-2 (1762)
693-5	202/B/1-3 [112/6, 12, 14]	3 songs: Das Privilegium (N. D. Giseke); Die Landschaft; Belinde (K. W. Müller): 1762-5, in Clavierstücke verschiedener Art, i (Berlin, 1765)
696	195	Zwölf geistliche Oden und Lieder als ein Anhang zu Gellerts geistliche Oden und Liedern mit Melodien (no.4: L. F. F. Lehr, nos.8, 10-11: A. L. Karschin), 1764 (Berlin, 1764/R1973) [*830]; some songs ed. in B, D
697	232	Phillis und Thirsis, cantata, 2 S, 2 fl, bc, 1765 (Berlin, 1766)
698	202/D	Bachus und Venus (H. W. von Gerstenberg), 1766, in Musikalisches Vielerley (Hamburg, 1770) 269
699	201 [264]	Der Wirth und die Gäste (Bleim), 4 solo vv, kbd, 1766 (Berlin, 1766, rev. 2/1790) and in Notenbuch zu des akademischen Liederbuches ersten Bändchen (Dessau and Leipzig, 1783); also in D-B for 4 solo vv, insts
700-01	200/10, 20	Belise und Thrysis: An eine kleine Schöne (Lessing): before 1767 (1789); 700 also as Allgütiger! gewohnt Gebet zu hören, autograph, B
702-8	200/6, 8, 11-12, 15, 17, 19	7 songs (J. H. Röding, J. H. Lütkens, C. D. Ebeling, J. C. Unzer), after 1767 (1789)
709-11	202/C/1-3	3 songs: Der Unbeständige ('W.'); Phillis (von Kleist); An die Liebe (von Hagedorn): c1768, in Unterhaltungen (Hamburg, 1768-70)
712-17	202/C/4-9	6 songs (some by D. Schiebeler), 1769, in Unterhaltungen (Hamburg, 1768-70)
718-21	202/C/10-13	4 songs (Schiebeler, Karschin, von Gerstenberg, D. P. Scriba), 1770, in Unterhaltungen (Hamburg, 1768-70)
723	237	Der Frühling, cantata (Wieland), T, str, bc, 1770-72 [*688]
724-9	202/E/1-6	6 songs (D. B. Münter), 1772-3, in D. B. Münters erste Sammlung geistlicher Lieder mit Melodien (Leipzig, 1773) [*797]
730-32	202/O/2; 202/F/1-2	3 songs: Klagelied eines Bauern (Miller); Vaterlandslied (F. G. Klopstock); Der Bauer (Miller): c1773, 731-2 in Göttinger Musen-Almanach ... 1774 (Göttingen, 1774); 732, autograph, Mбs, with 736-8, 739-5
733	196	[42] Übersetzte Psalmen mit Melodien (J. A. 269 Cramer), 1773-4 (Leipzig, 1774) [*774, *796, *798, *831-2]; selections ed. in B, D
734-5	200/9, 22	Der Frühling (Miller), 91773-82; Die Grazien, cantata (von Gerstenberg), 1774: (1789)
736-7	202/G/1-2	Die Schlummernde (J. H. Voss): Lyda (Klopstock): 1774, in Göttinger Musen-Almanach ... 1775 (Göttingen and Gotha, 1775); cf 732

	202/...?	Trinklied für freye (Voss), 1773, in Musen-Almanach, ed. J. H. Voss (Hamburg, 1776); cf 732
739	236	Selma, cantata (Voss), S, 2 fl, str, bc, ?1775 [*739-5]
739-5	202/I/2	Selma (Voss), 1775, in Musen-Almanach, ed. J. H. Voss (Hamburg, 1776) [*739]; cf 732
740-43	200/13, 21: 202/O/1, 4	4 songs: Trinklied (L. C. H. Hölty), 1775-82; An Doris (von Haller), Morgenroths (C.F. Cramer), ?1775-6: Da schlägt des Abschieds Stunde (Metastasio, trans. J. J. Eschenburg), ?1775-6: 740-41 (1789)
744-5	202/H; 200/1	An den Schlaf, 1776: Todtengräberlied (Hölty), 1776-82; 744 in Die Muse, i (Leipzig, 1776), 745 (1789)
746	202/J	Selma, 1777, in Musen-Almanach, ed. J. H. Voss (Hamburg, 1778) [not same as 739 or 739-5]
747-8	200/14, 5	Aus einer Ode zum neuen Jahr; An die Grazien und Musen (Gleim): ?1777-82 (1789)
749	197	[30] Geistliche Gesänge (C. C. Sturm) (Hamburg, 1780) [*795, *798-9, *833-4]; selections ed. in B, D
750-51	202/K/1-2	Fischerlied (C. A. Overbeck); Tischlied (Voss): 1780, in Musen-Almanach, ed. J. H. Voss (Hamburg, 1781)
752	198	[30] Geistliche Gesänge, ii (Sturm) (Hamburg, 1781) [*795-7, *807, *826]; selections ed. in B, D, and ed. H. Roth (Leipzig, 1922)
753-4	202/L/1-2	Lied (F. L. von Stolberg); Das Milchmädchen (Voss): 1781, in Musen-Almanach, ed. J. H. Voss (Hamburg, 1782)
755-60	200/2-4, 7, 16, 18	6 songs: Lied der Schnitterinnen (Gleim); Nonnelied; Das mitleidige Mädchen (Miller); Bevelise and Lysidor (J. A. Schlegel); Mittel, freundlich zu werden (Gleim); Ich hoff auch Gott mit festem Muth (E. von der Recke): 755-7, by ?1782, 762, 1785, all (1789)
761-2	214; 231	Fürsten sind am Lebensziele, aria, S, str, bc, lost: Freudenlied (auf die Wiederkunft des Herrn Dr. C. aus dem Bade), 2 S, bc, 1785
763	—	[Die Alster] (von Hagedorn), and Harvestehude (von Hagedorn): ?c1788 [cf Busch, 211ff]
764	202/N/1-12	12 Masonic songs, 1788, in Freymaurer-Lieder mit ganz neuen Melodien von den Herren Capellmeister Bach, Naumann und Schulz (Copenhagen and Leipzig, 1788), also in Allgemeines Liederbuch für Freymaurer, iii (Copenhagen, 1788) [misattrib. W. F. E. Bach in Miesner, cf Busch, 181ff]
765-6	202/O/3, 5	Kommt, lasst uns seine Huld besingen (J. A. Cramer); Die schönste soll bey Sonnenschein
767	213	D'amor per te languisco, arietta, S, 2 fl, bc, F-Pc; in NV 64 with added pts. for 3 vn

possibly authentic

768	—	An der Mond: Sophiens Reise auf der See [Ich sah durch Tränenbache], D-B
769	—	Weil Gott uns das Gesicht verlieh, aria, B
770	—	Se amore per lei t'accende, cancionetta, B
771	—	Nachahmung einiger Stellen des anderen Psalms, von Kohler [Der Herr ist meines Lebens Kraft] (?Kohler), B

CHORAL

All those formerly at the main source, Berlin, Singakademie, are lost (further information in Miesner); 774-826 are for solo vv, chorus, orch, 827-40 are mostly for chorus, orch; the Passions, incl. much material by J. S. Bach and Telemann, are lost, unless otherwise indicated.

772	215	Magnificat, S, A, T, B, SATB, 2 fl, 2 ob, 2 hn, 3 tpt, timp, str, bc, 1749, ed. G. J. D. Pölchau (Bonn, 1829-30); tpt, timp and most of hn parts added later [†776, †782,

270, 284, 285

284-6

H	W		
		†807, †817]; alternative version of 'Et misericordia', *D-B*, 1780–82; ed. G. Darvas (Budapest, 1971), ed. in SBA	
773–4	205–6	Der Zweyte Psalm, SATB; Der Vierte Psalm, S, A, bc: by 1761, in Musikalisches Allerley (Berlin, 1761) [*733]	
775	238	Die Israeliten in der Wüste (D. Schiebeler), oratorio, solo vv, SATB, 2 fl, 2 ob, bn, 2 hn, 3 tpt, timp, str, bc, 1769 (Hamburg, 1775); ed. G. Darvas (Budapest, *c*1970)	284, 285, 286
776	233	Passions-Cantata (Die letzten Leiden des Erlösers) (L. Karsch), solo vv, SATB, 2 fl, 2 ob, 2 bn, 3 hn, timp, str, bc, 1770, *A-Wgm*, *DK-Kk* [†722]	285
777	240	Auferstehung und Himmelfahrt Jesu (C. W. Ramler), oratorio, S, T, B, SATB, 2 fl, 2 ob, bn, 2 hn, 3 tpt, timp, str, bc, 1777–80 (Leipzig, 1787); ed. G. Darvas (Budapest, 1974)	285
778	217	Heilig, SATB, SATB, 2 ob, bn, 3 tpt, timp, str, bc, 1778 (Hamburg, 1779); ed. in SBA; used in 2 cantatas from 823 and 824; cf 804, 814	285, 286
779	239	Morgengesang am Schöpfungsfeste (Klopstock), ode, solo vv, SSTB, 2 fl, 2 vn, 2 va, vc, bc, 1783 (Leipzig, 1784)	285, 286
780	204	Zwey Litaneyen aus dem Schleswig-Holsteinischen Gesangbuche, SATB, SATB, bc, 1786 (Copenhagen, 1786) [*802]; cf 871	285
781	203	[14] Neue Melodien zu einigen Liedern des neuen Hamburgischen Gesangbuchs, 1v, bc, 1787 (Hamburg, 1787) [see Busch, 178f]	
782	—	St Matthew Passion, by 1768–9 [†772]	
783–5	—	3 Passions: St Mark, by 1769–70; St Luke, by 1770–71; St John, by 1771–2	
786	—	St Matthew Passion, by 1772–3	
787–9	—	3 Passions: St Mark, by 1773–4; St Luke, by ?1774–5; St John, by 1775–6	
790	—	St Matthew Passion, by 1776–7 [†686/14]	

H	W	
791–3	—	3 Passions: St Mark, by 1777–8; St Luke, by 1778–9; St John, by 1779–80
794	—	St Matthew Passion, by 1780–81, sketches, *B* [†686/23, †796]
795	—	St Mark Passion, by 1781–2 [†749, †752/6, 26, 29]
796	—	St Luke Passion, by 1782–3, incl. recit and aria, autograph, *B* [†733, †752, †794]
797	—	St John Passion, by 1783–4, incl. 2 arias, recit, *B* [†752, †724]
798	—	St Matthew Passion, by 1784–5 [†733, †749]
799	—	St Mark Passion, by 1785–6 [†749, †826/4]
800	234	St Luke Passion, by 1786–7, *D-Bds* [incl. indication of borrowed material, inc. autograph and †686/21]
801	—	St John Passion, by 1787–8
802	235	St Matthew Passion, by 1788, ? composer's last work [†780/1]; inc. autograph, *D-Bds* [incl. indication of borrowed material], copy *A-Wgm*
803	244	Oster-Musik (Cochius), cantata, 1756
804–5	241–2	Oster-Musik, cantata, by 1776; Oster-Musik, cantata, by 1778; 804 incl. 778, 805 partly borrowed from J. S. Bach
807	243	Oster-Musik, cantata, by 1784 [†752/14, †772, †inc. cantata from 824]; pt. ii lost
808	—	MSS of Oster-Musik for 1768–9, 1771, 1775, 1781–2, 1787, lost, mostly borrowed from other works
809–11	248; 245	3 Michaelis-Musik, cantatas, *c*1769–*c*1772; 809 sources inc.; 811 lost
812	247, 212	Michaelis-Musik, cantata, *c*1775, incl. w212, aria
814	246	Michaelis-Musik, cantata, by 1785 [incl. 778]
815	249	Weihnachts-Musik, cantata, 1775
816	—	At least 4 lost MSS of Weihnachts-Musik
817	—	Herr, lehr' uns thun, cantata, 1769, in NV 65, collab. G. A. Homilius, lost [†772]
818	—	Der Gerechte, ob er gleich, cantata, 1774, *D-B*, *Bds*, after (2) Johann Christoph Bach

Meine Seele erhebt den Herrn, cantata, in NV 65, collab. 'Hoffmann', lost

820

At least 4 lost MSS of Sonntagsmusik

821-4 | 250-53; —

c50 congratulatory cantatas, variously entitled Einführungsmusik, Jubelmusik, Serenata, Oratorio, Musik am Dankfest, Trauungs-Cantate, Dank-Hymne, Geburtstags-Cantate, 1768-87, in NV 56-9, occasional works for Hamburg, A-Wgm, D-B, Hs; often incl. 856 and much borrowed material

825 | 207 — Veni, Sancte Spiritus, after 1767

826 | 208 — 4 Motteten, nos.1-3 after 1767, no.4 c1781 [*686/30, 53, 9; *752/3; *799]; no.3 (Bonn, c1823)

827-8 | 218-19 — Einchöriges Heilig; Sanctus: after 1767; 827 *chorus from J. S. Bach: Magnificat

829 | 216 — Spiega, Ammonia fortunata, occasional work, 1770

830 | 221 — Mein Heiland, meine Zuversicht, ?Sonntagsmusik, 1771 [*696/12; ? part of cantata listed in NV 65]

831 | 222 — Wer ist so würdig als du, 1774 [*733/4]

832 | 223 — Zeige du mir deine Wege, 1777 [*733/9]; ? part of Sonntagsmusik, 1777

833 | 225 — Gott, dem ich lebe, 1780 [*749/9]; attached to 857

834-5 | 226-7 — Amen, Amen, Lob und Preis; Leite mich nach deinem Willen: 1783 [*749/4]; ? part of Sonntagsmusik 1783; 835 ed. G. Pölchau (Vienna, 1820)

836-7 | 228-9 — Meinen Lebenszeit verstreicht, 1783; Meinen Leib wird man begraben, ?1788: funeral music [*686/37]

838 | — — Merkt und seht, D-B, inc.; ? from Passion

839-40 | 209-10 — Antiphonia, 4vv; Amen, 4vv: lost

841 | — — Wirf dein Anliegen auf, in NV 65, arr. of anon. motet, lost

842 | p.96n — 10 Choräle (Grafen von Wernigerode), 4vv, by 1767, autograph, PL-WRu

843 | — — Naglet til Kors paa Jorden, chorale, by 1781, in Kirke-Melodierne til den 1778 udgangne Psalmebog (Copenhagen, 1778); ed. in Busch, suppl.

844 — 3 chorales, by 1785, in Vollständige Sammlung der Melodien ... des neuen allgemeinen Schleswig-Holsteinischen Gesangbuchs (Leipzig, 1785); ed. in Busch, suppl.

845 — Chorale, by 1786, in Vierstimmige alte und neue Choralgesänge (Berlin, 1786) [cf Busch, 176-7]

847 — Tpt and timp pts. added to C. H. Graun: Te Deum, after 1756, in NV 66, lost

848 — Inst introduction to Credo of J. S. Bach: B minor Mass, 1768 or later, D-B

850 — 2 recits in NV 89, for 2 cantatas by C. F. C. Fasch, lost

854 — Various acc. recits added to works by other composers, listed in NV 66, lost

doubtful or spurious

855 — Hilf dass ich folge, 4vv, c1725, B [transposition with new text of Was mein Gott will from Cantata bwv144]

856 | 220 — Veni, Sancte Spiritus, 1760 [by Telemann]; cf 821-4

857 — Selig sind die Todten, cantata, ? before 1781, A-Wn, used with 833 as funeral music, by 1781 [? by Telemann]

858 — Missa, Wgm

859 — Die Pilgrime auf Golgatha, oratorio, D-Mbs [? by Telemann]

860 — Passion cantata [St Mark Passion], KNu (as St Matthew Passion) [? by Telemann]

861 — So gehst du nun, cantata [misattrib. C. P. E. Bach in EinerQ; by J. E. Bach]

862-3 — Ecce cui iniquitatibus; Miserere mei, frag.; B

864 — Kommt, lasst uns anbeten, motet, PL-Wu

865 — 11 motets, D-ARk [? by J. E. Bach]

866 — Der Todt Jesu, aria, RH [from larger work]

866-5 — Sey mir gesegnet, aria, S, str, Bds

THEORETICAL WORKS

H	W		
867	121	Miscellanea musica, B-Bc; technical exercises collected by Westphal, incl. 285 and various sketches, some for 536	
868	254	Versuch über die wahre Art das Clavier zu spielen mit Exempeln und achtzehn Probe-Stücke in sechs Sonaten erläutert, i (Berlin, 1753/R1957, reissues 1759, 1780, rev. 2/1787) [for Probe-Stücke, see 70, 75, 2nd edn., incl. 292–7; cf 873]; Eng. trans. ed. W. J. Mitchell, as Essay on the True Art of Playing Keyboard Instruments (New York, 1949) [incl. printed revs. by C. P. E. Bach]	254, 258, 261, 269, 271, 275, 286–7
869	257	'Einfall, einen doppelten Contrapunct in der Octave von 6 Tacten zu machen, ohne die Regeln davon zu wissen', c1757, in F. W. Marpurg: Historisch-kritische Beyträge zur Aufnahme der Musik, iii (Berlin, 1757/R1970) [a permutational scheme of composition]; trans. in E. Helm: 'Six Random Measures of C. P. E. Bach', JMT, x (1966), 139	
870	255	Versuch über die wahre Art das Clavier zu spielen ... in welchen die Lehre von dem Accompagnement und der freyen Fantasie abgehandelt wird, ii (Berlin, 1762/R1957, reissues 1780, 1787, rev. 2/1797); Eng. trans., ed. W. J. Mitchell, as Essay on the True Art of Playing Keyboard Instruments (New York, 1949) [incl. printed revs. by C. P. E. Bach]	254, 258, 261, 269, 271, 275, 286–7
871	204	Zwey Litaneyen aus dem Schleswig-Holsteinischen Gesangbuche, SATB, SATB, bc, 1786 (Copenhagen, 1786) [contains nearly 100 different harmonizations of 1 motif; cf 780]; ed. in SBA	

doubtful or spurious

H	W		
872	—	Gedanken eines Liebhabers der Tonkunst über Herrn Nichelmanns Tractat von der Melodie (Nordhausen, 1755) [pamphlet ? by G. Leopold in response to C. Nichelmann: Die Melodie nach ihrem Wesen sowohl, als nach ihren Eigenschaften (Danzig, 1755)]	
873	256	Von der Fingersetzung, B-Br [Westphal's copy of exx. accompanying 868]	
874	258	Kurze Anweisung zum General-Bass, B-Br [in Westphal's hand]	
875	—	Anleitung, so viel Walzer man will mit Würfeln zu componieren (Berlin, n.d.) [adaptation of J. P. Kirnberger: Allzeit fertige Menuetten- und Polonoisenkomponist (Berlin, 1757); see O. E. Deutsch: 'Mit Würfeln komponieren', ZMw, xii (1929–30), 595]	

BIBLIOGRAPHY

BurneyH

C. Burney: *The Present State of Music in Germany, the Netherlands, and United Provinces* (London, 1773, 2/1775); ed. P. Scholes as *Dr. Burney's Musical Tours* (London, 1959)

C. P. E. Bach: Autobiographical sketch, in C. D. Ebeling's trans. of the above as *Carl Burney's der Musik Doctors Tagebuch seiner musikalischen Reisen*, ii, iii (Hamburg, 1773); trans. W. S. Newman as 'Emanuel Bach's Autobiography', *MQ*, li (1965), 363 [source of the autobiographical quotations above]

[J. M. Bach, C. P. E. Bach's widow]: *Verzeichniss des musikalischen Nachlasses des verstorbenen Capellmeisters Carl Philipp Emanuel Bach* (Hamburg, 1790) [based on earlier lists by C. P. E. Bach and Johanna Maria]; repr. with notes by H. Miesner as 'Philipp Emanuel Bachs musikalischer Nachlass', *BJb*, xxxv–xxxvii (1938, 1939, 1940–48); facs. repr. with notes by R. W. Wade as *The Catalog of Carl Philipp Emanuel Bachs' Estate* (New York, 1981)

C. H. Bitter: *Carl Philipp Emanuel und Wilhelm Friedemann Bach und deren Brüder* (Berlin, 1868)

[F. Chrysander, ed.]: 'Briefe von K. Ph. E. Bach und G. M. Telemann', *Leipziger allgemeine musikalische Zeitung*, iv (1869), 176

A. Wotquenne: *Thematisches Verzeichnis der Werke von Carl Philipp Emanuel Bach (1714–1788)* (Leipzig, 1905/*R*1964)

H. Schenker: *Ein Beitrag zur Ornamentik* (Vienna, 1908)

H. von Hase: 'Carl Philipp Emanuel Bach und Joh. Gottl. Im. Breitkopf', *BJb*, viii (1911), 86

R. Steglich: 'Karl Philipp Emanuel Bach und der Dresdner Kreuzkantor Gottfried August Homilius im Musikleben ihrer Zeit', *BJb*, xii (1915), 39–145

O. Vrieslander: *Carl Philipp Emanuel Bach* (Munich, 1923)

H. Uldall: *Das Klavierkonzert der Berliner Schule* (Leipzig, 1928)

H. Miesner: *Philipp Emanuel Bach in Hamburg* (Heide, 1929/*R*1969)

E. F. Schmid: *Carl Philipp Emanuel Bach und seine Kammermusik* (Kassel, 1931)

A. Schering: 'C. Ph. E. Bach und das redende Prinzip in der Musik', *JbMP 1938*, 13

A. E. Cherbuliez: *Carl Philipp Emanuel Bach 1714–1788* (Zurich and Leipzig, 1940)

D. Plamenac: 'New Light on the Last Years of Carl Philipp Emanuel Bach', *MQ*, xxxv (1949), 565

K. von Fischer: 'C. Ph. E. Bachs Variationenwerke', *RBM*, vi (1952), 190

E. Beurmann: *Die Klaviersonaten Carl Philipp Emanuel Bachs* (diss., U. of Göttingen, 1952)

C. R. Haag: *The Keyboard Concertos of Karl Philipp Emanuel Bach* (diss., U. of California, Los Angeles, 1956)

G. Busch: *C. Ph. E. Bach und seine Lieder* (Regensburg, 1957)

W. S. Newman: *The Sonata in the Classic Era* (Chapel Hill, 1963, rev. 2/1972)

———: 'Emanuel Bach's Autogiobraphy', *MQ*, li (1965), 363

P. Barford: *The Keyboard Music of C. P. E. Bach* (London, 1965)

E. Suchalla: *Die Orchestersinfonien Carl Philipp Emanuel Bachs nebst einem thematischen Verzeichnis seiner Orchesterwerke* (Augsburg, 1968)

M. Terry: 'C. P. E. Bach and J. J. H. Westphal – a Clarification', *JAMS*, xxii (1969), 106

E. R. Jacobi: 'Five hitherto unknown Letters from C. P. E. Bach to J. J. H. Westphal', *JAMS*, xxiii (1970), 119

E. Helm: 'The "Hamlet" Fantasy and the Literary Element in C. P. E. Bach's Music', *MQ*, lviii (1972), 277

E. R. Jacobi: 'Three Additional Letters from C. P. E. Bach to J. J. H. Westphal', *JAMS*, xxvii (1974), 119

D. M. Berg: *The Keyboard Sonatas of C. P. E. Bach: an Expression of the Mannerist Principle* (diss., State U. of New York, Buffalo, 1975)

———: 'Towards a Catalogue of the Keyboard Sonatas of C. P. E. Bach', *JAMS*, xxxii (1979), 276

R. W. Wade: *The Keyboard Concertos of Carl Philipp Emanuel Bach* (Ann Arbor, 1981)

S. L. Clark: *The Occasional Choral Works of C. P. E. Bach* (diss., Princeton U., 1982)

H. G. Ottenberg: *Carl Philipp Emanuel Bach* (Leipzig, 1982)

See also bibliography to Family history, p.27ff.

CHAPTER TEN

Johann Ernst Bach (*34*)

Johann Ernst Bach was born in Eisenach and baptized on 30 January 1722; he was a son of (5) Johann Bernhard Bach (*18*). On 16 January 1737 he entered the Thomasschule in Leipzig and became a pupil of his uncle (7) Johann Sebastian (*24*). After studying law at the university he returned to Eisenach in 1742 and deputized, without pay, for his ailing father. In 1748 he became his father's official assistant and the next year his successor. He continued to practise as a lawyer as well, and in 1756 he was appointed Hofkapellmeister 'in view of his well-known skill and musical knowledge'. He wrote the foreword to Adlung's *Anleitung zu der musikalischen Gelahrtheit* (Erfurt, 1758). Because of the fusion of the courts, he travelled between Weimar, Gotha and Eisenach and worked with Georg Benda on the reorganization of the Hofkapelle. When it was dissolved in 1758, after the death of Duke Ernst August, he retained his title and undertook duties in the administration of the ducal finances. He died on 1 September 1777.

As a composer, Johann Ernst was abreast of the stylistic innovations of his time although, like Johann Sebastian's sons, he did not exclude contrapuntal writing. His vocal works are often highly dramatic and full of effects. His songs depend on the older tradition of Görner, Gräfe and Mizler; he wrote *galant* melodies full

of expressive word-painting with lively basses and often elaborate accompaniments. His Passion oratorio is modelled on C. H. Graun's well-known *Der Tod Jesu*.

WORKS

VOCAL

O Seele, deren Sehnen (Passion oratorio), 1764, ed. in DDT, xlviii (1914)

Cantatas: So gehst du nun; Straf mich nicht in deinem Zorn; Alles was Odem hat, *D-Bds*; Der Meer ist nahe, *B*; Die Liebe Gottes ist ausgezogen, *B*, ed. in SBA; Kein Stündlein geht dahin, *B*

Magnificat, *B*; Herzlich lieb hab ich dich (Ps xviii), *B*; Mass [Ky–Gl] on Es wolle Gott uns gnädig sein, *Bds*

Sammlung auserlesener Fabeln, i (Nuremberg, 1749) [pt.ii lost], ed. in DDT, xlii (1910)

11 motets, *ARk* [? by C. P. E. Bach, н865]

INSTRUMENTAL

3 Sonaten, vn, bc, pt.1 (Eisenach, 1770)

3 Sonaten, vn, bc, pt.2 (Eisenach, 1772)

2 fantasias and fugues, F, d, ed. D. Hellmann, *Orgelwerke der Familie Bach* (Leipzig, 1967)

Sonatas, kbd: A, *B*; D, ed. in NM, ii (1927); F, in Oeuvres mêlées (Nuremberg, 1755–65), vi [also attrib. C. P. E. Bach, н383·5]; f, ed. K. Geiringer, *Music of the Bach Family* (Cambridge, Mass., 1955); G, in J. U. Haffer, Oeuvres mêlées (Nuremberg, 1755–65), vi

10 org chorales

BIBLIOGRAPHY

H. Kühn: 'Vier Organisten Eisenachs aus Bachischem Geschlecht', *Bach in Thüringen* (Berlin, 1950)

G. Kraft: 'Bach, Johann Ernst', *MGG*

CHAPTER ELEVEN

Johann Christoph Friedrich Bach (49)

Friedrich, known as the 'Bückeburg Bach', was born in Leipzig on 21 June 1732. He was a son of Johann Sebastian (24) and Anna Magdalena Bach, and the third of their four sons to reach musical eminence. Taught music by his father, and well tutored in other subjects as well as music by his distant cousin Johann Elias Bach (39), Friedrich matriculated at the University of Leipzig to study law, probably in late 1749; but by early 1750 Sebastian was seriously ill, and Friedrich gave up his student career to accept a position as chamber musician to Count Wilhelm of Schaumburg-Lippe in Bückeburg, at a salary of 200 thalers. He remained in the service of that court until his death.

The Bückeburg court, though small, was among the most genuinely cultured in Germany, thanks to Count Wilhelm. Its predominantly Italian music was led by Angelo Colonna as 'Concert-Meister' and Giovanni Battista Serini as composer; Friedrich was at first only a member of the orchestra. When the Seven Years War broke out in 1756 the Italians departed, and their duties fell to Friedrich. The count, involved in the war as an outstanding commander, was not able to transfer the title of 'Concert-Meister' officially to Friedrich until 1759, when he took the occasion of his promotion to raise Friedrich's salary to 400 thalers and to stand godfather to his first son, Wilhelm Friedrich Ernst. Friedrich had married the singer Lucia Elisabeth

Münchhausen (1728–1803), daughter of a court musician, in 1755.

When the war ended the count was able to encourage the blossoming of music and intellectual life in Bückeburg. Friedrich gave performances twice a week from a repertory that included oratorios, cantatas, symphonies, operas and chamber music, mainly in the Italian style – by Tartini, Jommelli, Pergolesi, Hasse etc – but also by composers such as the Stamitzes, Haydn, Rolle, Holzbauer and Gluck. His own works, however, seem to have been received with indifference by the count, and he was not always content with the provinciality of little Bückeburg and his conditions of employment there. In 1771 Friedrich's creative life took a decided turn for the better with the arrival of Johann Gottfried Herder as court pastor and consistorial counsellor. The two became close friends, and Herder provided a series of texts for oratorios, cantatas and dramatic works that Friedrich set to music in careful collaboration with the poet. Another consolation to him during this time was the warm admiration of the count's new wife. But in 1776 Herder, responding to an invitation from Goethe, abandoned the limited horizons of Bückeburg and moved to Weimar. His departure was made more depressing for Friedrich by the death of the countess; the count himself died a year later.

By this time young Wilhelm Friedrich Ernst, 18 years old, had made good progress as a musician and needed the stimulation of other surroundings. The circumstances seemed appropriate for Friedrich to take a leave of absence, so in April 1778 he and Wilhelm travelled to England to visit Johann Christian. They went by way of Hamburg and visited Emanuel. Arriving

in London at the height of the musical season, they took full advantage of the city, hearing, among other attractions, Johann Christian's new opera *La clemenza di Scipione* and the Bach–Abel concerts in Hanover Square. Friedrich bought a pianoforte for himself, along with much new music, and became a confirmed admirer of Mozart. After some weeks in London he returned to Bückeburg, leaving Wilhelm in Christian's care.

In his last years at Bückeburg, under Count Philipp Ernst and the regent Countess Juliane, Friedrich was able to maintain a high standard of performance. He enjoyed the friendship of K. G. Horstig, who had succeeded Herder at the court. Horstig's obituary–biography of Friedrich, which refers to his 'uprightness, magnanimity, obliging nature and courtesy', is the most valuable primary source of information about the composer's life. Friedrich died on 26 January 1795 of an 'acute chest fever'.

When J. C. F. Bach arrived at the Bückeburg court at the age of 18, he had been imbued with the contrapuntal style of his father, and with the north German seriousness of expressive purpose exemplified by Emanuel; yet at Bückeburg he found himself in Italianate musical surroundings: lyrical melody, with homophonic textures and slow harmonic rhythms. It is therefore no surprise that his first solid body of work is a compromise – or, in successive works, an alternation – between northern and southern stylistic ideals. Towards the end of his career his style became increasingly Classical, partly because of the influence of Johann Christian. His attraction to Mozart and Gluck was illustrated after his return from London by his Bückeburg productions of *Die Entführung aus dem Serail* and *Iphigénie en Tauride*.

Friedrich was an outstanding virtuoso of the keyboard, yet the sonatas and short keyboard pieces he chose to have published are mainly lightweight, verging on the *galant* style (though some show the influence of C. P. E. Bach's expressive style). Also rather superficial is his chamber music, in spite of the remarkably forward-looking independence of its individual parts. His keyboard concertos and symphonies, especially his last symphony (1794), show him in the progressive last stage of his career: not an innovator, but certainly under the influence of Haydn and Mozart. Hardly a single genre of vocal music was neglected by him. In his sacred and secular songs he did not altogether escape the aridity of the *Odenfabrikanten* who filled the popular collections of his time; but where there was a chance for dramatic expression, as in the accompanied recitatives of his 'monodramas' (solo cantatas), he showed real imagination. The choral compositions, especially the oratorios on texts by Herder, are essentially conservative and lyrical in style but laid out with real dramatic understanding.

WORKS

Catalogue: H. Wohlfarth: 'Neues Verzeichnis der Werke von Johann Christoph Friedrich Bach', *Mf*, xiii (1960), 404; repr. in *Johann Christoph Friedrich Bach* (Berne, 1971) [HW]
Edition: *J. C. F. Bach: Ausgewählte Werke*, ed. G. Schünemann, Fürstliches Institut für Musikwissenschaftliche Forschung, ser.3 (Bückeburg, 1920–22) [AW]
Sources: principal MSS in *D-B, Bds*; most lost MSS not recovered after World War II; for full information see HW

      Musikalisches Vielerley, ed. C. P. E. Bach (Hamburg, 1770): HW VII/1, VIII/2, X/3, XI/1–2, XII/3–7, XIX/1
      Musikalische Nebenstunden, i–iv, ed. J. C. F. Bach (Rinteln, 1787–8): HW I/5, IX/2–3, XI/4–7, XII/13, XVIII/3 and 6, XIX/2

ORCHESTRAL

HW	
I/1–20	20 syms., nos.7–9, 11–19 MSS lost; nos.6, 10, 20 facs. edn. ed. H. Wohlfarth (Bückeburg, 1966)
II/1–5	5 concs., kbd, orch, no.3 lost
III	Concerto, kbd, ob, orch, lost

Works

313

BIBLIOGRAPHY

K. G. Horstig: 'Nekrolog auf den Tod Johann Christoph Friedrich Bachs', *Nekrolog der Deutschen auf das Jahr 1795*, ed. A. H. F. von Schlichtegroll (Gotha, 1797)

G. Schünemann: 'Johann Christoph Friedrich Bach', *BJb*, xi (1914), 45–165

——: 'Friedrich Bachs Briefwechsel mit Gerstenberg und Breitkopf', *BJb*, xiii (1916), 20

——: *Thematisches Verzeichnis der Werke von Johann Christoph Friedrich Bach*, DDT, lvi (1917) [with monograph on the composer]

G. Hey: 'Zur Biographie Johann Friedrich Bachs und seiner Familie', *BJb*, xxx (1933), 77

U. Wolfhorst: 'Ein Orgelgutachten von Johann Christoph Friedrich Bach', *Mf*, xiii (1960), 55

W. S. Newman: *The Sonata in the Classic Era* (Chapel Hill, 1963, rev. 2/1972)

H.-J. Schulze: 'Frühe Schriftzeugnisse der beiden jüngsten Bach-Söhne', *BJb*, l (1963–4), 61

H. Wohlfarth: *Johann Christoph Friedrich Bach* (Berne, 1971) [incl. list of works]

CHAPTER TWELVE

Johann Christian Bach (50)

I Germany and Italy

Johann Christian Bach was born in Leipzig on 5 September 1735. He was the youngest son and the eleventh of the 13 children of Johann Sebastian Bach and his second wife, Anna Magdalena. Nothing is known of his schooling, but his second cousin Johann Elias (39), who lived with the family from 1738 to 1743, may have assisted with his education. Probably, in accordance with family tradition, he began lessons in keyboard playing and theory with his father in 1743 or 1744.

After his father's death in 1750, Johann Christian (who had inherited a generous share of the estate, including three harpsichords) left Leipzig to live with his brother Carl Philipp Emanuel in Berlin; under him he studied composition and keyboard playing. His performances, according to Gerber, were much admired in Berlin; his compositions of this period include keyboard pieces and concertos.

In 1754 (according to a note in C. P. E. Bach's *Ursprung*, supported by Gerber), Johann Christian went to Italy; possibly he travelled with an Italian lady singer. Few details are known of his early years there, but probably he spent some time in Bologna, studying under Padre Martini; his correspondence with Martini, written in tones of affection and respect, starts with a letter from Naples in 1757 and continues with others from Milan

in the following years (in *I-Bc*). He also acquired a patron, Count Agostino Litta, of Milan. Martini's tuition and Litta's influence directed Bach towards a safe career as a church musician. By 1757 he had been received into the Roman Catholic faith, and in June 1760 he was appointed one of the two organists at Milan Cathedral. As organist Bach was not required to compose; most of his liturgical works were in fact written before his appointment.

Bach was not, however, as attentive to his cathedral duties as Count Litta wished, and was absent from Milan during much of 1761. His career was already moving in another direction. He had received an invitation to compose a work for the Teatro Regio in Turin and his first opera, *Artaserse*, was given there on 26 December 1760; the libretto, like several that Bach was to set, was by Metastasio. He was next commissioned to write an opera for Naples, to celebrate the name day of Charles III of Spain: this was *Catone in Utica*, performed at the Teatro S Carlo on 4 November 1761 and revived there in 1764. It was a great success, and proved to be Bach's most widely performed opera, with other revivals in Milan (1762), Pavia, Perugia and Parma (1763), and Brunswick (1768). While in Naples Bach was apparently specially attentive to a ballet dancer, Colomba Beccari, whom he had first met in Turin. The success of *Catone* and Hasse's inability to gain leave of absence from Vienna to fulfil a commission led to Bach's writing a second opera for Naples, *Alessandro nell'Indie*, which, preceded by a cantata (also by Bach), was given on 20 January 1762 in celebration of the King of Spain's birthday. The reception of this opera, although less enthusiastic than that for *Catone*, was sufficiently warm

for the S Carlo administration to seek permission to re-engage Bach for the following season. But by then he had received offers from Venice and London, and in May 1762 he petitioned the cathedral authorities in Milan for a year's leave of absence to compose two operas for the King's Theatre in London.

II London, 1762–72

Unlike the court theatres of the European mainland, the opera houses in London were managed on a commercial basis. It was doubtless because of the need for economy that, for the first three months of the 1762–3 season, Bach was engaged in the presentation only of pasticcios (they included items of his own composition). Burney suggested that the delay in producing his own operas may have been occasioned by lack of faith in the available singers. The first of his contracted operas, *Orione*, was given on 19 February 1763, with considerable acclaim ('every judge of Music perceived the emanations of genius' – Burney) and the second, *Zanaida*, on 7 May. At the end of the season the management of the King's Theatre changed hands and, as one of the new directors was the composer Giardini, who was unfavourably disposed towards potential rivals, particularly non-Italians, Bach was not re-engaged. He was invited to return to Naples for the 1763–4 season, but preferred to remain in London. His activities had not been confined to the King's Theatre. The dedication of his op.1 concertos to Queen Charlotte, who was of German birth, shows that by March 1763 he enjoyed royal favour and patronage, and within a year he was able to advertise himself as the queen's music master. On 15 December 1763 he

317

obtained a privilege for the publication of his works.

During his first year in London Bach lodged with the director of the King's Theatre, Colomba Mattei. On her return to Italy, he moved to new lodgings in Meard's Street, Soho, which he shared with his compatriot, Carl Friedrich Abel, the composer and viola da gamba player who had lived in London since 1758. This friendship, which may have dated back to their boyhood days in Leipzig, was to have a major impact on London's concert life. Their first joint concert, which included an unidentified serenata in two acts by Bach, was at the Great Room in Spring Gardens on 29 February 1764. Two months later the eight-year-old Mozart arrived in London for a stay that was to last until July 1765; during that time he not only established a warm personal relationship with Bach but also fell under his influence as a composer. They are known to have improvised jointly at least once. No formal master–pupil relationship seems to have existed, but the charm of Bach's personality and the quality of his music clearly attracted the young Mozart.

In 1764 the management of the King's Theatre changed hands, and Bach's services were again called upon. He contributed to the two pasticcios that opened the season, and on 26 January 1765 his new opera *Adriano in Siria* had the first of its seven performances. Perhaps Bach's popularity had raised the expectations of the public too high and 'the opera failed. Every one seemed to come out of the theatre disappointed' (Burney); but the songs published separately enjoyed considerable success.

Three days earlier Bach, assisted by Abel, had directed the first concert in the subscription series

organized by Teresa Cornelys at Carlisle House, Soho Square. They gave ten concerts that year; in 1766 the number was increased to 15 and it remained at that level until 1781, when only 12 concerts were given. The concerts took place on Wednesdays from January to May except in Holy Week. Bach and Abel alternated as director, and much of the music performed was of their own composition, including Bach's cantatas, his op.3 symphonies (published in 1765) and later his op.18 symphonies. The concerts remained at Carlisle House for three seasons; in January 1768, when Bach and Abel took over the management, they moved to Almack's Assembly Rooms in King Street, St James's, where the Bach–Abel Concerts (as they became known) remained until 1774.

January 1765 also saw the first performance of the ballad opera *The Maid of the Mill* at the Theatre Royal, Covent Garden; Bach's contributions, a song and a duet, brought his art to a wider audience than those that frequented the King's Theatre or the fashionable concerts of the nobility and gentry. In 1766 he reached a still wider public with the songs he composed for Mrs Weichsell to sing in Vauxhall Gardens; altogether he published three collections of Vauxhall songs.

In autumn 1766 the soprano Cecilia Grassi, later to become Bach's wife, came to London for a season as prima donna for the serious operas at the King's Theatre. Poor health prevented her from taking part in Bach's new opera, *Carattaco*, first performed on 14 February 1767. The work was only a limited success; the public was more interested in Piccinni's comic operas. Bach apparently also supplied the music for an operetta, *The Fairy Favour*, presented at Covent Garden

on 31 January before the four-year-old Prince of Wales, making his first visit to a theatre.

Since his arrival in England Bach had always been ready to help his professional colleagues by taking part in their benefit concerts (his 'expressive and masterly', but not brilliant, keyboard style is interestingly discussed by Burney, ii, p.866). On 2 June 1768 at a concert at the Thatched House Tavern in St James's Street in aid of the oboist J. C. Fischer, he played a 'Solo on the Piano Forte', using an instrument probably by Zumpe: apparently this was the first time that the piano was publicly used as a solo instrument in London. Bach's op.5 sonatas were published, in 1766, as 'pour le clavecin ou le piano forte'.

In autumn 1769 Cecilia Grassi returned to London, having sung in Palermo and Naples since her departure in 1767. Bach too returned to the King's Theatre. He contributed not only to the two pasticcios that began the season but also joined with Guglielmi in arranging the London première of Gluck's *Orfeo ed Euridice*, supplementing the music so that it would be 'of a necessary length for an evening's entertainment'. Although their additions, inserted between the scenes of Gluck's opera, ran counter to Gluck's 'reform' principles (Burney remarked on the damage done to the 'unity, simplicity, and dramatic excellence of this opera'), the arrangement enjoyed a considerable public success. There were 13 performances in 1770, six in 1771 and three in 1773, and on 4 November 1774 this version was given at the S Carlo theatre in Naples.

In 1770 Bach presented a series of oratorio performances at the King's Theatre on Thursdays in Lent and in Easter week, competing with the well-established

series on Wednesdays and Fridays at Drury Lane and Covent Garden. The repertory consisted of a Passion by Jommelli, Pergolesi's *Stabat mater* and Bach's own oratorio *Gioas, rè di Giuda*. Cecilia Grassi was prevented by illness from taking part in the first of the three performances, on 22 March. The oratorio venture was not a commerical success, and Bach, who at the 'express command' of the queen played a concerto on the organ between the acts, suffered a public humiliation when his style of organ playing – markedly different from the Handelian tradition – was hissed by the audience and laughed at by the boys in the chorus. *Gioas* was revived in January 1771, but after two more oratorio evenings in Lent Bach abandoned the form.

The following spring Johann Baptist Wendling, first flautist in the electoral orchestra at Mannheim and husband of Dorothea Wendling, the prima donna of the Mannheim Opera, visited London; he, with Bach, Abel and the cellist J.-P. Dupont, held a benefit concert in May 1771. Wendling lodged with Bach and Abel in King's Square Court during the first part of his stay in London and moved with Bach to his new home in Queen Street, Golden Square, before April 1772. On 6 April 1772 Wendling and Cecilia Grassi took part in the first performance of Bach's cantata *Endimione* at the King's Theatre.

III Mannheim and London, 1772–8

In 1772 Bach received a commission for an opera for the name day celebrations of Elector Carl Theodor in Mannheim, possibly as a result of his collaboration with Wendling. He accepted, and arrived in Mannheim in August or September (possibly having visited Italy

during the summer), where he almost certainly enjoyed the hospitality of the Wendlings; according to Mozart's mother, Bach fell in love with their daughter, Augusta (*b* 1756). The first performance of the opera, *Temistocle*, was given on 4 or 5 November, before a distinguished audience and with an excellent cast; it was so successful that it was revived in November 1773, and Bach was invited to return to write a new opera for 1774. This was *Lucio Silla*, also first performed on 4 November. The libretto was the one written by Giovanni de Gamerra for Mozart in 1772 and adapted, as was Metastasio's for *Temistocle*, to the Mannheim taste by the court poet Mattia Verazi. *Lucio Silla* was less successful; but Mozart examined the score in 1777, and his letter of 13 November makes clear his high opinion of it. Other works from Bach's periods at Mannheim include the cantatas *Amor vincitore* and *La tempesta*.

Between his visits to Mannheim Bach maintained his usual busy round of activities in London. His duties at court included giving music lessons to the queen and her growing family, directing the Queen's Band, accompanying the king's flute playing, and contributing both as composer and performer to chamber music for the queen's entertainment in the evenings.

In summer 1773 Bach and Cecilia Grassi visited the west of England: they performed in Blandford on 14 July and in early October appeared at the Salisbury Musical Festival, where Bach 'favoured the company with an elegant performance on the harpsichord'. He revisited Blandford in 1776. His marriage to Cecilia may have taken place shortly after the 1773 journey; by January 1774 he had moved to 80 Newman Street and Abel elsewhere. In that month the Bach–Abel concerts

returned to Carlisle House, Soho, now vacated by the bankrupt Mrs Cornelys and a cheaper venue than Almack's. This was to be their home for only one season. On 28 June 1774 Bach, Abel and Giovanni Andrea Gallini acquired a property on the corner of Hanover Street and Hanover Square, Bach and Abel each providing a quarter of the capital of £5000, and had a new concert hall built in the garden. On 1 February 1775 it was inaugurated by the first concert of the new season of Bach–Abel concerts. The move was not a financial success; Bach had overreached himself, and was not helped by a fall in the receipts for the concerts, which suffered from the competition of the new Monday series at the Pantheon. On 12 November 1776 the syndicate was dissolved; the Bach–Abel concerts remained at the Hanover Square Rooms, but declined rapidly in popularity, as the sharp drop in receipts after 1778 shows. It has been suggested that they were able to continue only because of support from the Earl of Abingdon, Gallini's father-in-law.

Bach continued to take part in benefit concerts for his colleagues. The first performance of his cantata *Cefalo e Procri* was given at Hanover Square on 26 April 1776 for the 'Benefit of Signora Salis'; it was performed twice in May 1777 (it also formed part of Tenducci's Bach Commemoration on 17 May 1786). In that month Bach appeared on the London concert platform on no fewer than ten occasions, and *Orione* was revived on 24 May. The following season he presented a new opera, *La clemenza di Scipione*, which began a run of eight performances on 4 April 1778; between the sixth and seventh Bach presented a new cantata, *Rinaldo ed Armida*, at the Hanover Square Rooms.

323

In 1776 Padre Martini had asked Bach for a portrait for his private collection; according to Bach it was finished in May 1776, but it was not until July 1778 that he despatched it to Bologna, in the care of the castrato Francesco Roncaglia. The artist was his friend Thomas Gainsborough, who also executed a second portrait of him; one is still in Bologna (see fig.13), the other in the Earl of Hillingdon's collection. A bust of Johann Christian almost certainly dates from this time too; Johann Christoph Friedrich Bach, who formerly owned it, visited his brother in London in summer 1778 (leaving his son Wilhelm Friedrich Ernst in London with his uncle).

IV The last years

Bach's compositions had been performed and published in Paris for more than a decade, and in 1778 he received a commission to write an opera for the Académie Royale de Musique. He visited Paris in August of that year to hear the singers who were to take part; Mozart, then in Paris, wrote to his father of Bach's and his mutual delight in meeting, commenting on his affection for Bach and his pleasure in Bach's friendly praise of him. Bach wrote his new opera in London and returned to Paris in August 1779; the first performance of *Amadis de Gaule* was given on 14 December, before Queen Marie Antoinette. The opera was much criticized, partly because of the revisions that had been made to Quinault's 1684 libretto, partly because, given at the height of the Gluck–Piccinni controversies, it pleased neither side. It was withdrawn for revision after three performances, returning to the stage for four more a month later. However, Bach's first attempt at a French

13. *Johann Christian Bach: portrait by Thomas Gainsborough (1727–88)*

opera was a disaster neither for the Opéra nor for him: according to Brenet, he was engaged on a new commission at the time of his death.

Back in London, Bach's name appeared on the list of composers for the coming season in the King's Theatre advertisements in autumn 1779, 1780 and 1781; but he never again composed for that theatre. The Bach–Abel concerts continued their decline in popularity, although Bach and his music still figured prominently in public concerts. On 17 May 1779 at the Hanover Square Rooms Tenducci considered it to his advantage to include several works by Bach – a symphony for two orchestras (in the op.18 set, *c*1781), a Scotch Air, a quintet and *Amor vincitore* – in his benefit concert.

Bach's declining fortunes suffered another blow when, as the result of a rumour that he was about to give up his house in Richmond, the local tradesmen pressed for the settlement of their accounts; it was found that Bach's housekeeper had forged receipts for over £1000 and absconded with the money. He was in serious financial straits; his music was no longer in demand at the opera house, where the dominant figure was Sacchini, and his position as a leading teacher had been undermined by the advent of J. S. Schroeter, a pianist and composer to whom Bach had earlier given generous help and advice 'and assisted . . . as a friend, for his heart was too good to know the littleness of envy' (that comment of Mrs Papendiek is one of many in her memoirs referring to Bach and his activities in court circles, in which, as in London's artistic community and particularly its German-biassed part, he was treated with admiration and affection).

His health began to decline in 1781, and he moved to

Paddington for a change of air. In November he made his will, leaving everything to his wife; he died on 1 January 1782, and was buried on 6 January in St Pancras Churchyard. His debts, amounting to some £4000, were never fully repaid. Neither the Bach–Abel concerts, which his widow continued for one season with Abel, nor the benefit performance at the King's Theatre on 27 May 1782 contributed significantly to their reduction. The queen helped to meet immediate expenses and enabled Cecilia Bach to return to her native Italy in summer 1782.

Bach's death – noted by Mozart as 'a loss to the musical world' – went almost unnoticed by the London public, whose appetite for novelty was no longer satisfied by the music of a man who had lived and worked among them for nearly 20 years. Mrs Papendiek noted that 'this man of ability in his profession, of liberal kindness in it, of general attention to friends, and of worthy character, was forgotten almost before he was called to the doom of us all, and every recollection of him seems buried in oblivion'.

v Church music and oratorio

By the time Bach left Italy in 1762 he had composed almost all his Latin church music. With the exception of two solo cantatas, all the works are settings of liturgical texts with orchestral accompaniment, and demonstrate the range of styles used by composers of church music in Italy at the time. The most conservative feature is the writing for chorus. Movements in the so-called Palestrina style or 'strict style' are to be found in three works of 1757. In the Requiem (or Ingresso) and Kyrie in F, a plainsong cantus firmus appears in long notes in

327

the bass in two movements ('Requiem' and 'Te decet'), 'scartato e mutato' (i.e. used freely), according to a letter from Bach to Padre Martini; this type of composition was required of all applicants for membership of the Accademia Filarmonica of Bologna, with which Martini was closely associated. (There is no record of Bach's having applied.) In the responsorial portions of the invitatory ('Regem cui omnia vivunt'), the cantus firmus appears in the upper voices but never in the bass; in the responses of the three *Lezioni* imitative counterpoint without cantus firmus is used. The influence of the Roman school is also evident in the Kyrie double fugues of 1757. Elsewhere Bach's choral fugues follow the traditional 18th-century ecclesiastical style of Fux and Martini; they appear mainly in the concluding movements of lengthy works. Double fugues are used in the earliest works; single fugues predominate from 1758. All are relatively short and lack extended episodic development, though the double fugue for eight-part chorus concluding the *Dies irae* is quite substantial. In Bach's other, homophonic choral movements the chief musical interest is often found in the accompanying figuration, but there is also often antiphonal writing, notably in the double-choir music of the *Dies irae*.

In the standard style for Catholic church music of the time, all Bach's sacred works except the shortest are divided into series of movements; sometimes they occupy unusual key relationships, moving progressively around the circle of 5ths. He often followed the contemporary practice of relating the first and last movements thematically, for example in the *Laudate pueri* in G (1760), and the *Dixit Dominus* (1758), where the

favourite device of bringing back the opening material at 'sicut erat in principio' ('as it was in the beginning') is strengthened by a fugal coda on the word 'Amen'. Where soloists are used, movements employing them predominate. A considerable number of these are for two or three solo voices. Those from works written in 1757–8 are in the comparatively simple chamber duet style, but the duets and trios in the two *Gloria* settings of 1759 are highly sophisticated and original. The *Dies irae* contains the only movement for a quartet of soloists. Most of the solo movements, however, are for a single voice, and are in the expressive manner favoured in Italian church music: they show the young Bach at his most inventive, and responding to the mood of the text. Most are in standard aria form, without da capo; a few, where the text allows, adopt a fully written-out three-part plan with contrasting middle section. One such, 'Cor mundum' from the *Miserere*, sets the central impassioned prayer ('Ne projicias me in facie tua') as an *allegro moderato* in C minor against calmer outer sections in F major ('Cor mundum crea in me, Deus' and 'Redde mihi laetitiam salutaris tui'), which use Bach's favourite Lombardic rhythm. The arias show a wide range of expression, from the *aria cantabile* to the *aria di bravura*, and cadenzas are common.

Obbligato instrumental accompaniments appear in many of Bach's church compositions. They may include short passages for a pair of flutes or a solo organ, a full-scale violin solo (*Gloria* in D), a concertante aria with two violins and cello (*Gloria* in G) and, in the aria 'Intellectus bonus' from the *Confitebor*, a chamber accompaniment of six instruments.

Bach's solitary oratorio, *Gioas, rè di Giuda*, was an

attempt to adapt the Italian oratorio to the Handel-dominated English tradition. The solo numbers are in the operatic manner traditional to Italian oratorio; the choral items, most of them to texts added to Metastasio's libretto, lean heavily on the style of the church music, and indeed three of them contain reworkings of music from the *Miserere*, the *Dies irae* and the *Gloria* in D.

VI Operas

As a composer of Italian opera Bach was a traditionalist, preferring to follow current fashions, rather than an innovator. All ten of his Italian operas conform in essentials at least to the Metastasian type of *opera seria*. The operas he composed in Italy are all settings of revised versions of Metastasio's most popular librettos. The first, *Artaserse* (Turin, 1760), shows the most revisions: the dialogue is considerably shortened, and some of Metastasio's elegant but impersonal aria texts are replaced by others, more subjective in tone if less polished in diction. Like earlier settings of the opera, Bach's has a large number of arias, but the aria forms show a move away from the da capo types. It may be that the larger proportion of arias in da capo form found in the two operas for Naples reflect that city's greater conservatism. Bach's early success derived less from his musico-dramatic skill and the perfection of his musical forms than from the quality of his melodic invention, of which notable examples are to be found in the exquisite melancholy of 'Confusa, smarrita' (*Catone in Utica*) and the restrained grace and dignity of 'Non sò d'onde viene' (*Alessandro nell'Indie*; Mozart later commented on the beauty of Bach's setting).

In his first opera written to meet the taste of London audiences, *Orione* (1762), Bach turned away from the more orthodox *opera seria*. The subject involved the stage depiction of ritual, and gave him the opportunity to supply important parts for the chorus. The orchestra too assumed a larger role, with richer figuration, a greater prominence given to wind instruments, and the novel use of english horns and clarinets (Burney remarked on 'the richness of the harmony, the ingenious texture of the parts, and, above all, the new and happy use he had made of wind-instruments'). There are few da capo arias and, while the Metastasian ideal of elegant objectivity is observed in most solo items, the depiction of Retrea's grief in 'Più madre non sono' shows an interesting move towards the closer identification of the characters with their predicament. In the revised version (1777) this trend is taken further when Orion is allowed to die on stage. *Carattaco* (1777), with its large choral scenes, has much in common with *Orione*.

Temistocle (1772) is the most sumptuous of Bach's Italian operas. He clearly revelled in the opportunities afforded by the virtuosity of the Mannheim singers and orchestra and produced vocal numbers of extreme difficulty with accompaniments of unprecedented richness. The aria for Themistocles at the end of Act 1 is an extreme example, being virtually a double concerto for tenor, bassoon and orchestra lasting more than 12 minutes. In a number of ways, however, *Temistocle* shows a return to the purer Metastasian opera that he had begun to put behind him in his London operas *Orione* and *Carattaco*: almost all the arias are in da capo form and the chorus has an insignificant role. But the revisions by the Mannheim court poet of the ends of Acts 2 and 3

enabled Bach for the first and only time to compose extended finales. *Lucio Silla* (1774), with its very few da capo arias and more important role for the chorus, is musically on a smaller scale, and that may account for its lack of success. Both these operas have parts for the rare *clarinetto d'amore*.

La clemenza di Scipione (1778), too, with no da capo arias, shows the Metastasian *opera seria* at a late stage (and again possibly reflecting the taste of London audiences): the action is simplified, the dialogue reduced, the chorus has a dramatic function and the arias are almost all short. Arsinda's great second-act scena and aria with flute, oboe, violin and cello obbligato is a glorious exception to this general move towards more directness and economy in expression (the resemblance between this and 'Martern aller Arten' in Mozart's *Die Entführung aus dem Serail*, 1782, may be noted). The thematic link between the overture, the first scene of Act 1 and the final chorus represents an attempt to provide a special unity to the work.

Like Gluck's *Armide*, Bach's *Amadis de Gaule* (1779) was a setting of a libretto written for Lully. Its original five acts were compressed into three, and in the traditional French style there are divertissements at the end of each. The recitative is all orchestrally accompanied. The orchestra is imaginatively used; Bach seized upon every opportunity to exploit instrumental colour, particularly in the delightful ballet music. The choral writing too is impressive in quality and extent. Yet the compromise between the French conception and Italianate detail is often uneasy, and Bach clearly was handicapped by the absence of set-piece arias in the Italian style in the opera's scheme.

VII Orchestral music

At the beginning of Bach's career as an orchestral composer, there was little difference between the operatic overture and the orchestral symphony. Both were usually written in three movements in a fast–slow–fast pattern; Bach never really adopted the four-movement Mannheim–Viennese pattern. His first set of six overtures (published by Walsh soon after his arrival in England), some dating from his Italian years, some from his early London years, shows brilliant invention, formal mastery and melodic charm, and was immediately successful with English audiences. However, the six symphonies op.3 make it clear that by 1765 Bach was beginning to recognize the concert symphony as a different genre from the opera overture. The two share a brisk Allegro, an Andante and a quick finale in 2/4 or 3/8 time; but in detail the first movements at least are rather different. The triadic themes and insistent *forte* of the beginnings of the operatic overtures give way to a greater thematic variety in op.3, and the melody-and-bass texture of the overtures is succeeded by a fuller texture and greater use of thematic development in the symphonies. Full sonata-form recapitulations appear in some of the first movements; previously Bach had favoured a binary structure in which the recapitulation had begun only with second-subject material.

All the symphonies of the two sets published in Amsterdam as opp.6 and 8 appear to date from before 1769. They are generally on a larger scale and more serious in tone than op.3. Op.6 no.6 is the most serious of all, with its fiery, energetic outer movements and its sombre Andante, and is unique in Bach's orchestral

output in using minor keys in all three movements. It is one of the most significant of the remarkable series of G minor symphonies written about this time by (for example) Haydn, Mozart, Rosetti and Vanhal.

Bach published a number of miscellaneous orchestral works, sometimes called symphonies, sometimes overtures. Thus about 1769 came the overture to *Carattaco*, a piece of great vigour, which appears in various versions, one of them serving as the overture to *Temistocle*. A set of three overtures or symphonies, appearing as op.9 (and later as op.21) is of great distinction, the little Bᵇ symphony–overture to *Zanaida* (1763) being of particularly vivacious charm, while no.2 in Eᵇ is a work of true symphonic dimensions, opening with a spacious Mannheim-style crescendo (an earlier example may be found in op.3 no.5) and ending with an extended minuet. Other works of a similar calibre, published both in England and on the Continent, show Bach's growing mastery of orchestral effect and formal neatness.

The peak of Bach's purely orchestral output, however, is to be found in the late op.18 collection of Six Grand Overtures published in London. Late in publication, that is; individual works date from 1769 onwards, up to at least 1779. No.2, written for *Lucio Silla* (1774), is Bach's finest operatic overture, with its sophisticated phrase structure, melodic distinction and richness of colour. No.4 in D is a taut and vigorous work, and no.6 incorporates material from *Amadis de Gaule*. No less distinguished among the set are the three grandiose Mannheim-influenced overtures for double orchestra, which exploit all possible contrasts of space and time between the two differently constituted

orchestras: one of strings, oboes, bassoon and horns, one of strings and flutes (the latter often used for echo effects). Bach's use of the same music in the overtures to different operas, and his habit of rearranging works with different combinations of movements, as well as his publishers' tendency to reissue works under different numbers, has complicated the study of his symphonic output; the existence of many dubiously attributed works in manuscript (as by simply 'Bach', 'Pach' or 'Back' etc) confuses the matter further.

Bach's feeling for orchestral colour attracted him to the *symphonie concertante* in the 1770s. As early as 16 April 1773 one of his compositions in this genre, much associated with Mannheim and Paris, was performed at the Concert Spirituel, and he composed many more. The number of solo instruments varies from two to nine and the orchestra always includes at least two pairs of wind instruments. Most of these works are in three movements; about a third are in the *galant* two-movement form. Many were written for leading London soloists, including J. C. Fischer and others of Bach's circle. Their style is apt to be leisurely. The most successful of them are the most Italianate, with no more than four solo instruments; larger solo groups created problems that Bach appeared reluctant to attempt to solve, resorting to cliché or the pedantic making of points of imitation. Yet their melodic invention and orchestral writing is highly attractive. Bach's attitude to the solo group was never rigid and it was his regular procedure to supplement it with an instrument or two from the tutti if it suited his purpose.

Apart from one concerto each for flute, and cello,

and two each for oboe and bassoon, Bach composed composed solo concertos only for keyboard. Those of his Berlin period and the doubtful two published in Riga (which have also been ascribed to J. C. F. and C. P. E. Bach) exhibit the serious, somewhat angular style of the north German concerto of the time, and have little in common with his London concertos. Some of the concertos of his op.1 set, published in London in 1763 as a kind of preliminary flourish to justify his appointment as music master to the queen, may have been composed in Italy. As a whole, the set sent the English concerto off on a new path, quite different from the traditional one of Handel's concertos or of the composers of the London school.

The fourth and sixth, the only works in this set with three movements, are entitled 'Concerto o Sinfonia', and have first movements in ritornello form. However the first movements of the other four concertos establish the form of Bach's own later concertos, and may have influenced that of Mozart. The plan of the Classical concerto sonata form, with its orchestral and solo expositions and flexible attitude to motivic development and repetition, is already present in all its essentials. The opening allegros of opp.7 and 13 pursue the same pattern, now broadened and deepened, and the introduction of new thematic material to start the dominant section of the solo exposition is an innovation in some of the op.7 concertos. The op.7 no.2 concerto is almost certainly the one Bach wrote to play on the organ in the oratorio *Gioas*. Bach's most dramatic and developed concertos are nos.2 and 4 of the op.13 set, three-movement Classical concertos in miniature, with dramatic and highly developed first movements; in accordance with

the growing interest in national song Bach incorporated sets of variations on popular Scottish songs in both these works.

VIII Keyboard and chamber music

Throughout his career Bach was a player and teacher of keyboard instruments; and that is reflected in his output of instrumental music. Much of his published work was designed to meet the needs of his pupils and other amateur performers, and his accompanied sonatas in particular (keyboard with violin or flute, sometimes with cello), though always well written, are decidedly modest in scale and scope. (Most of the works in this genre published after Bach's death must be regarded as highly suspect.) It was no doubt Bach's accompanied sonatas that Leopold Mozart had in mind when he urged his son to write in Bach's manner, praising his 'natural, easy and flowing style' and 'sound composition'.

Bach's two sets of solo keyboard sonatas, opp.5 and 17, each open with an easy piece, presumably designed to encourage amateur performers of limited technique to purchase the publications. Both sets are described as 'for harpsichord or pianoforte', but the C minor Sonata op.5 no.6, with its prelude, fugue and gavotte structure, would seem to have been conceived for the harpsichord – unless composed to meet the conservative English taste for fugues, it may belong to the 1750s. Most of the sonatas are in two movements and in the lyrical vein of that favourite *galant* form. The three-movement works are more demanding both musically and technically, and the C minor Sonata op.17 no.2 is a particularly powerful work. The young Mozart arranged three of the op.5 sonatas as concertos, probably in 1772 (κ107).

Bach's output includes a set of six trios for two violins and viola or continuo, published in London by 1763 and later in Paris and Amsterdam. While owing something to the Baroque trio sonata, they are each in the *galant* two-movement form (a slow movement followed by a minuet); they have stylistic resemblances to the notturnos of G. B. Sammartini. Virtually all Bach's quartets involve one or two flutes and strings. Those of the op.8 set, possibly composed for J. B. Wendling, are elegant, unpretentious works in two movements, as are the three quartets originally published in 1776 along with works by Abel and Giardini. The four posthumously published quartets op.19, in three movements, are rather more substantial, doubtless reflecting the sophisticated taste of Lord Abingdon, for whose private concerts they were written, and perhaps also Haydn's influence.

Outstanding among Bach's chamber works, however, are the six quintets op.11, for flute, oboe, violin, viola and continuo, dedicated to that famous connoisseur the Elector Palatine Carl Theodor. One (no.4 in E♭) was composed, according to Mrs Papendiek, for a chamber music evening with the Queen's Band; others may also have been. There is no discernible Mannheim influence on these pieces, whose scoring is unique for their time. They are in Bach's most warm and graceful style, of exceptional melodic charm and formal elegance, and are scored with much sensitivity, ingeniously exploiting (with thematic material specially apt to the purpose) the various available combinations of instrumental colour, often in dialogue patterns. Half of them are in two movements, half in three. Two further quintets, published posthumously as op.22, are also highly character-

338

istic works, and represent early examples of obbligato keyboard parts in concerted chamber music; associated with them, in other publications, are a piano quartet and a sextet with keyboard, violin, cello, oboe and two horns, an attractive work that has often been ascribed to Bach's brother J. C. F. Bach. In most of these works the cello is not always tied to the bass line. Besides his true chamber music, Bach contributed to the repertory of the wind (or military) band, with a number of marches and two sets of works: a collection of 'symphonies' (including music arranged from Gluck and other composers) issued in 1780 and one of 'Military Pieces' or quintets published posthumously.

IX **Reputation**

Johann Christian Bach enjoyed a high reputation, particularly as a composer of instrumental music, in his lifetime; his slow movements especially were regarded as music for the connoisseur. After his death his music faded from public notice, as Haydn (and later Mozart) came to be seen as the chief representatives of the later 18th century. As his own father's music came into the repertory writers lamented that Johann Sebastian's youngest son should have composed works lacking the high seriousness of his father's as well as the originality of those of his brother, Carl Philipp Emanuel; they came to be regarded as facile and decadent. A succeeding view acknowledged that Johann Christian, being of a later generation and having been exposed to, and amenable to, a greater measure of operatic influence than any other of the Bachs, could legitimately have written music in a different style; but the same view regarded him merely as an interesting minor figure of the lower

foothills of the mountainous achievement of the mature style of Mozart. In a broader historical perspective he can be seen as a highly significant figure of his time, the chief master of the *galant* style, who produced music of elegance, formality and aptness for its social purpose, and was able to infuse it with both vigour and refined sensibility.

WORKS

(printed works published in London unless otherwise stated)

Catalogue: C. S. Terry: *John Christian Bach* (London, rev. 2/1967/R1980 by H. C. R. Landon) [T] [T numbers show the page no./no. of the incipit on the page and are not Terry's numbers; in a group the number of the first incipit only is given; roman numerals denote corrigenda pages]

Sources: principal MS sources are listed; items listed in T as in *D-BNu* and autographs in *D-Hs* were destroyed in World War II, and *D-SW/824–9* and *D-W/Rl 349* are missing; contrary to Landon, items cited in T as in *D-W* are still there but differently numbered. Items in T not listed here are duplicates or misattributions.

Numbers in the right-hand column denote references in the text.

*– autograph

SACRED VOCAL

T	(aria arrangements given only if not in T)	
		327–30
199/4		
200/6	Attendite mortales, motet, T, orch, c1770, *D-Bds*, 1st aria arr. from Carattaco	
—	Beatus vir (F), S, A. T, B, SATB, orch, 1758, *CH-E*; movt 6 = r202/5, Dispersit; movt 7 = r202/4, Gloria Patri	
202/1	Confitebor tibi Domine (E♭), S, A, T, B, SATB, orch, 1759, *E, D-Mbs, F-Pn*; ed. in SBA	329
202/3	Credo (C), SATB, orch, *CH-E, I-BGc* Sala E.2.10 (with Gloria, r204/1, and Kyrie, r204/8, headed 'Messa'); ed. in SBA	
202/4	Dies irae (c), S, A, T, B, SSAATTBB, orch, 1757, *CH-E, D-Dlb, Mbs, ?*GB-Ob*, partial **I-Bc* DD97; ed. J. Bastian (Mainz, 1972); movt 9 with new text = r201/4, Confitebor *Bc, Gi(l)*; ed. S. van Marion (Hilversum, 1973)	328
202/6	Dixit Dominus (D), S, A, T, B, SATB, orch, 1758, *CH-E, I-Bc, Gi(l)*; ed. S. van Marion (Hilversum, 1973)	328
203/3	Domine ad adiuvandum (G), S, A, SATB, orch, 1760, *CH-E*	
203/2	Domine ad adiuvandum (G), S, A, SATB, orch, 1758, lost	
204/3	Gloria in excelsis (D), S, A, T, B, SATB, orch, 1759, *CH-E, I-Gi(l)* (inc.); ed. in Vos (1969), ii, 77; movt 2 = r205/5, Laudamus te	329, 330
204/1	Gloria in excelsis (G), S, A, T, B, SATB, orch, *CH-E* (inc.), *Zz, D-B, BNms, DS, LBm, F-Pn, I-BGc* Sala E.2.10 [see Credo, r202/3, and Kyrie, r204/8], *BGc* Antisala B.VI.8, *?USSR-KAu*; ed. in SBA; movt 4 = r203/4, Domine Deus	329
204/8	Kyrie (D), S, T, SATB, orch, *CH-E, I-BGc* Sala E.2.10 [see Credo, r202/3, and Gloria, r204/1], *Gi(l), PAc*; ed. M. A. H. Vos (St Louis, 1972)	
205/2	Larvae tremendae (D), motet, S, orch, *CH-E* [dated 1782]	
206/3	Laudate pueri (E), S, orch, Milan, 12 Aug 1758, lost	
206/1	Laudate pueri (G), S, T, orch, 1760, *E, D-B, DS*	328
—	Laudate pueri (B♭), S, orch, *I-Gi(l)*	
199/1	Let the solemn organs blow (W. Dodd), anthem for Magdalen Chapel, c1764, in *The Christian's Magazine*, vi (1765), 140	
206/4	[3] Lezioni del officio per gli morti: Parce mihi, Domine (B♭), S, A, SATB, orch, 1757; Taedet animam meam (F), S, A, B, SATB, orch, 1757; Manus tuae (C), S, A, T, SATB, orch, 1757 [movt 5 of no.3 = r204/5, Gratias agimus, *CH-E*]; all *E*	328
207/1	Magnificat (C), SATB, SATB, orch, 1758, **GB-Lbm, Lcm*; ed. A. Fodor (Budapest, 1978), ed. in SBA	
207/2	Magnificat (C), SATB, SATB, orch, c1758, **Lbm* (inc.)	
207/3	Magnificat (C), S, A, T, B, SATB, orch, 1760, *CH-E, *GB-Lbm, Lcm*; ed. F. van Amelsvoort (Hilversum, 1960), W. Ehret (New York, 1973)	
207/5	Miserere (B♭), S, A, T, B, SATB, orch, 1757, *CH-E, D-Mbs*; movt 2 = r203/5, Et secundum; movt 5 = r202/2, Cor mundum; movt 7 = r206/7, Libera me de sanguinibus	329, 330
—	Pater noster, 1757, sent to Padre Martini 6 Sept 1757, lost	
208/4	Regem cui omnia vivunt (F), invitatory, S, A, T, B, SATB, orch, 1757, *CH-E*; movt 2 with new text = r199/2, Ad coenam agni; movt 4 with new text = r199/3, Ad coenam agni; movt 6 = r208/3, O lux beata Trinitas; movt 8 = r203/6, Exultet coelum; movt 10 = r207/6, Nisi Dominus	328

T

208/5	Requiem, Te decet hymnus and Kyrie [Messa de' morti] (F), SSAATTBB, orch, c1757, CH-E, D-Mbs, *GB-Ob Tenbury MS 888; ed. in SBA	327, 328
209/3	Salve regina (Eb), S, orch, c1758, Lbm	
209/1	Salve regina (F), S, orch, A-Wn	
209/5	Si nocte tenebrosa (F), motet, S/T, orch, CH-E, (S/T, b only; different 2nd aria), D-B, GB-Lbm	
210/2	Tantum ergo (F), S, orch, 1757, CH-E	
209/7	Tantum ergo (G), S, orch, 1759, E	
210/3	Te Deum (D), SATB, SATB, orch, 1758, *GB-Lbm (inc.)	
210/5	Te Deum (D), S, A, T, B, SATB, orch, 1762, Lbm, CH-E, D-Mbs; ed. A. M. Müller (Augsburg, 1968)	

(spurious)

202/7	Domine ad adiuvandum (C), SATB, str, GB-Lbm	
204/6	Messa a più voci (Ky-Gl) (G), SATB, orch, Lbm [dated 1741]	
204/7	Messa in pastorale (Ky-Gl) (D), SATB, orch, Lbm [dated 1740]	
208/6	Salve regina (D), S, S, A, T, B, SSAATB, orch, Lbm [dated 1740]	

DRAMATIC

CG – London, Covent Garden Theatre   KT – London, King's Theatre
HAY – London, New Theatre in the   SC – Naples, Teatro S Carlo
     Haymarket

(3-act operas unless otherwise stated)

† – favourite songs published shortly after first performance

217; xl	Artaserse (after Metastasio), Turin, Regio, 26 Dec 1760, *GB-Lbm (inc.), I-Nc (1 aria), Tf, P-La (2 copies); ov. in Six Favourite Overtures (1763)	316, 330
222; xlii	Catone in Utica (after Metastasio), SC, 4 Nov 1761, D-BS, Wa, F-Pc, I-Nc (2 copies: 1761 version without recits; 1764 version with recits, Acts 1 and 2 only), P-La (2 copies: 1761 version, 1764 version); ov. = r277/10	316, 330
212; xxxii	Alessandro nell'Indie (after Metastasio), SC, 20 Jan 1762, F-Pc, I-Mc, Nc, P-La; ov. in Six Favourite Overtures (1763)	316, 330
237; xlvii	Orione, ossia Diana vendicata (G. G. Bottarelli), KT, 19 Feb 1763, †, GB-Lbm, Ob Tenbury MS 348 (both inc.); ov. arr. in Six Favourite Overtures (1763)	317, 323, 331
241; xlix	Zanaida (Bottarelli), KT, 7 May 1763, †; ov. = r269/1	317, 334

T

211; xxxi	Adriano in Siria (after Metastasio), KT, 26 Jan 1765, †, P-La	318
—	The Fairy Favour (masque, T. Hull), CG, 31 Jan 1767, perf. by children as afterpiece, music lost	319
221; xlii	Carattaco (Bottarelli), KT, 14 Feb 1767, †, *B-Bc, GB-Lbm (both inc.); ov. (n.d.)	319, 331, 33.
226; xliv	Gioas, rè di Giuda (oratorio, 2, after Metastasio), KT, 22 March 1770, †, A-Wgm, Wn, *GB-Lcm (inc.)	321, 329, 336
238/3; xlviii	Temistocle (M. Verazi, after Metastasio), Mannheim, Hoftheater, 4 or 5 Nov 1772, D-B, Dlb, DS, F-Pc (Act 1), *GB-Cfm 23.J1.11–12 (Acts 1, 3), US-NH; ov., D-DS = r278/3; vocal score ed. and adapted E. Downes, H. C. R. Landon (Vienna, 1965); ov. ed F. Stein, EDM, 1st ser., xxx (1956)	322, 331, 334
232; xlv	Lucio Silla (Verazi, after G. de Gamerra), Mannheim, Hoftheater, 4 Nov 1774, DS 60.1-3; ov. in Six Grand Overtures, op.18 (c1781); ov. ed. F. Stein (Leipzig, 1925), G. Beechey (London, 1971)	322, 332, 334
229; xliv	La clemenza di Scipione, KT, 4 April 1778, op.14 (1778/R1972); ov. as 1st movt of no.1 of Deux sinfonies à grande orchestre, op.18 (Amsterdam, c1785); ov. ed. in Diletto musicale, xcvi (1968); scene 'Arsinda', ed. R. Meylan (Frankfurt am Main, 1971)	310, 323, 332
215; xxxiii	Amadis de Gaule, after Quinault), Paris, Académie Royale de Musique, 14 Dec 1779 (Paris, c1780/R1972), F-Po (Acts 1–2, rev., ballet music; some material from cantata Cefalo e Procri, 1776)	324, 332, 334

Material inserted in operas and pasticcios

252/2	[Ferradini: Demofoonte, Milan, 26 Dec 1758]: Misero pargoletto, aria, A-Wgm Q2685, D-SWl 832	
250/5	[Cafaro: Ipermestra, Naples, 1761]: Abbiamo penato, aria, I-Mc Noseda B36 3	
273/2	[Il tutore e la pupilla (pasticcio, Bottarelli), KT, 13 Nov 1762]; ov., from Cantata a 3 voci per festeggiare, with new 2nd movt, GB-Lbm, in Six Favourite Overtures (1763)	
273/8; 1	[Astarto, rè di Tiro (pasticcio, Bottarelli), KT, 4 Dec 1762]; ov., from Alessandro nell'Indie, D-B and elsewhere, in Six Favourite Overtures (1763): Deh, torna in te stesso, qt, based on r224/7 from Catone in Utica; Io so ben, duet, lost; Per quel primiero affetto, aria, lost; Deh, seconda, duet, lost	
273/5	[La cascina (pasticcio, Bottarelli), KT, 8 Jan 1763]: ov., in Six Favourite Overtures (1763)	

272/5 [Galuppi: La calamità de' cuori, KT, 3 Feb 1763]: ov., in Six Favourite Overtures (1763); Pupilla vezzosa, aria, †, GB-Lbm Add.31717

1 [Issipile (opera, Metastasio), Naples, 26 Dec 1763]: Per il bosco, aria, ? music lost; Caro se vuoi così, aria, I-Nc

244/1 [Menalcas (pastoral, J. Harris), Salisbury, 22 or 24 Aug 1764]: Relentless Death, aria: Muse divine, aria; See him falling, chorus; Cease, cease your tragic measures, aria; Swaynes be gay, chorus: D-LEb GO.S.42; arias based on r237/2, 237/6 from Orione, 241/3 from Zanaida

225/1; xlii [Ezio (pasticcio, after Metastasio), KT, 24 Nov 1764, †]: Non sò d'onde viene, aria, r214/8; Se il ciel mi divide, aria, r214/5: from Alessandro nell'Indie

245/3 [The Maid of the Mill (pasticcio, compiled by S. Arnold, I. 319 Bickerstaffe), CG, 31 Jan 1765]: Trust me, aria, based on r236/1 from Orione: My life, my joy, duet

li / 219/3; xlii [Zophilette (pasticcio, Marmontel), Paris, 1765]: ? music lost
Berenice (pasticcio), KT, 5 Jan 1765, †]: Confusa, smarrita, aria, r224/5, from Catone in Utica

246; li [The Summer's Tale (pasticcio, R. Cumberland), CG, 6 Dec 1765, †]: So profound an impression, aria; Yes, 'tis plain, duet, based on r213/8 from Alessandro nell'Indie; Nature, when she gave us pleasure, aria, based on r241; from Zanaida, pubd as See the kind indulgent gales (c1768)

238/1; xxlviii [Sifare (pasticcio), KT, 5 March 1767, †]: Fiumicel che 's ode appena, aria, r223/2, from Catone in Utica; Se è ver, aria, r214/4, from Alessandro nell'Indie; Per quello stesso labbro, aria; Dovea svenario allora, aria, r224/1, from Catone in Utica

li [Tom Jones (pasticcio, J. Reed, after H. Fielding), CG, 14 Jan 1769, †]: Thirst of wealth, aria; Blest with thee, aria, r220/4, from Carattaco; When I'm in nuptial union join'd, aria

231/2 [Piccinni: Le contadine bizzarre, KT, 7 Nov 1769, †]: Sono in 320 mar, aria, based on r223/3 from Catone in Utica

231/3 [L'Olimpiade (pasticcio, after Metastasio), KT, 11 Nov 1769, 320 †]: Quel labbro adorato, aria

234; xlvi [Gluck: Orfeo ed Euridice (Bottarelli), KT, 7 April 1770, †, P-La; also SC, 4 Nov 1774, I-Nc]: Non è ver, il dir talora, aria; Chiari fonti, aria; Accorda amico, aria; Più non turbo, aria; based on r213/3 from Alessandro nell'Indie; Sulle sponde del torbido Lete, aria; Non temer, amor lo guida, aria; Obliar l'amato sposo, aria; La sventura del figlio, scena

with chorus, r251/5, *D-B (inc.), probably intended as opening of pasticcio

li [Amelia (pasticcio, R. Cumberland: The Summer's Tale, London, 14 Dec 1771]: music lost

245/2 [The Flitch of Bacon (pasticcio, compiled by W. Shield, H. Bate), HAY, 17 Aug 1778]: No, 'twas neither shape nor feature, aria, based on r250/4, J. C. Bach's transcription of M. Mortellari: Io ti lascio

(doubtful)

— [Ifigenia o le barbare furie]: Arrestatevi, scena with chorus, D-B P1004

253/4 [Cleonice (? pasticcio), KT, 26 Nov 1763]: Tu parti, mio ben, duet, B, Bds, GB-Lbm; by F. Bertoni

— [Demofoonte (Metastasio)]: Non dura una sventura, aria, US-AA M1505.B12.D4, ? for M. Vento: Demofoonte, KT, 2 March 1765 [according to London Stage, all music by Vento]

253/2 [?L'Olimpiade]: Quel labbro adorato, aria, D-Llh, different from r231/3

319

CANTATAS AND SERENATAS

(cantatas unless otherwise stated)

244/6 Ode on the Auspicious Arrival and Nuptials of ... Queen Charlotte [Thanks to the God who rules the deep] (J. Lockman), S/T, SAB, vn, bc, ?*GB-Lbm [Charlotte arrived 8 Sept 1761; no perf. date known]

— Cantata a 3 voci per festeggiare il felicissimo giorno natalizio di sua Maestà cattolica (?Passeri), 2 S, T, chorus, orch, Naples, 12 Jan 1762, P-La [see ov. to Il tutore, r273/2]; La pace all'alma mia, aria, I-Nc; lib, Nn

— Gli orti esperidi (?Passeri, after Metastasio), Naples, S Carlo, 320 1765, lost, cited in F. de Filippis and R. Arnese: Cronache del Teatro di S Carlo: 1737–1960, i (Naples, 1964), 37

248/3 Endimione (serenata, after Metastasio), 3 S, T, SATB, orch, 319 London, King's Theatre, 6 April 1772; rev. Mannheim, Hoftheater, 1774, with scene by Jommelli; D-DS (with Jommelli scene); *of pt.1 without ov. but with duet [not in Tl, GB-Cfm 23.J.13; arr. of ov. in Six Grand Overtures, op.18 (c1782); ov. ed. in The Symphony 1720–1840, E/ii (New York, 1983)

T

247/2 Amor vincitore (?Verazi), 2 S, SATB, orch, Schwetzingen, ? 322, 326
Aug 1774, *A-Wgm*, *D-DS*, *F-Pc*

li Cefalo e Procri (?Bottarelli), 2 S, A, orch, London, Hanover 323
Square Rooms, 26 April 1776, *US-Wc*; ed. E. S. Derr
(Ann Arbor, 1970); Già Febo, recit, Vo cercando, aria,
pubd as Aurora: a Favorite Cantata, r247/1 (c1819), ? from
MS, *GB-Lbm*; material from Scorsa 'o tutta la selva, acc.
recit, Già Febo, acc. recit, and Vo cercando, aria, used in
Amadis de Gaule; Sconsolata, andai vagando, aria, rev. in
Orpheus and Eurydice as Comfortless is ev'ry thought
(pasticcio assembled by William Reeve), London, Covent
Garden, 1792, *Lcm*

— La tempesta (Metastasio), S, orch, Mannheim, c1776, *A-Wgm* 322
Q3700, *D-Bim* Bach, J. C. 1; in G. J. Vogler: *Betrachtungen
der Mannheimer Tonschule* (1778), July, pls.x–xvi, Aug,
pls.vii–xvi

250/2 Rinaldo ed Armida, 3vv, orch, London, Hanover Square 323
Rooms, 20 May 1778; lost except Serba, o caro, aria,
B-Bc 3707; incl. Ebben si vada ... Io ti lascio [see
'Transcriptions']

243/1 Happy morn, auspicious rise, 2 S, T, chorus, *GB-Lbm*; arr. of
ov. in oratorio Gioas, rè di Giuda

(spurious)

249/7 L'Olimpe, SATB, 2 hn, 2 cl, str, *D-B* (2 MSS, late 18th
century)

OTHER VOCAL

Chamber duets

— [9] Duetti, 2 S, bc, ?c1760, *I-Gi(l)* M.2.14, *Nc* 170 (nos.1–4), *F-Pc* D9638(3) (not no.8): 1 Chi mai di questo core; 2 Che
ciascun per te sospiri; 3 Trova un sol; 4 Io lo sò; 5
Ascoltami, oh Clori; 6 Eccomi alfin; 7 Parlami pur; 8 Lascia
chi'io posso; 9 Ah che nel dirti addio [nos.2, 5 rev. as op.4
nos.5, 6; others different from opp.4, 6]

259/1 Sei canzonette a due, 2 S, bc, op.4 (1765)/R1982 with
introduction by E. S. Derr): 1 Già la notte; 2 Ah rammenta
oh bella Irene; 3 Pur nel sonno almen talora; 4 T'intendo si
mio cor; 5 Che ciascun per te sospiri; 6 Ascoltami, oh Clori;
ed. E. Reichert (Wiesbaden, 1958)

T

260/2 Sei canzonette a due, 2 S, bc, op.6 (1767): 1 Toma in quel
l'onda; 2 Io lo sò; 3 E pur fra le tempeste; 4 Trova un sol; 5
Chi mai di questo core; 6 S'infida tu mi chiami

Miscellaneous arias

250/6 Accender mi sento, *GB-Lbm*
— Ah che gli stessi numi ... Cara ti lascio, A, orch (c1785)
— A quei sensi di gloria, *A-Wn*
251/2 Caro mio bene, *A-Wn*
247/1 Infelice ... Là nei regni, Mez, kbd 4 hands, pubd as A
Favourite Scene and Rondo on the Duke of Nivernois Air
(c1783), [? red. of orch score]
252/3 O Venere vezzosa (Horace, trans. Bottarelli), in Sei ode di
Oratio ... da Signori Bach ... Holzbaur (c1775)
— Sventurata in van mi lagno, S, 2 hn obbl, orch, *D-B* P1155
(after 1773)

(*doubtful or spurious*)

— Amiche solitudine ... Verdi pianti, *I-Gi(l)*
iii Al si barbaro colpo ... Morte vieni, *A-Wgm* Q2683, *US-AA*
M1613.B13 M6 17 —
— Fosca Nube, che in alto s'aggira, *A-Wgm* Q2688
251/3 Hvad fasligt qval mitt hjerta plågar, *S-Skma*
251/4 La sorte spietata, in B. Mengozzi: *Méthode de chant du
Conservatoire* (Paris, 1803), 204
251/7 Mi scordo i torti miei ... Dolci aurette, acc. recit and rondo,
Mez, orch, *D-B* (attrib. J. C. Bach). *WRtl*; from G.
Gazzaniga: Perseo e Andromaca; attrib. Gazzaniga in Six
Favorite Italian Songs ... Mr Tenducci (1778) without
concluding allegro; ed. L. Landshof (Leipzig, 1930)
252/1 Misera, misera, *S-Skma*
— Nel cammin di nostra vita, S, orch, *I-MAav*
— Non temer, bell'idol mio, S, ob, orch, *GB-Er* W13
252/6 Parto, ma se tu m'ami, *D-B*
252/7 Principe non temer ... Con si bel nome, B
— Questa da te l'ho impregata, *A-Wgm* Q2687
— Se quel folle ... Figlia, oh diol, S, orch, *I-MAav*
[9] Solfeggi ... del Sig. Giovanni Bach in Genova 1781, S, bc,
Gi(l) SS.A2.7 (G8)
253/3 Sospiri del mio cor, *D-LI/h*
253/5 Una semplice agnelletta, B

Vieni, dell'amorosa Glicera ... Di gioventù desia, *A-Wgm* Q3700, pp.96–128

— Vo sokando, S, orch, *I-Nc*

— Vò cercando, *D-MÜu* Bach 14 (attrib. J. C. Bach); from Piccinni: La buona figliuola maritata

256/3 When an angry woman's breast [Neptune] (c1775)

Vauxhall songs

254/1 A Collection of [4] Favourite Songs sung at Vaux Hall by 319 Mrs. Weichsell (1766): 1 By my sighs; 2 Cruel Strephon; 3 Come, Colin; 4 Ah, why shou'd love

254/5 A Second Collection of [4] Favourite Songs sung at Vaux Hall 319 by Mrs. Pinto and Mrs. Weichsell (1767): 1 In this shady blest retreat; 2 Smiling Venus; 3 Tender virgins shun deceivers [rev. of Non è ver, r220/4, from Carattaco, later pubd as Blest with thee (c1769), r255/6, from Tom Jones (pasticcio)]; 4 Lovely yet ungrateful swain

255/2 A Third Collection of [4] Favorite Songs, sung at Vaux Hall 319 by Miss Cooper (1771): 1 Midst silent shades; 2 Ah, seek to know; 3 Would you a female heart inspire; 4 Cease awhile, ye winds, to blow [pubd separately (c1800); nos.1, 2, 4 ed. L. Landshoff (Leipzig, 1930)]

Folksong settings

256/2 Farewell, ye soft scenes: a Celebrated Air by Mr Bach (? 1790), Eng. rev. of r231/3 from L'Olimpiade

257/2 See the kind indulgent gales: a Favourite Song sung by Mrs Weichsell at Vaux Hall Gardens (c1780), Eng. rev. of r241/3 from Zanaida

— The Braes of Ballanden [Beneath a green shade] (T. Blacklock), A, ob, vn, va, vc, pf (1779); in W. Shield: Rudiments of Thorough Bass (?1800); ed. R. Fiske (London, 1969)

257/– The Broom of Cowdenknows [How blyth was I each morn] (S.R.'), A, 2 fl, 2 vn, bc (c1784); ed. R. Fiske (London, 1969)

— I'll never leave thee (R. Crawford), A, 2 fl, 2 vn, bc (c1784); ed. R. Fiske (London, 1969)

256/– Lochaber [Farewell to Lochaber] (A. Ramsay), A, 2 fl, 2 vn, bc (c1785); ed. R. Fiske (London, 1969)

— The Yellow-hair'd Laddie, lost; attrib. Bach in Storace: Gli equivoci, 1786, *A-Wn*; arr. in 3rd movt of pf conc., op.13 no.4, r296/4

Transcriptions

250/2 Ebben si vada ... Io ti lascio, acc. recit and rondo, Mez, ob, pf, orch, *A-Wn*, *B-Bc*, *US-NYp*, formerly *D-BNu*, *F-Pc*, *GB-Lbm*, pubd as The Favourite Rondeau [sung] by Mr Tenducci (c1778); ? from cantata Rinaldo ed Armida; expanded version of Ombra felice ... Io ti lascio from M. Mortellari: Arsace, 1775, of r245/2, Flitch of Bacon; rondo also as First Favourite Rondo [Venus, Queen of tender passion], Mez, ob, hpd (?c1785); ed. L. Landshoff (Leipzig, 1930)

251/1 Al mio bene (after G. Roccaforte: Antigona), rondo, Mez, pf, orch, as Rondeau ... sung by Mr Tenducci at Messrs Bach and Abels Concert ... 1779 (1779); vocal score in A Select Collection of the Most Admired Songs, i (Edinburgh and London, c1785); original by V. Ciampi or F. Bertoni, see Oldman (1961)

253/6 Wenn nach der Stürme Toben, aria, S, kbd, in J. A. Hiller: Deutsche Arien und Duette (Leipzig, 1785); transcr. of Allor che il vincitore, r229/4, from La clemenza di Scipione

SYMPHONIES AND OVERTURES

333–6

277/4 Ov. (D), 2 ob, 2 hn, str, no.1 in The Periodical Overture in 8 Parts (1763)

272/2 Six Favourite Overtures (1763): ovs. from the operas: 1 Orione; 2 La calamità; 3 Artaserse; 4 Il tutore; 5 La cascina; 6 Astarto (= Alessandro nell'Indie); no.3 in VI Sinfonie a più stromenti composte da vari autori, op.12 (Paris, 1761)

276/3 Sym. (C), 2 ob, 2 hn, str, *CH-E*; 1st movt = 1st movt of no.46 in Sinfonie a più stromenti composte da vari autori (Paris, after 1769, before 1772)

262/1 Six simphonies (C, D, Eb, Bb, F, G), 2 ob/fl, 2 hn, str, op.3 319, 333, 334 (1765); ed. in Diletto musicale, cclxxix–cclxxxiv (1975); also arr. hpd as Six Overtures Composed and Addapted for the Harpsichord (before 1769), ed. S. Staral (Graz, 1980); = r347/2

275/3 An Overture in 8 Parts (D), 2 ob, 2 hn, str (1766); corrected version of Periodical Overture no.xv (1766) [pubd by Bremner]

264/1 Six simphonies (G, D, Eb, Bb, Eb, g), 2 ob/fl, 2 hn, str, op.6 333 (Amsterdam, 1770), in Breitkopf suppl. 1770: nos.3–5 = op.8 nos.1, 5, 6; nos.4, 5 in Breitkopf suppl. 1766: no.3 in Breitkopf suppl. 1767, ed. in NM, ccxxxix (1973); nos.4, 5

281/3 Sym. (B♭), 2 ob, 2 hn, str, attrib. 'Sigre Giuseppe Baach', A-Wgm; attrib. Lang in Breitkopf suppl. 1767

— Sym. (B♭), 2 ob, 2 hn, str, D-Bds, SW!; attrib. Maldere (Paris and Lyons, 1764)

— Sym. (B♭), 2 hn, str, I-MAav; in Breitkopf suppl. 1767; attrib. Ricci (1768)

— Sym. (E♭), A-KR; attrib. Malzart in Breitkopf suppl. 1767; many other attribs.

— Notturno (E♭), M (as Cassatio); incipit in Breitkopf suppl. 1767; as Cassatio dulcis attrib. Haydn, hIII:Es10, D-Gd

281/6 Sym. (E♭), 2 ob, 2 tpt, str, S-Skma

281/9 Sym. (E♭), 2 ob, 2 hn, str, Skma; attrib. J. Stamitz, DTB, iv, Jg.iii/1 (1902), xl

282/2 Sym. (E♭), 2 ob, 2 hn, str, Skma

283/3 Sym. (E♭), 2 tpt [? or cl], hns, bns, str, D-W

— Sym. (E♭), A-Kr (attrib. J. C. Bach), ST (attrib. I. Fränzl), D-Mbs (attrib. Haydn), Rtt (attrib. V. Pichl); attrib. Filtz in Breitkopf suppl. 1766

— Sym. (E♭), 2 ob, 2 hn, str, CH-Zz

— Sym. (E♭), A-Z; attrib. Haydn, hI:Es2; attrib. G. van Swieten in Breitkopf suppl. 1782-4; attrib. Vanhal (n.d.) [pubd by Betz]

— 12 syms. (C, C, G, D, D, A, F, F, B♭, B♭, E♭, E♭), 2 ob, 2 hn, str, I-Rdp; see Holschneider (1961); many other attribs.

335

SYMPHONIES CONCERTANTES

(instruments listed as concertato; ripieno)

284/1 Sinfonie concertante (G), 2 vn, vc; 2 ob, 2 hn, 2 vn, 2 va, b (Paris, by 1772), I-MAav; ed. J. A. White (Tallahassee, 1963)

284/4 Simphonie concertante (A), vn, vc; 2 ob, 2 hn, str (Paris, by 1775), GB-Lbm; ed. A. Einstein (London, 1934); = r289/3

284/6 Concert ou symphonie (E♭), 2 vn, ob; 2 fl, 2 hn, str (Paris, 1773); ed. F. Stein (London, 1935); also as pf conc., r290/1, r300/8

286/1 Sym. conc. (C), 2 vn, vc; 2 fl, 2 ob, 2 hn, str, D-Hs (lost), GB-Lbm (inc.); = r290/8

286/4 Sym. conc. (G), ob, vn, va, vc; 2 fl, 2 hn, str, D-Hs (lost)

— Sym. conc. (G), 2 vn; 2 fl, 2 hn, str, I-MAav [not = r286/4]

286/8 Sym. conc. (E), 2 vn, vc, fl; 2 ob, 2 hn, str, D-Hs (lost), GB-Lbm (inc.); = r290/6; ed. in The Symphony 1720–1840, E/ii (New York, 1983)

287/2 Sym. conc. (F), ob, bn/vc; ob, 2 hn, str, D-Hs (lost), GB-Lbm; ed. F. Dawes (London, 1973); = r289/2

287/7 Sym. conc. (B♭), ?vn, vc; 2 cl, bn, 2 hn, str, D-Hs (lost) [see White (1958)]

288/4 Sym. conc. (E♭), 2 vn; 2 ob, 2 hn, str, Hs (lost), I-MAav; also as bn conc., r288/4

288/7; iiv Notturno (E♭), 2 ob, 2 tpt, 2 vn, 2 va, vc; 2 vn, b, *A-Wn, GB-Lbm; ed. J. A. White (Tallahassee, 1963); 1st movt not = r290/7

289/4 Sym. conc. (C), fl, ob, vn, vc; 2 fl, 2 cl, 2 bn, 2 hn, str, by 1775, Lbm; ed. R. Maunder (London, 1961)

289/7 Sym. conc. (B♭), ob, vn, vc; pf, 2 fl, 2 hn, str, by 1780, Lbm (inc.)

290/2 Sym. conc. (D), 2 fl, 2 vn, vc; 2 hn, str, Lbm, I-MAav; ed. in The Symphony 1720–1840, E/ii (New York, 1983)

290/4 Sym. conc. (E♭), fl, ob, bn; 2 hn, str, GB-Lbm; attrib. Haydn, hI:Es14

290/9 Sym. conc. (E♭), 2 cl, bn, ob; 2 ob, 2 hn, str, Lbm; ed. J. A. White (Tallahassee, 1963)

— Concerto a più istrumenti (D), 2 vn; 2 fl, 2 ob, 2 hn, str, I-MAav; not = r290/2

(doubtful)

335-6

CONCERTOS   317

292/1 Six concerti (B♭, A, F, G, C, D), hpd, 2 vn, vc, op.1 (1763); no.4 ed. A. Mann (New Brunswick, NJ, 1953)

286/7 Conc. (D), fl, 2 hn, str, *D-B (dated 1768; 1st movt, inc.), ?*F-Pn (2nd movt only); ed. R. Meylan (Vienna, 1958)

293/4 Sei concerti (C, F, D, B♭, E♭, G), hpd/pf, 2 vn, vc, op.7 (1770); no.5 ed. C. Döbereiner (Leipzig, 1927), H. Illy (Rome, 1967), A. Fodor (Budapest, 1980); no.6 ed. in Antiqua (1954)

295/1 A Third Sett of Six Concertos (C, D, F, B♭, G, E♭), hpd/pf, 2 vn, vc (2 ob, 2 hn, ad lib), op.13 (1777); 3rd movt of no.4 = arr. of folksong, The Yellow-hair'd Laddie; nos.2, 4 ed. L. Landshoff (Leipzig, 1933, 1931)

298/1 5 concs. (B♭, f, d, E, G), hpd, str, *D-B; no.2 ed. in NM, clxx (1954)

300/8 Conc. (E♭), pf, 2 fl, 2 cl, bn, 2 hn, str, B, GB-Lbm (inc.), S-Skma; = r209/1; version of sym. conc., r284/6

301/1 Conc. (E♭), kbd, str, hns ad lib, D-Dlb; ? as ler concerto (E♭), hpd, str, op.14 (Paris, n.d.) [cited in RISM as op.13 no.6], in Breitkopf suppl. 1781

310/9 Quartetto (G), vn, 2 vc, kbd (Offenbach, 1783); issued in 2 edns. by J. C. Luther: (1) vn, va, vc, hpd; (2) arr. vn, in Three Favorite Quartetts and One Quintett (1785); ed. in Antiqua (1951); = r311/5

307/4 Four quartettos (C, D, G, C), op.19 (1784): nos.1, 3 for 2 fl, va, vc; no.2 for fl, ob/fl, va, vc; no.4 for 2 fl, vn, vc; arr. hpd/pf, fl, vc (c1787); ed. in Organum, iii/63-4, 66, 68 (1962); no.2 ed. in HM, cxix (1954); nos.1, 3 ed. S. Sadie (London, 1961)

311/6 Sonata (Bb), 2 vn, vc, no.1 in Six Sonatas ... by Messrs Bach, Abel and Kammel (1777) [no.2 ? also by J. C. Bach; see Breitkopf suppl. 1778]

330/5 Sonata (Bb), harp, (vn, vc)/hpd, no.6 in Musical Remains: or The Compositions of Handel, Bach, Abel, Giuliani, &c (?1796); 1st movt earlier version of sestetto, r302/1

317/2 Trio (C), fl, fl/vn, vc, no.1 in Two Trios ... Selected by T. Monzani (c1800); ed. R. de Reede (Winterthur, 1980)

314/5 Six trios (Bb, A, Eb, G, D, C), 2 vn, va/bc, op.2 (1763), also as op.4 (Amsterdam, 1767), in Breitkopf suppl. 1766 as first 6 of set of 12 (see also r317/5); ed. W. Höckner (Locarno, 1963); nos.2, 4, 6 ed. in HM, xxxvii (1949)

317/5 6 trio sonatas (G, D, E, F, Bb, Eb), 2 vn, bc, I-Mc; nos.3-4, Gi(l); in Breitkopf suppl. 1766 as second 6 of set of 12 (see also r314/5)

317/7 Trio sonata (G), 2 fl, b, Mc, Gi(l) (2 vn, b)

318/8 Trio sonata (F), 2 va, bc, formerly Singakademie, Berlin, destroyed

313/1 Six sonates (F, G, D, C, D, Eb), hpd, vn/fl, vc, op.2 (1764); ed. in Diletto musicale, dhxxi-dhxxvi (1978); no.3 ed. in Collegium musicum, xix (New York, 2/1955); 1 ed. in NM, cxcii (1957)

322/1 Six Sonatas (Bb, C, G, E, F, D), hpd/pf, vn, op.10 (1773) [for transcrs. see Sei quartetti, op.17]; nos.1-5 ed. L. Landshoff (London, 1939)

335/1 Six Duetts (D, G, Eb, Bb, A, C), 2 vn (by 1775), also as op.13 (Paris, c1775); attrib. G. Kennis in Breitkopf suppl. 1768; ed. in NM, cxxvi, cxl (1937-8)

323/5 Sonatas (C, A, D, Bb), hpd/pf, vn, vc, nos.1-4 in Four Sonatas and Two Duetts, op.15 (1778); nos.1, 2 ed. in Diletto musicale, ccclxxvii-ccclxxviii (1979); no.4 ed. in Collegium musicum, xix (Leipzig, n.d.)

325/1 Six Sonatas (D, G, C, A, D, F), hpd/pf, vn/fl, op.16 (1779/R1961); nos.1, 2 ed. in NM, i (1927); no.4 ed. in NM, ciii (1933)

326/3 Sonatas (C, D, Eb, G), hpd/pf, vn/fl, nos.1-4 in Four Sonatas and Two Duetts, op.18 (1781)

336/6 4 canzonettes (F, Eb, G, Bb), 2 vn, GB-Lbm, arrs. of Sei canzonette, op.6, see r260/2, nos.1, 4, 3, 2

332/4 [7] Sonate (F, D, G, A, G, D, F), hpd, vn, I-Mc; no.1 ed. in Mekota (1969), 264

— Sonata (A), hpd, vn, Mc; 2nd movt = r333/5

(doubtful or spurious)

— Sonata (F), ob, vn, va, vc, Gi(l)
— Sonata (D), 2 vn, va, vc, Gi(l)
— Sonata (Eb), eng hn, vn, va, vc, Gi(l)
— 4 trio sonatas (C, F, A, Eb), 2 vn, vc, Gi(l)
— 3 sonatas (D, F, c), hpd, vn, vc, Gi(l)
— 2 sonatas (Bb, G), hpd, vn, Vc; = J. S. Schroeter's op.2 nos.4, 2; no.1 = r319/9

331/2 Sonata (D), hpd, vn, D-B (2 copies: 1 as Sonata; 2 [dated 1771] as Trio); as Sonata ed. in Mekota (1969), 243

— 6 sonatas (C, G, F, Bb, Eb, D), hpd, vn, PExp
— Sonata con cembalo o spinetta (F), probably vn, hpd, Mc (inc.)

279/10 Trio sonata (F), 2 vn, bc, S-Uu, attrib. 'Sign Back' [not sym. as in T]

319/4 Trio sonata (Bb), 2 vn, bc, GB-Lbm, by C. P. E. Bach (w158, H584)

319/7 Trio sonata (Bb), 2 vn, bc, D-Mbs

319/9 Divertimento (Bb), 2 vn, bc, A-Wgm, arr. of J. S. Schroeter's op.2 no.4

320/5 Trio sonata (Bb), 2 vn, bc, D-Mbs
320/4 Trio sonata (Eb), 2 vn, bc, S-Skma
320/6 Trio sonata (Eb), 2 vn, bc, formerly in Socznik collection, Gdańsk, ?lost; attrib. Wagenseil in Breitkopf catalogue 1762

320/9 Trio sonata (Bb), fl, vn, b, D-Kf; ed. H. Kölbel (Zurich, 1968)
321/1 Trio sonata (Eb), hpd, vn [not 2 vn as in T], Mbs; as Sonata ed. in Antiqua (1951)

— Sonata, gui, vn (c1770)

327/5 Six Sonatas (C, G, D, A, Eb, Bb), hpd/pf, vn/fl, op.19 (1783)

T

329/1 Three [= 6] Sonatas [i–ii] (C, D, F, G, A, B♭), hpd/pf, vn, op.20 (c1785)

332/1 Sonata (F), hpd, fl, B, also attrib. C. P. E. Bach (H597) and W. F. Bach; ed. K. Marguerre (Celle, 1960)

331/5 Sonata (D), vn, bc, Bds, ?lost

337/1 3 sonatas (D, G, C), fl, vn, A-Wn

344/2 Trois sonates (E♭, B♭, D), hpd/pf, vn, op.21 (Paris, after 1785)

352/2 Sonata (C), hpd, vn, in The Feast of Apollo (c1788)

KEYBOARD 337

345/7 5 opera ovs. (Orione, Zanaida, Artaserse, La cascina, Astarto [= Alessandro nell'Indie]), arr. hpd/org in Six Favourite Opera Overtures (1763)

338/1 Six sonates (B♭, D, G, E♭, E, c), op.5 (1766/R1976; ed. E. G. Heinemann (Munich, 1982); nos.2–6 ed. L. Landshoff (Leipzig, 1925)

340/5 2 duets (G, C): 2 kbd; kbd 4 hands; in Four Sonatas and Two Duetts, op.15 (1778); no.1 ed. S. Hudnik (Mainz, 1935); no.2 ed. in NM, iv (1938), ed. W. Weismann (New York, 1943), ed. in SBA

341/1 Six Sonatas (G, c, E♭, G, A, B♭), op.17 (1779/R1976); previously pubd as op.12 (Paris, 1773–4); ed. E. G. Heinemann (Munich, 1982); nos.2–6 ed. L. Landshoff (Leipzig, 1927)

343/3 2 duets (A, F), kbd 4 hands, in Four Sonatas and Two Duetts, op.18 (1781); 1 ed. in NM, cxv (1935), ed. in SBA Weismann (New York, 1943), ed. in SBA

— 6 minuets (c, C, d, g, C, C), 2 polonaises (B♭, E♭), aria (a), B P672, attrib. J. C. Bach; also attrib. J. C. Bach in Verzeichniss des musikalischen Nachlasses ... Carl Philipp Emanuel Bach (Hamburg, 1790), see BJb, xxxv–xxxvii (1938, 1939, 1940–48); ed. S. Staral (Graz, 1981)

(doubtful or spurious)

358/4 Sonata (B♭), I-Bc

— Solo (a), D-Bds

— Sonata (A♭), I-Bc

— Toccata (b♭), Bc

— Canzonette with Variations (?c1765), also attrib. C. P. E. Bach

---

T

355/8 Sonata (F), 1768, I-Mc

— Ov. (C), in Periodical Overtures for the Harpsichord, Pianoforte (c1775)

350/8 Five Sonatas and One Duett (D, F, B♭, C, E♭, C) ... by Mr Bach (c1780); 1st movt of no.5, CH-E 66-12 = 1356/5; probably by W. F. E. Bach

— Four Progressive Lessons ... and Two Duetts (C, F, D, G, D, G) (c1782); no.4 uses theme from rondo 1250/4, by M. Mortellari, transcr. J. C. Bach; probably by W. F. E. Bach

— Menuetto (F), in Sammlung vermischter Clavierstücke von verschiedenen Tonkünstlern auf das Jahr 1782, i (Nuremberg, 1782), B-Bc; ed. S. Staral (Graz, 1981)

— Minuetto (D), in Journal de clavecin par les meilleurs maitres, i (Paris, 1782), F-Pn; ed. S. Staral (Graz, 1781)

343/7 Sonata ... qui represente la bataille de Rosbach (F) (c1782), also attrib C. P. E. Bach (w272, H381) and Graun

349/1 Six Progressive Lessons (1783); by C. P. E. Bach: Probestücke (w63, H70) incl. in Versuch (w254, H868)

— Méthode ou recueil ... pour le forte-piano ou clavecin ... composé ... par J. C. Bach et F. P. Ricci (Paris, c1786/R1974); unlikely J. C. Bach had anything to do with text of exx.; pieces in pt.i unattrib; pieces in pt.ii = C. P. E. Bach's Probestücke for Versuch; J. C. Bach's name taken from 1349/1

T

356/2 Sonata (F), no.1 in Six Sonatas ... by Bach, Benda, Gzaun, Wagenseil, Hasse and Kernberger [sic] (1799); arr. of C. P. E. Bach's Sinfonia (w175, H650)

348/4 Fugue (F), on B–A–C–H (Leipzig, c1809), D-Dlb

352/5 Alla polacca (G), Bds; by J. C. F. Bach

352/6 Variazioni (C), Dlb 3374-T-10

353/1 Rondeau ... con [12] variazioni (C), Dlb 3374-T-11, attrib. J. C. Bach; (c1770), attrib. Joseph Dietz [on theme from J. C. Fischer's Ob Conc., no.1]

356/2 Allegro vivace (C), CH-E; ed. S. Staral (Graz, 1981)

356/3 Sonata (C), E

356/4 Andante (f), E; ed. in Mekota (1969); ed. S. Staral (Graz, 1981)

356/6 XI Variationen über eine bekannte Ariette von J. C. Bach (C), D-B P706

356/7 Ballo Montezuma, A-Wgm

353/2 Variazioni (F), kbd 4 hands, I-PEsp

— Six sonates (E♭, G, B♭, D, C, F), kbd 4 hands, c1764, formerly B-Br (lost)

BIBLIOGRAPHY

BurneyH; *EitnerQ*; *FétisB*; *GerberNL*

The Lyric Muse Revived in Europe (London, 1768)

G. Vogler, ed.: *Betrachtungen der Mannheimer Tonschule* (Mannheim, 1778–81/*R*1974)

ABCDario Musico (Bath, 1780)

C. Cramer, ed.: *Magazin der Musik* (Hamburg, 1783–6/*R*1971–4)

R. J. S. Stevens: *Recollections* (MS, *GB-Cpl*)

H. Angelo: *The Reminiscences of Henry Angelo* (London, 1828–30)

Earl of Mount Edgcumbe: *Musical Reminiscences* (London, 4/1834)

MacKinlay: *Mrs. Cornely's Entertainments at Carlisle House, Soho Square* (London, *c*1840)

J. Jesse: *Memoirs of the Life and Reign of King George III* (London, 1867)

C. F. Pohl: *Mozart und Haydn in London* (Vienna, 1867/*R*1970)

C. Papendiek: *Court and Private Life in the Time of Queen Charlotte* (London, 1887)

A. Paglicci Brozzi: *Il regio ducal teatro di Milano nel secolo XVIII* (Milan, 1894)

M. Schwarz: *J. Christian Bach: sein Leben und seine Werke* (Leipzig, 1901)

——: 'Johann Christian Bach', *SIMG*, ii (1900–01), 401–54

M. Brenet: 'Un fils du grand Bach à Paris en 1778–1779', *Guide musical*, xlviii (1902), 551, 571

H. Saxe-Wyndham: *The Annals of Covent Garden Theatre from 1732 to 1897* (London, 1906)

C. von Mannlich: *Lebenserinnerungen* (Berlin, 1913)

H. Abert: 'Joh. Christian Bachs italienische Opern und ihr Einfluss auf Mozart', *ZMw*, i (1919), 313

A. Einstein: 'Mitteilungen der deutsche Musikgesellschaft, Ortsgruppen München', *ZMw*, iv (1921–2), 121 [précis of lecture by L. Landshoff on Bach's secular vocal music]

G. de Saint-Foix: 'A propos de Jean-Chrétien Bach', *RdM*, x (1926), 83

H. Schökel: *J. Christian Bach und die Instrumentalmusik seiner Zeit* (Wolfenbüttel, 1926)

F. Tutenberg: *Die Sinfonik Johann Christian Bachs* (Wolfenbüttel, 1928)

C. Terry: *John Christian Bach* (London, 1929 [review by H. Miesner in *ZMw*, xvi (1934), 182]; rev. 2/1967/*R*1980 by H. C. R. Landon [review by S. Sadie in *MT*, cviii (1967), 330])

A. Wenk: *Beiträge zur Kenntnis des Opernschaffens von J. Christian Bach* (diss., U. of Frankfurt am Main, 1932)

E. Reeser: *De zonen van Bach* (Amsterdam, 1941; Eng. trans., 1949)

H. Wirth: 'Bach, Johann Christian', *MGG*

——: 'Johann Christian (Jean Chrétien) Bach', *Revue internationale de musique*, new ser. (1950), no.8, p.133

H. Blomstedt: 'Till kännedomen om J. C. Bachs symfonier', *STMf*, xxxiii (1951), 53

S. Sadie: 'The Wind Music of J. C. Bach', *ML*, xxxvii (1956), 107

R. Seebandt: *Arientypen Johann Christian Bachs* (diss., Humboldt U., Berlin, 1956)

F. van Amelsvoort: 'Johann Christian Bach en zijn oratorium Gioas', *Mens en melodie*, xii (1957), 300

J. A. White jr: *The Concerted Symphonies of John Christian Bach* (diss., U. of Michigan., 1957) [incl. edns. of 3 syms. concertantes]

E. O. D. Downes: *The Operas of Johann Christian Bach as a Reflection of the Dominant Trends in Opera Seria 1750–1780* (diss., Harvard U., 1958)

E. J. Simon: 'A Royal Manuscript: Ensemble Concertos by J. C. Bach', *JAMS*, xii (1959), 161

J. LaRue: 'Major and Minor Mysteries of Identification in the 18th Century Symphony', *JAMS*, xiii (1960), 181

The London Stage 1600–1800 (Carbondale, Ill., 1960–68)

A. Holschneider: 'Die Musiksammlung der Fürsten Doria-Pamphilj in Rom', *AMw*, xviii (1961), 248

C. B. Oldman: 'Mozart's Scena for Tenducci', *ML*, xlii (1961), 44

W. Haacke: *Die Söhne Bachs* (Königstein im Taunus, 1962)

P. M. Young: 'Johann Christian Bach and his English Environment', *GfMKB, Kassel 1962*, 32

H.-J. Schulze: 'Frühe Schriftzeugnisse der beiden jüngsten Bach-Söhne', *BJb*, i (1963–4), 61

S. Kunze: 'Die Vertonungen der Arie "Non sò d'onde viene" von J. Chr. Bach und W. A. Mozart', *AnMc*, no.2 (1965), 85

E. Warburton: 'J. C. Bach's Operas', *PRMA*, xcii (1965–6), 95

B. S. Brook, ed.: *The Breitkopf Thematic Catalogues, 1762–1787* (New York, 1966)

B. Matthews: 'J. C. Bach in the West Country', *MT*, cviii (1967), 702

E. S. Derr: *J. C. Bach: Cefalo e Procri (London, 1776): a Critical Edition* (diss., U. of Illinois, 1968)

N. J. Fujisawa: *Johann Christian Bach: London ni okeru kareno katsudo to ongaku* [Life and works in his London years] (diss., Tokyo U. of Arts, 1968)

B. A. Mekota: *The Solo and Ensemble Keyboard Works of Johann Christian Bach* (diss., U. of Michigan, 1969) [incl. corrections and additions to Terry's catalogue]

352

Bibliography

M. A. H. Vos: *The Liturgical Choral Works of Johann Christian Bach* (diss., Washington U., 1969)

E. Warburton: *A Study of Johann Christian Bach's Operas* (diss., U. of Oxford, 1969)

P. M. Young: 'Johann Christian, der Englischer Bach', *Musa–mens–musici: im Gedenken an Walther Vetter* (Leipzig, 1969), 189

——: *The Bachs: 1500–1850* (London, 1970)

N. Krabbe: 'J. C. Bach's Symphonies and the Breitkopf Thematic Catalogue', *Festskrift Jens Peter Larsen* (Copenhagen, 1972), 233

R. Fiske: *English Theatre Music in the Eighteenth Century* (London, 1973)

I. S. Baierle: *Die Klavierwerke von Johann Christian Bach* (diss., U. of Graz, 1974)

J. Bolen: *The Five Berlin Cembalo Concertos P 390 of John Christian Bach: a Critical Edition* (diss., State U. of Florida, 1974)

B. Matthews: 'The Davies Sisters, J. C. Bach and the Glass Harmonica', *ML*, lvi (1975), 150

H. Brofsky: 'J. C. Bach, G. B. Sammartini, and Padre Martini: a *Concorso* in Milan in 1762', *A Musical Offering: Essays in Honour of Martin Bernstein* (New York, 1977)

E. S. Derr: 'Zur Zierpraxis im späten 18. Jahrhundert', *ÖMz*, xxxii (1977), 8

D. J. Keahey: *The Genoa Manuscripts: Recently Rediscovered Trios of J. C. Bach* (diss., U. of Texas (Austin), 1977)

A. Schnoebelen: *Padre Martini's Collection of Letters in the Civico Museo Bibliografico Musicale in Bologna* (New York, 1979)

S. W. Roe: *The Keyboard Music of J. C. Bach: Source Problems and Stylistic Development in the Solo and Ensemble Works* (diss., U. of Oxford, 1981)

D. McCulloch: 'Mrs Papendiek and the London Bach', *MT*, cxxiii (1982), 26

S. W. Roe: 'J. C. Bach, 1735–1782: Towards a New Biography', *MT*, cxxiii (1982), 23

E. Warburton: 'J. C. Bach's Latin Church Music', *MT*, cxxiii (1982), 781

H.-J. Schulze: 'Wann begann die "italienische Reise" des jüngsten Bach-Sohnes?', *BJb*, lxix (1983)

CHAPTER THIRTEEN

Johann Michael Bach

Johann Michael was born in Struth on 9 November 1745. He came from a Hessian line of Bachs which can be traced back to Caspar Bach (*d* Struth, 1640). Geiringer's description of him as a son of Johann Elias Bach (*39*) is incorrect; there was probably some connection with the Wechmar Bachs, although none has been proved. Johann Michael began travelling at an early age, visiting the Netherlands (in about 1767, where he had some contact with the music publisher Hummel), England and America. On his return he studied law at the University of Göttingen, where he came into contact with Forkel. He practised law in Güstrow (Mecklenburg), evidently also working as a composer, and by 1793 he was Kantor and organist in Tann; his *Kurze und systematische Anleitung zum General-Bass und der Tonkunst überhaupt* was published at Kassel in 1780. It is not known when he went to Elberfeld, where he was a professor (probably music teacher at the Gymnasium) until his death in 1820. As a composer and theorist Johann Michael represents in a derivative way a style similar to that of (11) Johann Christoph Friedrich Bach (*49*). He had two sons who were musicians, Johann Georg and Georg Friedrich (see List of musicians, p.2).

Johann Michael Bach

WORKS

6 Klavierkonzerte, C, G, D, F, D, B, op.1 (Amsterdam, 1767)
Concerto, kbd, B♭, *D-Bds* [with final fugue on B–A–C–H]
2 cantatas: Gott fähret auf mit Jauchzen; Jehova, Vater der Weisen: *Bds*

BIBLIOGRAPHY

H. Lämmerhirt: 'Ein hessischer Bach-Stamm', *BJb*, xxxiii (1936), 78

CHAPTER FOURTEEN

Wilhelm Friedrich Ernst Bach (*84*)

Wilhelm Friedrich Ernst, a son of (11) Johann Christoph Friedrich Bach (*49*), was born in Bückeburg and baptized on 27 May 1759. He was the only one of Johann Sebastian's grandsons of any musical importance. He studied with his father and in 1778, after a brief stay with C. P. E. Bach in Hamburg, went to live with (12) Johann Christian (*50*) in London, working there as a piano virtuoso and teacher. After his uncle's death at the beginning of 1782 he began a long concert tour which took him in particular through the Netherlands and to Paris. In 1787 he became music director in Minden, near his home town. On Friedrich Wilhelm II's visit to that city in 1788 he composed the cantata *Westphalens Freude*, which made such an impression on the king that he appointed Bach Kapellmeister and harpsichordist at the court of Queen Friedrike of Prussia in Berlin; in 1797 he assumed a similar post at the court of Queen Luise (in 1795 he had applied unsuccessfully for the professionally more attractive position of Hofkapellmeister at Bückeburg). He was chiefly responsible for the music training of the Prussian princes until 1811, after which he lived in retirement in Berlin on a pension of 300 thalers. As the last musically significant descendant of Johann Sebastian he attended the dedication of the Bach monument in Leipzig on 23 April 1843; he died in Berlin on 25 December 1845.

Many of his numerous compositions, most of them written in London and Minden, were circulated in print (as well as manuscript copies) in his lifetime. In Berlin he also played an influential role in the musical life of the city. His compositions are not without conventional features, notably in their use of strict contrapuntal writing; his style is generally vapid and does not approach the originality of his two famous uncles and mentors, Johann Christian and Carl Philipp Emanuel.

WORKS

VOCAL

Trauer-Cantate, on the death of Frederick the Great (Minden, 1787)

Westphalens Freude (Die Nymphen der Weser), for Friedrich Wilhelm II of Prussia, 1788 (Rinteln, 1791)

Columbus oder die Entdeckung von America, T, B, chorus, orch, 1798, *GB-Lbm*

Concerto buffo, B, toy insts, orch, *Lbm*

L'amour est un bien suprême; Ninfe se liete, S, orch, *Lbm*

Vater unser, T, B, choir, orch, *Lbm*, ed. in SBA

Lieder: Auswahl deutscher und französischer Lieder und Arietten (Berlin, n.d.); Rheinweinlied (Berlin, n.d.); Wiegenlied einer Mutter, ed. K. Geiringer, *Music of the Bach Family* (Cambridge, Mass., 1955); 12 Freymaurer-Lieder (Copenhagen and Leipzig, 1788) [wrongly attrib. C. P. E. Bach as w202]; others, *Lbm*

INSTRUMENTAL

Orch: 2 sinfonias, C, G, *GB-Lbm*; 2 suites, E♭, B♭, *Lbm*; ballet-pantomime, *Lbm*; 3 pf concs., Conc. for 2 pf, all formerly *D-B*

Chamber: Sextet, E♭, 2 hn, cl, vn, va, vc, ed. K. Janetzky (Halle, 1951); 6 Sonatas, hpd/pf, vn, vc, op.1 (London, 1785); 3 sonates, hpd/pf, vn, op.2 (Berlin and Amsterdam, n.d.); Trio, G, 2 fl, va, ed. in HM, lvii (1951); Sinfonia, C, vn, pf, *GB-Lbm*

Kbd: 5 Sonatas and 1 Duett (London, c1780); XII grandes variations sur un air allemand populaire (Berlin, n.d.); Andante, a, kbd 4 hands, ed. A. Kreutz (Mainz, n.d.); Das Dreyblatt, F, pf 6 hands, ed. K. Geiringer, *Music of the Bach Family* (Cambridge, Mass., 1955); Grand sonata, E♭, 1778; Variations on 'God save Frederick our King'; A Favourite Overture, and Divertimento, kbd 4 hands, both *Lbm*; other small pieces, *Lbm*

(*doubtful*)

Four Progressive Lessons . . . and Two Duetts (c1782) [also attrib. J. C. Bach, т350/8]

BIBLIOGRAPHY

G. Hey: 'Zur Biographie Johann Friedrich Bachs und seiner Familie', *BJb*, xxx (1933), 77

H. Wohlfarth: 'Wilhelm Friedrich Ernst Bach: Werkverzeichnis', *Schaumburg-Lippische Heimatblätter*, xi/5 (1960), 1

——: 'Wilhelm Friedrich Ernst Bach', *Schaumburg-Lippische Mitteilungen*, xvi (1964), 27

Index

Index

Index

Index

Index

Index